ROADS TO PROSPERITY

Great Lakes Books

A complete listing of the books in this series can be found online at wsupress. wayne.edu

ROADS TO PROSPERITY

Economic Development Lessons from Midsize Canadian Cities

Gary Sands and Laura A. Reese

Wayne State University Press
Detroit

ISBN 978-0-8143-4359-3 (paperback)
ISBN 978-0-8143-4441-5 (hardcover)
ISBN 978-0-8143-4360-9 (e-book)

Library of Congress Control Number: 2017938186

Wayne State University Press
Leonard N. Simons Building
4809 Woodward Avenue
Detroit, Michigan 48201-1309

Visit us online at wsupress.wayne.edu

In memory of Douglas Caruso and Malcolm Matthew
Professional planners, dedicated teachers, and good friends

Contents

Tables

Figures

Maps

Acknowledgments

The work presented here benefitted from financial support from a number of sources. We have received several grants from the Canadian Embassy's Faculty Research Grant Program, which provided resources for US scholars doing work on and in Canada. Separate grants were also received from the Québec / United States University Grant Program through the Québec Government Office in Chicago. Additional financial support was provided by Wayne State University and Michigan State University.

While each of these sources has been important, funding from the Canadian Embassy's Faculty Research Grant Program has been especially vital. The corpus of research presented here represents the fruits of that grant program, which aimed to foster cross-border research linkages, present Canadian work to US audiences, and develop scholarship (and scholars) in the United States focusing on Canada. The Embassy Faculty Research Grant program was discontinued in 2013. We hope that this book will serve as a testament to the lasting value of that program's support.

In particular, we would like to thank Dr. Dan Abele of the Canadian Embassy in Washington and Dennis Moore, Public Affairs Officer at the Canadian Consulate in Detroit. Over the years, their support and encouragement for our work has been invaluable.

We also owe a great deal to all those individuals who assisted our research by generously giving their time, knowledge, and understanding. There are far too many local officials, planners, economic development specialists, and academics for us to try to list them individually. We want to thank them for their assistance.

There are, however, a number of individuals who deserve recognition for their extraordinary contributions to this effort. Doug Caruso (Planner for the City of Windsor and adjunct planning faculty member at Wayne State University and the University or Windsor) and Mal Matthew

(Planner for the Borough of North York and Professor at the University of Windsor) provided invaluable assistance helping us to understand Canadian cities and their context. Professor Pierre Filion of the University of Waterloo not only provided essential insights and critiques, but also helped to bring us into contact with professional and academic planners across Canada.

Over the years we also benefitted from the capable research assistance provided by a number of individuals, both at Wayne State University and the University of Michigan. These include Jessica Faist-Witt, Maranda Holtsclaw, Kathryn Huttenga, T. J. Knezek, Bradon Martin, and Moushumi Roy.

1

Introduction

Canadian urban areas are very different places to those in the United States. Hence, the notion of the "North American City" can be of only limited value and may be potentially misleading.

Goldberg and Mercer, 1986, 239

[T]hese factors suggest that the Canadian experience is likely to be highly relevant to conditions in the United States.

Tomalty and Mallach, 2015, 2

Cities have, for decades, pursed policies to promote healthy local economies, retain and attract residents and businesses, and foster economic growth. Local economic development policies have tended toward the faddish as city officials emulate their neighbors and even communities across the nation or world in the quest for the silver bullet to ensure economic stability, sustainability, and expansion. This books presents several decades of research on economic development policies in Canadian cities (with comparisons to US cases when appropriate) to assess how some of the most common local economic development strategies and policies have succeeded (or more typically failed) to achieve the goals just noted. Two central findings are emphasized: that, indeed, there are no silver bullets or one best way to achieve local economic success, and that local officials are better off focusing on the basics of government: good services, strong schools, safe communities, and enhancing the local quality of life.

While the primary focus of the research is on midsize Canadian cities, the book rejects the supposed "exceptionalism" of Canadian cities— an argument suggesting that the history and nature of Canadian urban areas is essentially unique and incomparable to other, particularly US, urban areas. While the trajectories may be different, cities across North America are facing the same global changes with similar effects on economic systems. Urban challenges such as economic growth, sprawl, deindustrialization, and environmental quality are common across cities in North America and beyond. Governing regimes and urban power systems are important frames for understanding how policies are made and cities across the world continue past practices even when clearly better alternatives are available. While there is strong evidence that there are important differences between cities and policy responses in Canadian and US cities—racial histories and ethnic divisions are very different with implications for urban policy making, for example. Nevertheless, Canadian urban areas can provide a useful counterfactual for those interested in understanding metropolitan areas in the United States. The research presented here does not address questions of culture or political structure; these are accepted as givens. Nor do we attempt to verify that the differences highlighted by Goldberg and Mercer continue to distinguish between Canadian and American metropolitan areas (1986). Rather, the aim is to analyze midsize Canadian cities to develop a better understanding of their nature and functioning. In some cases, the analysis leads to the identification of specific policies that might be useful to other cities. In other cases, it leads to conclusions about why specific policy transfers are unlikely or impossible.

The research focuses on the two decades between 1991 and 2011. The end date of 2011 was selected because it is the last year for which comprehensive demographic and socioeconomic data are currently available at the appropriate geographic scale. The 1991 baseline was chosen to provide sufficient time for trends to develop and be observed. That year was also the beginning of an extended period of economic growth in Canada.[1] Thus, the reported trends occurred during a period when generally increasing economic well-being was the norm, rather than the exception.

---

1. The Great Recession of 2008–09 had considerably less impact in Canada than it did in the United States.

In both Canada and the United States, cities owe their existence to the next higher level of government, the province or the state. The national level of government has relatively little direct involvement with the cities. Provincial governments provide a broad framework of enabling legislation that establishes the parameters of what is expected of cities and other governmental units.

This book has two primary concerns. The first is to provide a basic understanding of the state of midsize Canadian urban areas, largely from an economic development perspective. In particular, we attempt to identify trends and tendencies, especially those resulting from global restructuring, that have affected them over the two decades from 1991 to 2011. Although specific economic development strategies are discussed, our intent is not to evaluate the effectiveness of these strategies in individual cities. Rather, we consider midsize urban areas as a whole. Our assessments are drawn from aggregate data.

The second objective is to identify the ways in which these communities have been affected by public policies. Are there specific public policies that have significantly altered the trajectory of these urban areas to prevent decline or maintain prosperity? Or are policy outcomes only capable of achieving marginal changes, limited by global economic realities, historic inertia, and place luck?

URBAN POLICY AND GLOBALIZATION

Urban policy making is inherently limited by path dependency and the natural advantages (or disadvantages) of cities as they take their places in the urban hierarchy. Increasing social and economic globalization adds a rapidly changing external environment over which individual cities or even urban regions, no matter how integrated, have little control. Yet place and politics still matter and livable, sustainable, and governable cities will be those that find room within these forces for effective local efforts to address and perhaps even shape change. Throughout this volume, the discussion is framed by two concepts: (1) globalization and its impacts on economic change and (2) the rise of the New/Knowledge Economy.

The increasingly global nature of economic production drives the shift from manufacturing to knowledge employment, challenges the sustainability of urban regions, stimulates immigration flows, divides cities and workers into "haves" and "have nots" depending on their readiness to embrace economic change, and intensifies the competition between cities and regions for workers, residents, and capital investment. The shift from a manufacturing to a tertiary or service-based economy is fact; the pace of change, and the extent to which a knowledge-based economy ensures current and future economic sustainability, is still very much open to debate within both academic and policy circles. The changing global economy raises a host of critical questions related to cities. How rapid and complete has the shift been from manufacturing to knowledge-based employment, and has the process taken place differentially between types of cities or across space? Do urban areas with more knowledge, more technological or creative jobs, or more skilled residents fare better economically? Do larger numbers of New Economy workers and employers assure future economic growth and sustainability? And most importantly, are there effective policies to address the challenges raised by changing global circumstances, and whose interests are represented in making or selecting among those policies?

Population and knowledge employment increasingly cluster in urban centers at the expense of non-urban areas and smaller cities, creating impacts on a host of other urban issues: the environment, green space, and regional sustainability; political representation within and between cities; and the future economic viability of the entire urban system and concomitant public policies to ensure it. It appears likely that Canadian urban conflicts will continue to focus on large city/small city polarization with serious implications for public policy at all levels of government (Filion, 2010). For larger cities this portends increasing power on the provincial and national scene, expanding demands for social and built environment infrastructure (potentially placing pressure on current green spaces), and exacerbating conflicts between powerful city regions and provinces. At the same time the smaller have-not cities will call for economic aid and greater policy intervention in the economy. To the extent that larger cities attract the bulk of the country's immigration, this also sets up a potential cultural conflict between areas with diverse racial and ethnic groups and those more homogeneously composed of "native" Canadians.

Declining and stable urban areas deploy economic development initiatives to counter disinvestment and in some cases adapt land use and services to dwindling population and economic activity. Meanwhile, growing metropolitan regions must deal with the financial, environmental, and quality of life implications of development in the present context, characterized by limited public sector budgets for new or upgraded infrastructures, crippling traffic congestion and concern about different forms of pollution and climate change. Growth of some cities may occur at the expense of others. How these changes affect the general urban system within Canada is inherently related to equity as globalization creates urban winners and losers.

Most contemporary discussions of globalization and cities turns at some point to the issue of immigration. To Richard Florida, immigration and its attendant diversity and presumed tolerance is a driving force behind innovation, quality of life, and economic growth. For countries such as Canada with limited internal population growth, there is a more direct economic need for the skills immigrants bring with them. If immigration is truly a primary economic driver, then where immigrants choose to locate is also an important feature of inter-city equity. This research highlights the importance of immigration to knowledge-based economies and suggests the significance of differential location choices, while at the same time providing a cautionary note about the limits of relying on immigration as an economic development panacea. In short, it may be a strategy that works for some cities but not for others.

CHARACTERISTICS OF MIDSIZE URBAN AREAS

The Canadian urban system has evolved in ways that are quite different from that in the United States. As a whole, Canada's population is just one-tenth that of the US population (33.1 versus 311.6 million in 2011). Canada has just seven metropolitan areas with populations over one million and twenty-four Census Metropolitan Areas with populations of 125,000 or more. The urban system is completed by 114 Census Agglomerations that each have a population between 10,000 and 125,000. (In the United States, there are five metropolitan areas with populations of more than five million, 383 other Metropolitan Statistical Areas with populations over 50,000, and 541 Micropolitan Statistical Areas, with populations of 10,000 to 50,000.) Despite the smaller number of urban areas, Canada is just as urbanized as the United States. Canada's largest urban area, Toronto, includes one of every six Canadians; the New York metropolitan area is home to one of every 16 Americans.

Some Canadian metropolitan areas have experienced significant population growth over the past half-century. Both Calgary and Edmonton were clearly in the midsize category in 1951, with populations of 129,000 and 160,000, respectively. Even twenty years later, neither city had a population of more than 440,000. By 2011, however, Calgary had a population of almost 1.1 million; at a population of 812,000, Edmonton was clearly no longer midsize. Some population declines have also occurred, but none have been on the scale of Detroit or Cleveland. Overall, the composition of the midsize category has remained remarkably stable in recent years.

This book is primarily concerned with research that focuses on midsize Canadian urban areas, those with populations between 50,000 and 500,000.[2] There are several reasons for this choice. As a group, these communities vary considerably in their demographic and physical characteristics, their development histories and economic well-being. This provides the opportunity for useful comparisons. The range of available policy options are broadly similar across the group, with more options than among smaller communities but fewer choices than those available to larger urban areas. But there are differences due to variations in population, age, and provincial legislation.

The choice of this population range is admittedly somewhat arbitrary. The population dynamics of these communities can result in substantial changes in the qualifying communities after every census. For

_____

2. In 1991, the largest of these metropolitan areas, London, Ontario, had a population of just under 400,000. In some instances comparisons to larger Canadian or American cities are included.

example, based on the 2011 census, there were seven additional midsize urban areas in the specified range. In 2011, there was still a substantial gap (roughly 244,000) between the largest midsize urban area, Kitchener, and the next largest CMA, Hamilton. Although no communities "outgrew" the midsize classification, both Calgary and Edmonton have done so in the recent past.

The 1996 Canadian census reported forty-two metropolitan areas (Census Metropolitan Areas and Census Agglomerations) in the target population range, from Saint-Hyacinthe, Quebec (50,000), to London, Ontario (399,000). The average population size was 143,000. During the previous five years (1991–96), the population of these urban areas increased by an average of just over 5 percent. Seven communities experienced a population decline, while five saw their populations grow by more than 20 percent. Several of the metropolitan areas that nominally fall within this size range have been excluded from the analysis. Communities such as Oakville Ontario, which are also included in the definition of a consolidated urban area (in this case, Greater Toronto), are not included. Also excluded are consolidated cities (Chatham-Kent, Ontario; Cape Breton, Nova Scotia; Ft. McMurray, Alberta) because the densely settled core of these areas has a much lower population than their total population would suggest.

The majority of these urban areas are located in the provinces of Ontario (14), Quebec (8), and British Columbia (6). Prince Edward Island and Manitoba have no urban areas in this size range, but each of the other provinces has at least one. About one-third of the urban areas are located within 100 kilometers of one of Canada's three largest urban areas: Montreal, Toronto, and Vancouver. In some instances, the midsize metro areas serve as satellite centers, providing lower-cost housing within commuting range of the major metropolis. Barrie, Abbotsford, and Saint-Jean-sur-Richelieu are in this category. Five provincial capitals are included in the group.

These midsize urban areas had a total population of some seven million in 2011, about the same as the Greater Toronto area. Two of every nine Canadians currently reside in one of these communities. The research reported here focuses on the midsize urban areas but occasionally makes comparisons to US metropolitan areas of similar size. In addition, we also relate midsize Canadian cities to Toronto, Montreal, and Vancouver. The chapter on planned communities primarily considers developments in the Toronto and Montreal areas, although the Riverside East case study is located in Windsor Ontario, one of the midsize urban areas. Some of the key characteristics of these metropolitan areas are summarized in Table 1.1.[3] The average growth rate for the midsize communities between 1991 and 1996 was close to the national average. There were half a dozen midsize urban areas that lost population during this period: Sault Ste. Marie and Sarnia, both located on the border with Michigan, each recorded a population decline of 1.6 percent. Three of the four urban areas that recorded gains of more than 20 percent were in British Columbia.

The proportion of immigrants in the midsize metro areas is, on average, well below the comparable national figure. Given that three-quarters of international immigrants settle in one of the three largest Canadian urban centers, this is not surprising (Statistics Canada, 2003). Urban areas with large proportions of immigrants include three Ontario urban areas, Kitchener (21.6 percent), Windsor (20.4 percent), and Guelph (20.3 percent). The Quebec midsize metropolitan areas are particularly low in their share of immigrants; in Saguenay and Shawinigan the proportion of immigrants is less than one percent.

Table 1.1 Midsize Canadian Urban Areas, 1996

	Midsize Urban Areas			Canada
	Mean	**Minimum**	**Maximum**	
Population	143,125	50,027	398,616	29,611,000
Change 1991–96	5.7%	-1.6%	22.2%	5.6%
Immigrants	10.1%	0.6%	21.6%	17.4%
Visible Minorities	3.9%	0.4%	12.7%	11.2%
University Degree	11.6%	6.3%	21.0%	15.6%

Source: Statistics Canada.

---

3. The complete list is provided in Appendix A, Table 1.

The proportion of visible minorities in the midsize urban areas is also well below the national average. Nevertheless, three of the communities with high proportions of immigrants—Abbotsford (BC), Windsor, and Kitchener—are also among the top with respect to visible minorities. Sherbrooke is the only Quebec urban area where the proportion of visible minorities is greater than 1 percent. The proportion of visible minorities (as well as immigrants) is relatively high in communities that are home to major universities.

MIDSIZE COMMUNITY PROFILES

The Canadian midsize urban areas that are the focus of this research comprise a highly diverse group of cities. The first part of the book is devoted to developing a typology of these communities. It may, however, be useful to introduce at least a generalized classification scheme to assist readers who are not familiar with this group of communities. Five broad functional categories are identified and representative examples of the different categories are briefly described (see Table 1.2). The typologies are not rigorously defined and the boundaries between them are often not distinct. For example, some of the provincial capitals are also home to research universities and thus could have been classified as university centers. Likewise, some of the metro areas classified as university communities have economies that are quite diverse; however, they are widely known for their academic institutions.

Regional Centers

The largest group of midsize cities, fourteen of the forty-two, can be described as regional centers that provide somewhat specialized goods and services to the surrounding areas. They are often located at some distance from Canada's largest urban areas; in some cases, due to growth of the largest metropolitan areas, these midsize areas now find themselves within the commuter-shed of the major urban areas. These regional centers tend to have diversified economies, with no readily identifiable economic specialization, or serve as retail and wholesale trade centers; two examples are provided below.

Table 1.2 Typology of Midsize Canadian Urban Areas

Regional Centers	Manufacturing	Resource	University	Capital
Barrie	Brantford	Abbotsford	Guelph	Fredericton
Belleville	Drummondville	Chilliwack	Kingston	Halifax
Cornwall	Granby	Greater Sudbury	Kitchener[4]	Regina
Kamloops	Oshawa	Kelowna	Peterborough	St. John's
London	Saint-Hyacinthe	Lethbridge	Saskatoon	Victoria
Moncton	Saint-Jean-sur-Richelieu	Medicine Hat	Sherbrooke	
Nanaimo	Sarnia	Prince George		
North Bay	Shawinigan	Red Deer		
Saguenay	St. Catharines			
Saint John	Windsor			
Sault Ste. Marie				
Thunder Bay				
Trois-Rivières				

Moncton. The Moncton Census Metropolitan Area, with a population of 138,000 in 2011, is the largest urban area in the province of New Brunswick and the fastest growing. The City of Moncton accounts for about half of the metro population. The city has experienced several cycles of economic boom, spurred by its role as a transportation center (shipbuilding in the first half of the nineteenth century and railroads in the twentieth century). The 1970s and 1980s saw several closings—the Canadian Forces Base Moncton, the Eaton's distribution center, and the Canadian National Railway locomotive repair yard—resulting in the loss

---

4. Because the data employed throughout are for Census Metropolitan Areas, data for Kitchener also include the cities of Waterloo and Cambridge.

of thousands of jobs. The local economy began to recover in the 1990s, based on growth in the insurance, information technology, health care, higher education, tourism, and trade sectors.

The City of Moncton currently concentrates its economic development efforts on two locations: the city core, which is the focus of office and hotel development, and the suburban Magnetic Hill area, where tourist attractions and shopping malls have developed. The city is officially bilingual, which has been instrumental in the attraction of more than three dozen call centers to the area (Patriquin, 2016). The two local universities and two regional medical centers are also major employers. The largest shopping mall in Atlantic Canada is located in suburban Moncton. Improvements to the transportation infrastructure, particularly a new bridge across the Petitcodiac River, have contributed to the rise in development activity in the city center.

Nanaimo. The early history of Nanaimo is based on the exploitation of natural resources, first coal and then lumber, which were shipped from the city's excellent harbor. By the late twentieth century, the Nanaimo economy declined along with these industries. In the 1990s, the city functioned primarily as a wholesale and retail trade center for the central part of Vancouver Island. Over the past quarter century, economic development efforts have focused on downtown and waterfront renewal, technology industries, and tourism. The city has partnered with Google to increase public access to municipal data. The University of Vancouver Island (Malaspina University-College until 2008) has almost 20,000 students on its three campuses; it has been an active partner in economic development efforts.

The numerous visible indications of improvement in and around the city center are reflected in the strengthening of the local economy since 2000. The current population of 98,000 is an increase of about 13,000 since 2001. Incomes have increased by more than 40 percent during the same period, and numerous tech firms have been established in Nanaimo; however, most are small, often with fewer than five employees.

Manufacturing Centers

Ten of the midsize urban areas are identified with manufacturing employment. Half of these communities are located in Ontario and half in Quebec. The Ontario cities, especially those along the Highway 401 Corridor from Windsor to Oshawa, have strong ties to the motor vehicle manufacturing industry. Manufacturing wages in these communities are generally higher than those in the Quebec manufacturing centers. Several of the Quebec urban areas have faced sharp declines in their original industrial base; finding replacements for the lost jobs has been difficult; Shawinigan is an example of this type of city.

Brantford. Brantford's location between the steel mills in Hamilton and the abundant electrical power from Niagara Falls was critical to the city's early growth as a manufacturing center. In the early years, Brantford was noted for the manufacturing of agricultural implements by firms such as Massey-Harris and Verity Plow. Several of these heavy manufacturing industries closed or suffered bankruptcy in the 1980s and 1990s. In recent years, several consumer product firms, including Proctor & Gamble and SC Johnson, have established manufacturing facilities in the community.

Until 1999, Brantford did not have a local university; in that year, Wilfrid Laurier University established a satellite campus in downtown Brantford. Current enrollment, mostly undergraduate, is about 2,800 full-time students. Enrollment is expected to decline as a result of the decision of Nipissing University to discontinue offering a teacher training degree at Laurier Brantford.

The city center location of Laurier Brantford, including several student residence halls, was part of an effort to revitalize the downtown area. The university occupies a number of historic buildings around the city park and has constructed several new buildings as well. Heritage preservation efforts suffered a significant setback when forty-one historic building were demolished in 2010.

Shawinigan. In many respects, Shawinigan is typical of Quebec manufacturing centers. The city is located at the falls of the Saint Maurice River, about nineteen miles north of the St. Lawrence River. The development of hydroelectric power to take advantage of the 165-foot drop in the Saint Maurice River at this location made Shawinigan attractive to energy intensive industries, including aluminum, carborundum, and chemicals. Since the 1920s, local manufacturing activity has declined steadily with the exception of a brief period during the Second World

War. The loss of industrial employment opportunities has only been partially offset by new jobs in the tourism and hospitality sectors.

In 1998 and 2002, several municipalities were amalgamated into the present city of Shawinigan. The population of the Census Agglomeration is just 56,000 and has been declining since 1991. The median age in Shawinigan is 50.3 years, roughly ten years above the national figure. Less than 1 percent of the population lists their mother tongue as English. Fewer than 500 Shawinigan residents were born outside of Canada; just 75 of these immigrated in the last five years. Visible minorities comprise only 0.6% of the population.

Natural Resources Centers

Eight of the midsize cities serve as natural resource centers, and most are located in Western Canada; Price George (BC) and Greater Sudbury (ON) are examples. Because most of these resource-based urban areas are relatively remote, they also serve as regional centers for trade and services.

Greater Sudbury. The mining of nickel ore has largely determined the fortunes of Sudbury. First discovered during the construction of the transcontinental railroad in 1883, nickel quickly supplanted forestry as the mainstay of the local economy. Over the next century, Sudbury endured a number of boom-bust cycles as worldwide demand for nickel fluctuated. A lengthy miners strike in 1978 encouraged the municipal government to pursue economic diversification.

Smelting operations caused extensive environmental damage. The air pollution and consequent acid rain destroyed virtually all of the vegetation and blackened the landscape for miles around. Remediation efforts began in 1972 and have included the planting of more than nine million trees. By 2010, about ten percent of the area had been restored, leaving almost 120 square miles to be rehabilitated.

In 2001, Greater Sudbury was created by the amalgamation of half a dozen settlements with adjacent township areas. The resulting municipality covers 1,300 square miles and includes some 330 lakes of twenty-five acres or more. The largest population center is the former city of Sudbury, which includes about two-thirds of the new municipality's total population of 160,000.

Prince George. Located in the interior of British Columbia, 450 miles north of Vancouver, Prince George was founded in the early 1800s as a trading post of the North West Company. The city grew as a regional service and distribution center and is informally known as the capital of Northern British Columbia because of the concentration of government services. Lumbering activity in Prince George began to increase in importance after World War II, with the opening of the first pulp mill there in 1964. Lumbering declined sharply as a result of the Mountain Pine Beetle infestation in the 1980s and 1990s. Exploration for oil and gas in the area suggests that natural resources may continue to play an important role for this community.

Although natural resources are important to Prince George, in recent years the local economy has become increasingly oriented to services. Services, particularly medical and educational, are important components of the Prince George economy today. The University of Northern British Columbia was founded in 1990 and has an enrollment of about 4,000 students. UNBC has emerged as one of the top-ranked undergraduate universities in Canada. Provincial and federal government offices also make a significant contribution to the economy.

With a population of 72,000, Prince George contains almost 82 percent of the metropolitan area population. The CMA population has increased by 22 percent since 1991. At about 13 percent, the First Nations population in Prince George is almost double the proportion of visible minorities (7 percent) in the community. Recent immigrants to Canada make up just 1.1 percent of the CMA population. In recent years Prince George has had one of the highest crime rates in Canada. This has been attributed to the transient nature of much of the population.

Provincial Capitals

Five of the midsize urban areas are provincial capitals. (Four of the other capitals exceed the specified population range, while the population of Charlottetown [PEI] was below the minimum size.) The provincial capitals benefit from relative economic stability and a well-educated labor force.

Halifax. The Halifax Regional Municipality was created in 1996 and is the largest municipality in Atlantic Canada. About three-quarters of the CMA population of 390,000 is located in the urban core, centered on Halifax and Dartmouth. The urban core is relatively dense and walkable; over one-quarter of the downtown population walks to work. The substantial number of tourists visiting the city contribute to the well-used and lively downtown. The rural areas of the regional municipality include historic population centers such as Peggy's Cove and Cole Harbour.

As the largest metropolitan area in the Atlantic provinces, Halifax has a diverse economy, including trade, public services, shipping, and shipbuilding and higher order services, such as banking, education, and health care. The largest concentration of employment is found in the Halifax central business district. With six universities in the city, which enroll almost 33,000 students, Halifax could easily be thought of as a university town. Dalhousie (15,500 students) and St. Mary's (7,600) have the largest enrollments. Population growth in Halifax has been modest, about 7 percent, since the turn of the century. Recent immigrants make up just 2 percent of the total population; Asia and Europe are the largest sources of immigrants to Halifax.

Victoria. The economy of Victoria has been highly dependent on the public sector. In addition to the provincial government, the federal government (including the Department of National Defense), municipal governments, and public school districts are also major employers. Esquimalt, just west of Victoria, has been the West Coast home of the Canadian Navy for 150 years. The two universities in Victoria have a total enrollment of 23,700, most at the University of Victoria, and employ about 5,000. Service industries, such as tourism and health care, also play an important role in the economy. The technology sector, which benefits from the universities, several national research laboratories, and the naval base, is the most important private sector employer.

Unlike Halifax, there has not been any significant reorganization of local governments in the Victoria Census Metropolitan Area. The thirteen municipalities in the CMA have a number of cooperative agreements but have resisted amalgamation. The city of Victoria, with a population of some 80,000, represents less than one-quarter of the metropolitan area population of 345,000. Five out of every six residents is a European Canadian; visible minorities (12 percent) and aboriginal groups (6 percent) compose the balance. The CMA's population has grown by more than 10 percent since the turn of the century; immigrants make up about 18 percent of the population and account for about one-third of the recent growth. Victoria has the third-highest proportion of residents over the age of 65 among Canadian municipalities.

University Centers

Canada's leading universities are generally located in its largest cities; McGill University (Montreal), the University of British Columbia (Vancouver), and the University of Toronto, for example, are regularly ranked among the top fifty universities in the world. There is some form of post-secondary education available in all the midsize metropolitan areas;[5] however, universities play major roles in the community identity of six of the midsize urban areas.

Kingston. Located at the eastern end of Lake Ontario, Kingston is home to Queens University and the Royal Military College, which together enroll almost 27,000 students. The Department of National Defense is the largest employer in Kingston (9,600 employees), followed by Queens University. Public sector employment also includes several prisons and the Ministry of Health and Long Term Care. Tourism and culture are important parts of the economy as well.

The population of the Kingston CMA is about 160,000, with just over three-quarters residing in the city of Kingston; amalgamation of the city with the surrounding townships occurred in 1998. Ninety percent of the population is of white, European descent; visible minorities and aboriginal peoples make up the balance. Because of the large number of students and military personnel, population turnover in Kingston is well above the Canadian average. Population growth has averaged just over 1 percent annually in recent years, well below the Ontario growth rate.

Sherbrooke. The University of Sherbrooke, with 35,000 graduate and undergraduate students, is one of the largest francophone universities in Canada. Together with the much smaller (anglophone) Bishop's

---

5. The only post-secondary institution in Saint-Hyacinthe, however, is the University of Montreal Veterinary School.

University, the combined post-secondary population represents 20 percent of the total population of the CMA. The city of Sherbrooke recognizes the importance of universities to the community; its strategic plan gives priority to integrating the two campuses into their neighborhoods and to retaining their graduates in the Sherbrooke community.

Sherbrooke is well connected to other parts of Quebec and to the United States by road and rail. Despite the important role of education and health care in the local economy, Sherbrooke is also a major manufacturing center, with many small to midsize firms producing pulp and paper. Sherbrooke offers a wide variety of outdoor recreation and sports activities.

Sherbrooke is the largest municipality in the Eastern townships and the largest center for trade and services. Amalgamation in 2002 pushed the population of the city to 155,000; the metropolitan area population is just over 200,000. Over 90 percent of the population is francophone. Recent immigrants represent about 2 percent of the population; many of these immigrants are from non-francophone countries.

These profiles provide a sense of the nature of the midsize communities that serve as the base for most of the research in this book. More detail on general types and specific cities is provided in individual chapters. Before describing the organization of the book and content of the chapters, a note about the data underlying the analysis is warranted. The time period for the analyses presented here is typically from 1996 to 2011, although there are variations in the data based on changes in the Canadian census. For example, the content of the 2011 census enumeration was limited; most socioeconomic data for 2011 are based on the National Household Survey, which utilizes a much smaller sample than the census. Each chapter identifies the time period and source of data employed in the analyses contained therein. Some of the data (typically based on survey research and case studies) were collected at only one time period in the 2000s—again, this is fully explained in each chapter. Some of the variation in the years of data collection results from the fact that the research for this book was conducted over more than two decades. To the extent possible, data have been updated since the research was originally conducted, but again, that is not possible in all cases due to limits in data availability and the cost of conducting new surveys and case studies.

ORGANIZATION OF THE BOOK

Chapter 2 describes the economic base of the forty-two midsize urban areas and how their classification has evolved over the past two decades. A community's economic base is defined by above-average concentrations of employment in broadly defined industrial sectors. Among the midsize urban areas, a substantial number are found to have an economic base dependent on primary (agriculture, forestry, fishing, and mining) and secondary (construction and manufacturing) industries. Tertiary (services) economic activity, while widespread, seldom defines the economic base of these communities.

Chapter 3 shifts the focus from industrial to occupational structures. This approach facilitates the identification of economic activity that reflects the burgeoning New Economy. While many of the occupations that make up the knowledge/information economy tend to concentrate in larger metropolitan areas, some of the midsize urban areas have been successful in attracting and retaining these jobs. The chapter explores the connections between New Economy occupations and economic prosperity. While the midsize urban areas with relatively high proportions of New Economy jobs may be better positioned to move forward in the twenty-first century, they are not necessarily more prosperous at the present time.

In Chapter 4, the relationship between measures of city-center success and community economic prosperity is explored. The downtown area of a city is typically the most important place in the community, one that is perhaps best known to outsiders. We find that a well-regarded city center is not always associated with a prosperous metropolitan area. Moreover, some of the attributes that have the greatest influence on the reputation of the city center are not easily employed as local economic development strategies. For example, many successful core areas are found to be in close proximity to a major research university; creating such a facility is not an easy task.

The next three chapters consider specific economic development strategies that communities might employ. In Chapter 5, creative class economic development strategies are examined. As is the case with many other critical examinations of the creative class model, it is difficult to verify that the process actually functions in the way the model specifies. Nevertheless, creative class strategies are found to offer some potential benefits to midsize urban areas.

The presence of foreign-born populations in midsize urban areas is the subject of Chapter 6. A number of midsize urban areas have adopted economic development strategies that focus on attracting immigrants. While the actual numbers of foreign born are relatively small in the midsize urban areas, the relationships between immigrants and economic prosperity are complex. Both the timing of the move to Canada and the region of origin prove to be important.

Chapter 7 looks at different organizational models for the management of commercial districts, both city centers and neighborhood shopping districts. The chapter provides a comparison of Business Improvement Areas (BIAs; the most common organizational model in Canada) with Downtown Development Authorities (DDAs), the predominant model in Michigan and elsewhere in the United States. Differences in governance and financing are found to make each of the models suitable for a different purpose. A Canada/US comparison is employed in this chapter because it is critical to understanding the different forms of commercial district management organizations. BIAs are the most prevalent in Canada, while the pertinent comparison organizations— DDAs—are more common in the United States. This chapter also examines BIAs in cities of all sizes in Canada because of insufficient numbers of BIAs in midsize cities.

Chapter 8 examines New Urbanist approaches to urban development and redevelopment. This higher-density, mixed-use, pedestrian oriented paradigm may provide an alternative to the predominant suburban model (low-density, single-use, auto-dependent) of development that has predominated across North America since the middle of the last century. Thus, the chapter focuses on the role of residential design in creating a livable and attractive city. Again, because of the limited number of New Urbanist developments in the midsize cities, the analysis includes neighborhoods in some of the larger Canadian cities.

In Chapter 9, casino gambling is examined as a potential new engine of economic growth, based on comparisons between Ontario and

Michigan. A Canadian/US comparison is again employed in this chapter to allow for exploration of the larger legal frameworks that represent alternatives affecting how casinos are used in their host cities and whether or not they represent an effective economic development "bet."

The final chapter brings together the themes developed throughout the book, providing specific policy implications and general insights. Not surprisingly, there is no "one size fits all" characterization of midsize Canadian urban areas or for ensuring their economic prosperity.

2

The Evolving Economic Base of Midsize Canadian Cities

Further, in spite of the declining importance of manufacturing in Canada in terms of both GDP and total labour force, its growth has continued in absolute terms, albeit at a lower rate than that of services. Rather than being viewed as mutually exclusive activities, goods production and service production have come to be recognized as two essential elements of modern integrated production systems.

Coffey and Shearmur, 2006, 249

Over the last few decades, a number of trends—globalization, deindustrialization, the knowledge economy, and advances in technology, especially communications—have had substantial impacts on urban areas across North America. Some have argued that these changes are making the world "flatter" as the importance of place diminishes (Friedman, 2005). In the new economy based on knowledge and information, less importance may be attached to a specific location that provides access to natural resources or transportation infrastructure. Rather, communication and information technologies allow individuals and firms to choose locations that offer an attractive climate or other amenities. For many functions, however, it is clear that place continues to matter a great deal. Indeed, the recent reversal of the population declines in many large North American cities suggests that the new knowledge-based economies will continue to favor places where there are more opportunities for serendipitous meetings, unexpected synergies, and intellectual spillovers.

Larger urban areas seem to be better positioned than midsize and smaller metropolitan areas with respect to economic restructuring.

Nevertheless, in recent years, most of the Canadian midsize metropolitan areas have continued to gain population and jobs, albeit at widely different rates. This chapter examines the employment structure of midsize urban areas between 1996 and 2011 and how they have evolved over time. It examines the relative economic performance of these urban areas to determine which types of communities have been able to achieve higher rates of growth and prosperity. We address the following questions:

- How has the economic base of midsize Canadian cities changed in the face of the pressures of globalization and deindustrialization?
- What is the relationship between a community's economic base and its relative prosperity?
- Can the economic well-being of these communities be explained by the socioeconomic characteristics of their populations?
- Does a location close to a major metropolitan area provide agglomeration benefits for midsize metro areas?

The next section defines the concepts and variables used in the analysis, followed by a section that examines the changes in the economic base and the economic health of these communities. The fourth part of the chapter considers the effect of proximity to a large urban area on the economic prosperity of the entire urban area. We then consider whether an analysis based on changes in employment (rather than industry) leads to different conclusions. The chapter finishes with a discussion of the implications of these findings for public policies related to economic development.

FRAMEWORK AND VARIABLES

There are strong indications that place still matters. Agglomeration economies provided Pittsburgh and Detroit with sufficient advantages to ensure their dominance for many generations in the steel and automobile manufacturing industries. Similar factors appear to apply to Silicon

Valley and financial service centers like New York and London. A great deal of sorting out is continuing in larger metropolitan areas, with the ongoing development of world cities like New York and second-tier centers like Chicago and Toronto. Meanwhile, cities like Detroit, Hamilton, and St. Louis have yet to find a way to reinvent themselves according to a twenty-first-century model.

In some instances, major metropolitan areas have incentivized corporate relocations. For example, Chicago used tax breaks to lure Boeing's headquarters to that city. Less successful major cities, such as Detroit, have relied heavily on subsidies to attract and retain businesses (Sands and Reese, 2012). For the most part, however, economic development incentives appear to be less important in larger cities. Business-friendly public policies (e.g., low tax rates, accommodating development regulations), amenities, agglomeration economies, and a large skilled labor force obviously do matter in firm location decisions, but incentives targeted to a particular firm are often not necessary. Targeted economic development policies are more common in less populous metropolitan areas.

Where do these trends leave the midsize metropolitan areas? Such cities seem to be too large to disappear completely but generally seem to lack the critical mass and resources necessary to adapt and prosper in the new economy. Several scenarios are possible. At one extreme, urban areas that are highly dependent on a single industry, particularly those related to natural resources, may suffer an abrupt decline when the resources are exhausted or the plant closes. Some midsize urban areas will retain their twentieth-century economic base and, at least in the short run, maintain or regain a measure of prosperity. In time, the lack of change in these urban areas will lead them to a long, slow decline. Other urban areas will experience a change in their employment profile, because they have been able to develop a new specialty. For these areas, the result may be relative improvement in economic well-being.

In addition to its current economic base, a community's prospects for economic growth and prosperity are likely to be related to its geographic location. Many midsize metropolitan areas are relatively isolated, while others are located in close proximity to Canada's three largest urban centers. In the Windsor–Quebec City corridor, the midsize metro areas are not only close to Toronto and Montreal, but also close to each other. This may provide a more advantageous location than northern British Columbia or New Brunswick.

The economic prospects of a community may also be related to the socioeconomic profile of its residents. A well-educated population may be closely linked to a community's economic progress. Richard Florida (2002b) has suggested that communities also benefit from diversity. While there are multiple dimensions of diversity, the ones considered here are visible minorities, same-sex couples, non-Christian religions, and foreign-born populations. Other socioeconomic measures, such as home ownership, home values, creative occupations, and commuting mode, are also tested.

Local economic development efforts are often most concerned with growth—increasing employment opportunities, tax base, or income—to improve economic well-being for residents and create prosperous communities.[1] But for communities that have reached their peak, local economic development may be focused on replacing lost jobs and retention of existing employment opportunities. This can be a difficult task, one that often requires attracting a new mix of industries. Some communities may choose to focus on improvement of the quality of life of community residents.

Since 1991, midsize urban areas have experienced significant growth in population, employment, and income (Table 2.1). This growth has varied across time as well as space. All of these cities had more jobs in 2011 than in 1991. The highest rate of employment growth occurred between 1996 and 2001, but was almost flat between 2006 and 2011. On the other hand, the highest rates of population and income growth occurred in this five-year period, when job growth was negligible.

Deindustrialization, the absolute loss of manufacturing jobs from the local labor market, is one of the most important economic trends in recent decades. Across North America, manufacturing's share of the gross national product has declined as production has moved overseas to lower wage areas. Between 1991 and 2011, manufacturing employment in Canada fell by

---

1. Recent work by UN Habitat broadens the concept of economic prosperity to include quality of life and equity considerations. See UN Habitat, 2012.

TABLE 2.1 Trends in Midsize Metropolitan Areas, 1996–2011

	Percent Change			
	1991–1996	1996–2001	2001–2006	2006–2011
Population	5.7%	3.9%	7.4%	8.6%
Employment	3.3%	37.1%	11.0%	1.0%
Median Income	4.6%	12.5%	20.4%	39.0%

Source: Statistics Canada

almost half a million jobs, a 22 percent decline. During this period Canada added a total of almost 3.4 million jobs; as a result, manufacturing's share of total employment fell from 14.7 to 9.2 percent. Canada's three largest metropolitan areas lost almost one-quarter of their manufacturing jobs, with Montreal suffering the largest decline, 29.4 percent.

Most midsize urban areas were more successful at retaining manufacturing jobs. On average, manufacturing employment declined by 17.7 percent. The net loss of manufacturing employment for all forty-two midsize urban areas was about 76,000 jobs, fewer than the 89,000 manufacturing jobs lost by the Montreal CMA. Three communities—St. Catharines-Niagara (49.9 percent), Nanaimo (54.1 percent), and Belleville (61.6 percent)—each lost half or more of their manufacturing jobs between 1991 and 2011. About one-third of the midsize urban areas, led by Chilliwack (43.1 percent), Red Deer (46.6 percent), and Lethbridge (51.6 percent), experienced absolute increases in manufacturing employment.

The impact of losing manufacturing jobs may be offset by job growth in other areas, in particular higher order services. Canada had a net employment gain of almost 3.4 million jobs between 1991 and 2011. Business services jobs—finance and insurance, real estate and professional business services—increased by 735,000 to a total of 2.35 million. In 2011, total business service employment was greater than total manufacturing employment. About half of the growth in business services (358,000 jobs) occurred in Canada's three largest metro areas, where the concentration of business service employment was above the national average.

All but two of the midsize urban areas experienced a net gain in business service employment. Sault Ste. Marie had a 6 percent decline and Belleville an 18 percent loss. Business service employment more than doubled in Red Deer, Lethbridge, Kelowna, and Medicine Hat. Eighteen other cities had increases that exceeded the national growth average of 45.6 percent. In eighteen of the midsize urban areas, the number of manufacturing jobs exceeded business service employment in 2011.

Local economies consist of more than just manufacturing and business service jobs, however. To better understand the nature of these economies, this section takes a closer look at the economies of the midsize urban areas. While the concepts examined here are generally part of the standard lexicon of economic developers and policy analysts, there are multiple definitions of key terms. Because the different definitions can lead to different interpretations and conclusions, the specifications of key variables used are provided below.

Economic Prosperity

To provide a simple measure of economic prosperity, an index was calculated, including three variables: median household income, percent of the labor force that is employed, and the share of market income (that is income not from public sources such as employment insurance or public assistance).[2] Each of the variables is measured in such a way that higher scores are indicative of greater prosperity. The score for each of the components is divided by the comparable national value to derive a location quotient. The three location quotients are each multiplied by 100 and then summed. When the resulting index value equals 300, the local economy is performing at a level comparable to the national economy.

Economic Base

The concept of a community economic base is a familiar one to planners and economic developers. Since the middle of the last century, practitioners have sought to understand the workings of the local economy by dividing economic activity into basic and service components (Blumenfeld, 1955; Mattila and Thompson, 1955). Basic economic activity

---

2. A similar index has been used in other studies of Canadian metropolitan areas. See, for example, Institute for Competitiveness and Prosperity, 2002.

generally is considered to include the goods and services that are produced for export, that is, those activities that bring money into a community; the balance of the economy serves local needs (Andrews, 1953; Mattila and Thompson, 1955). While there are numerous issues regarding the specification of basic and service activities, as well as the appropriate geographic definition of a local economy (Blumenfeld, 1955), there is a broad consensus that basic industries are key to the growth and prosperity of a community.

Although much of the economic base literature has traditionally focused on manufacturing and natural resources as basic industries, a broader definition may also be appropriate (Thompson, 1967). The export industries that bring revenue into the community may be educational or financial services. Retirement communities and centers of tourism may also be an essential component of a community's economic base. Table 2.2 identifies the specific industry codes that comprise each of the categories

Figure 2.1 compares the 1996 employment structure of the midsize urban areas with that of Canada as a whole and the average for the three largest Canadian metropolitan areas: Toronto, Montreal, and Vancouver. Employment in service industries makes up just over 60 percent of all jobs in the three largest Census Metropolitan Areas, but just under half (48.3 percent) of the total in the midsize urban areas. The midsize urban areas have higher proportions of their employment in manufacturing and wholesale and retail trade than either Canada as a whole or the major urban centers.

With the majority of jobs in the service industry, a more detailed breakdown will be helpful in characterizing the local economies. In the following analysis, service employment is divided into three groups: business services (including finance and insurance; real estate; professional, scientific, and technical services; and management of companies), health and educational services, and all other services, including public administration.

Six industry groups (natural resources, manufacturing, trade, business services, health and education services, and other services) are used to define the economic base or specialization of each community. Location quotients (lq) for each industry group are calculated by dividing the percent of local workers in an industry by the corresponding national

CHAPTER 2

Table 2.2 Components of Economic Base Categories

	Code	Industry
Natural Resources	11	Agriculture, forestry, fishing and hunting
	21	Mining, quarrying, oil and gas extraction
	22	Utilities
Manufacturing	23	Construction
	31–33	Manufacturing
Trade	41	Wholesale Trade
	44–45	Retail Trade
Business Services	52	Finance and Insurance
	53	Real Estate
	54	Professional, Scientific and Technical
	55	Management of Companies and Enterprises
Education and Health Care	61	Educational Services
	62	Health Care and Social Assistance
Other Services	48–49	Transportation and Warehousing
	51	Information and Cultural Industries
	56	Administrative and Support, Waste Management and Remediation
	71	Arts, Entertainment and Recreation
	72	Accommodation and Food Services
	81	Other Services
	91	Public Administration

percentage (see also Leigh, 1963). Any industry with a location quotient of 1.3 or higher (that is, where the local proportion of employment is at least 30 percent higher than the national figure) is considered to be a basic industry. Urban areas that had no industry that had a share of employment that was more than 30 percent above average (lq>1.3), or that had two different specializations, were classified as diversified.

Table 2.3 summarizes the distribution of midsize metropolitan areas by economic base in 1996. The largest group comprised a dozen

Figure 2.1 Employment by industry, 1996

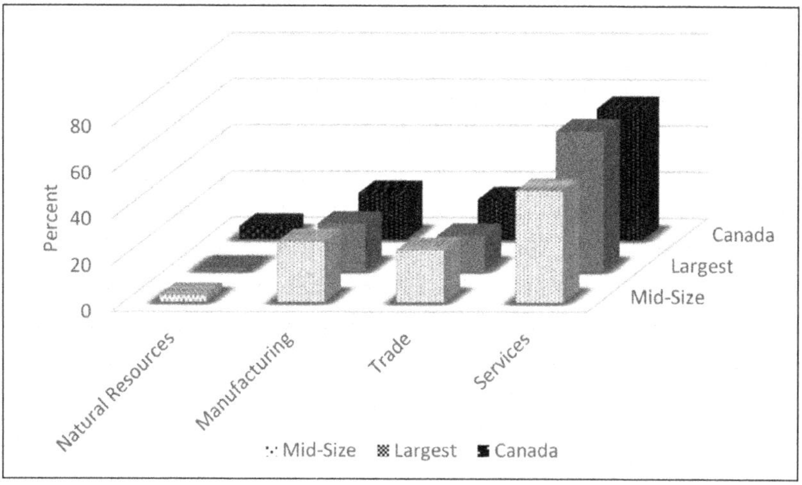

Source: Statistics Canada

manufacturing centers. All of these were in Ontario and Quebec, Canada's industrial heartland. There were eight urban areas where natural resource industries dominated, mostly in Western Canada. Eight communities had a diversified economic base. Education/health care was the next most common specialization, including six metro areas. Six metro areas specialized in trade, and two recorded specializations in other

Table 2.3 Community Economic Base, 1996

	West	Ontario	Quebec	Maritimes	Total
Natural Resources	7	1	-	-	8
Manufacturing	-	7	5	-	12
Trade	2	3	-	1	6
Business Services	-	-	-	-	-
Education/Health	3	1	-	2	6
Other Services	-	1	1	-	2
Diversified	-	4	2	2	8
Total	12	17	8	5	42

Source: Statistics Canada

services. None of the midsize metro areas had an economic base where business services were predominant.

These results are generally consistent with expectations. Local economies that rely on manufacturing and natural resources together represent almost half of the forty-two midsize metros. Almost all the communities with an economic base in manufacturing are located in the Canadian heartland, stretching from Windsor to Quebec City (Filion, 2010). There are two distinct clusters of manufacturing cities, one in southern Ontario and the other in Quebec. These differ in the types of manufacturing activities, with the Ontario cluster much more closely tied to the automobile industry. Natural resource communities are located predominantly in Western Canada.

Diversified economies, those in which no single industry dominates, accounted for eight of the metro areas. Higher education / health care services and trade centers are found in every region except Quebec. Higher order services employment (business services) was not found in sufficient numbers to be classified as the economic base of any of these metro areas.

ECONOMIC RESTRUCTURING

By 1991, services accounted for just under half (48.8 percent) of Canadian jobs (Figure 2.2). Natural resources, goods producing (manufacturing and

Figure 2.2 Services as a proportion of total employment, 1991–2011

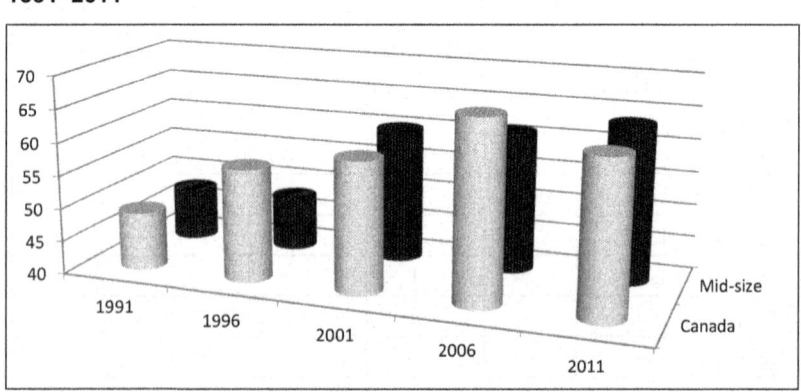

Source: Statistics Canada

Table 2.4 Employment Profile Canada and Midsize Metropolitan Areas, 1996–2011

	Canada				Midsize Metros			
	1996	2001	2006	2011	1996	2001	2006	2011
Natural Resources	5.6%	4.7%	4.1%	4.8%	3.3%	3.5%	3.5%	3.4%
Manufacturing	20.0%	19.8%	12.9%	16.1%	25.5%	20.3%	19.2%	16.9%
Trade	17.4%	15.8%	15.5%	15.7%	23.0%	16.0%	16.0%	16.1%
Business Services	12.0%	12.3%	12.5%	13.4%	12.1%	10.3%	10.6%	11.2%
Health/ Education	16.9%	16.4%	16.8%	18.5%	12.2%	18.1%	18.7%	20.3%
Other Services	28.1%	31.1%	38.2%	31.5%	23.9%	31.9%	31.9%	32.1%

Source: Statistics Canada

construction) industries, and wholesale and retail trade accounted for the balance. Over the next twenty years, there was a substantial increase in the share of jobs in services. By 2011, services provided 63.4 percent of Canadian jobs. Services' share of employment in the midsize urban areas was 48 percent in 1991, but by 2011 it had increased to almost 64 percent.

Trends in employment share for Canada and the midsize metropolitan areas are presented in Table 2.4. Nationally, the employment share by industry is relatively stable. There was a substantial decline in the relative number of manufacturing jobs between 2001 and 2006, with a corresponding increase in the share provided by other services. For the entire period, each of the service categories recorded an increase while the natural resources, manufacturing, and trade sectors each declined.

Among the midsize urban areas, the proportion of jobs in natural resources and business services remained relatively stable between 1996 and 2011.[3] Manufacturing and trade employment experienced relative declines of 8.6 and 6.9 percentage points, respectively. Both the health/

---

3. See Appendix A, Table 2 for changes in manufacturing and business service employment in each midsize metropolitan area.

Table 2.5 Change in Dispersion Measures, 1996–2011

	Mean		Standard Deviation		Range	
	1996	2011	1996	2011	1996	2011
Natural Resources	3.3%	3.4%	2.8%	2.2%	10.5%	9.2%
Manufacturing	25.4%	16.8%	7.2%	5.1%	26.3%	21.2%
Trade	23.0%	16.1%	2.9%	1.3%	10.9%	5.3%
Education & Health Care	23.8%	11.2%	4.9%	1.9%	23.7%	7.3%
Business Services	12.1%	20.3%	2.7%	3.2%	11.4%	15.2%
Other Services	12.1%	32.2%	5.2%	4.1%	21.9%	18.3%

Source: Statistics Canada

education and other service categories increased their share of total employment by about 8 percent. As a result of these substantial and rapid shifts, the industry profile of the midsize cities became much more like that of the nation as a whole. There are other indications that employment profiles are becoming more similar. Table 2.5 shows that the distribution of the proportional share of total employment for most of the industry groups became much tighter over the course of the decade. For most industries, both the standard deviation and the range decreased between 1996 and 2011. The only exception was in business services where both measures increased. While there continue to be distinct differences in the employment profiles of the midsize urban areas, these differences are becoming less prominent. Measures of dispersion, such as the range between highest and lowest employment share, have decreased for every industry except business services.

The rapid growth of service industries resulted in changes in the economic base classification of most of the midsize urban areas (Table 2.6). Just twenty of the midsize urban areas had the same economic base in 2011 as they did in 1996. Manufacturing (eight of twelve), diversified (six of eight), and natural resource (five of eight) local economies had the same economic base during this fifteen-year period. (See Appendix A, Table 3 for a complete list of the economic bases of all midsize

Table 2.6 Change in Economic Base, 1996–2011

1996–2011	Natural Resources	Manufacturing	Trade	Health/ Education	Other Services	Diversified	TOTAL
Natural Resources	5	-	-	-	-	3	8
Manufacturing	-	8	-	-	-	4	12
Trade	1	-	-	1	1	3	6
Health/Education	1	-	-	1	-	4	6
Other Services	-	-	-	-	-	2	2
Diversified	-	-	-	2	-	6	8
TOTAL	7	8	0	4	1	22	42

Source: Statistics Canada

communities.) None of the trade or other service-based economies continued to have the same economic base; only one of the six urban areas where health and education services dominated in 1996 remained in this category.

Among the communities that experienced a change in economic base over the decade, the largest increase occurred in the number of diversified economies. Fourteen urban areas moved into the diversified category, with all other economic specializations contributing to the increase. The number of local economies relying on natural resources increased from seven to ten, in most cases as a result of the growth of the energy economy in Western Canada.

Note that these changes in economic base are based on relative rather than absolute changes in employment. None of communities experienced a net decline in employment. Trois-Rivières, Quebec, was the only urban area where employment growth was less than 10 percent. There were net losses of trade jobs in sixteen metro areas and of manufacturing jobs in fourteen. But only two of the latter group, Sarnia and St. Catharines-Niagara, had an economy based on manufacturing in 1996. Among the urban areas shifting from an economic base of health care/education to one that is diversified, all experienced an increase in health and education employment over the decade. The shift in classification resulted from the even larger increases in other industries. Similarly, urban areas where the economic base changed from trade to diversified experienced growth in trade employment, but at slower rates than some of the services; only Belleville, ON, actually saw an absolute decline in wholesale and retail trade jobs.

Overall, the employment structure of the midsize urban areas has become more homogenous and increasingly similar to the national economy since 1996. While the 1996 employment profile of the midsize metropolitan areas suggested that they functioned as centers of trade and services, by 2011 these distinctions had largely dissipated. The energy boom in recent years resulted in an increase in the number of communities where natural resources employment defines the economic base. Uneven employment growth across industries has lessened the dominance of the key industry. Over half of the midsize urban areas no longer have a distinct economic base; that is, they do not have any industry in which local employment is at least 30 percent higher than the national average.[4] Although some have had success in attracting business and financial service jobs, this industry is not dominant in any of the midsize metropolitan areas.

ECONOMIC BASE AND ECONOMIC PROSPERITY

What have been the consequences of these transformations in terms of economic prosperity? Which communities are better off, those that are able to successfully diversify or those that have been able to adapt to changes brought on by globalization and deindustrialization? Are the new employment opportunities that have been added sufficient to allow these communities to grow and prosper? Or have the urban areas that have retained their traditional economic base enjoyed greater prosperity?

---

4. A smaller location quotient does not indicate an absolute decline; it simply means that the local employment growth is occurring at a slower rate than the national average.

Table 2.7 Average Prosperity Score by Region, 1996–2011

	1996	2001	2006	2011
Maritimes	318	294	301	301
Ontario	326	304	303	297
Quebec	293	286	289	277
West	316	298	305	306
All Midsize	316	297	301	295

Table 2.7 provides the average economic prosperity score of the midsize metropolitan areas by region. Initially, the midsize metro areas' prosperity scores were substantially above the national average; Quebec communities were the only ones that had prosperity scores below the national average. Ontario communities had the highest average prosperity score.

Over the next five years, the average prosperity index fell from 316 to 297. Because the Economic Prosperity Index reflects relative health, this change reflects slower growth in these communities than the national average, rather than an actual decline in the prosperity of the midsize cities. The midsize cities' prosperity scores were particularly affected by lower growth in income and the share of income from private, non-government sources. There was a modest recovery over the next five years; only the Ontario communities experienced a decline in the 2001–06 period. The average prosperity score for all midsize urban areas declined to 295 in 2011. Communities in Central Canada declined while there was a slight increase in Western Canadian cities.

When categorized by economic base (Table 2.8), the same cyclical pattern is evident. With the exception of communities whose economic base was other services, midsize metropolitan areas experienced a relative decline in average economic health scores between 1996 and 2001. Between 2001 and 2006, all of the urban areas recorded a small improvement. In the most recent five-year period, natural resources communities had an increase in average prosperity scores. Manufacturing cities experienced the largest declines, an average of 15 points. The communities with economic bases in services, as well as diversified economies, were just slightly below the average for all midsize urban areas.

Table 2.8 Trends in Prosperity Scores by Economic Base, 1996–2011

Economic Base	Average Health Score			
	1996	2001	2006	2011
Natural Resources	315	295	303	307
Manufacturing	318	300	303	288
Trade	314	nil	nil	nil
Business Services	nil	nil	294	mil
Education/ Health Care	327	296	301	294
Other Services	302	304	304	294
Diverse	311	297	299	294
All Midsize	316	297	301	295

Source: Statistics Canada

The average economic ratings obscure some important differences. For example, the Ontario manufacturing communities in 1996 had an average Economic Health Index of 336, which subsequently declined to an average value of 300 in 2011. At the end of the period, although their 2011 prosperity scores had declined, Guelph and Kitchener ranked well above the other three manufacturing cities. The five Quebec manufacturing cities, on the other hand, began with an average index of 287 (49 points below their Ontario counterparts). By 2011, the average index value for the Quebec cities had decreased to 278, but the gap between Quebec and Ontario manufacturing centers was cut in half.

Ten urban areas maintained a prosperity index of at least 300 throughout the period. Five of these (Barrie, Guelph, Kingston, Kitchener, and Oshawa) are in Ontario and four in Western Canada (Prince George, Red Deer, Regina, and Victoria). Halifax is the only city in the Maritimes with consistently above-average prosperity scores.

ECONOMIC HEALTH AND COMMUNITY ATTRIBUTES

In the previous section, we described the sets of variables that are used in the following examination of what attributes of a community are related to its economic health. There are clear differences among the mid-size communities in each of the dimensions considered (economic base and economic well-being). In some instances, geography is an important factor. In this section we examine the relationships among the variables through correlation and regression analysis. We address the following questions:

- Which community characteristics are associated with differences in community economic well-being?
- Are there specific attributes more likely to be found in economically healthy communities?

Understanding these relationships can be used to inform public policy decisions. Table 2.9 presents the significant correlations between specific demographic attributes and the Economic Prosperity Index (EPI) in census years from 1996 to 2011. The highest correlations are between the Economic Prosperity Index in different years. Each possible pair of indexes is correlated at the highest level. Despite the significant fluctuations in the EPIs for individual urban areas that were noted previously, there appears to be considerable path dependency in this measure.

Additional variables considered include total population, proportions of immigrants and visible minorities (measures of diversity), and proportion of university graduates (measure of skill or talent). Total population in 1991 and 1996 show similar patterns of correlations: they are significantly correlated initially but the strength of the correlation diminished over time. There are no significant population correlates in 2001 or 2006. The 2011 population, however, is significantly correlated in all four years, with the strength of the correlation steadily decreasing.

The current proportion of immigrants is significantly correlated with prosperity in each census year; in 2001 and 2006, the correlation remains significant in subsequent years. Visible minorities are positively

Table 2.9 Significant Demographic Correlates of EPI, 1996–2011

	Prosperity Index 1996	Prosperity Index 2001	Prosperity Index 2006	Prosperity Index 2011
Prosperity Index 1996	1	.731**	.514**	.615**
Prosperity Index 2001		1	.743**	.711**
Prosperity Index 2006			1	.717**
Prosperity Index 2011				1
Population 1991	.635**	.477**	.324*	
Population 1996	**.649****	.502**	.346*	
Population 2011				**.311***
Visible Minorities 2001		**.575****	.389*	.462**
Visible Minorities 2006			**.343***	.423**
Visible Minorities 2011				**.522****
Immigrants 1996	**.349***			
Immigrants 2001		**.613****	.362*	.420**
Immigrants 2006			**.360***	.421**
Immigrants 2011				**.444****
University 1996	**.340***	.347*		
University 2001		**.471****		.417**
University 2006				.420**
University 2011				**.513****

**Significant at 0.01
*Significant at 0.05

Source: Statistics Canada, Canadian Census

and significantly correlated with the EPI starting in 2001; the strength of these relationships increases between 2006 and 2011. With the exception of 2006, there is a significant correlation between the proportion of university graduates and the current EPI; the 2001 and 2006 proportions are also significantly correlated with the 2011 EPI.

Perhaps the most interesting aspect here is the lagged relationships. Population in 1991 continues to be significantly related to economic prosperity in 2006; immigrant and visible minority populations show similar results. Although the population of university graduates is significantly related to current prosperity in three of the years, the relationship in subsequent years does not always remain significant.

The concurrent and lagged measures of economic specialization were correlated with economic prosperity (Table 2.10). The correlation between the current measure of business services and the prosperity index was positive and significant in three of the four years. The only other concurrent correlation that significant was a negative one between manufacturing employment and prosperity in 2011.

Several variables were significantly correlated with the prosperity score five years later. By far the strongest correlation was between the prosperity score and the score recorded five years earlier. That is, the economic health of the community five years earlier exhibited the highest degree of correlation with present health. This relationship appears to extend over even longer time periods; the 1996 health scores were significantly correlated with the 2006 prosperity score at the .001 level.

DISCUSSION

From the point of view of planners and policy makers, the statistical relationships described above are somewhat discouraging. Overall, community economic health scores are most strongly correlated with the economic health score from five years earlier. There is nothing that can be done to change a past that reflects the accumulation of historical choices and "place luck" (Reese and Ye, 2011). The opportunities to alter this path dependency by public policy decisions seem limited. Some of the strongest positive correlations (e.g., metropolitan population, university graduates) are not really policy variables. The significant negative correlation with manufacturing employment should not lead to the conclusion that a community should adopt policies aimed at eliminating existing manufacturing jobs.

There are issues of critical mass (which may be measured by population, income, or economic activities) that limit the potential of many midsize cities. Historic accidents as well as conscious choices, by private interests and public policies, further limit the scope of actions. This is not to say that nothing can be done to improve the economy. Rather,

Table 2.10 Correlations of Economic Prosperity and Industry

	1996		2001		2006		2011	
	Correlation	sig.	Correlation	sig.	Correlation	sig.	Correlation	sig.
Business Services 1996	0.510**	0.001	0.376*	0.014	0.337*	.029	0.434**	0.004
Manufacturing 1996							-0.380*	0.013
Business Services 2001	0.504**	.001	0.311*	.045			0.570**	.000
Manufacturing 2001							-0.428**	.005
Manufacturing 2006							-0.387*	.011
Health/Higher Ed. 2006	0.406**	.008					0.468**	.002
Business Services 2011	0.605**	.000	0.589**	.000	0.448**	.003	0.582**	.000
Manufacturing 2011							-0.353*	.022
Trade 2011	-0.354*	.021	-0.390*	.011				
Prosperity Index 1996			0.731**	0.000	0.514**	0.001	0.615**	0.000
Prosperity Index 2001	0.731**	.000			0.743**	.000	0.711**	.000
Prosperity Index 2006	0.514**	.001	0.743**	.000			0.717**	.000
Prosperity Index 2011	0.615**	.000	0.711**	.000	0.717**	.000		

*Correlation significant at .05
**Correlation significant at .01

it recognizes that meaningful change, at either the metropolitan or city center level, will be slow, uncertain, and difficult.

This analysis perhaps raises more questions than it answers. At the metropolitan level, it is clear that the local economic structure does affect economic prospects: resource-based economies are likely to be volatile, while manufacturing economies, at least those tied to the automobile industry, are likely to continue to struggle. Diverse economies (those with more than one industry specialization) and those based on professional services can be expected to continue to enjoy above-average economic health. Communities with no discernible economic specialization, on the other hand, may face the most difficult challenges.

Just as economic conditions are changing, both absolutely and relative to the national average, local economic structures are also evolving. Is there a relationship between changes in the industrial composition of a local economy and its economic well-being? Can communities diversify or develop entirely new specializations? Or do past decisions and "place luck" limit the potential of midsize cities to reinvent themselves to meet the challenges of the new globalized and deindustrialized economy?

There is also a need for a better understanding of causal connections and the potential for public policies that will encourage positive changes. Disaggregating the measures of economic well-being as well as the industry categories may be essential to improving understanding. The presence in a community of a large research university (or hospital) may indeed make a significant contribution to overall community economic health, but a recommendation to create such an institution *de novo* would be unrealistic—economies of scale and limited funding are obvious obstacles. Fostering growth in professional services employment may not be a strategy that can be successfully pursued by all midsize cities, especially those close to large urban centers (Sands, 2007a).

In the short run, policy options for realizing changes in the community economic base appear limited. Attracting new industries or firms that will add jobs to the local economy is a lengthy and difficult process, especially in competitive markets. Even today, firms are not entirely footloose and will seek locations that provide access to their particular set of suppliers, labor force, and markets. Providing public support for firms in declining industries will not ensure that they grow or even survive (Reese and Sands, 2007).

The prospects for bringing about economic restructuring are some-what brighter in the longer run. As the national economy continues to shift from natural resources and manufacturing to higher order services, midsize cities may see growth not only as spillovers from larger metropol-itan areas but also from increasing demand from the local market area. Ensuring the availability of an educated and skilled labor force (itself a long term project) and focusing on maintaining and improving quality of life will make the community more attractive and viable.

3

Prosperity and the New Economy

Today we are evolving rapidly into a post-industrial, knowledge-based society as our economies are steadily shifting from material- and labor-intensive products and processes to knowledge-intensive products and services. A radically new system for creating wealth has evolved that depends upon the creation and application of new knowledge.

Duderstadt, 2015, 9

The previous chapter examined the relationships between community economic base, industrial restructuring, and the relative prosperity of urban areas. Despite substantial economic restructuring, natural resources and goods producing (manufacturing and construction) industries continue to define the economic base of more than 40 percent of the midsize Canadian urban areas. Although natural resources employment in the midsize communities decreased slightly (about 1 percent), seventeen of these urban areas experienced an increase in this category, primarily as a result of the energy boom in Western Canada. Aggregate manufacturing employment in midsize communities declined by 17 percent, with twenty-nine of the forty-two midsize urban areas recording reductions in the number of manufacturing workers over the past two decades. Despite these declines, half of the midsize areas remained above the national average of 9.2 percent in manufacturing employment, led by Granby at 24.6 percent and Drummondville at 21.7 percent.

In most midsize metropolitan areas, there has been a complementary increase in the importance of services industries in their economic profile. Across North America, communities of all sizes have experienced absolute and relative growth in services employment. Excluding natural resources, manufacturing, and trade, 63.3 percent of all Canadian jobs were in services industries in 2011. The comparable figure for midsize urban areas was slightly higher at 63.6 percent. The proportion of services jobs was highest in three provincial capitals—Victoria (74 percent), Fredericton (73.1 percent), and Halifax (72.3 percent), along with Kingston (73.8 percent). The lowest proportions of services employment are found in the small manufacturing centers in Quebec, including Granby (48.5 percent) and Drummondville (49.1 percent).

This chapter considers the relationships between growth in the services sector employment and the economic prosperity of the midsize urban areas. Because of the wide variety of jobs that fall under the services umbrella, we give particular attention to the occupations that are representative of the New Economy. While there is little consensus on which jobs should be included in the definition of New Economy, most definitions typically include business services, information technology, and other knowledge and technical occupations. Richard Florida's (2005a) conceptualization of the creative class is extremely broad, comprising over half of total employment in some US metropolitan areas. Here, however, we will use a much narrower definition, one that focuses on creative and knowledge occupations. In addition, since many New Economy occupations require university or other post-secondary training, we use the proportion of university graduates to assess the metropolitan area's potential to be successful in transitioning to the New Economy.

This chapter considers the following questions:

- Is the prosperity of midsize urban areas a function of their New Economy and creative job base?
- Are there particular occupations that better explain differences in the relative prosperity of these communities?
- Are midsize metropolitan areas close to major urban centers more likely to attract creative jobs than more remote communities?

UNIVERSITY DEGREES

In 1991, 13.4 percent of Canadians over the age of 15 possessed a university degree. University graduates were most likely to be found in the larger metropolitan areas. Each of the three largest Canadian metropolitan areas had a higher proportion of university graduates than the national average, led by Toronto, where 18.7 percent of the adult population had a bachelor's degree or higher. The proportion of university graduates in midsize metropolitan areas ranged from 18.7 percent in Fredericton, NB, to just 5.2 percent in Shawinigan, QC. Four other midsize communities had 15 percent or more of their adult population with university degrees.

By 2011, the proportion of university graduates in Canada had increased to 20.9 percent from 13.4 percent. Increases in the proportion of university graduates in the largest metropolitan areas were even greater; for example, the proportion of university degree holders in Toronto and Vancouver rose by about eleven percentage points, to 29.9 percent and 27.7 percent, respectively. The proportion of university degree holders rose in all of the midsize cities with increases ranging from 2.6 percentage points in Saskatoon to 15.9 percentage points in Barrie. Fredericton continued to have the highest proportion of university graduates (28.4 percent) and Shawinigan the lowest (8.6 percent).

There is a positive and significant relationship between a university-educated workforce and the Economic Prosperity Index for the midsize metropolitan areas. The correlation between the two has risen from 0.353 in 1991 to 0.514 in 2011. Moreover, there is a strong correlation (generally 0.4 to 0.5) between the proportion of university graduates and subsequent EPI scores. For example, the correlation between university graduates in 1991 and the 1996 EPI scores is 0.509; even in 2011 the correlation is 0.438.

CREATIVE OCCUPATIONS

The traditional economic base analysis defined by industries does not provide a completely accurate picture. Industries such as higher education, health care, business services, and finance, insurance and real estate are more representative of the New Economy than manufacturing or natural resources. However, employment in these industries is not homogeneous; they may also include a substantial number of jobs that do not fit the Creative definition, ranging from clerks to laundry workers to janitors. The use of occupational data makes it possible to focus on the higher skilled occupations in these industries, as well as identifying the high-tech occupations within the manufacturing industries.

In general terms, New Economy jobs include technology, knowledge, and creative activities that can provide the economic foundation for a prosperous and sustainable local economy. While these jobs typically require university credentials or specialized training, determining specifically what constitutes a New Economy occupation is not necessarily clear-cut. There is no single "correct" answer. Choices with respect to which job categories to leave in or leave out of the definition are just as likely to be based on data availability as on their conceptual relevance. Richard Florida (2002b, 2005b) has offered several different definitions of creative class membership. The creative class may include engineering and information technology workers, university faculty, as well as artists, performers, and musicians.

Here we adopt a narrow definition of creative occupations, one that is limited to creative and performing artists, design professionals, writers, and photographers. The specific Statistics Canada occupation codes are provided in Table 3.1.[1] Knowledge- or information-based employment, including computer and information technology, librarians and archivists, university faculty, and management consultants, are not included.[2]

These occupation data report employment by residence of the workers rather than by location of the jobs. As a result, a community could have a large number of New Economy workers and no New Economy jobs (or vice versa). While such an extreme condition is unlikely, commuting to jobs outside of the Census Metropolitan Area or Census

---

1. Appendix A, Table 4 presents the proportion of creative jobs in all forty-two midsize urban areas.

2. When these additional occupations were included as creative occupations, the results were similar to those presented here.

Table 3.1 New Economy Occupations, by Statistics Canada Codes

	1991–2006	2011
Architects, landscape architects, land surveyors	C05	215
Authors & Writers	F021	5121
Creative & Performing Artists	F03	513
Photographers	F121	5201
Announcers	F13	523
Creative Designers	F14	524

Source: Statistics Canada

Agglomeration could distort the results to some degree. These occupations represent a very small proportion of the total work force in most communities; nevertheless, most of the midsize metropolitan areas include at least some employment in these occupational categories.

In 1991, there were about 177,000 creative workers in Canada, representing 1.25 percent of total employment (Table 3.2). Almost half of these jobs (84,000) were in one of the three largest Census Metropolitan Areas. Over the next two decades, the number of creative workers in Canada increased by more than 61 percent, to a total of 286,000. Creative jobs in Toronto, Montreal, and Vancouver increased by 53,000, to 137,000, a 63 percent rate of growth. During the same period, total employment in Canada and its three largest CMAs rose by 17 percent and 23 percent, respectively.

In 1991, creative jobs accounted for an average of 1.15 percent of total employment in midsize urban areas, ranging from about 2 percent in St. John's and Sherbrooke to just 0.72 percent in Cornwall and Sault Ste. Marie (Appendix Table A3). Three provincial capitals (Victoria, Regina, and Halifax) were also among the top five in creative employment share. Eight of the ten lowest ranked urban areas were in Ontario.

Twenty years later, the average for all midsize urban areas had increased by four-tenths of a percentage point. Only the provincial capitals

Table 3.2 Creative Occupations, 1991 and 2011

	1991		2011		Change	
	Total	**Creative**	**Total**	**Creative**	**Total**	**Creative**
Canada	14,220,230	177,335	16,595,035	286,320	16.7%	61.5%
3 Largest CMA	4,749,215	84,105	5,860,690	137,225	23.4%	63.2%
42 Midsize	2,985,876	34,475	3,546,310	55,883	18.8%	62.1%

Source: Statistics Canada

of Victoria and Halifax remained in the top five for New Economy jobs. The substantial growth in creative employment that occurred in Nanaimo, Barrie, and Kelowna moved them to the top of the ranking. Brantford and Fredericton also recorded gains in creative employment of more than half a percentage point. Sixteen of the urban areas experienced declines in their relative share of employment in this category, with the largest decreases occurring in Sherbrooke (0.91 percentage points) and Saint-Hyacinthe (0.64 percentage points). These two communities, along with Saguenay and Shawinigan, recorded absolute as well as relative declines in Creative employment.

Occupational Correlates of Economic Prosperity

The top panel of Table 3.3 shows the correlations between the proportion of New Economy jobs and the Economic Prosperity Index. Beginning in 2001, the aggregate proportion of New Economy jobs is positively and significantly correlated with the concurrent Economic Prosperity Index. The lower part of this table presents the lagged correlations, showing that some of the correlations remain significant over time. For example, the 1991 proportion of New Economy jobs is significantly correlated with the prosperity scores in 1996, 2001, and 2011 (but not 2006). As noted previously, New Economy employment has tended to increase steadily overall, as well as in most of the midsize urban areas. The Economic Prosperity Index, however, has fluctuated from one year to the next, with an overall downward trend in most midsize metro areas. Despite the fact

Table 3.3 New Economy Occupations and Economic Prosperity, 1996–2011

New Economy Occupations	Economic Prosperity Index			
	1996	2001	2006	2011
1996	.113 (.476)			
2001		.474** (.002)		
2006			.345* (.025)	
2011				.512** (.001)
1991	.417** (.006)	.320* (.029)	.234 (.136)	.353* (.022)
1996		.261 (.095)	.218 (.166)	.140 (.375)
2001			.383* (.012)	.467** (.002)
2006				.440** (.004)

**Significant at 0.01
*Significant at 0.05

Source: Statistics Canada, Canadian Census

that the two measures are moving in different directions, the correlations are uniformly positive.

Table 3.4 reports the correlations between specific New Economy occupation categories and current and future levels of the Economic Prosperity Index. Only the statistically significant correlations are reported here. Figures in bold type represent significant correlations between occupations and the concurrent prosperity levels.

In general, computer and information technology occupations tend to be significantly correlated with both concurrent and future levels of economic prosperity.[3] Management consulting jobs are also significantly correlated with the EPI beginning in 2001, and have continued to be significant in subsequent years. The proportion of university professors in several years is significantly related to prosperity measures in later time

---

3. There are a number of instances of statistically significant correlations with the EPI in earlier years; however, these relationships do not appear to be relevant.

Table 3.4 Specific Occupations and Future Economic Prosperity, 1996–2011

Category	Year	1996	2001	2006	2011
Computer Occupations	1991	.319*			
	1996		.378*	.331*	
	2001		.511**	.410**	.418**
	2006			.413**	.431**
	2011				.442**
Library and Information Occupations	2006				.410**
Management Consultants	2001		.533**	.456**	.449**
	2006			.372*	.478**
	2011				.359*
Professors	1991	.320*	.305*		.342*
	2001		.533**	.455**	.449**
	2006			.372*	.478**
Artists	1991	.333*		.362*	.467**
	2001			.374*	.484*
	2006			.306*	.513**
	2011				.401**
Design	2006				.492**
	2011				.437**

**Significant at 0.01
*Significant at 0.05

Source: Statistics Canada, Canadian Census

periods. For the remaining New Economy occupation categories, the results are occasionally but not consistently significant.

Occupational Structure and Changes in Economic Prosperity

We now consider the relationships between occupational structure and *changes* in the Economic Prosperity Index. Over the decades, there were substantial changes in the EPI for most of the midsize urban areas. The average change was a decline of about twenty-one points, or about 7 percent.

Table 3.5 New Economy Occupations and Change in EPI

	Change		
	1996–2001	**2006–2011**	**1991–2011**
Designers 2006		-.444**	
Artists 2006		.325*	
Change			
Designers 2001–2006		.307*	
Artists 1991–1996	-.308*		
Artists 1996–2001		.429**	-.331*
Total 2006–2011		.352*	
Total 1991–2011			.554**

**Significant at 0.01
*Significant at 0.05

Source: Statistics Canada, Canadian Census

Only one of every six midsize metro areas recorded a net increase in its EPI between 1996 and 2011.[4]

Table 3.5 presents the correlations between occupational variables and changes in EPI; only the statistically significant results are presented. Unlike the correlations with the absolute levels of the EPI, there are few variables that have a statistically significant correlation with current or future levels of EPI change. The 2006 proportions of creative and performing artists and design professionals are both significantly correlated with change in EPI over the next five years; however, the correlations have different signs. There is a negative relationship between designers and 2006–2011 prosperity change; for arts professionals, there is a positive correlation. None of the other New Economy occupations have a significant relationship with change in EPI.

Changes in the proportion of creative and performing artists and design professionals are the only occupational changes that have a

---

4. Recall that the EPI compares the local indicators to the comparable national averages; the actual number of communities with absolute improvements is greater than the number with relative improvement.

significant relationship with changes in EPI. Generally, a change in an occupational measure is related to a change in the prosperity measure in the subsequent five-year period. The correlations with changes in the proportion of artists are inconsistent, however. Change in the total proportion of New Economy jobs between 1991 and 2011 is significantly related to changes in EPI over the same period. Again, the relationship is positive even though the indicators are moving in different directions.

Similar to the results of other studies (Sands, 2009; Reese and Sands, 2007b), the single most consistent predictor of future economic prosperity is current economic prosperity. These results suggest that the current New Economy employment data do not provide a strong indicator of future economic prosperity. As was the case with measures of industrial structure discussed in the previous chapter, there are clearly other factors at work. Although changes in economic fortunes do occur, for the most part it is likely that well-off communities will continue to prosper, while struggling communities will seldom realize substantial gains in economic well-being.

These findings may be relevant to local economic development strategies. A strategy to increase the number of jobs in professional service industries or jobs in the arts and other creative fields will not automatically lead to improvements in city prosperity. (This result is another reminder that local economic development is a difficult task.) The finding that New Economy *occupations* are more strongly correlated with economic prosperity than are New Economy *industries* could be useful to local economic developers. Even traditional manufacturing can make a large contribution to economic prosperity if it increases employment for engineers and designers. None of the variables considered were reliable predictors of future changes in economic prosperity.

CREATIVE OCCUPATIONS
AND ECONOMIC PROSPERITY

In most of the midsize metropolitan areas, the number of information science and high-tech jobs is greater than the number of creative workers. This section considers the relationships between these creative jobs and

Table 3.6 Highest and Lowest Proportions of Creative Workers, 1991–2011

1991	% Creative	2001	% Creative	2011	% Creative
Victoria	1.565%	Victoria	2.242%	Barrie	1.624%
Regina	1.477%	Halifax	1.549%	Nanaimo	1.579%
Halifax	1.327%	St. John's	1.440%	Kelowna	1.561%
Saskatoon	1.203%	Kelowna	1.405%	Fredericton	1.462%
London	1.198%	Nanaimo	1.306%	Halifax	1.452%
Cornwall	0.683%	Prince George	0.749%	Sarnia	0.685%
Thunder Bay	0.652%	Saint-Jean-sur-Richelieu	0.686%	Chilliwack	0.671%
Brantford	0.649%	Saguenay	0.635%	Saint-Hyacinthe	0.500%
Sault Ste. Marie	0.646%	Cornwall	0.595%	Shawinigan	0.339%
Shawinigan	0.541%	Shawinigan	0.548%	Cornwall	0.181%
Average	0.945%	Average	1.059%	Average	1.025%

Source: Statistics Canada

community prosperity. The largest number of creative jobs are included in the Statistics Canada category of professional occupations in creative and performing arts (see Appendix Table 3.2). Additional creative occupations include creative designers, authors and writers, announcers, and managers in these fields. Although architects and landscape architects are sometimes counted as creative professionals, no significant relationship was found here between these occupations and measures of economic health.

In 1991, creative occupations made up just under 1 percent of the jobs in the midsize urban areas. Three provincial capitals topped the rankings (Table 3.6). Shawinigan QC had the smallest proportion of creative workers. The next four places were held by Ontario metropolitan areas.

Over the next two decades, the number of creative workers increased by 25.7 percent. Absolute increases occurred in all but nine of the midsize metropolitan areas. During the same period, total employment in these communities rose by 19.8 percent, resulting in a slight gain in the creative proportion of employment. By 2011, Halifax was the only one of the original communities to remain in the top five. The majority of the bottom five metros also changed, with only Cornwall and Shawinigan remaining. In each of these urban areas, creative and performing artists (including actors, dancers, musicians, and painters) and creative designers (including fashion and theater designers, graphics designers, and illustrators) are the two largest categories.

The upper panel of Figure 3.1 presents the relationship between the proportion of all creative occupations and the Economic Prosperity Index in 1991. Although there is a positive relationship between the two variables, the trend line is relatively flat. The R-square value is just 0.1383, meaning that only just under 14 percent of the variance in prosperity is accounted for by creative occupations.

Two decades later, the scattergram for 2011 (lower panel) indicates a much stronger and more positive relationship. The trend line slopes upward more sharply and the R-square value is 0.3361. Even though creative occupations remain a small proportion of total employment in midsize urban areas, the importance of their relationship to economic prosperity has increased substantially.

CITY REGIONS AND ECONOMIC PROSPERITY

Given Canada's large geographic area and relatively small population, it is not surprising that there are substantial regional differences across the country. Central Canada–Ontario and Quebec–has enjoyed relative prosperity largely due to the concentrations of manufacturing and financial services located there. The Maritimes and Western Canada, on the other hand, have had a greater reliance on natural resources. In recent decades, the West has enjoyed considerable prosperity due to its energy resources; the long-term decline of fisheries has had a negative effect on the Maritimes.

Employment concentrations in creative occupations are typically found in large metropolitan areas. Small cities are thought to be at a considerable disadvantage in attracting and retaining such jobs. As a result,

Figure 3.1 Creative occupations and economic prosperity

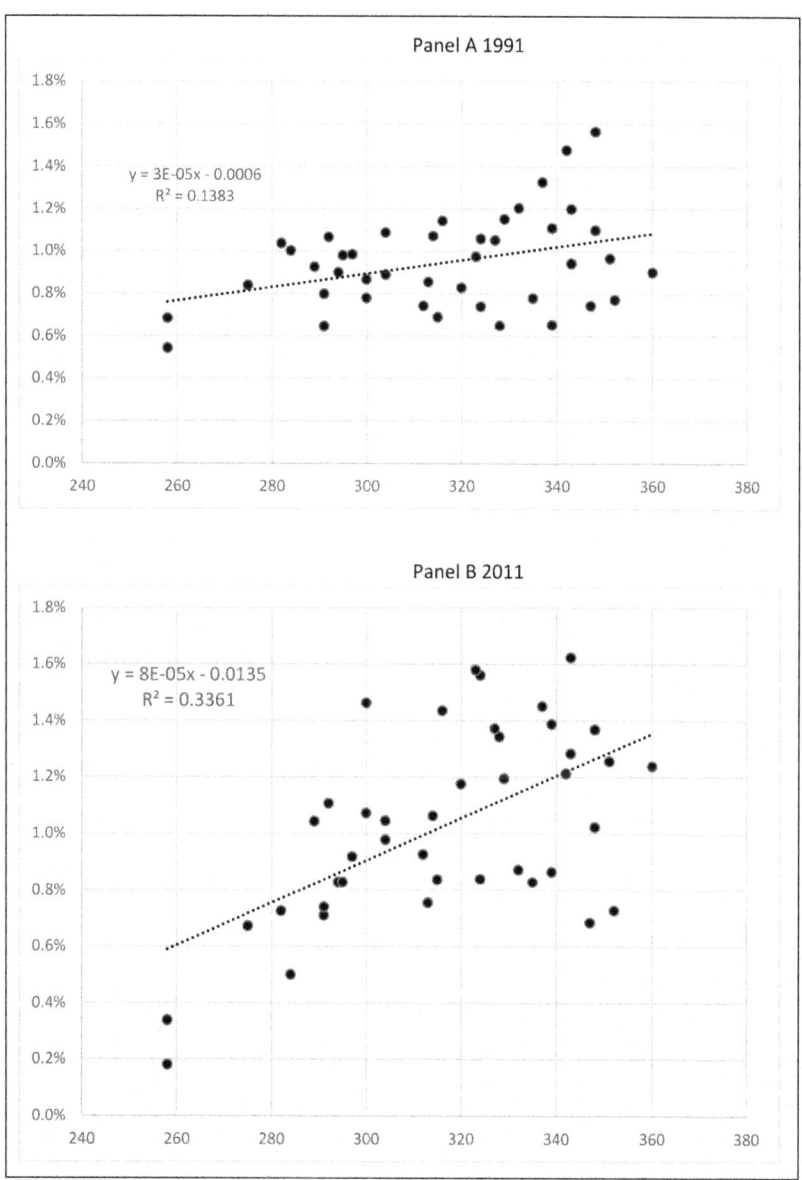

Source: Statistics Canada

major metropolitan areas seem likely to increase their dominant position. As job opportunities in these fields continue to grow, smaller urban centers may become competitive in attracting creative workers, especially if they are relatively close to a large urban center.

In this part of the analysis, we consider the regional effects of New Economy employment by examining economic prosperity in midsize urban areas in the same province as the three largest Canadian cities—Toronto, Montreal, and Vancouver. Canada's three largest CMAs have attracted above-average proportions of New Economy jobs and enjoy levels of economic health that are also above the national average. But what about the nearby, smaller urban areas? Are these CMAs and CAs experiencing any positive benefits of their proximity to the major metropolitan areas?

In this chapter, the term *City Region* is used to denote a subsystem of urban areas close to the major urban centers of Montreal, Toronto, and Vancouver, which together account for over one-third of the total Canadian population. Historically a manufacturing and government center, Toronto (the capital of Ontario) has become an increasingly important financial and business services center over the last quarter-century. Montreal is the largest metropolitan area in francophone Canada. Although Montreal has retained much of its manufacturing base, population and economic growth have been relatively flat in recent decades. Cultural and creative industries are an important part of the city's economy. Vancouver has benefitted in recent years from the economic growth of the Pacific Rim. The metropolitan area growth rate has exceeded that of the other two large metropolitan areas. Service industries are the most important component of the local economy.

Each of these metropolitan regions has a number of peripheral metropolitan areas that are close enough to a major center to be influenced by it, but are far enough away that they are not just suburbs. Indeed, these peripheral cities initially developed as independent cities separated from the larger urban center by what was then a significant distance. The economic fortunes of these midsize urban areas are linked to the larger ones through commuting and commercial ties, as well as their provision of lower-cost housing alternatives. The specific metropolitan areas included in each city-region are identified in Table 3.7.

Table 3.7 Satellite and Remote Midsize Urban Areas

Province	Satellite	Remote	
Quebec	Drummondville	Saguenay	
	Granby	Shawinigan	
	Saint-Hyacinthe	Trois-Rivières	
	Saint-Jean-sur-Richelieu		
	Sherbrooke		
Ontario	Brantford	Barrie	North Bay
	Guelph	Belleville	Peterborough
	Kitchener	Cornwall	Sarnia
	Oshawa	Greater Sudbury	Sault Ste. Marie
	St. Catharines-Niagara	Kingston	Thunder Bay
		London	Windsor
British Columbia	Abbotsford	Chilliwack	
	Nanaimo	Kamloops	
	Victoria	Kelowna	
		Prince George	

Source: Statistics Canada

In examining these relationships, two different approaches are used. First, satellite metropolitan areas (those closest to the major urban centers) are compared to the balance of midsize metropolitan areas in the same province. The second approach compares the relative prosperity of the midsize areas closest to the major urban centers in comparison to the major city. Here, the base for each index (location quotient) is the corresponding value for the regional metropolis; that is, incomes in the Quebec satellite urban areas are compared to that of Montreal, while in British Columbia, the comparison is to Vancouver. Because both Toronto and Vancouver have Economic Prosperity Index scores above the national average (315 and 307, respectively, in 2011), comparing the smaller cities to the large city score lowers the EPI for the midsize cities. In the case of Montreal, however, with a 2011 index of 285, using its

Table 3.8 Demographic Characteristics of Satellite and Remote Metro Areas

	Population		Visible Minorities		Immigrants		University Graduates	
	1996	2011	1996	2011	1996	2011	1996	2011
Ontario Satellite	175,451	199,505	7.1%	12.5%	14.9%	18.5%	17.6%	18.9%
Ontario Remote	90,715	111,538	4.6%	5.6%	13.5%	11.3%	13.5%	13.6%
Quebec Satellite	74,573	100,478	5.8%	12.4%	10.0%	17.1%	18.3%	18.0%
Quebec Remote	143,034	157,685	2.8%	5.8%	12.1%	10.7%	14.7%	17.0%
British Columbia Satellite	79,573	100,478	3.1%	2.9%	5.7%	4.0%	13.6%	13.1%
British Columbia Remote	120,087	117,977	2.0%	1.2%	2.5%	1.5%	17.4%	12.6%

Source: Statistics Canada

Economic Prosperity Index score as the base for the location quotient raises the scores for the midsize metropolitan areas.

Satellite and Remote Urban Areas

Table 3.8 provides a comparison between the satellite and remote urban areas in the three provinces. Ontario is the only province in which the average population of the satellite metro areas is larger than that of the remote communities. The average population of remote Ontario metropolitan areas grew more rapidly between 1996 and 2011, narrowing the gap between the two. In the other provinces, population growth was more robust among the satellite communities. The average population of the remote British Columbia metros actually declined slightly.

With respect to the presence of visible minorities and immigrants, the satellite metros have higher proportions of both than their more remote

Table 3.9 Highest and Lowest Average Location Quotients

	Average Industrial Location Quotients							
	1996		2001		2006		2011	
	High	Low	High	Low	High	Low	High	Low
Ontario Satellite	Mfg.	Serv.	Mfg.	Nat Res	Mfg.	Nat Res	Mfg.	Nat Res
Ontario Remote	HEH	Serv.	HEH	Nat Res	Serv.	Nat Res	HEH	Nat Res
Quebec Satellite	Mfg.	Nat Res	Mfg.	Nat Res	Mfg.	Nat Res	Mfg.	Nat Res
Quebec Remote	Mfg.	Nat Res	Mfg.	Nat Res	Bus Serv.	HEH	Bus Serv.	HEH
British Columbia Satellite	Nat Res	Serv.	Serv.	Mfg.	Serv.	Mfg.	Serv.	Bus Serv.
British Columbia Remote	Nat Res	Bus Serv.	Nat Res	Mfg.	Nat Res	Mfg.	Nat Res	Bus Serv.

counterparts. The proportions of visible minorities have increased in these Central Canada metro areas while declining in British Columbia. The immigrant percentages also decreased in British Columbia, as well as in the remote urban areas in Central Canada. In 2011, the satellite metros in all three provinces had higher proportions of university graduates than the remote communities; the difference, however, is substantial only in Ontario.

There are also differences in the economic bases of these communities. Table 3.9 compares the highest and lowest average location quotients for each pair of metropolitan areas. In 1996, manufacturing was generally the most prominent economic base in Central Canada (with the highest average industrial location quotient), while natural resource industries were highest in British Columbia. Over the next fifteen years, manufacturing continued to be prominent in the satellite communities in Ontario and Quebec. Natural resources continued high in the remote British Columbia urban areas, but were the lowest in Ontario and Quebec satellite communities. New Economy industries such as business services were prominent in remote areas of Quebec in 2006 and 2011, but were the lowest category throughout British Columbia in 2011. Overall, however, there is little indication of significant differences in the role of New Economy industries between satellite and remote urban areas.

The patterns are clearer when New Economy occupations are considered (Table 3.10). Quebec midsize urban areas consistently have a lower proportion of New Economy jobs than either Ontario or British Columbia metro areas. The total proportion of New Economy jobs is consistently higher among the satellite metropolitan areas than it is in communities that are more remote. The same is true for all three subcategories in Ontario and British Columbia; in Quebec, arts occupations are slightly more likely to be found in the remote urban areas.

With the exception of the Quebec satellite communities, the proportion of New Economy jobs increased between 1996 and 2011, with the average increases smaller in the remote urban areas of Ontario and British Columbia. Among the specific occupational categories, there was generally a decline in the relative proportion of jobs in the creative and performing arts category and an increase in the design occupations.

Trends in the average Economic Prosperity Index scores for these communities are reported in Table 3.11. To the extent that there are positive economic benefits to communities in close proximity to major metro areas, the satellite metropolitan areas would be expected to have higher EPI scores than the more remote communities. This is indeed the case for the Ontario cities and, starting in 2001, for the Quebec urban areas. The pattern is different in British Columbia, where the satellite metropolitan areas start with a higher EPI score, but the difference virtually disappears in the later years.

Over time, there is a downward trend across all categories, with the exception of a modest (two to five point) increase between 2001 and 2006 in every category except the Ontario satellite urban areas. The differences between the satellite and remote community averages decline in Ontario and British Columbia but increase in Quebec.

Table 3.10 New Economy Occupations in Satellite and Remote Urban Areas

| | New Economy Jobs | | | | | | | |
| | Arts | | Design | | Other | | Total | |
	1996	2011	1996	2011	1996	2011	1996	2011
Ontario Satellite	0.53%	0.41%	0.45%	0.58%	2.64%	3.42%	3.62%	4.41%
Ontario Remote	0.51%	0.41%	0.39%	0.58%	2.07%	2.22%	2.97%	3.31%
Quebec Satellite	0.49%	0.24%	0.49%	0.67%	1.79%	1.83%	2.77%	2.74%
Quebec Remote	0.49%	0.32%	0.73%	0.49%	0.92%	1.60%	2.14%	2.41%
British Columbia Satellite	0.56%	0.57%	0.44%	0.94%	1.91%	2.94%	2.91%	4.45%
British Columbia Remote	0.51%	0.40%	0.38%	0.69%	1.23%	1.76%	2.12%	2.85%

Source: Statistics Canada

Prosperity Measures in Satellite Communities

We now turn our attention to the satellite urban areas in the three provinces. For this part of the analysis, the prosperity of the midsize urban areas will be measured against that of the nearby major metropolitan area. That is, the location quotients for the five communities close to Montreal will use that city's median income, market income share, and employment rate as the basis for comparison, rather than the corresponding

CHAPTER 3

Table 3.11 Average Economic Prosperity Index Scores, Satellite and Remote Urban Areas

	Average Economic Prosperity Index				
	1996	2001	2006	2011	1996–2011
Ontario Satellite	343	316	312	308	-35
Ontario Remote	320	299	300	292	-28
Quebec Satellite	292	289	292	277	-15
Quebec Remote	294	280	285	266	-28
British Columbia Satellite	333	295	297	299	-34
British Columbia Remote	307	295	298	297	-10

national figures. The Regional Prosperity Index scores are presented in Table 3.12.

The Regional Prosperity Index scores differ from their national counterparts in several respects. The downward trend in the EPI scores (see Appendix A, Table 4) is not as widespread in the RPIs; nor is the cyclical pattern. The range of RPI scores is considerably narrower, indicating that the economic fortunes of these midsize urban areas follow those of the nearby large metropolitan areas more than the nationwide trends.

The peripheral urban areas around Montreal generally had Economic Prosperity Indexes in 1996 that lagged Montreal; only Saint-Jean-sur-Richelieu had an overall index score above 300. Over the next five years, all of the smaller urban areas enjoyed substantial increases in their EPIs (see also Morazain, 2002). By 2006, however, all of the areas experienced a decline of ten points or more. Drummondville, Saint-Hyacinthe, and Sherbrooke experienced further declines between 2006 and 2011. Drummondville had the lowest EPI among the Quebec municipalities in each census year. Saint-Jean-sur-Richelieu had the highest index score in all four years and was the only community with an index consistently above 300. Montreal's index values have been quite close to the national averages throughout this period, so that the smaller urban areas in

Table 3.12 Regional EPIs, 1996–2011

		Economic Prosperity Index			
		1996	2001	2006	2011
Montreal	Drummondville	289	299	286	278
	Granby	293	305	291	293
	Saint-Hyacinthe	292	305	291	286
	Saint-Jean-sur-Richelieu	300	314	304	305
	Sherbrooke	297	310	294	285
Toronto	Brantford	288	280	280	279
	Guelph	309	309	310	303
	Kitchener	299	297	299	299
	Oshawa	308	306	308	307
	St. Catharines-Niagara	288	285	285	273
Vancouver	Abbotsford	289	285	298	294
	Nanaimo	281	260	289	276
	Victoria	298	297	307	297

Quebec have essentially the same economic health indexes they would have if they were being compared to national figures.

The communities in Ontario recorded relatively high prosperity scores, despite being compared to Toronto. Guelph and Oshawa had EPI scores above 300 in all four census years; Kitchener's scores were just below 300. The Prosperity Index scores for most communities are remarkably consistent over time. Brantford experienced a decline of eight percentage points between 1996 and 2001. St. Catharines-Niagara's score fell by twelve points between 2006 and 2011, leaving this community with the lowest score of any of the peripheral urban areas.

Each of the peripheral British Columbia municipalities had an Economic Health Index below that of Vancouver throughout the fifteen-year period. Victoria in 2006 was the only instance when the index for any of the communities was above 300; Abbotsford and Nanaimo also recorded their highest scores in that year. All three British Columbia urban areas had a decline in their prosperity scores in the last five years. Nanaimo's score declined by thirteen points; only Brantford has a lower Economic Health Index score in 2001. The cyclical pattern on Nanaimo's prosperity scores can be seen in the other two urban areas, but to a lesser degree.

NEW ECONOMY JOBS AND ECONOMIC HEALTH

What is the relationship between New Economy jobs and economic health in these urban areas? In 1991, New Economy jobs averaged about 3 percent of the total for these peripheral metropolitan areas, ranging from 1.5 percent in Abbotsford to over 5 percent in Guelph. Victoria and Kitchener also had high proportions of New Economy jobs. Sherbrooke, at just under 4 percent, had the largest proportion among the Quebec urban areas.

All of these smaller centers had an absolute increase in New Economy jobs between 1991 and 2011; the proportion of New Economy jobs almost doubled to 6 percent of the total in 2011. Relative increases were the lowest in Saint-Hyacinthe and Drummondville. Victoria and Kitchener had the largest percentage point increases (more than five) by 2011. The proportion of New Economy jobs in Nanaimo more than tripled.

Bivariate correlations between the proportion of New Economy jobs and economic health scores are positive and statistically significant in 1996 and 2011. Table 3.13 presents the correlations between the current proportion of New Economy jobs and local economic health at some point in the future. The proportion of New Economy jobs in 1991 is significantly correlated with economic health in all three subsequent periods. Lower but still significant correlations result from the 1996 New Economy jobs. There is again a strong correlation in the 2001 to 2006 comparison.

This table also suggests that there is considerable path dependency involved; there is a significant correlation between the health indexes at different points in time. Simply put, high levels of economic health in any one year are likely to result in high levels of economic health five and ten years later. The proportion of university graduates is a good leading indicator of economic health in 1996 and 2006. Not surprisingly, the

Table 3.13 Correlations between EPI Scores and New Economy Jobs, City Regions

New Economy Jobs	1996	2006	2011
1991	.767**	.803**	.676*
1996	.687**	.738**	.628*
2001		.793**	.637*
2006		.789**	.637*
2011			.522

*Correlation significant at .05
**Correlation significant at .01

proportion of manufacturing jobs is negatively correlated with economic health in later years, although this is not statistically significant.

DISCUSSION

The foregoing analysis provides some answers to the initial research questions:

- Do the peripheral areas of these urban regions enjoy any "spill-over" benefits from the large urban areas?

For the most part, the peripheral urban areas continue to have relatively higher proportions of manufacturing jobs (most of which these areas have been able to retain) and generally lower proportions of New Economy jobs. Peripheral metro areas that had relatively high proportions of New Economy jobs in 1991 (Victoria, Guelph, and Kitchener) were the most successful in attracting more such jobs, suggesting an element of path dependency. There are other mitigating factors to consider, however. Guelph and Kitchener are within commuting distance (seventy to eighty kilometers) of Toronto, though admittedly lengthy; they are also the location of major universities. Victoria is anomalous because of its status as provincial capital and its well-developed tourist industry. Like Nanaimo,

Victoria requires commuting by air or water to Vancouver. The five Quebec peripheral metros gained only 2,650 New Economy jobs, well below the 49,500 jobs in this category that the Montreal CMA gained. Similar disparities exist in the other city regions. The small city with the greatest increase in New Economy jobs—Saint-Jean-sur-Richelieu—is within easy commuting distance of Montreal (forty kilometers) and is increasingly serving as a bedroom community. In this case, the place-of-residence data may provide a less meaningful description than would place of work data.

Relative to national measures of economic well-being, all three of the large metropolitan areas have recorded improvement since 1996. The Economic Health Index scores for Toronto and Vancouver have remained well above parity with the national figures in each census year. Montreal has also improved but remains close to the national average.

- Is the prosperity of midsize urban areas a function of their New Economy and creative job base?

What do these results indicate for economic development strategies that focus on attracting New Economy jobs to smaller urban areas? Is it possible to conclude that increasing the proportion of New Economy jobs would provide smaller urban areas with an advantage in terms of future economic prosperity? Unfortunately, the answer is probably not. Although correlation analysis suggests that New Economy jobs may be reasonably good indicators of future economic health, past economic prosperity is also significantly correlated with future economic prosperity.

Moreover, the nature of New Economy jobs makes them problematic as potential economic drivers for small urban areas. Services employment is arguably less vulnerable to offshoring than manufacturing, but much of this employment benefits from face-to-face contacts (proximity to markets) and agglomeration (clustering); these characteristics are difficult to create from scratch (see Gottlieb, 2001; Elfring and Hulsink, 2003). Similarly, while economic benefits may accrue to capital cities and university towns, basing one's economic development strategy on attracting a major research university or a new seat of government does not seem practical.

With respect to other measures, serious questions of the direction of causation remain. For example, does an active arts scene cause economic prosperity, or does a prosperous economy generate more opportunities for cultural activity? Although the evidence is limited, a plausible case could be made for the latter. This is an important question in the design of local economic development strategies.

4

City Centers

A downtown commercial district is the most visible indicator
of a community's economic and social health. Its vitality and
commercial success is an asset when recruiting new residents,
enticing tourists, and stimulating new investment, businesses
and industries.

Heritage Canada the National Trust, 2014

The concept of a downtown, or central business district (CBD), was
well established in larger North American urban areas by the end
of the nineteenth century. City centers separated commercial activity—
retail, office, and government—from residential land uses (Fogelson,
2001). Throughout North America, the CBDs of most metropolitan
areas reached their peak by the middle decades of the last century. By
the middle of the twentieth century, changes in transportation and communication technologies, along with rising incomes, made low-density
peripheral development the norm in North American metropolitan areas
(Gruen, 1964; Filion, Bunting, and Warriner, 1999).

Urban cores, defined by tall buildings, concentrations of government and private-sector offices, and large-scale and specialty retailing,
took shape in most cities by the 1920s. Core areas are characterized by
functions that are large (serving a population greater than the immediate neighborhood), specialized (providing goods or services that are not
found elsewhere in the area), or both. This clustering of activities within
close proximity facilitated face-to-face communication and the physical exchange of goods. It also attracted ancillary activities such as attor-
neys, accountants, and the like. Government, especially the courts, also

attracted related professional services. Inter-city train terminals located downtown and other forms of mass transit encouraged the development of hotels and other facilities for travelers.

Increasing vehicular congestion and competition from outlying business districts emerged as concerns in the 1920s and 1930s (Fogelson, 2001). As the post–World War II suburban boom created new competition for center city retail and office activities, planners turned their attention from managing congestion to revitalizing increasingly uncompetitive city centers. The city center typically retains important government and economic functions, as well as a high proportion of the property tax base and often employment. It is the focus of the local transportation network and the location of heritage buildings.

Nevertheless, most city centers have experienced declines, often substantial, both absolutely and relative to their share of metropolitan wide activity. Corporate offices, retail units, and service establishments are now more often found in suburban locations. This decentralization of economic activity is characteristic of urban areas of all sizes, from the largest metropolis to small towns.

The consequences of these trends are more substantive than nostalgic. A declining center city can affect the image of the entire metropolitan area and its ability to attract investment and residents. It offers residents fewer choices of goods and services. Local governments also suffer from the loss of economic activity and tax base. Eventually, the decline can lead to blight and physical deterioration, with a lack of adequate public and private resources to address the problem.

Public policies have sought to promote core area revival throughout the latter half of the twentieth century. While particular emphasis has often been placed on retail commercial activities, planners have also sought to attract or retain employment in the core areas. Such efforts, however, have met with only limited success outside of a small number of metropolitan areas.

The waning importance of city centers and the consequent narrowing range of functions that they offer gave rise to three distinct types of revitalization strategies. One strategy concentrated on an adaptation to automobile accessibility. During the 1950s and 1960s, many cities built radial expressways and widened arterial roads meant to channel flows of cars toward downtowns, increasingly well provided with parking spaces. More recently, a number of communities have introduced new public transit systems, including subways (e.g., Washington, Baltimore) and light rail (Atlanta, Buffalo, Calgary, San Diego), generally focusing on the downtown core.

A second strategy attempted head-on competition with suburban retail developments. Policy makers became convinced that to stem the retail hemorrhage to the suburbs, downtowns had to gloss their image and embrace suburban shopping formulas (Black, Howland, and Rogel, 1983; Gillette, 1985; Gruen, 1964; Robertson, 1993; Anderson, 1964; Wilson, 1966). New retail facilities, mimicking an already well-established suburban shopping formula, were being introduced to core areas. This strategy was grounded in the assumption that by replicating conditions found in suburban shopping centers, core areas could compete successfully with suburbs. In a number of communities, downtown (retail) business associations were established to coordinate opening hours, promotions, and publicity. Shopping streets were pedestrianized, either by closing them to all vehicular traffic or by widening sidewalks. Some cities developed suburban-style enclosed shopping malls. The modernization efforts of the time inspired confidence that downtowns would remain the foremost retail destination (or at least among the foremost) within the metropolitan region.

A third strategy focused on accentuating the distinct identity of the core area (see Abbott, 1993 for an alternative five-phase history; see also Carmon, 1999; Filion, 1993). Increasingly, planning interventions emphasized a preservation or enhancement of the uniqueness of the physical features of core areas within rapidly suburbanizing metropolitan regions and the targeting of markets where cores enjoyed competitive advantages (Lockwood, 2000; Milder, 1997; Palma, 2000a; Palma and Hyett, 1997). This reorientation signaled a mounting recognition that downtowns could no longer compete with the suburbs on their terms but that downtown revival would rest on their distinction from the suburban realm in terms of the nature of their activities, a more compact-built environment, and the predominance of pedestrian movement for intra-core journeys (Robertson, 1995).

IDENTIFYING SUCCESSFUL CORES

In large measure, the special characteristics of the core areas of North American cities are related to their physical form. The downtowns that emerged in North American urban areas during the last decades of the nineteenth century were relatively compact, even in the largest cities. Because of their predominantly pedestrian orientation, vertical rather than horizontal expansion was favored. Market forces, in particular high land values in the city center, contributed to the high-rise form of the downtown skyline. A substantial portion of the urban area's (middle and upper class) population came to the city center on a regular basis, making congestion a dominant feature (Fogelson 2001).

The physical environment of these core areas contributes to their success in three different ways. First, it promotes a pedestrian-induced synergy between different categories of users and the types of activities present in the core, as well as among these activities. Second, the historical and pedestrian-friendly character of core areas constitutes an important drawing force for tourism, the presence of which in turn contributes to a further enhancement of their appeal by raising their overall level of activity. And third, the more that cores provide a distinct alternative to other districts in the predominantly dispersed urban areas, the better positioned they will be to attract people seeking settings and shopping experiences that differ from those available in the suburbs.

A number of North American downtowns have managed to retain, or even expand, their level of activity in the face of suburbanization by virtue of extraordinary public transit accessibility advantages, historically high concentrations of employment and retail, and, in some measure, successful revitalization initiatives (Fogelson, 2001: 383; Smerk, 1965; Teaford, 1990: 93–105). The examples that most readily come to mind are concentrated among larger metropolitan regions such as New York, Chicago, San Francisco, Boston, Philadelphia, Toronto, and Montreal.

The urban form of midsize metropolitan areas has experienced more dispersion than that of their larger counterparts. Dispersion is defined as the combination of low overall density, intense land use specialization, overwhelming automobile reliance, a decentralization of activities, and an absence of clear metropolitan-wide accessibility, density, and land value gradients (Bunting and Filion, 1999; Filion, Bunting, and Warriner, 1999). Especially in this class of cities, the classic core-focused accessibility pattern has given way to a more fully car-reliant and diffused distribution of journeys, consistent with decentralization (Gottdiener and Klephart, 1991; Lloyd, 1991). The drawing power of the core area has generally fallen well below levels enjoyed in major suburban concentrations.

MEASURING SUCCESS

Despite the importance of city centers, there have been only limited systematic attempts to assess the vitality of these special places. One such effort is a Web-based survey of urban professionals in Canada and the United States that asked respondents to rate the relative importance of specific attributes of core areas and to identify midsize urban areas with successful city centers (Filion et al., 2004). The survey also attempted to identify quantitative measures of the health of core areas. The urban professionals surveyed were generally in agreement about which urban areas had successful downtowns. They also concurred on the identification of those attributes that were most relevant to achieving a reputation for a high level of success. Both categories of response are inherently subjective, however, and as a result they may be difficult to apply to other areas.

Survey respondents were asked to provide a numerical rating (on a seven-point scale) for the city centers with which they were familiar. Although the resulting ratings are subjective, the results overall are at least broadly representative for most communities. Of the approximately 200 cities included in the sample, only a small number were rated as successful by more than a handful of the respondents. The nineteen core areas considered successful by at least half of the survey respondents from their home region are listed in Table 4.1. Only three Canadian midsize cities are included in this group, but all of them are in the top eleven.

These responses confirm the widespread observation that the vast majority of the core areas of small metropolitan regions face serious difficulties. Some of the successful cores have retained their vitality by retaining distinct market niches. Rather than serving as the focal point for

Table 4.1 Small Urban Areas with Successful Cores

Rank	City	Rank	City	Rank	City
1	Madison, WI	8	Victoria, BC	14	Athens, GA
2	Burlington, VT	9	Santa Fe, NM	15	State College, PA
3	Halifax, NS	10	Charlottesville, VA	16	Santa Barbara, CA
4	Boise, ID	11	Kingston, ON	17	Fort Collins, CO
5	Savannah, GA	12	San Luis Obispo, CA	18	Wilmington, NC
6	Iowa City, IA	13	Chattanooga, TN	19	Rochester, MN
7	Asheville, NC				

Source: Filion et al., 2004

the metropolitan area, they have been sustained by meeting the needs of specialized markets. All highly rated cores possess at least one of the following assets: a university that is in, or close to, downtown; a location in a metropolitan region with a strong tourist (or visitor) orientation; a well-preserved historical district; and a state capitol or provincial legislature. In justifying their selection of successful downtowns, respondents also alluded to the presence of cultural activities, art galleries, and live entertainment, as well as natural features (particularly waterfronts).

Respondents were also asked to select (from a list of nineteen items) the city center characteristics that led them to regard an area as successful. Table 4.2 summarizes the relative importance of these items and also indicates the extent to which they can be facilitated by public policies or actions. It is notable that most of the "Very Important" items are those that are not typically public sector responsibilities. Conversely, many commonly employed strategies, such as parking and transit, are regarded as having little value, despite their widespread use.

Assessing the success of core areas requires at least an implicit agreement as to what standards of measurement are to be used. Some of the most common measures of success may be ambiguous, however. For

Figure 4.1 Victoria, BC, city center waterfront

example, while traffic congestion is unlikely to be viewed as a positive attribute for any core area, high levels of pedestrian activity are clearly an attribute of healthy core areas. Similarly, historically high land prices and commercial rents may be effective barriers to revitalization efforts. There appears to be general agreement on several basic attributes of successful core areas, however.

The first of these is that a successful core area is one that is *used*. This can be measured by the occupancy rates of downtown properties, for both ground level and upper floors of existing buildings. In a successful core area, these uses are likely to be dynamic—high levels of turnover are to be expected.

The second criterion is that the successful downtown area will be *valued*. This will be reflected in property values, sales activity, and rents. Levels of investment, especially private investment, are important.

Third, a successful core area must have an active public life; that is, high levels of pedestrian activity for extended periods. This criterion suggests certain physical attributes for the core area: it must be relatively compact and high density; it must be pedestrian friendly (including sidewalks, diverse streetscapes, a clean and safe environment, etc.); and

Figure 4.2 Kingston, ON, city center

it must provide a variety of discretionary activities (cultural and civic events, festivals, dining and entertainment).

INFLUENCING SUCCESS

Planners and public officials in both Canada and the United States place a high priority on restoring and maintaining the health of the core areas of their cities. Although economic and societal changes, especially in employment and retailing, over the last fifty years have significantly altered the functions of most downtown areas, the core area continues to have symbolic value as one of the most important places in the community. Indeed, many suburban communities are consciously attempting to create downtown developments to provide a sense of place and identity.

Of the nineteen characteristics included in the survey, there is considerable variation in both of these dimensions. In some instances, the listed attributes include those that might be paired but in fact represent quite different things. For example, active retail is a desired result that is probably not directly amenable to policy intervention. Street-oriented

Table 4.2 Revitalization Strategies

		Degree of Importance		
		Very Important	**Important**	**Not Important**
Degree of Control	Direct	• Pedestrian Environment	• Green Space • Civic Events	• Social Services • Public Offices • Transit • Parking
	Indirect	• Street-Oriented Retail • Cultural Activities	• Tourist Activities	• High Density Residential • Educational Presence • Retail Mall
	None	• Active Retail • People on Sidewalks • Employment	• Historical Character • Strong Neighborhood • Architectural Quality	

Source: Filion et al., 2004

retailing, however, could be facilitated by public policies. Similarly, the objective of having many people on the sidewalks can be encouraged by policies directed at the creation of a pedestrian-oriented environment.

Table 4.2 categorizes the survey responses on these two dimensions. It seems clear that most of the attributes in the survey are either not important or beyond the ability of planning and public policies to influence. (The assignments are clearly subject to debate.) One conclusion from this exercise would be to prioritize the types of interventions that receive the most attention from planners. Initiatives to improve the public realm (pedestrian environment, green space) would seem to be deserving of more attention than parking or transit improvements.

Core areas that have suffered decline may aspire to be many things as a result of concentrated public and private efforts. It is clear, however, that they cannot hope to become what they once were—the dominant center of commercial, government, and office activity for their metropolitan region. Rather, their choices would seem to be limited to developing a new specialization, serving only a portion of the former market.

A basic measure of the success of a city center is that it must be a location that attracts people. As office employment and retail activity have declined in most downtowns, planners have attempted to tap new markets. Many communities have pursued strategies to increase the residential population of the core area. Theaters, restaurants, coffee shops, sports facilities, and bars and clubs attract, and are attracted by, a residential population, particularly one that is relatively young and affluent.

An alternate strategy involves developing a concentration of entertainment or tourist-oriented activities in the downtown. This alternative, which probably applies to a smaller number of cores, is to find new specializations that contribute to the maintenance of activity levels and property values. This may be thought of as the adaptive reuse, rather than restoration, of the downtown core. Tourism as well as conventions, cultural/arts facilities, and entertainment specializations are obvious examples of this reinvention. And while cultural/arts facilities may not be enough to anchor downtown prosperity, they can be harnessed to bolster struggling city centers (Ganning, 2016).

Over time, planners have shifted their focus from regulation of development and the reduction of congestion in the city center to efforts to ensure that the downtown remains competitive with new suburban business centers (Gruen, 1964; Abbott, 1993; National Main Street Center, 1998). Attempts to replicate suburban models of development—for example, the introduction of enclosed shopping malls and abundant parking—in the core areas typically have met with only limited success (Teaford, 1990; Bunting and Millward, 1999). By the 1980s, local governments and private interests adopted new strategies to revitalize city centers, including convention centers, sports venues, and increasing residential populations (Keating and Krumholz, 1991; Suchman, 2002; Turner and Rosentraub, 2002; Knack, 1998). Other communities promoted entertainment to make their downtown the leading center in the metropolitan area (Hannigan, 1998; Beyard, 2001). The effectiveness of these newer strategies has been, at best, mixed, especially in midsize urban areas.

CITY CENTER HEALTH
AND COMMUNITY CHARACTERISTICS

Before considering the relationship between core area health and community prosperity, we discuss how the city center ratings vary with other community characteristics, specifically population, regional location, and economic specialization. Table 4.3 presents the average core rating by population size and region. As population size increases, core area ratings also increase. Core area ratings are above the average for all midsize urban areas only for the largest of these metropolitan areas.

The differences between regions are even larger. While the city center average rating in the Maritimes was 525, in neighboring Quebec the average was just 356. All five urban areas in the Maritimes had an average core area rating of 450 or more. In Quebec, the individual ratings ranged from 500 in Trois-Rivières to 200 in Shawinigan.

Core area ratings also vary with economic specialization. The highest-rated downtowns are found in metropolitan areas with diversified economies; manufacturing communities have the lowest-rated cores. Somewhat unexpectedly, natural resources–based communities have a higher

Table 4.3 Core Area Rating by Population Size and Regional Location

Population	Average Core Rating	Region	Average Core Rating	Economic Base	Average Core Rating
All Midsize	405	Maritimes	525	Manufacturing	315
Less than 80,000	348	Quebec	356	Nat Resources	407
80,000 to 130,000	389	Ontario	395	Health/ Higher Education	368
More than 130,000	461	West	433	Diversified	438

average core rating than communities where hospital and university employment predominates.

COMMUNITY ECONOMIC HEALTH
AND CITY CENTER HEALTH

While there is a positive correlation between the overall economic health of a community (as measured by the prosperity index described in Chapter 2) and the perceived success of its downtown, the results are not statistically significant. That is, an economically prosperous community does not always have a successful downtown, and a strong core area can exist in a community with below-average economic indicators.

Table 4.4 presents the socioeconomic measures that are statistically significant correlates of downtown health. Because the core area ratings were compiled in 2003, correlations for both 2001 and 2006 are presented. Notably, the correlation between the core area health rating and the community health indexes for 2001 and 2006 was positive but not significant. A number of other demographic and socioeconomic variables were tested, none proved to have a significant relationship with economic health.

The highest correlations are with proportions of community residents with a university degree and commuting by transit. Transit use is a key variable from a public policy perspective (Hartley et al., 2016).

Table 4.4 Correlates of City Center Health

Variable	Correlation	Sig.	Variable	Correlation	Sig.
EPI 2001	.238	.133	EPI 2006	.293	.083
Transit use 2001	.548	.000	Transit use 2006	.536	.000
University 2001	.728	.000	University 2006	.706	.000
Metro pop. 2001	.332	.034	Metro pop. 2006	.326	.032
Home value 2001	.210	.049	Home value 2006	.323	.040

While the correlations are highly significant, the direction of causation probably runs from a healthy downtown to higher transit use, rather than transit use improving downtown quality. Communities with healthy downtowns, particularly when they are significant employment centers, are able to support a public transit system. But investing in transit improvements will not necessarily make a city center more successful, if there is no reason to go there. Home values and metropolitan population are the only other significant measures. Larger, better-educated communities thus are likely to have a healthier core area, as are communities with higher home values.

CASE STUDIES

To better understand the differences in core area ratings, case studies will consider the characteristics of several city centers in more detail. Kingston, Ontario; Victoria, British Columbia; and Halifax, Nova Scotia, were thought to have the most successful core areas among the midsize Canadian cities. We compare these highly regarded urban core areas to nearby communities that survey respondents considered to be less successful—Brantford, Ontario; Kamloops, British Columbia; and Moncton, New Brunswick. The latter two had city centers that were rated about the middle of the ranking of all midsize urban areas included in the survey, while Brantford received the lowest ranking of any of the cities in the survey.

Community Characteristics

Table 4.5 presents select demographic and socioeconomic information for these six case study communities. The cities with successful core areas typically have a larger population and a lower percentage of homeowners, but higher home values. The higher rates of commuting via public transit in the urban areas with the more successful cores most likely reflect the importance of the city center in terms of employment. Cities with healthy downtowns are not necessarily better off economically, at least as measured by such indicators as higher median incomes or lower unemployment rates, than the comparison cities.

Table 4.5 Community Profiles of Case Study Core Areas

	Halifax	Moncton	Kingston	Brantford	Victoria	Kamloops
Population 2001	116,292	61,046	114,195	86,417	74,125	77,281
Percent of Metro Area	33%	34%	78%	73%	24%	89%
Increase 1996–2001	4.7%	2.9%	1.2%	2.0%	0.8%	1.2%
Population Density	$1,506/k^2$	$433/k^2$	$254/k^2$	$1,208/k^2$	$3,766/k^2$	$260/k^2$
Median Age	36.5	37.9	37.6	37.5	40.3	37.9
Median HH Income	$38,900	$40,000	$46,000	$43,900	$34,300	$46,500
Visible Minorities	10.4%	1.9%	4.7%	4.2%	9.7%	5.9%
Immigrants	10.5%	3.1%	12.4%	13.0%	20.7%	10.3%
Unemployment Rate	7.7%	8.2%	7.5%	6.8%	8.6%	10.1%
Public Transit Commuters	13.3%	3.6%	4.2%	3.2%	12.0%	3.4%
% Homeowners	40%	58%	58%	67%	38%	71%
Average Home Value	$170,802	$101,100	$158,363	$136,482	$207,139	$152,303
Tourism Index	26	24	22	4	52	18
Street Retail Index	20	8	48	3	36	15

Sources: Statistics Canada, Filion et al., 2004

Filion and colleagues identified several characteristics of healthy core areas (2004). The Street Retail Index is measured by the number of blocks of retail commercial frontage that offers opportunity for "window shopping." Among the three case study pairs, the more successful downtown clearly dominates on this measure. Kingston has the most street retail activity while Brantford has the least.

Tourism orientation is based on the number of hotel rooms available in the downtown core. Here, there are clear differences between Kingston and Brantford and Victoria and Kamloops. The difference in hotel accommodations between Halifax and Moncton is small, however.

Historic character was also identified as an important attribute of a successful core area. It reflects not only the presence of heritage buildings, but also how these assets are maintained. Each of the successful city centers has a large number of heritage sites that play an important role in their downtowns. Moncton and Brantford have fewer historic buildings and Brantford has only recently begun to recognize their importance. Kamloops, the newest of the case study cities, simply has few heritage assets.

Every core area of the case study communities has a waterfront location. The successful cores make good use of these assets, providing opportunities for both active and passive recreational opportunities. Although the waterfront areas in Brantford and Kamloops are extensive, they are not well integrated with other downtown activities.

Having a university in or near downtown and being a provincial capital are also common attributes of successful communities (Pink-Harper, 2015). Only Kingston and Halifax have a major university adjacent to their core areas. Brantford is developing a branch of Wilfrid Laurier University, which includes residential as well as classroom facilities. Halifax and Victoria are provincial capitals, and Kingston was once the capital of Canada and continues to serve as an important regional government center.

REVITALIZATION STRATEGIES

Core area revitalization strategies have evolved over the past half-century (Filion et al., 2004; Abbott, 1993; Robertson, 1999). Many communities

Figure 4.3 Brantford, ON, city center

sought to introduce the advantages of plentiful parking and climate-controlled retail environments in the city center. This emphasis on replicating suburban models of development in core areas met with limited success, however, particularly in midsize urban areas (Wells, 2000; Burayidi, 2001; Teaford, 1990). Core areas offering the same retail opportunities as suburban malls, but without free parking, were unable to attract suburban residents downtown to shop.

By the 1980s, local government and private interests sought to revitalize city centers by pursuing new functions and activities. Development of convention centers and sports venues was a common approach to downtown revival (Turner and Rosentraub, 2002). Residential development was encouraged in many areas in an effort to extend the level of activity in downtown beyond the Monday to Friday workweek (Suchman, 2002; Knack, 1998). Other communities sought to promote their downtown as the leading entertainment center in the metropolitan area (Hannigan, 1998; Beyard 2001). The success of these strategies has been, at best, mixed (Robertson 1999).

Current efforts at downtown revitalization continue to give high priority to increasing the number of residents in the core and to marketing downtown as an entertainment center for the metropolitan area (Haque, 2001; Keating and Krumholz, 1991). There has also been increased emphasis on design considerations, including the use of street furniture and other amenities to imbue the core area with a distinct sense of place and to preserve and adaptively reuse historic properties (Paumier, 2004). Business associations or quasi-public authorities are often seen as an essential ingredient of success (Alexander 1986). An increasingly important strategy in some communities is the use of financial incentives to attract private investment (Ministry of Municipal Affairs and Housing 2000).

Table 4.6 lists a number of specific downtown revitalization strategies and indicates their use by the case study communities. Often a feature of a successful city center will be widely adopted (Robertson, 1999; Reese and Ye, 2011) by less successful city centers, with the expectation that it will provide the same benefits as in more successful communities. As a result, strategies have become ubiquitous and unique approaches that set one core area apart from the others are difficult to find.

Table 4.6 Utilization of Revitalization Strategies

	Successful			Unsuccessful		
	Halifax	Kingston	Victoria	Moncton	Brantford	Kamloops
Pedestrian Precinct	X		X	X	X	X
Parking Structures	X	X	X	X	X	X
Enclosed Mall	X		X	X	X	X
Sports Facilities	X				X	X
Casino Gambling	X		X	X	X	X
Office Employment	X		X	X	X	X
BIA	X	X		X	X	X
Number of Strategies	7	2	5	6	7	7

Distressed communities typically employ more different revitalization strategies as compared to the communities that are regarded as successful. They appear to choose any and all strategies that might contribute to core area improvement. But, at the end of the day, the results are often discouraging. No matter how many different approaches are tried or how well they are implemented, the differences in perceived quality of the city centers remain. There may be no causal connection between the public policies and core area health, or the causal connections may run in the opposite direction, with struggling city centers producing more policy initiatives. In any event, public policies may have only limited potential to effect marginal improvements. The following section describes some of the more popular revitalization strategies and assesses their potential.

Pedestrian Friendly Streets

One of the most basic strategies for a successful, sustainable downtown is the creation of attractive pedestrian precincts, typically offering wide sidewalks, distinctive paving, benches, streetlights, banners, and flowers. These features are used to identify the city center as a special place, distinct from the rest of the city. The primary indicator of a healthy and successful downtown is an active pedestrian scene (Lorch and Smith, 1993; Joh et al., 2011; Peach and Petach, 2016). No matter how many people are attracted to a downtown, if they have no human presence on the streets, the core area is unlikely to be considered a success. But if the streets in the city center have extensive pedestrian traffic, it will be taken as a sure sign that it is an interesting and vital place.

Closing streets to vehicles and other pedestrian friendly features in the city center can support street level human activity, but it may not be sufficient to ensure success. Sidewalk treatments, benches, and other street furniture provide an attractive setting in the Moncton city center, but one that attracts few users. In Kingston, the sidewalks in some parts of the city center are narrow and in poor repair, but this does little to deter their use.

Heritage Promotion and Tourism

In recent decades, many communities have "discovered" the importance of preserving heritage properties and sites. Because city centers are often the site of original settlements, the core is likely to be the location of the largest number of historic buildings and sites. The successful core areas studied here actively promoted their heritage properties as important elements of the city center. These efforts not only provide potential tourist attractions but also help to ensure the distinctive character of the downtown, setting it off from homogenized suburban alternatives (Birch, 2002).

An obvious limitation of this strategy is that many communities have relatively few significant heritage sites. Moncton and Kamloops are both comparatively new cities, with few structures dating from the nineteenth century. It seems unlikely that heritage promotion strategies can make a significant contribution to revitalization efforts in such communities. Nevertheless, maintenance of the distinctive urban fabric in the core, including the street pattern and building setback lines, is likely to be an important strategy even in relatively new cities.

Increasing tourism is also an attractive strategy for downtown revitalization. This mercantilist strategy sees tourists (adopting a broad definition of tourism that includes business travelers and convention goers) as contributing to the local economy through spending on accommodations, meals, and entertainment activities (Houston, 1998; Loukaitou-Sideris and Sodreli, 2012). Tourists are also likely to spend some of their time as pedestrians and shoppers in the city center, if there are appropriate destinations available. Not surprisingly, the city centers with the best reputations are also the ones that have the most tourist activity. Halifax, Victoria, and Kingston each attract more than one million tourists annually. While tourism strategies are attractive, it seems unlikely that many communities will be able to increase tourist activity to levels comparable to these cities with successful core areas.

Sports and Entertainment Centers

Many cities have accepted the demise of the core as an employment and retail center, electing to pursue downtown revitalization that focuses on entertainment and other activities that bring people to the city center. These may include a range of entertainment options (sports venues, restaurants, casinos, theaters, nightlife, and cultural events) that appeal to

Figure 4.4 Guelph, ON, city center, Old Quebec Street

residents and visitors alike. Universities and hospitals can be considered attractions as well. Employment opportunities may also bring some local residents to the city center on a regular basis.

The limitations to this strategy in midsize cities are related to both scale and competition. Not every city can realistically expect to be successful in creating an entertainment environment that will attract visitors from an extensive market area (Hannigan, 1998). The market potential for casino gambling, amusement parks, and convention centers is, after all, finite. As these strategies are adopted by more communities, markets become saturated, making it difficult to attract visitors to locations that lack other distinctive attributes.

Enclosed Shopping Malls

A clear example of the importance of tactical details is provided by the enclosed shopping malls that many communities built in the 1970s and 1980s (West and Orr, 2003). Of the five case study cities where malls have been built, only the one in Victoria appears to be successful as a focus for revitalization efforts. The Bay Center there is well connected to the street; a number of shops are accessible only from the street,

Figure 4.5 Victoria, BC, tourist-oriented retail

rather than from the interior of the mall. The Halifax mall, on the other hand, is at best only marginally successful. The enclosed malls in Brantford and Kamloops are inwardly focused and contribute little to active street life. These malls also are plagued by high vacancy rates and the conversion of retail space to office or other uses. While Moncton has two enclosed malls at the fringe of its core area, both are highly suburbanized and separated from the core by large expanses of surface parking.

Parks and Open Space

Public open space is another important component of the urban fabric, particularly in the city center. But it is likely to be the quality of the open space rather than its quantity that matters most. Centennial Park in Kingston is only a small part of the downtown area, but it is actively used because of the adjacent hotels, ferry docks, and marina. The resulting high level of pedestrian activity attracts vendors and people-watchers. Brantford and Kamloops, in contrast, have much more extensive waterfront park areas adjacent to their city centers, but they lack easy accessibility and programmed activities.

Densification

As central business districts have declined, the proliferation of abandoned buildings, vacant storefronts, and surface parking lots has contributed to a negative image of the core. The remaining viable activities and
uses become isolated. Restoring the urban fabric through development
regulations, design controls, and heritage preservation can help to restore
continuity among key activities.

An important element of such strategies is to ensure that the area
selected for concentrated development is of an appropriate size. While
larger cities may be successful in expanding their concentrated downtown core areas (Shaw and Williams, 1994; Houston, 1998; Ford, 2003),
this appears more difficult to accomplish in smaller cities. The success
of strategies based on densification is likely to depend on concentrating
efforts on a compact cohesive area, one that is likely to be considerably
smaller than the city center was at its peak. It may be difficult to accept
(and to accurately define) a smaller core area that is viable.

Using public improvements to define an excessively large city center
is likely to dilute the effect and be counter-productive to revitalization
efforts. The approach, employed by both Victoria and Brantford, of dividing the core area into distinct districts, can be effective in addressing this
issue. The locations of the arena in Moncton and the arena and casino in
Brantford contribute little to downtown activity because they are physically separated from other downtown activities. Physical barriers, whether
they are surface parking lots or rail lines, inhibit pedestrian traffic.

Regional Planning and Development Strategies

The sustainability of the core area is also influenced by metropolitan development trends. Peripheral commercial development located close to
highway interchanges competes with the city center (Lang, 2003). These
centrifugal forces may be difficult to counter in the absence of strong
regional planning or regional government (Rusk, 1993).

Municipal consolidations have occurred in most of the case study
communities, not only adding suburban development to the central city
tax base but also bringing peripheral sites within the jurisdiction of a

single planning authority. Municipal amalgamations have taken place in four of the urban areas within the past decade. Suburban development had been well established prior to amalgamation and continues on the periphery of even the more successful city centers.

Consolidating multiple jurisdictions has not always eliminated competition between the downtown core and peripheral locations. An amalgamated government may, as in the cases of Kingston and Halifax, locate local government offices throughout the municipality, reducing the concentration of these activities in the city center. Government restructuring where more than one significant city center previously existed may not eliminate competition between these locations (Reese, 2004). For example, the Halifax Regional Municipality continues to plan for downtown activities in the former city centers of both Halifax and Dartmouth. The City of Kamloops consciously considers the needs of the North Kamloops area in its commercial revitalization efforts and the allocation of new municipal sports facilities. In each case, public policy choices limit the ability of the downtown core to attract investment necessary to ensure its sustainability.

Residential

Many communities have adopted policies to increase residential uses in their city center. This is seen as a means to extend downtown activity beyond the traditional nine-to-five workweek, increasing both market potential and foot traffic. The loss of manufacturing, retail, and office activities from the core can provide opportunities for new developments or adaptive reuse of existing structures.

In the more successful city centers there are more residents than in the distressed communities (Table 4.7); the number of residents in all instances is relatively small, however. Economic indicators (incomes, housing values, and rents) consistently favor the more successful city in each pair. The Halifax and Kingston city centers in particular have been able to attract significant numbers of higher income households. The largely lower income residents of the core areas of Brantford and Kamloops contribute less to retail vitality.

Living downtown may be expensive (or require costly subsidies to be affordable), however. It may cause conflicts between residents and some

Table 4.7 Core Area Residential Characteristics, 2001

	Halifax	Kingston	Victoria	Moncton	Brantford	Kamloops
Population	4,004	1,222	2,965	1,212	5,956	1,241
Change 1991–2001	*16%*	*3%*	*-12%*	*-7%*	*25%*	*33%*
Households	2,725	797	2,208	891	4,055	842
Change 1991–2001	*44%*	*27%*	*13%*	*35%*	*39%*	*38%*
Median Income	$37,680	$23,754	$38,573	$21,458	$22,387	$21,745
As percent of city	*98%*	*59%*	*116%*	*49%*	*65%*	*47%*
Average Home Value	$176,000	$83,700	$265,000	$96,000	$156,000	$136,000
As percent of city	*103%*	*73%*	*177%*	*71%*	*75%*	*89%*
Average Rent	$861	$583	$782	$532	$569	$460
As percent of city	*126%*	*104%*	*121%*	*86%*	*84%*	*71%*

Source: Statistics Canada

Figure 4.6 Kingston, ON, city center residential

activities, such as bars and clubs. The lack of neighborhood amenities is also likely to inhibit efforts to increase the downtown population. Downtown residents require amenities that may not currently exist in the core area, including groceries and personal service establishments. All types of residential development cannot be expected to have the same positive effects on the city center. Social housing, retirement homes, and homeless shelters will make less of a contribution to city center vitality than high-end condominium or loft developments. Strengthening neighborhoods adjacent to the core may be as effective a strategy as putting more housing in the city center itself.

One characteristic that stands out is the greater amount of street-oriented commercial frontage in the more successful city's cores. An extensive retail scene seems to be a strong indicator of downtown health. Likewise, the number of downtown hotel rooms, relative to population size, also consistently favors the more successful city in each pair. Both of these measures seem to be amenable to public policy intervention; for example, zoning regulations can be used to ensure that space is reserved for retail or hotel uses. Nevertheless, the actual causal linkages are not clearly established.

The connections between specific attributes and a positive image for the city center are rather tenuous. Providing a tourist- or shopper-friendly environment clearly seems important. But simply creating pedestrian streets (as in Brantford) or hotel rooms (Kamloops) is just as clearly not sufficient to achieve the desired objective. The sustainability of pedestrian-friendly retail, however, depends on ensuring that the pedestrians become customers, not just passersby. The public sector can, at best, organize and regulate the setting in which the private sector activities will take place.

There are a number of factors that may actually favor sustainable downtown areas. Even those city centers that have suffered from demographic and economic decline (as well as bad planning) may possess some inherently attractive aspects. The relatively small size typical of city centers in this population range provides opportunities for functional pedestrian districts with a mix of activities. Center city land values in many small and midsize urban areas are typically not so high (at least relative to those at the periphery) as to preclude new development. Especially in midsize Canadian urban areas, the availability of public (bus) transit focused on the downtown core may be an asset, but one that probably is limited to city center employees. Another advantage of the midsize urban core is that it is readily accessible to all areas of the region. In a market that will support only one of a particular business, a downtown location might be the most favorable.

KINGSTON AND BRANTFORD

We now take a closer look at the city centers of two of these metropolitan areas, Kingston and Brantford. Kingston, Ontario, is a city with a well-regarded urban core area, while the Brantford city center had the lowest average score of any Canadian downtown. Kingston, located about 250 kilometers (150 miles) east of Toronto, was once the capital of the province of Canada and continues to be a regional center for many provincial services. Public sector employment in Kingston includes employees of Queens University, the Royal Military College, five prisons, and OHIP, the provincial health insurance agency. The city also has a strong tourist orientation, including heritage sites and port facilities for cruises through the Thousand Islands recreational areas.

Brantford, on the other hand, emerged as a manufacturing center, taking advantage of its proximity to the Hamilton steel mills and abundant hydroelectric power from Niagara Falls. Although the original heavy manufacturing of agricultural equipment has moved elsewhere, Brantford continues to have one of the highest concentrations of manufacturing jobs among the midsize cities. Brantford is not far from several larger cities, including Hamilton, St. Catharines, and even Toronto. These larger centers make it difficult for Brantford to attract regional retail, health, and education facilities.

Brantford has implemented almost every city center revitalization fad in recent years. Some, such as pedestrian streets, enclosed shopping malls, and structured parking, have met with at best marginal success. The charity casino and arena, while more successful, are not well integrated with the downtown. Similarly, the riverfront open space development is detached from the core area. The conversion of historic homes on the fringes of downtown to office use is a good example of heritage conservation, but little has been done to preserve the remaining Victorian era commercial blocks in the core.

The core of Brantford covers a thirty-five-block area. Victoria Park provides a large gathering space used for concerts and other public events. Retail options in the core are severely limited, with both Eaton's and Woolworth's having closed their downtown stores. Retail uses formerly were located along Colborne and Dalhousie Streets, but what little retail activity that remains now is largely concentrated in an enclosed mall, built on the site of the former Eaton's department store. Downtown remains a major employment center, however, as the result

of the introduction of a number of call center operations that have located in unused retail space in the downtown mall. There is no identifiable pedestrian-oriented retail street in the core area.

Redevelopment of the area south of the core (but physically separated from it by a substantial difference in elevation) has provided sites
for a gambling casino, a municipal ice arena, and a suburban-style retail
development. The Brantford urban area has undergone a municipal consolidation in recent years. That has brought all of the peripheral development activity into the central city tax base.

Kingston, on the other hand, has avoided many of these popular
solutions. Voters rejected redevelopment for an enclosed downtown
shopping mall (Filion et al., 2004) and there is neither a casino nor, until
recently, an arena in downtown. Public park space on the waterfront is
limited, with much of the lakefront occupied by high-density residential, hotels, marinas and cruise ship terminals. Kingston has built several,
rather undistinguished, parking structures in the core; sidewalks are often
narrow and in poor repair. The city has, however, been aggressive in heritage conservation efforts throughout the core area,

The relative success of Kingston's core area may be attributed to several factors. The amount of street-oriented commercial frontage is an important attribute of successful city core areas (Lorch and Smith, 1993).
The more extensive the retail scene, the more likely the core area is to be
able to attract the large volumes of pedestrian traffic that are the hall-
marks of downtown health. The variety of retail establishments (many
small shops) and continuity of the retail spaces (that is, not broken by
parking lots and vacant stores) may be more important than the quality
of street furniture and sidewalk width (Black, Howland, and Rogel,
1983). Kingston has much more core area retailing, a total of forty-eight
block fronts, than Brantford, which has only three. It is not surprising
that pedestrians are a more common sight in Kingston.

Street life in Kingston clearly benefits from tourist activity. A wide variety of cruises, from day trips to four-day cruises, depart from Kingston.
The more robust tourist market in Kingston is reflected in the presence
of five hotels (a total of 729 rooms) in the downtown core; Brantford
has only one hotel with 95 rooms downtown. Tourists are a particularly

attractive market since they are likely to be interested in spending money in local shops, as well as not spending time in a hotel room. Permanent residents also make an important contribution to the success of downtown Kingston (Birch, 2002). There, the city center has been able to attract significant numbers of higher-income households to high-density condominium developments. Home values in Kingston's core are about 75 percent higher than the citywide average (Sands, 2007b). The largely lower income residents of the core areas of Brantford contribute less to retail vitality. In Brantford, the median household income of downtown residents is half the citywide figure and both rents and values in the core are well below average.

Brantford's municipal government has been quite active in efforts to promote the core area. Although incentives are available to private firms, most of the development activity has involved public investment. The city has attempted to attract private investment to downtown by waiving development charges and making grants to encourage investments (Sands et al. 2014). The city has created demand for considerable amounts of office space in the downtown, particularly in vacant retail facilities, and supported renovation of a historic theater for live performances. Brantford has embarked on a second phase of core area revitalization.

Perhaps the most important of these new initiatives is the development of a new campus for Wilfrid Laurier University that presently occupies several buildings scattered through the downtown area. Additional development, including new construction and rehabilitation of existing structures, will increase both classroom and residential facilities to serve an eventual student population of 1,800 to 2,000. The city developed a new civic square to complement the existing Victoria Park, which many consider to be overused. The city purchased the struggling shopping mall in order to convert it into municipal offices, but later sold it to Laurier Brantford for campus expansion (Gamble, 2014).

ANN ARBOR AND OAKVILLE

Two successful midsize urban area cores, Ann Arbor, MI, and Oakville, ON, were excluded from the original survey because they are part of

Figure 4.7 Brantford, ON, Harmony Square

larger consolidated metropolitan areas. Nevertheless, respondents volunteered them as examples of successful city centers. The lessons learned from these very successful downtowns are instructive and applicable to midsize cores in both countries. The examination of Ann Arbor is useful because it represents a core area that is not well represented among the Canadian cities; it benefits from the presence of a large university and multiple healthy shopping districts in combination with a high percentage of renters, relatively high unemployment in the core, and limited public transit. Table 4.8 summarizes some of the demographic and economic characteristics of these two cities. Substantial differences are evident between the successful and struggling communities, as well as between the Canadian and American cities.

Both cities with successful core areas are prosperous, with relatively high incomes and housing costs and with low unemployment. The population of Oakville is growing much more rapidly than that of Ann Arbor. The substantial university population in Ann Arbor accounts for the relatively low average household size, low proportion of elderly residents, and higher proportion of renter households than in Oakville. Although Ann Arbor has some of the highest rents and housing values of any central

Table 4.8 Ann Arbor and Oakville City Profiles, 2000/2001

	Ann Arbor	Oakville
Population	114,024	144,738
Change in 1990s	+3.9%	+20.8%
Households	45,693	49,260
Percent 65+	7.4%	10.9%
Median Household Income	$46,300	$84,000
Unemployment Rate	4.0%	4.5%
Public Transit Commuters	6.6%	13.3%
Percent Homeowners	45%	81%
Median Home Value	$178,500	$306,200
Median Rent	$696	$1,019

Sources: Statistics Canada, US Census

city in Michigan, the figures are well below those of Oakville. The high proportion of Oakville public transit commuters largely reflects intercity commuting, primarily to Toronto.

City Center Characteristics

Ann Arbor's central business district, as defined by the Downtown Development Authority, covers all or part of 67 blocks, a total of about 271 acres. The district abuts the central campus of the University of Michigan. There are four subareas within the DDA: Kerrytown, Main Street, South University, and State Street. Each of these areas has a distinct "personality" and serves a distinct niche market. Although recent developments in the core area have been mid- to high-rise structures, downtown Ann Arbor retains a number of older and historic buildings that contribute to a human-scale, pedestrian-friendly environment.

As recently as the early 1980s, the central business district had two department stores, as well as numerous smaller shops. Both city and county offices, including courts, are located in the downtown area. Numerous professional offices and the headquarters of financial institutions are also located in the core. Currently the city center is seen as a cultural and entertainment center, with an emphasis on museums, concert halls, and galleries. Downtown Ann Arbor also has an extensive resident population. Four of every five blocks in the core have some resident population. There are several hotels in the downtown area, contributing to the area's population base and helping to promote downtown as a round-the-clock activity area. The University of Michigan contributes both residents and activities that attract residents to downtown.

The downtown core of Oakville, as defined by the Business Improvement Association (BIA), consists of a dozen blocks on either side of Lakeshore Road, encompassing about twenty acres. Additional businesses are located on some of the cross streets. Surface and public parking structures are located primarily north of Lakeshore, leaving the primary shopping street with an unbroken facade of pedestrian-oriented retail. The one exception is the Towne Square at Lakeshore and George Street. This plaza area provides space for outdoor cafes and seating areas, as well as a link to the historic residential area that lies between the downtown and the lakefront.

Downtown Oakville provides specialty retailing; restaurants and entertainment venues are also important components of the downtown core. There are some 400 businesses in the downtown, including clothing and specialty shops, restaurants and cafes, professional offices, personal services, and financial institutions. A number of public facilities (library, theater) and some office developments are located immediately west of the BIA area. Residential uses within the core are limited to the south side of the BIA area.

The functional core of Oakville appears to be substantially larger than the area covered by the Business Improvement Association, however. Sixteen Mile Creek on the west is the location of a large marina and parklands that connect to lakefront parks. A number of historic buildings and museums are located along Navy Street, which parallels the creek on the east. High-density residential development is located to the west of the creek. Commercial uses also extend along Lakeshore Road to the east.

Table 4.9 presents summary statistics for the Ann Arbor and Oakville cores, comparing each of them to their respective citywide figures. The index number represents the ratio between the value for the core area and the citywide figure, with 100 representing equivalent figures for the

Table 4.9 Ann Arbor and Oakville Core Area Profiles, 2000/2001

	Ann Arbor		Oakville	
	Value	Index	Value	Index
Population Change	+2.6%	65	+12.6%	26
Percent 65+	8.9%	120	25.8%	237
Household Change	+6.8%	70	+19.9%	67
Family Households	8.6%	16	54.1%	65
One Person Households	70.5%	199	44.2%	276
Median Household Income	$11,232	24	$59,157	70
Homeowners	18.6%	41	18.6%	52
Median Home Value	$350,000	196	$549,500	179
Median Rent	$642	92	$1,057	104
Built in 1990s	6.8%	158	4.0%	17
% Transit Commuters	1.7%	26	10.5%	87
Labor Force Participation	56.2%	85	62.3%	87
% Unemployed	5.2%	130	2.0%	44
% Knowledge Workers	73.3%	93	69.8%	107

Sources: US Census, Statistics Canada

two areas. For example, the unemployment rate for Ann Arbor core area residents is about 30 percent higher than the city of Ann Arbor average.

Both Ann Arbor and Oakville record high index values for median home value, and in Oakville, the core surpassed citywide figures for median rent. One-person and non-family households are much more common in the downtowns than in the rest of each city. The proportion of elderly residents is higher in both downtowns but substantially so in Oakville. Ann Arbor's core has a much higher proportion of new housing than is the case elsewhere in the city. Ann Arbor city center residents are much more likely to be unemployed and somewhat less likely to be in the labor force than other Ann Arbor residents or downtown Oakville residents.

About 70 percent of the downtown residents in both cities are employed in knowledge-based occupations, including managerial and professional occupations, education, health care, and the arts. That is slightly below the citywide figures of more than 75 percent in this classification in both Ann Arbor and Oakville. Nevertheless, they are both well above the comparable national figures of 49 percent for Canada and 59 percent for the United States.

City Center Plans and Policies

Oakville and Ann Arbor each have a long-standing commitment to growth management and quality development. Both communities have stringent standards for new development and are regarded by the development community as difficult to work in. According to the Oakville Economic Development Alliance, "Oakville prides itself on meticulous planning to insure a promising future" (Oakville Economic Development Alliance, 2000). Nevertheless, both cities have pursued a number of different strategies to promote their downtown economy (Table 4.10).

There are a number of significant differences, however. Ann Arbor has adopted a planning strategy that emphasizes increasing densities in the downtown core area. The plan favors mixed-use developments with substantial residential components. The city has also invested heavily in structure parking. Congestion levels in the core area are not seen as a major problem.

Oakville, on the other hand, sees its Old Oakville area as a location for small-scale development, with locally owned shops and services that offer a variety of unique shopping and dining opportunities. Whereas two parking structures have been built, surface parking (not on Lakeshore) is still viable. Plans do not contemplate increasing the density of either the commercial core or the adjacent residential areas.

Ann Arbor. The Downtown Development Authority, which is responsible for administering the district, has formulated a plan to maintain the character and quality of the core area that includes public improvements, design guidelines for private development and historic preservation, and promotional activities. (The latter are primarily the responsibility of the four sub-area associations.)

Table 4.10 Economic Revitalization Strategies, Ann Arbor and Oakville

	Ann Arbor	Oakville
Streetscape Improvements	X	X
Pedestrian Streets	X	X
Parking Structures	X	X
Farmers' Market	X	X
Enclosed Mall		X
Cultural Facilities	X	X
Sports Venues		X
Entertainment	X	X
Convention Center		X
Residential, Market Rate	X	X
Residential, Affordable	X	
Downtown Plan	X	X
DDA/BIA	X	X
TOTAL	10	12

The DDA has direct responsibility for constructing and maintaining a range of public improvements, including street furniture, sidewalks, landscaping, parking structures, transportation, and other infrastructure improvements. These developments are supported by revenues from the tax increment financing district that is coterminous with the DDA.

Mixed-use new development is encouraged by the DDA, with a particular emphasis on street-level retail uses and increasing the residential base of downtown. Priority is given to retail that meets the needs of core area residents and promotes interaction between merchants and residents. A broad range of housing to meet the needs of a variety of household types and incomes is also encouraged. Developing linkages between downtown residents and surrounding neighborhoods is another priority of the DDA.

Oakville. Overall planning for the municipality of Oakville identifies three major commercial centers: Old Oakville, Midtown, and Uptown. These retail centers each have distinct roles, and future developments should re-inforce them. New retail commercial development in North Oakville will serve primarily the new population in that area and will not include major retail facilities that would compete with these existing centers.

The Town of Oakville continues to see the Old Oakville Down-town as a primary location for (primarily upscale) specialty retailing and restaurants. Several strategies (Randolph Group, 1997; Oakville, 2002) have been identified to strengthen the downtown core, including

- Promoting tourist activities
- Promoting the upscale heritage theme of the core
- Improving connections between the commercial core and the waterfront
- Improving traffic patterns and parking
- Strengthening neighborhoods adjacent to downtown

In addition, the citywide policies related to heritage preservation, urban aesthetics, and environmental management also implicitly con-tribute to strengthening the core.

DISCUSSION

Downtown revitalization policies cannot rely on a "quick fix" or de-pend on a "magic bullet" to resolve longstanding and complex prob-lems. Rather, a diverse range of strategies, applied over a long period, may initiate the virtuous cycle that is necessary for sustaining a healthy core. Urban areas that have more successful cores also have residents with higher incomes and better education, and higher levels of economic growth, along with more diverse and stable economies. These attributes have greater potential to support downtown locations for restaurants, entertainment venues, and cultural activities. That, in turn, can foster success in other downtown activities, such as specialty retail and resi-dential. The development of downtown as a neighborhood will in turn contribute to other types of retail growth. A downtown that is diverse and active will continue to attract the investment required to sustain it as a distinct place in the metropolitan framework.

Despite these potential advantages, not every community can aspire to a downtown that is the regional leader in terms of measures such as retail sales or employment. Indeed, recent research notes that having more amenities such as professional symphonies and ballet and opera companies is correlated with attraction of "knowledge class" residents (Nelson et al., 2016). This, however, is a strategy that can only be applied to large downtowns serving regional markets. For many midsize city cores, a different metric of success will be required. Some of the factors that might be considered in designing effective strategies are described below. While there are clearly no simple answers to the problems of downtown revitalization, it is possible to identify a number of principles that seem to be applicable in a wide variety of situations.

The case studies provide a rather mixed picture with respect to the potential contribution of public policies and economic development strategies to the health of core areas. Ann Arbor and Oakville have the ability to be more selective in the development allowed, emphasizing both design and growth controls. So is the potential for a successful downtown area just a matter of "place luck," of being located in a prosperous urban area? Or are there specific actions that can be expected to make a significant difference in the prospects for the downtowns of middle size urban areas? The case studies suggest a number of relevant principles for the design of successful core area revitalization strategies:

- A successful core area is likely to be one that has a distinct physical appearance, regardless of the market niche it serves. A downtown that retains its historic character (providing a physically distinctive environment) is more likely to be successful. The distinct physical character that often exists in core areas helps to establish the identity of the downtown as a special place (Filion and Hoernig, 2003). The street and building patterns in downtown create an attractive environment. Well-designed public spaces and buildings contribute to the success of the core (Paumier, 2004). Both

Oakville and Ann Arbor have made conscious efforts to retain the distinct character of their downtowns.

- The absence of detrimental policies (such as urban renewal that removes historic structures, traffic schemes that discourage pedestrian activity, retail precincts interrupted by surface parking or blank building walls) can contribute to the health of the core. Planning initiatives that implicitly attempt to create a suburban environment in the cores seem generally inimical to the success of traditional city centers.

- The image of the core is as important as the reality. The reputation of a city and its core area is complex and unlikely to be formed based on a single attribute. There may also be a significant time lag in any change in perceptions, so that current circumstances may not adequately reflect the basis for the reputation. With this caveat in mind, there nevertheless seem to be some general observations that can be drawn from these case studies.

- The initial assessment of the health of these core areas was based on a survey of urban experts from across Canada and the United States, most of whom were "outsiders" whose image of the city centers may have been based on limited firsthand experience. The way in which a community is described in the popular or professional literature, assessed by travel agents and convention planners, or how it is discussed at professional meetings will affect the external image of the community. Moreover, there is little doubt that a reputation (good or bad) is likely to endure beyond the time when it accurately reflects reality.

- A downtown that serves a range of populations and markets, through the promotion of variety in land uses and activities, will be more sustainable and have a greater potential for success than more narrowly focused core areas. Markets vary by time of day, day of the week, and season of the year. Attracting residents to downtown locations generally will require the existence of activities (retail, restaurants, and entertainment) that may also serve other market segments: downtown workers, tourists, and residents of the metropolitan area.

- Downtown revitalization efforts must be approached at an appropriate scale. The historic core may represent too large an area to be successfully revitalized. Particularly in a downtown that has experienced a long period of decline, there may simply be too much downtown to revitalize. Strategic choices must be made to ensure that the necessary critical mass of activity is achieved. In slow-growing markets, strategies based on encouraging development at multiple locations, with the expectation that the spaces in between will be filled in, are unlikely to produce the desired results. Large-scale revitalization projects may not be as cost-effective as a series of smaller scale initiatives. Major investments in parking facilities or sports arenas may not be as effective as money spent on landscaping and comfortable seating.

- But it is not just the city center's reputation with outsiders that matters. The way that the core area is perceived by residents of the urban area can be equally important. If the downtown is generally thought to be a place to be avoided by local residents, it seems unlikely that it will be able to have a positive image to outsiders.

- The city center is likely to become—or remain—healthy and sustainable only if it is seen as a priority for the community. Successful city centers will rarely occur by chance. They must receive high levels of attention and investment to ensure their continued prosperity. The Trinity area in Moncton and the Southwest district in Kamloops both provide locations for new retail developments that are strongly supported by the respective municipal governments. The city of Victoria has encouraged new residential development in West Victoria across the Inner Harbor from downtown; the provincial government has relocated a number of agencies to the Selkirk waterfront area. Local residents believe that these policies have had negative impacts on the city center. Kingston, on the other hand, has been much more focused on the Princess Street retail core.

- Whereas the public sector may have an important role in revitalization efforts, the sustainability of downtown also requires interest and participation by the private sector—whether investors, residents, employees, or shoppers. The concept of partnerships also extends to the community broadly defined—the customers, employees, and residents who will use the city center. Developing support for downtown revitalization among these constituent groups may be difficult, but it is important. The implicit goal of most core revitalization efforts is a city center that is actively and visibly used. This cannot be achieved without the support of the public.

- No one organization, or type of organization, can single-handedly bring about the revitalization of an older urban core area. Efforts to revitalize the city center are not just the domain of the public sector. Government initiatives must be undertaken in cooperation with the private sector, civic leadership, and the nonprofit community as well.

- An organization that is an effective downtown advocate (e.g., BIA, DDA, merchants association) is probably a prerequisite for success. Although there are substantial differences between the Canadian BIA and the American DDA (see Chapter 6), these differences do not seem to have a significant impact on their relative effectiveness. While having some downtown advocate appears to be important, as is the relationship of this entity to the municipal government, neither organizational structure seems to be inherently superior. The maintenance of existing public areas and facilities is also important. In a number of the case study communities, an active and professional BIA appears to be a key participant in revitalization efforts. The more effective BIAs have adopted a broad mission that may include physical and fiscal planning, research, and advocacy in addition to traditional promotion and design activities. While no guarantee of success (Victoria's city center does not currently have a BIA; Moncton has one of the more effective ones), a BIA or equivalent mechanism to marshal the support of the downtown business community can make a substantial contribution to revitalization efforts.

- Successful cores are likely to be able to attract higher quality developments than their struggling counterparts. It is clear that both Ann Arbor and Oakville are in a position to pick and choose

among development proposals. Even with substantial induce-
ments, a struggling downtown may not be able to attract the same
quality of development as one that is more successful.

- A healthy core is likely to benefit from favorable demographics.
The presence of middle- and upper-income residents is likely to
be more important than simply having people living in the core.
High proportions of knowledge workers were also associated with
successful core areas. It is unlikely that a desirable mix of residents
can be attracted to a downtown that does not already possess a
certain critical mass of activities.

- While there is often a university presence in healthy cores, that
does not seem to be essential. However, downtowns without a
university may have different demographic characteristics. For
example, Ann Arbor's downtown, which clearly benefits from
having a major university close by, is thriving with few family
households and low labor force participation. Oakville, on the
other hand, has been able to attract a relatively high proportion
of family households and higher labor force participation to its
successful core area.

- Finally, the case studies suggest that even a struggling core area
may be perceived as having some level of success, so long as there
are tangible signs of improvement. Brantford is hoping to increase
core activity by bringing educational institutions and new public
facilities to the core. While these big-ticket public investments
include an element of risk, there are signs that some positive spinoffs are occurring. The potential for success of these strategies is
not clear, however. Certainly not every community can aspire to
be a major entertainment center. Other activity generators, such
as universities and government offices, may be more appropriate
strategies.

CONCLUSIONS

Few midsize city centers anywhere in North America are likely to achieve
the recognized level of success represented by Halifax, Kingston, or

Victoria. The core areas of these midsize Canadian cities can be expected to continue to be highly regarded. The visible signs of success—extensive pedestrian activity, a variety of retail and entertainment options, community events, and private investment—will likely sustain these city centers, allowing them to adapt to changing circumstances. There are, however, some hopeful indications for those cities whose cores are less well regarded. Planning and public policies for the revitalization of the city centers can result in improvements to even the most distressed community. Through public investments and bringing post-secondary educational institutions to the city center, Brantford may be successful in increasing the sustainability of at least a portion of its core area. Downtown Moncton is a major employment center for its metropolitan area, but has had limited success in extending downtown activity beyond the workday. The Kamloops city center seems to be slowly achieving its modest goals as a vital residential neighborhood. In each of these instances, the downtown core is becoming a "finer place," one that is sustainable and better suited to the needs of community residents. And an improvement in the quality of life would seem to be an appropriate measure of success.

The nature of the city center's built environment is of equal importance. Some attributes are well understood, regardless of specific community characteristics. The core area must be perceived to be, and actually be, clean and safe. It must be relatively compact, with a continuity of activities. Extensive "dead" areas of parking or blank walls should be avoided. It must be legible to all types of users, with adequate signage and well-defined edges.

For most communities the downtown is also viewed as an important place, one that is a focus of considerable attention. From the perspective of urban professionals, the extent of pedestrian traffic in the core seems to be the major consideration in city center well-being. While it is not the only measure, it is an important one. Strategies for maintaining and increasing foot traffic deserve closer examination. A useful place to start is the presumption that a successful city center will serve multiple markets—residents of the downtown, the metropolitan population, downtown workers (including students), and tourists. Each of these populations will be represented in different proportions in each midsize city center. Public policies that seek to increase any of these markets must consider what each is looking for in the downtown and how they will use it. The opportunities offered by the city center must be tailored to meet the desires of each segment of the market. Retail commercial establishments may be important, but grocery stores are likely to be more relevant to city center residents than tourists. Service establishments (dry cleaners, barbershops) may serve multiple markets (residents and workers), while entertainment activities have the broadest market potential.

City center improvement strategies must consider the types of uses that are appropriate for different market segments. Consideration must also be given to whether a particular use "creates" or follows market potential. A souvenir shop will flourish only if there is a reason for a tourist market to exist. A wine and cheese specialty shop will do well only if there are higher income residents nearby. While there may be opportunities for retail commercial development, they must be exploited with close attention to the potential markets to be served. Certainly the prospects for destination retail in the city center are limited in most midsize cities (see Beyardi, 2001; Philips, 2002; and Kent and Brown, 2009).

The singular characteristics of the city center should be emphasized. Where possible, heritage buildings should be preserved and put to active use. Design details should distinguish the downtown as a special place. Pedestrian activities should be facilitated. The potential of the city center is not the same in all communities. Geographic location, historic development patterns, the accumulation of public and private decisions, as well as the nature of the local economy all affect what the city center is and what it can readily become.

Planning for city center sustainability also requires careful consideration of how success should be defined. Plans that envision a return to downtown retail dominance may be just as unrealistic as plans that feature heritage tourism in a 1950s downtown or rely on development of expensive mass transit systems. The city center is a complex economic and social space. Selecting appropriate strategies for city center revitalization efforts will depend on the primary function of the core. In each of the cities studied, the core area is more or less explicitly in competition with other parts of the city and metropolitan area for development, employment, and retail activity. For most of these functions, the city center represents only one possible location in the urban area. It will be necessary to determine the priority for development of retail, office, and residential uses in the core as opposed to other locations in the jurisdiction. Though many communities share the goal of a strong and vital city center, there are simply no one-size-fits-all strategies or criteria for success.

5

The Creative Class

If vague concepts are vaguely understood, then their meaning will always be in doubt. If there is no agreement on how to define and measure the creative class, there is little prospect that it will provide useful public policy guidance. If no one knows how the creative class is constituted, or how their presence relates to economic growth, there are likely to be no effective policy levers.

Reese and Sands, 2008: 6

Two distinct but related concepts have emerged to frame discussions of urban economic restructuring and prosperity in the twenty-first century. The first is the growth of the New Economy defined by knowledge-based and high-tech industriwes. In the early 1990s, Edward Glaeser and others (Glaeser et al., 1992; Feser, 2003) began to advocate economic development strategies based on investments in education and skills development (Pink-Harper, 2015). Many of these often highly specialized jobs simply did not exist fifty years ago, but they are now seen as the engines of economic prosperity in the twenty-first century (Chappele et al., 2004; Erichek and McKinney, 2004; Duderstadt, 2005).

The second concept focuses on occupations in creative and cultural fields. Richard Florida has argued that attracting and retaining talented individuals (which he defines as being members of the creative class) will in turn attract the twenty-first-century, New Economy employment opportunities that are essential to the prosperous communities of the future (Eakin, 2002; Lever, 2002; Luciani, 2006; Scott, 2006). The presence of this creative class is seen as an essential component of economic vitality (Glaeser and Mare, 2001; Ley, 2003; Florida, 2005a, 2014). Rather than depending on highly immobile natural resources or heavy industries, municipalities are urged to focus on information and creativity to foster economic growth. Although researchers have found little direct evidence of these connections (Sands and Reese, 2008), one would expect that cities with large creative class populations would be more prosperous than those urban areas still tied to the old economy.

Many cities across North America, of all sizes and circumstances, appear to be jumping on the creative class bandwagon (Eakin, 2002; Peck, 2005; Sands and Reese, 2008). Academics, however, continue to explore several basic substantive and methodological issues related to this economic development nostrum. Among the issues raised are the following questions: How should the creative class be defined? How can it best be measured? Are the presence of creative class and economic growth really related? If there is a relationship, what is the causal order? What explicit local policies will actually attract creative class? And can all cities aspire to be attractive to creative individuals?

This chapter begins by taking a step back from the policy debate to consider different criteria that can be used to define the creative class. Inherently a theoretical construct, "creative class" must be operationalized before it can be used to design and evaluate local policies. While Florida's operationalizations have generally been opaque, a number of other scholars have begun to chip away at the concept in an effort to come up with replicable and reliable definitional and measurement schemes (see, for example, Markusen et al., 2008). Looking across the growing creative class literature, several methodologies for measurement have been employed: analysis of census and other economic data, business, and quality of life indicators; case studies and other descriptive efforts; and surveys of business leaders and other experts (Glaeser and Mare, 2001; Florida, 2005b; Peck, 2005; Rausch and Negrey, 2006; Sands and Reese, 2008; Markusen et al., 2008). Thus far, however, this research provides little overall sense of the relative validity of the creative class concept.

The second half of the chapter directly takes up the economic development policy relevance of the creative class. Creative class strategies are attractive because *any* city has the potential to become a thriving, creative place, one that will prosper and grow for decades to come. The task at hand, then, is to be an attractive location for younger, educated, New Economy and creative individuals; this can be done, it is argued, by offering a diverse, tolerant, and amenity-rich community. Practicing *tolerance* and developing amenities will attract residents with *talent*, leading to an expanded *high-technology* sector, ultimately stimulating economic growth, which can support investments in even more amenities, creating an ever more positive economic cycle. At least, this is the doctrine offered to cities as the *au currant* road to prosperity (Florida, 2002b; Nelson et al., 2016).

But the connections and processes required for this growth chain to operate have not been sufficiently tested empirically. Assumptions embedded within creative class arguments have raised many questions among academics and other policy evaluators (Ley, 2003; Peck, 2005; Thomas and Darnton, 2006; Scott, 2006, among many others). This chapter attempts to unpack some of the assumptions behind the creative class by examining the success that midsize Canadian urban areas have attained in attracting and maintaining a creative class population.

IN SEARCH OF THE CREATIVE CLASS

Identifying reasonable expectations regarding what midsize metropolitan areas might be able to achieve in attracting the creative class and competing effectively in the twenty-first-century economy is a critical endeavor (Scott, 2006). Most league tables of competitive and successful metropolitan areas seldom include those with fewer than a quarter-million residents. Yet cities of all sizes and locations have apparently bought into the creative class as a means of stimulating economic growth (Eakin, 2002; Peck, 2005). What can these smaller cities reasonably expect to achieve?

This research examines the nature of the creative class in midsize Canadian urban areas using four measures. First, occupational and demographic profiles of midsize Canadian Census metropolitan areas identify differences in the creative workforce. In particular, measures of talent (educational attainment, occupational mix) and diversity (immigration, racial/ethnic mix, lifestyle) are considered. Trends in these dimensions are compared to standard measures of economic prosperity such as employment and income growth (Moss, 1997). Second, a variety of creative class accoutrements are coded for each community: coffeehouses, art museums and stores, ethnic restaurants, independent bookstores and the like, as well as the city center evaluations described in Chapter 4. Finally, site visits and case studies in a sample of Canadian municipalities assess the extent of creative class "on the ground." These three measurement systems are then compared for consistency and reliability. Specific research questions include the following:

- Are rankings on different indicators correlated?
- Do the same municipalities come up high on all of the creative class indicators?
- How do the different measurement criteria relate to overall economic health and growth?
- Which measurement or combination of measurements appears most reliable?

Research empirically testing creative class arguments is relatively limited but increasing. Much of it has been as polemical as Florida's original (see Ley, 2003; Luciani, 2006; Peck, 2005, as examples); other studies, however, have deconstructed the creative class dynamic using both extant literature (Thomas and Darnton, 2006) and empirical data (e.g., Rausch and Negrey, 2006; Stern and Seifert, 2007; Markusen et al., 2008; Sands and Reese, 2008). Assessments of Florida's economic development paradigm tend to focus on three distinct questions (see Reese and Sands, 2008, for a more detailed discussion):

- What is the nature of the creative class and what are the most relevant measures of it?
- Is there an identifiable connection between the inputs (creative class) and desired outcomes (economic growth and prosperity)?
- What public policies and programs are most useful in attracting and building the creative class?

Much of the case for creative class-based strategies rests on the presumption that, in the new era where knowledge industries are the primary engine of economic growth, there are fewer restrictions on where economic activity can locate. Place continues to matter, but it is no longer just those places that provide accessibility to natural resources or transportation that prosper. Rather, it is places that offer superior access to other talented people and a rich variety of amenities that will enjoy economic growth (Florida, 2002b: 4–8).

The measurement question is fairly straightforward, if not effectively answered to date: If there are causal connections (not simply statistical relationships) between economic success and the creative class, what exactly *is* the creative class? Will we know it when we see it? Valid measurements of the size and composition of the creative class are essential to the development of targeted implementation strategies. If creative class economic development strategies are not to be based on place luck or serendipity, the essential instrumental values must be identified. Florida suggests that tolerance (acceptance of different populations) and amenities (particularly lifestyle assets such as outdoor recreation and a vibrant local music and arts scene) are keys to successful creative class strategies. But it is not clear how tolerance is in fact measured, let alone how it can be enhanced. Although Florida uses different measures of population diversity to represent tolerance, the actual connection between diversity and tolerance is not well established. Nor is it clear which amenities are relevant and how these might be incorporated into public policy.

Empirical research has raised questions on a number of points related to measuring or operationalizing creative class. For example, on the input side of the equation, there is a lack of clarity in conditions that cause creative individuals to congregate and stay in a location over an extended period of time (Scott, 2006). What attributes of a place are most important for creative class individuals—services, arts, entertainment venues, street life, educational opportunities, recreational options, good scenery, climate? The answer is far from clear.

The internal components of Florida's diversity or "melting pot" indexes are also murky. Specifically, relationships between the presence of African Americans and economic growth or decline have not been fully explored (Madden, 2001; Thomas and Darnton, 2006); the impact of immigrants has not been examined by skill level (Borjas, 1995); the extent that ethnic and racial enclaves are voluntary and thus socially and economically beneficial has not been assessed (Qadeer, 2005); and it appears that race and ethnicity may relate differently to the other creative class indicators in the United States and other nations such as Canada (Sands and Reese, 2008). Measures of gays are also highly problematic due to reliance on census data that may well underrepresent single gays and fail to differentiate among different types of gay households (Thomas and Darnton, 2006; Sands and Reese, 2008).

Similarly, measuring tolerance remains problematic. Florida places considerable emphasis on the importance of tolerance as a factor in attracting and retaining the creative class. The logic is quite straightforward: creatives prefer to live in tolerant communities because they themselves often prefer unconventional lifestyles and tend to appreciate the diverse social and cultural milieu fostered by tolerant places. Although originally limited to measures of the gay population, the definition of diversity has expanded to include broader measures of diversity, such as the presence of immigrants and artists ("bohemians") in a community (Florida, 2002a). The result of this expansion has been to make the concept less clear (Thomas and Darnton, 2006). And this feature of creative class arguments has lacked empirical examination (see Sharp, 2007 and Reese and Zalewski, 2015 for US city exceptions). Numerous very practical questions remain to be addressed: Is diversity a suitable proxy for tolerance; that is, are more heterogeneous communities actually more tolerant? What variables constitute a useful measure of community tolerance? Is there a measurable relationship between indicators of community tolerance, creative class populations, and subsequent community prosperity?

Findings, particularly those related to measures of high technology and creativity, are quite sensitive to how variables are defined. For example, cities may come out higher or lower on creative class scales depending on what is categorized as high technology, whether services and manufacturing are considered separately, whether the metric used is cultural industries or cultural occupations, what time periods are used, and which particular set of cities or regions is examined (Chappele et al., 2004;

Markusen et al., 2008). Further, there appear to be substantial differences even among jobs generally considered to be high-tech. Employment in computer or aerospace manufacturing is inherently different than information technology or medical services (Sands and Reese, 2008).

Research attempting to identify and measure the extent of creative class populations among cities using the indicators implicit in the work of Florida and others has had mixed results. For example, while across cities there indeed seems to be an identifiable confluence of same-sex households and artistic occupations, tolerance (as measured by diversity) appears to be a very different concept (Sands and Reese, 2008). While diversity appears positively related to same-sex couples and creative employment, these variables are either not related to high-tech occupations at all (Sands and Reese, 2008) or inconsistently related, depending on time period (Rausch and Negrey, 2006). And research that has directly measured tolerance via the use of citizen surveys has failed to find a consistent relationship between various measures of tolerance and economic prosperity (Reese and Zalewski, 2015).

METHODOLOGY

Because Florida's initial and subsequent arguments about the importance of the creative class have focused on larger metropolitan regions and large central cities, it raises the question of whether the model is directly applicable to smaller urban areas. While it is possible that creative talent congregates in only the largest cities, Florida makes no such distinctions, and artistic or creative outposts are evident in smaller communities across Canada and the United States: Stratford, Ontario, and Santa Fe, New Mexico, for example. And more importantly, local officials in cities of all sizes are embracing creative class strategies. Before policy analysts can in good conscience recommend creative class strategies to local governments across the board, empirical data need to show that the model is widely applicable to cities of all types, scales, and sizes. Data for this part of the analysis are drawn from the Canadian Census (Statistics Canada, 1996, 2001), supplemented by data from Industry Canada (2002).

Demographic Measures of Creative Class

The operationalization of creative class, technology workers, tolerance, and diversity is at best a subjective enterprise. There are no widely agreed upon measures of these concepts, nor has Florida been particularly clear in either his early or later writing (indeed, he has offered different definitions) on specific indicators. Research using different operational schemes has resulted in different conclusions regarding the relationship between creative class and other measures such as technology and tolerance (Chappele, et al., 2004; Peck, 2005; Thomas and Darnton, 2006; Sands and Reese, 2008). The demographic indicators used here have been selected to provide the closest Canadian equivalents to the original US measures used in Florida (2002b) and closely mirror those used in previous creative class studies across larger cities in Canada conducted by a team of researchers including Florida (Gertler et al., 2002). Demographic indicators are presented in Table 5.1.

Several aspects of the demographic measurement scheme should be noted. First, diversity indicators have been used in creative class arguments not only to portray the racial and ethnic composition of a region, but also as a proxy for the concept of tolerance. Thus, it is assumed that areas with more diverse populations have residents that are more tolerant of such diversity (including variety in lifestyle preferences); logic suggests that individuals in these categories will prefer to locate where tolerance levels are higher; hence, they will receive greater acceptance. This presumption had limited empirical testing, however, and greater diversity may well not ensure greater tolerance. Just the opposite could occur depending on the direction of the causal relationship (if indeed there is one). Similarly, the mere presence of creative individuals does not mean that innovation and creativity emerge (Scott, 2006).

Second, the measures are based on industry rather than occupation. Again, this was done to maintain consistency with other work by Florida using Canadian data (Gertler et al., 2002). The creative class measure combines educational with industry measures based on empirical analysis indicating they are part of the same underlying concept (Sands and Reese, 2008). The measures of high technology are based on industry

Table 5.1 Operational Measures

Creative Indicators	High-Tech Industries	Diversity Measures	Economic Health/Growth
Arts companies	Manufacturing	Visible minorities	Population
Independent artists	Pharmaceuticals	Immigrants	Population change
University employees	Computers	Non-Christians	Average earnings
Graduate degrees	Aerospace	Blacks	Earnings change
Design service workers	Medical devices	Hispanics	Median family income
	Services	Arabs	Family income change
	Engineering	Asians	Unemployment
	Computer	Foreign born	Unemployment change
	Scientific consulting	Same sex couples	
	R&D services		

data that include all occupations within the industries. Finally, it should be noted that measures of change are only examined for the economic health and diversity variables, where 1996 census measures are available. Same-sex households were not included until the 2001 census.

In order to provide a set of measures that are reasonably comparable for urban areas that vary considerably in population, a location quotient was calculated for each variable. The location quotients compare a local value (expressed as a percentage) with the corresponding provincial value. Provincial values are used rather than national values because of the wide variation among provinces in much of the demographic data, particularly, as will be clear later in this analysis, for Quebec. Comparing cities to their respective provinces provides a more appropriate frame of reference; using national values would impose standardization inappropriately. If the local value is identical to the provincial value, the location quotient is unity. Location quotient values greater than one indicate the locality has an above average concentration of the particular variable, while values less than one occur when the locality is below average. The calculated location quotients generally range between 0.5 and 2.0.

Creative Class Amenities

Creative class amenities were tabulated for all of the metropolitan areas. A central component of the Florida argument (see Florida, 2014, for a more recent reemphasis) is that creative class individuals will be drawn to urban areas that contain particular amenities that serve their creative impulses and make the community more unique: "They are excited by opportunities for recreation and by fashionable consumption opportunities in the hip restaurants, bars, shops, and boutiques abundant in restructured urban neighborhoods" (Clark et al., 2002: 500). Such amenities include local coffeehouses and restaurants, independent bookstores and cinemas, art museums and art supply stores, and other cultural venues such as science centers, zoos, historical museums, and the like. All of these features enhance the cultural life of a community and do so in a way that makes it stand out from others. Non-creative (more generic) forms of similar amenities would include chain bookstores, coffee shops, restaurants, and movie venues that serve mass, homogenized audiences. Both creative and generic amenities were coded based on multiple websites for each city.[1]

Distinguishing between local and unique, as opposed to chain and generic, amenities can be rather subjective. The Appendix at the end of this chapter provides a discussion of the rules of thumb used for differentiating between local and chain establishments and also for differentiating coffeehouses from restaurants. Efforts to identify such amenities as bars, nightclubs, and ethnic restaurants failed primarily because the lines were too hard to draw in a reliable fashion. Almost no establishments serve only alcohol, so how much and what types of food distinguish between a bar and a restaurant, pub, or bistro is almost impossible to discern.

The importance of these amenities presumably is enhanced by concentration: "cool" districts may be more important than a similar number

---

1. The site www.foodinc.ca was the primary source for restaurant data; it is a national site that includes comparable lists of local dining opportunities.

Figure 5.1 Saint Hyacinthe, QC, cafes

of amenities spread across the entire metropolitan area. Thus we use a measure of core area health (Chapter 4) as an indicator of the potential appeal of a community to the creative class.

Community Site Visits

To augment the expert rankings of downtowns and other aggregate data, visits were made to a subset of nineteen of the cities, almost half of the total number of midsize urban areas (Table 5.2). These cities were selected based on a purposive sampling method that began with classification of cities by province. Again, the use of province as a frame is based on systematic variation in the health of cities by province. If cities were examined nationally, there would be no highly healthy midsize cities in Quebec (Sands and Reese, 2008). Within each provincial group, cities were selected to represent healthier, growing communities as well as slow or negative growth examples. Due to resource limitations, the analysis here focused on cities in Ontario, Quebec, and British Columbia. Obviously this does not represent a random sample and is used to provide a check on the other measuring systems. Each site visit lasted two to three days.

Table 5.2 Site Visit Communities

Brantford, ON	Drummondville, QC
Granby, QC	Guelph, ON
Halifax, NS	Kamloops, BC
Kingston, ON	Kitchener, ON
London, ON	Moncton, ON
Nanaimo, BC	Oshawa, ON
Sarnia, ON	Sherbrooke, QC
St. Catharines-Niagara, ON	Saint-Hyacinthe, QC
Saint-Jean-sur-Richelieu, QC	Victoria, BC
Windsor, ON	

Assessments were made of the quality and uniqueness of the downtown (visual demarcation, balance between retail commercial and entertainment venues, variety of entertainment and commercial establishments, walkability, integration of art and culture), nature of local housing (quality, variety, price), recreational amenities (water features, community parks, fairs and festivals), variety of restaurants, institutions of higher education, historic preservation, and planning quality (land use, integration and use of natural features, infrastructure maintenance). The site visits provided a visual reality check on the validity of demographic, downtown quality, and creative class amenities. Local officials were also interviewed at each site, although those data are not part of this analysis.

ANALYSIS

Are Community Rankings on the Different Indicators Correlated?

Formal analysis to identify which variables are the most relevant to understanding the creative class is confounded by the fact that many of these measures are highly correlated with each other. To address this issue, we subjected all of the variables that are potentially related to creative class to an exploratory and confirmatory factor analysis. Factor analysis is a

Figure 5.2 Nanaimo, BC, coffee houses and restaurants

statistical technique that is used to create index measures (factors) that combine related variables (see Appendix B). The index scores provide summary measures that minimize differences within the factors while maximizing differences between them.

The analysis identified five separate factors that reflect the underlying structure of the variables related to the creative class:

- gay/creative—employment in design, computer, and scientific services, arts companies and independent artists, and the number of same-sex households
- diversity—population that is black, Hispanic, Arab, Asian, and/ or foreign born
- engineering—employment in engineering and research and development
- high-tech manufacturing—employment in computer and aerospace manufacturing
- medical—employment in pharmaceutical and medical equipment manufacturing

The indexes derived from the factor analysis make clear that the presence of gay households is a conceptually different measure of diversity than racial or ethnic traits. Thus, the Florida Diversity Index, which includes measures of gays, bohemians (artistically creative people), and the melting pot (foreign born), is mixing conceptually unrelated variables, at least as applied to Canadian urban areas. Further, multiple concepts are required to represent a creative core of high technology and high-talent individuals. Talent, as measured by the percentage of the population with a college degree, does not load on any of the factors.

To reduce complexity, the amenity variables were also factor-analyzed, with two conceptually different factors emerging:

- unique amenities—independent bookstores, coffeehouses and restaurants, art house or non-chain cinemas, museums, zoos and aquariums, art galleries and studios, theaters and concert halls, and art supply stores
- generic amenities—chain bookstores, chain coffeehouses and restaurants, fairs and festivals

Other amenities related to the visual arts (movie houses, museums, galleries, and theaters) load with the locally unique amenities. The number of local fairs and festivals loads with the generic amenities. This result is not surprising since case study data indicated the presence of some type of festival in every community. While the themes may vary (hot air balloons and fireworks in some, downtown shopping days and cultural events in others), festivals have become almost *de rigeur*.

Correlations among the various creative class indicators generally reveal strong interrelationships (Table 5.3). First, the two amenities indexes are significantly correlated, indicating that those communities that have more locally unique features also have more entertainment amenities overall; that is, chains may locate in cities where there are more local amenities. Indeed, both amenity indexes relate to the other indexes in nearly identical patterns: greater amenities of any type are positively associated with more successful downtowns, more creative class individuals, and greater diversity. Neither amenity index is related

Table 5.3 Creative Index Correlation Matrix

	Cool Amenities	Generic Amenities	Downtown	Creative Class	Diversity	Engineering	Computer	Medical	University
Cool	1.00	.75**	.47**	.76**	.55**	.14	-.15	.04	.30
Generic	.75**	1.00	.42**	.54**	.73**	-.02	-.21	.09	.41**
Downtowns	.47**	.42**	1.00	.62**	.62**	.35*	.11	.00	.65**
Creatives	.76**	.54**	.62**	1.00	.45**	.18	.06	.16	.40**
Diversity	.55**	.73**	.18	.45**	1.00	-.14	.04	.21	.21
Engineering	.14	-.02	.35*	.18	-.14	1.0	-.28	-.14	.47**
Computer	-.15	-.21	.11	.06	.04	-.28	1.0	-.02	-.16
Medical	.04	.09	.00	.16	.21	-.14	.-02	1.0	.20
University	.30	.41**	.65**	.40**	.21	.47**	-.16	.20	1.00

*Significant at the .05 level
**Significant at the .01 level

to any of the measures of high-tech employment. Cities with more highly rated downtowns have significantly more creative class individuals and engineers. The presence of creative and diverse populations is also significantly and positively related. With the exception of the relationship between engineering employment and downtown quality, none of the high-tech employment indexes are related to any other measure of creative class or amenities, with the exception of a positive relationship between university employment and engineers. In sum, this relatively unsurprising analysis suggests that more amenities, regardless of type, better downtowns, and the presence of creative class individuals are significantly related. Contrary to many creative class arguments, high-tech employment, for the most part, is not associated with any other measure of creative class.

Do the Same Municipalities Score High on All Creative Class Indicators?

The aggregate analysis above becomes more interesting when the correlations are unpacked and the performance of individual cities becomes the

Figure 5.3 Brantford, ON, commercial street

context of analysis. A handful of cities emerge at the top of the group regardless of the indicator; Halifax, Victoria, Kitchener, and Saskatoon consistently are included in the top ten; Halifax appears in the top ten for twelve of the sixteen indicators; the other three cities each appear eleven times in the top ten. Interestingly, Halifax does not rank first among these cities for any single indicator, though it ranks second on two important indicators, its downtown and creative class indexes. More intriguing, of the four indicators on which Halifax does not claim a top-ten spot, two are related to the economy: overall economic health and change in economic health over the last two censuses.

Victoria, with four number-one rankings and one number-two ranking, outdoes Halifax (and every other city listed) in its overall "coolness." Victoria ranks first on downtown quality, creative class index, and total culture index. Like Halifax, Kitchener attains no number one rankings but ranks second on coffeehouses per capita and overall diversity. Saskatoon ranks second on bookstores and restaurants per capita, but it too lacks number-one rankings for any of the sixteen indicators. London claims ten spots on the various top ten lists, and Kelowna comes in at

Figure 5.4 Victoria, BC, downtown housing

eight. After these six cities, the list becomes less clear, as numerous cities have seven or fewer top ten appearances by indicator.

A handful of cities also emerge with the poorest performance across indicators; these cities are largely in Quebec, with a few in Alberta. Shawinigan claims eleven "bottom ten" spots; Saint-Jean-sur-Richelieu nine; Drummondville, Lethbridge, Medicine Hat, and Saint-Hyacinthe eight; and Sarnia and Trois-Rivières seven. Shawinigan is dead last on ten of the eleven indicators for which it is in the bottom ten, and is third from the bottom on the other indicator. Saint-Jean-sur-Richelieu, Lethbridge, and Saint-Hyacinthe each claim four next-to-last spots on indicators (because Shawinigan had claimed the last spot).

Looking across the lists of top- and bottom-ranked cities, a regional effect is suggested (see also Sands, 2007b). As will be discussed more fully later, many of the most poorly ranked cities are in Quebec. When the rankings are calculated by region—Ontario, Maritimes, Prairies, British Columbia, and Quebec—a pattern of nodal cities emerges. Within each region a relatively consistent set of cities top the rankings, representing the "best in class," so to speak; rankings on individual measures are far more consistent when used regionally. Larger urban areas are also more likely to be considered "cool."

On thirteen of the sixteen indicators, Victoria, Halifax, and Saskatoon, the "top three," appear within the top ten. The only three lists on which all three cities do not rank within the top ten are in the proportion of local to total bookstores, coffeehouses, and restaurants. Halifax is the only city of the top three that ranks in the top ten in the proportion of local to total bookstores, ranking eighth. For proportion of local to total restaurants, Victoria is sixth; it is also ninth for the proportion of local to total coffeehouses. Saskatoon is absent on all three local to total indicators. It seems that these cities, because of their size, are unable to escape the presence of generic and chain establishments.

The presence of diversity, however, does not necessarily mean the presence of "creativity," or a creative class. Only five of the metropolitan areas—the top three plus London and Kitchener—score highly on both the index of racial/ethnic diversity and on the creative class index drawn from Florida. The ways in which the lists deviate are more striking than their similarities. For instance, excluding the five cities listed above, the remaining five cities in the top ten on the creative class index drawn from Florida are Kelowna, Kitchener, Nanaimo, Peterborough, and Fredericton. For the index of racial/ethnic diversity, the remaining cities in the top ten are Windsor, St. Catharines-Niagara, Oshawa, and Abbotsford.

The only three indexes where the top three do not dominate—proportion of local to total bookstores, coffeehouses, and restaurants—seem to be populated mainly by Quebec cities: Saint-Hyacinthe, Granby, Saint-Jean-sur-Richelieu, Shawinigan, Trois-Rivières, and Saguenay. This may be a function of the relatively small size of the cities, however. The prevalence of generic and chain enterprises is reduced in small cities, so this connection would make sense. Indeed, with the exception of high rankings of Quebec cities on the aforementioned indexes, Quebec cities rank the most poorly of all cities across the majority of the sixteen indicators. Table 5.4 identifies the rankings of Quebec cities for a number of measures. Numbers in italics indicate that a city is in the bottom quartile for that particular index.

Table 5.4 Rankings of Quebec Cities

	Diversity	Health Change	Cool Amenities	Generic Amenities	Total Culture	Total Entertainment	Downtown	University	Economic Health	Creative Class
Drummondville	37	15	32	36	33	38	28	31	36	21
Granby	18	30	36	38	37	37	40	34	17	18
Saguenay	34	22	17	34	31	20	23	18	38	34
Saint-Hyacinthe	39	7	38	37	38	39	26	22	34	39
Saint-Jean-sur-Richelieu	35	3	39	39	39	36	36	27	28	30
Shawinigan	40	1	40	40	40	40	38	29	40	40
Sherbrooke	15	16	19	23	16	22	19	6	30	16
Trois-Rivières	32	35	18	31	15	34	10	15	39	33

As might be expected, index scores for total cultural amenities and total entertainment amenities are highly correlated. Nine of ten cities ranked in the top ten for total cultural amenities are also ranked in the top ten for entertainment amenities. Table 5.5 provides another way of looking at the consistency among the various indicators. Rank order correlations (Spearman's Rho) are presented for the ten cities highest on economic health. Logically, if the indicators were consistent and related to health, each city's ranking on one measure should be correlated with ranks on others. This is the case for only two of the indicators: rankings on generic and cool amenities are related, as are rankings on creative class and university employment. Rankings on the remaining indicators are completely unrelated, suggesting that they are measuring inherently different things. And none appear particularly good at predicting either economic health or change.

Figure 5.5 presents a visual representation of the consistency of the various indicators. The ten cities highest on the Economic Health Index are represented by the ten columns; their ranking on each measure is indicated on the vertical axis. The symbols in each column represent the

Table 5.5 Rank Order Correlations: Healthiest Cities

	Health Change	Downtown	University	Creative	Diversity	Cool	Generic
Economic Health	0.574	0.200	0.018	0.176	0.297	-0.139	-0.030
Health Change		0.102	-0.460	-0.064	-0.077	-0.421	-0.332
Downtown			-0.455	-0.564	-0.188	-0.515	-0.442
University				0.697*	0.539	0.479	0.394
Creative					0.576	0.479	0.333
Diversity						0.552	0.600
Cool							0.939**

*Significant at the .05 level, **significant at the .01 level

different demographic, amenity, and downtown health indicators used in the study as shown in the key. Each city would have eight distinct and visible symbols if they have different ranks on each of the measures. Shapes lying on top of each other show that the rankings involved are identical. A city that had the same rank on every indicator would have only one visible shape with the ranks on the other indicators lying underneath it. Thus, the number of shapes and the distance between them illustrate how consistently indicators are ranking cities.

Overall, half of the cities have six distinct ranks (or visible symbols): one has seven and three have five. In some cases, the space between the different indicator shapes is considerable, meaning that there is wide variation in how the different indicators rank these cities. The measures most likely to evidence overlapping ranks are the cool and generic amenities indexes, consistent with the forgoing analysis. The indicator with the greatest disparity in ranks is change in economic health; that is, it shows the greatest inconsistency in rankings relative to the other measures. Additionally, rank on economic health is often quite different than ranks on the other purported creative class measures. In short, economic

Figure 5.5 Indicator Scattergram

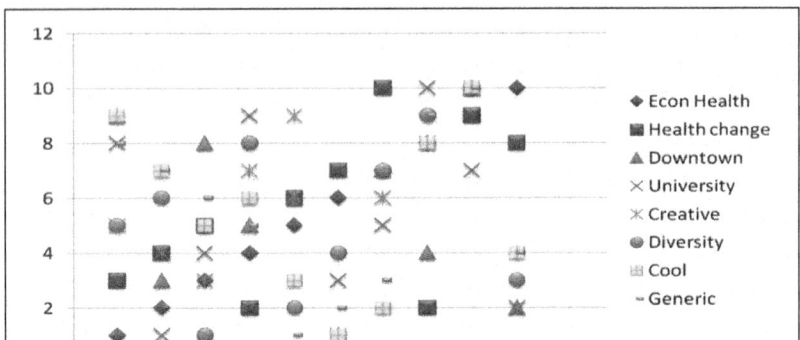

health appears most out of step with the other indicators. Finally, of the cities included, Guelph (the second to the last column) has the greatest consistency among indicators; all of the indicators are between seven and ten, indicating uniformly high ranks. The indicators for the rest of the cities show a much wider range.

Which Measurement or Combination of Measurement Systems Appears Most Reliable?

The answer to the question of which measurement scheme is most reliable is dependent on the purpose or goal of the analysis. Are we interested in assessing amenities? Are we analyzing the presence of particular populations, demographic traits, or skills? Or is the primary goal one of instructing local officials on the policies they need to pursue to increase or stabilize economic growth? Implicitly and explicitly, Florida's creative class arguments have presented local officials with a formula for economic prosperity: develop the tolerance and local amenities favored by the creative class, and creative class individuals will flock to the location, high-tech jobs will follow the creative class, and economic growth will ensue. This "virtuous path" to prosperity has, as its primary policy drivers, a tolerant culture and desirable urban amenities.

This logic seems fairly clear, even if actual implementation is murkier. Developing local arts and entertainment scenes, investing in special places (often the downtown), and fostering the creation of unique dining and shopping options are relatively straightforward. Academics and consultants have been essentially silent on how local officials are to foster tolerant environments, if indeed such aspects of the local milieu can even be measured and compared. The assessment of the reliability of the different operational schemes for measuring creative class is based both on the statistical analysis just presented as well as the site visits to particular communities.

Returning to the measurement question, it appears that indicators of high-tech employment are particularly unsuited to the task of measuring any aspect of the virtuous growth path. The various high-tech indicators are unrelated to creative individuals, diversity (as a proxy for tolerance), amenities, downtown quality, economic health, or economic growth. Many cities ranked in the top quartile of high-tech indicators are relatively uninteresting from a cultural standpoint, do not necessarily have robust economies, and are on the top ten list for relatively idiosyncratic, as opposed to systemic, reasons. For example, Shawinigan is a relatively isolated city in Quebec that has a great deal of high-tech employment but relatively little else that fits the creative class paradigm. Despite the presence of relatively large numbers of highly skilled individuals, the city continues to be isolated and lacking in the types of urban cultural amenities purported to attract the creative class. Indeed, levels of creative employment are quite low. In other cities with substantial proportions of high-tech employment, such as Windsor and Oshawa where auto manufacturing firms are located, there appears to be no synthetic connection to creativity, urban amenities, tolerance, diversity, or, indeed, economic growth.

The two indexes measuring entertainment and cultural amenities appear to be better indicators of creative class than high-tech employment, but these are problematic as well. Statistically, the two indexes are highly correlated. Cities with more unique local amenities also have more generic options. A variety of analyses were run in an effort to separate out the impacts of cool and generic amenities, including examination of each component indicator individually, using per capita figures, creating additive indexes rather than ones based on factor analysis, and so on. In all cases the effects of the different types of amenities were indistinguishable. Cities with more unique amenities have more generic ones; both types of amenities are correlated with static economic health (health in 1996 and 2001), and higher numbers of creative individuals and same-sex households. However, neither set of amenities is correlated with economic growth. It is also interesting to note that neither amenity measure is significantly correlated with population size. Thus, the most the correlation with the Economic Health Index may be saying is that entertainment venue owners are doing an accurate job of market analysis and thus locate in prosperous areas.

This, however, says nothing about the usefulness of either indicator in designing policies to attract creative class individuals. Since the Florida thesis would suggest that uniquely cool amenities attract the creative class while generic options should repel them, the lack of any distinguishable effects of the two variables implies that it doesn't matter much what types of amenities cities pursue as long as they have some. In short, a Starbucks, Tim Horton's, or McDonalds may be just as relevant to the creative class as a Babel Fish Bistro, a Fat Duck Gastro Pub, or Van Gogh's Ear (all in downtown Guelph).[2]

Based on an admittedly subjective (but reasonably consistent) assessment of the cities visited in the case studies, it appears, however, that the downtown quality index, the creative class index, and the location of university employees do the best job of identifying particularly desirable metropolitan areas. Victoria, Halifax, and Saskatoon consistently rank highly on each of the indicators. Tourism is particularly important in Victoria and Halifax: they represent major tourist destinations, contain Tier 1 higher education options, include heritage buildings, and incorporate local water resources into their downtowns. In short, they benefit significantly from "place luck" rather than good economic development policies. To be sure, local policies have enhanced downtowns, amenities, and economic health, but the cities had a great deal to work with in the first place.

Similarly, there are several cities that consistently rank poorly regardless of the indicator: Shawinigan, Saint-Jean-sur-Richelieu, Saint-

---

2. See Chapter 7 for a more extensive discussion of city center improvement strategies.

Figure 5.6 Saint-Jean-sur-Richelieu canal development

Hyacinthe, Drummondville, and Trois-Rivières. The primary common-
ality here is location in Quebec. Based on site visits to three of these
communities it appears that creative class measures do not work well
for the province of Quebec. Saint-Hyacinthe has a charming downtown
area with heritage buildings, an excellent and well-used farmers market,
and a variety of local (as opposed to generic) bars and restaurants. The
downtown also includes a reasonable array of retail shopping options
serving both local needs (pet store, stationery) and more upscale shopping (clothing and home furnishing stores). While the downtown area
of Saint-Jean-sur-Richelieu has not fully achieved its potential, the city
has an excellent farmers market, is working to more fully integrate its
canal-front location into the city, and has a growing new housing market
as the result of its proximity to Montreal. In short, both of these communities are far nicer than the creative class indicators would suggest. The
generally lower rank of another Quebec municipality—Granby—also
seems inconsistent with reality. The core of Granby is walkable and the
surrounding neighborhoods are attractive.

Outside of the problems with using these assessment measures for
Quebec cities, the case studies discovered other questionable results.

Several of the rankings on the cool local amenity index do not appear accurate: Saint-Hyacinthe, Granby, and Cambridge do not warrant their low rankings (the latter city is in Ontario), while Windsor, London, and Kitchener may not warrant higher ones.

Rankings on the downtown quality and health indexes are likely quite time bound in that they do not account for improvements or change in economic health since the 2001 census. For example, the Guelph downtown was rated very highly according to Canadian planning experts. However, the site visit noted a number of commercial vacancies and a general lack of reinvestment in the downtown area. Indeed, there appeared to be little awareness of the importance of the downtown to the city's health; local economic development efforts focus almost exclusively on the development of "employment lands" on the periphery. On the other hand, the poorly rated Nanaimo downtown is attractive and has clearly experienced significant local investment since the time of the planning survey. The local harbor front, shopping districts, and entertainment amenities are attractive and clearly increasing in quality and quantity over time. Similarly, cities high on the Economic Health Index—Oshawa and Windsor, for example—do not have particularly attractive cores, while the much lower ranked Nanaimo and Saint-Hyacinthe seem pleasant.

The creative class index appears to be the most accurate measure of local quality, with the most notable glitch being the placement of Saint-Hyacinthe in the bottom ten (most likely an artifact of the Quebec effect evident in all the indexes). Indeed, on this indicator Nanaimo is rated in the top ten, as are Kelowna, Peterborough, and Fredericton, places that did not necessarily rank highly on the other indicators. The university employment indicator also recognizes the quality of several places—Sherbrooke, Quebec, and Kingston, Ontario, for example—that do not necessarily rank highly on other indicators such as amenities and economic health. In short, then, it appears that measures of creative employment, same-sex households, and university employment reflect the quality of places more accurately than amenities, downtown quality, or general economic health.

SUMMARY

The forgoing analysis suggests some relatively simple answers to the questions posed earlier, as well as some conclusions about overall measurement and policy issues. First, to return to the questions driving the analysis:

- Are rankings on different indicators correlated?
  Sort of, but not completely
- Do the same municipalities come up high on all of the creative class indicators?
  Sort of, but not completely
- How do the different measurement systems relate to overall economic health and growth?
  Some correlate with health, none with growth
- Which measurement or combination of measurement systems appears most reliable in identifying "cool" communities?
  Creative employment, same-sex households, university employment

Several general lessons can be drawn from the forgoing analysis, all having implications for measurement of the creative class and for public policies to attract it. The most critical finding is that there appear to be serious problems with the creative class model that challenge the entire conceptual framework. While the purpose here is not to test or refute the creative class as a theory or economic development strategy but rather to test measurement schemes, the findings clearly call into question the overall approach. First, as defined by Florida, there does not appear to be a coherent mass called the "creative class," at least among midsize cities in Canada. Diversity (representing tolerance) is an inherently separate concept from any of the other creative class measures and includes racial (visible minorities) along with ethnic and immigrant variables. There is an identifiable confluence of same-sex households and artistic industries employment. Included within this index are some high-tech services but other high-tech employment is not part of the same underlying concept. Diversity is not related to high-tech employment and the latter is not related to the creative index. Finally, high-tech employment is not related to economic health and there is no correlation (let alone basis for suggesting causation) between improved economic health and any of the creative class indicators. In short, much of the creative class argument simply does not hold up under empirical analysis, probably the gravest finding of the research.

Other, more methodological findings also raise serious questions about using the creative class as a conceptual model, much less an economic development strategy, and are summarized below.

Nothing explains Quebec very well. Cities in Quebec are consistently among the lowest ranked on all of the measurement schemes. However, case studies suggest that, for many cities, the low rankings are unwarranted. Thus, it appears that the unique culture and language in Quebec, and perhaps the physical isolation of many of its communities, make the standardized indicators misleading. Measurement schemes specific to Quebec appear warranted.

Regions matter. The various measurement schemes perform far better within regions than between them. Except for three "super cities," index performance is more consistent when controlling for region. This suggests that, even beyond the province of Quebec, regionally specific indicators are required to fully assess creative class attributes.

Reliable measures include university location, same-sex households, and creative occupations. Based on correlation analysis and case studies, it seems that the creative class index and university employment most accurately distinguish between cool and not so cool cities. And to be clear, the creative class index includes creative employment and same-sex households, but not many of the other variables suggested by Florida, most pointedly high-technology employment. While the creative class index is related to diversity (proxy for tolerance), they are distinguishably different concepts.

High-tech occupations, amenities, and, to an extent, downtown quality don't matter. There is little to suggest that the path to prosperity, at least for midsize Canadian cities, lies in the attraction of high-tech jobs or workers. Nor does it seem that development policies based on creating unique local amenities would make much of a difference apart from general efforts to attract and retain an array of standard eating and entertainment options. Finally, while downtown quality is associated with creative class individuals, it is not related to either economic growth or health.

Creative class measures are not related to economic growth. Since none of the indicators here are significantly correlated with economic change over time (either growth or decline), it appears that focusing on the creative class, particularly amenities, high-tech jobs, or even educated university employees does not mean that a city is on the path to economic prosperity. Rather, it can be concluded that the indicators in this analysis do not say much about general quality of life for residents in a community nor ensure future prosperity.

Critical variables are missing. Because of the lack of significant correlations between the creative class indicators and economic change, it is likely that many important attributes are not measured by any of the creative class indicators. Items missing might include the quality of local primary and secondary schools, the quality of other local public services, crime rates, numbers of university-related individuals (faculty, staff, students) in relation to overall population, weather characteristics, proximity to other larger urban nodes, quality of transportation systems, presence of other types of households, particularly those with children (e.g., reproductive class as opposed to creative class), and other types of local development policies (Reese and Ye, 2011). Indeed, perhaps even finer measures of creative amenities are required, although the experience here suggests that such an effort would be extremely difficult and likely even more subjective.

Measures of creative class do not lead to helpful public policy recommendations. The analysis suggests that if cities are healthier, have higher creative employment, include more same-sex households, and a university (the more highly ranked the better), economic health (if not growth) will be higher. But if creative class individuals are not associated with particular local entertainment or arts amenities, if sexual preference legislation is similar across Canada, if universities and quality downtowns are largely historical artifacts representing significant sunk capital, then what does this say to cities about policies? The answer appears to be: very little.

To come full circle, then: Do we know the creative class when we see it? It appears that larger populations of individuals employed in creative occupations and same-sex households can be identified in metropolitan areas and that their presence is correlated with diversity and relatively high, but static, economic health. However, whether such individuals represent a true class or creative core, why they choose to locate where they do, what types of amenities (or other local features) attract and retain them, and how any of this relates to economic growth remains unclear. More importantly, even if we know the creative class when we see it, the implications for local economic development are still less clear. It might be possible to improve the operational definition of creative class, but it seems unlikely that the results will be more useful. The relationship with and implications of the creative class for economic development policy is explored in depth in the following sections.

CREATIVE CLASS AND ECONOMIC DEVELOPMENT STRATEGIES

> Cities must attract the new "creative class" with hip neighbor-hoods, an arts scene, and a gay-friendly atmosphere—or they will go the way of Detroit.
>
> Florida, qtd. in Dreher, 2002: 1

The appeal of economic development strategies based on creative class principles is obvious and understandable; the concepts have been described as "politically seductive" (Peck, 2005: 766). Given Florida's assessment of the imperative of creativity-led economic development, communities may feel that they have no choice but to adopt this message. One of the more attractive aspects of the rhetoric is that any and all communities have the potential to realize or at least enhance their creative resources and move up at least a few places in the rankings of cities provided by Florida. Moreover, encouraging creativity or engaging in "hipsterization strategies" (Peck, 2005) is, compared to other types of economic development strategies, relatively inexpensive and likely does not require that other strategies be abandoned.

The interest here is to determine whether Florida's conclusions and recommendations are actually useful to local policy makers, particularly those in small to midsize urban areas, which comprise a substantial part of where people live and work. In particular, there are several empirical preconditions that must be met for creative class to serve as a viable economic development strategy for a broad range of cities:

- the various elements of the "creative class" must be present within particular cities
- there must be some correlation between the presence of this creative class and measures of diversity, tolerance, and high-tech workers and industries
- there must be correlations between creative class, diversity, high technology, and some measure of actual economic health or growth

The first part of this chapter has examined the compatibility of different measures of creative class–related variables. We now consider whether these preconditions support the applicability of creative class strategies to cities, regardless of size or situation. In other words, are creative class economic development strategies a "one-size-fits-all" economic development solution? Are such strategies as appropriate for smaller and more isolated places such as Nanaimo, British Columbia, as they are for Austin, Texas (or Detroit, Michigan, for that matter)? Should all cities cultivate the creative class?

Trends and Fashions in Economic Development Policy

Provinces/states and cities have been competing to attract economic development for well over a hundred years. From the canal and road building era of the nineteenth century, through the industrial policy initiatives of the southern states that began in the 1930s, to the tax abatement and infrastructure grants of the last quarter of the twentieth century, localities have embraced a number of economic development doctrines, ranging from the well considered to the faddish. More contemporary trends in economic development policies and techniques have been well documented (see Reese and Rosenfeld, 2004; Peters and Fisher, 2005; Osgood et al., 2012; Reese and Ye, 2011, for examples). Academic observers and policy evaluators have focused on a relatively parsimonious set of recommended goals for economic development policies at the local level: diversifying the economic base and focusing on areas of competitive advantage (Voytek and Ledebur, 1991; Hill and Brennan, 2000); shifting local employment from manufacturing and heavy industry to high technology, knowledge-based, and creative industries (Florida, 2005b; Duderstadt, 2005); developing new, local capacity for entrepreneurship and human capital (Glazer and Grimes, 2005; Pink-Harper, 2015); and improving quality of life, culture, and urban amenities (Clark, 2011; Florida, 2005b).

Yet the most common state and, particularly, local economic development policies seem poorly suited to realizing these goals. Despite a call more than twenty-five years ago by Eisinger (1988) for a shift to demand-side policies, research since then clearly shows cities continuing to emphasize traditional industrial attraction incentives such as basic infrastructure and land development, promotion and marketing, and particularistic financial incentives (Clarke and Gaile, 1992; Blakeley, 1994; Reese and Sands, 2012; Peters and Fisher, 2005; Reese, 2006; Reese and Ye, 2015). Some local officials are embracing the most recent recommendations—focusing on amenities, tolerance, creativity, and quality of life—in large numbers. The spate of recent research on the topic, as well as the popularity of Florida as a speaker both nationally and internationally, however, certainly suggest that perhaps there is something new under the local economic development sun after all.

Research empirically testing "creative class" arguments is relatively new but appears to be increasing. Generally questions have been raised on a number of points:

- lack of clarity in conditions that cause creative individuals to congregate and stay in a location over a stable period of time (Scott, 2006)
- education and skill development appear more important than culture or amenities in economic growth (Glaeser et al., 2001; Pink-Harper, 2015)
- innovation appears just as likely in older manufacturing centers as newly creative cities (Chappele et al., 2004). And there are no sectors that corner the market on creativity—all sectors include, and indeed require, creative individuals (Luciani, 2006)

- the internal components of the diversity or melting pot indexes need unpacking; specifically, relationships between the presence of African Americans and economic growth or decline have not been fully explored (Madden, 2001; Thomas and Darnton, 2006), nor has the impact of immigrants been examined by skill level (Borjas, 1995), or the extent that ethnic and racial enclaves are voluntary been assessed (Qadeer, 2005)

- measures of gays are highly problematic due to reliance on census data that may well underrepresent single gays and fail to differentiate among different types of gay households (Thomas and Darnton, 2005)

- concerns that "cool" or "creative" is a transient state, available to only a few places at a time due to the potential for the creation of "a narrow range of cloned spaces world-wide" (Ley, 2003; Bell and Binnie, 2004: 1814; Rich, 2013)

- the assumption that the mere presence of diverse populations indicates that local residents really are more tolerant is tenuous at best (Rushbrook, 2002; Thomas and Darton, 2006; Reese and Zalewski, 2015); further, it is possible that extreme heterogeneity may not be conducive to innovation (Elfring and Hulsink, 2003; Scott, 2006)

- findings, particularly related to measures of high technology and creativity, are highly sensitive to how those variables are operationalized (for example, what is categorized as high tech and whether service and manufacturing were considered separately), what time periods are used, and which particular set of cities or regions are examined (Chappele et al., 2004).

At root, the creative class as an economic development tool presupposes a particular virtuous chain of forces leading to economic growth, as illustrated in Figure 5.7. While the chain itself has not been empirically tested in its current form, research has explored various aspects of it with mixed results (Thomas and Darnton, 2006). Overall, the model is rooted in the expectation of a linear relationship between investments in research and development and the creation of knowledge and innovation,

Figure 5.7 Hypothesized relationships

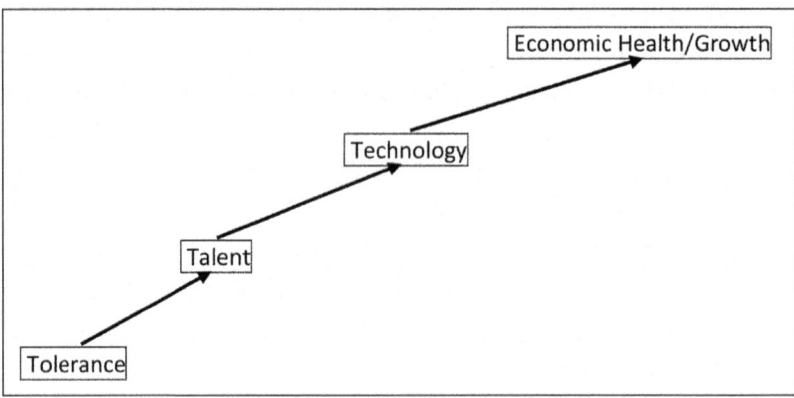

leading to competitive advantages, particularly in high technology, cul-
minating in economic growth (Malecki, 1997; Kresl and Singh, 1999).
And although some researchers have pointed to the need for feedback
loops and dead ends, these have not been incorporated into creative class
rhetoric (Myers and Rosenbloom, 1996; Lever, 2002). In essence, creative class arguments suggest that increased tolerance in a city should lead
to attraction of educated and creative workers; the resulting atmosphere
should then attract high technology companies and employees. As a result of these high-tech investments and the nature of the local population, increased economic growth is expected to occur.

ANALYSIS

The aspect of the creative class argument that does not appear to be supported in these cities, however, is the relationship between creative class,
high-tech workers, and economic health. Higher numbers of workers in
technology jobs, regardless of type, are not significantly correlated with
economic health in 2001. This says nothing about the trajectory of economic growth, however.

Table 5.6 shows correlations between various economic and demographic measures in 1996 with the 2001 creative class index. Not surprisingly, economic prosperity is highly path-dependent; cities that were
healthier in 1996 remain significantly healthier in 2001 regardless of the

Table 5.6 Creative Class and Change in Economic Health

	Gay/creative	Diversity	Engine/R&D	Comp/aero	Medical	Health01	Downtown	Health06
Health Change	-.18	.05	.03	.07	.14	.16	-.10	1.00
Diversity Change	-.37*	.05	-.22	-.03	.25	.14	-.11	.47**
Health 96	.53**	.63**	-.14	.02	.23	.95**	.31	-.16
Diversity 96	.48**	.99**	-.12	.04	,18	.65**	.19	.00
Black 96	.48**	.78**	-.11	.10	.17	.50**	.27	.01
Hispanic 96	.29	.87**	-.05	.05	.15	.51**	.05	.09
Arabic 96	.29	.88**	-.12	.00	.15	.48**	.19	.07
Asian 96	.55**	.86**	-.07	-.04	.14	.63**	.23	-.14
Foreign born 96	.50**	.94**	-.18	.07	.20	.63**	.12	-.02
Med pers income 96	.52**	.58**	-.14	.10	.28	.71**	.22	-.26
Med fam income 96	.37*	.51**	-.23	.08	.09	.84**	.15	-.18
Average earnings 96	.17	.50**	-.15	.16	.01	.70**	.01	-.14
Central city pop 96	.32*	.78**	-.22	.16	.11	.61**	.18	-.16
Fem labor force 96	.37*	.27	-.02	-.10	.11	.78**	.31	-.03
Employed 96	.37*	.40**	-.03	-.09	.43**	.65**	.27	.04
No public assist 96	.39*	.44**	-.01	-.06	.08	.88**	.34*	-.07

*Significantly correlated at .05
**Significantly correlated at .01

nature of the creative class population. Similarly, cities that were more diverse in 1996 remain significantly more diverse in 2001.

Examining change in the health index over the five years shows some interesting relationships, however. First, and most notably, improved economic health is not significantly related to any creative class or economic variables with the exception of change in the diversity index. This appears to support the assertion that high technology in particular does not necessarily mean the same thing as high growth (Chappele et al., 2004). Health change is also not significantly related to health status in either 1996 or 2001 (correlations are -.16 and .16, respectively). Cities with improving economic health were those that were becoming more diverse, however.

Individual economic and diversity indicators from 1996 are also shown to explore whether particular components of the indexes appear more determinative of 2001 creative class traits than others. For higher location quotients of same-sex and creative occupations, higher proportions of African Americans, Asians, and foreign-born residents generally appear most critical. More positive 1996 economic indicators are significantly correlated with the 2001 same-sex/creative factor. The 1996 median personal income is the most strongly related. None of the economic or demographic variables from the prior period are significantly related to 2001 high-tech employment, with the single exception that higher employment rates generally in 1996 are correlated with higher medical technology employment in 2001. The only variable associated with the existence of a healthier downtown is lower proportions of residents on public assistance in 1996.

Creative class arguments imply a salutary relationship between presence of the creative class and high-tech workers and economic growth. Indeed, the path to prosperity inherent in Florida's arguments is that creative and high-tech workers are drawn to areas rich in amenities. These individuals then attract other businesses (as well as bringing and creating their own) and economic growth ensues. The initial drivers in this chain of events are the presence of the types of cultural and entertainment amenities that attract the creative class along with an acceptance of diversity. Does this chain of events appear accurate for Canadian cities? The correlations in Table 5.7 suggest that the answer is, in large part, no.

Table 5.7 Economic Health Correlations

	Economic Health 1996	Economic Health 2001	Change in Health
Cool Amenities	.47**	.39*	-.26
Generic Amenities	.60**	.58**	-.09
Downtowns	.31	.28	-.10
Creative Class	.53**	.48**	-.18
Diversity	.45**	.65**	.05
Engineering	-.14	-.14	.03
Computer/aerospace	.02	.04	.07
Medical	.23	.27	.14
University employment	.33*	.33*	.00

*significant at .05
**significant at .01

There is a positive relationship between greater economic health in 1996 and 2001 and many of the creative class indicators: unique local and generic amenities, the creative class, and diversity indexes. Various forms of high-tech employment are not significantly related to economic health. These are static states, however. The critical issue is whether creative class factors are positively related to economic *growth*. The last column in the table shows no significant correlations between any of the creative class or amenity indicators and economic growth. What is causing differences in economic growth among midsize Canadian cities is unclear, but it is certainly not local cultural and entertainment amenities or the presence of creative or high-tech individuals.

SUMMARY AND CONCLUSIONS

By way of summary, it is useful to revisit the creative class propositions driving the analysis. First, are the creative class elements empirically identifiable by their presence in midsize Canadian cities? The answer to this question is a qualified yes, but not in the manner argued by Florida and others. There does seem to be an identifiable confluence of same-sex households (which does not necessarily measure the overall presence of "gays") and artistic occupations.

However, included in these occupations are some high-tech services, specifically computer and scientific consulting. The other high-tech occupations are not part of the same underlying concept, and several appear conceptually distinct. Diversity is an inherently separate concept from any of the other creative class measures and includes racial (black) as well as ethnic or immigrant variables.

Second, is there a correlation between creative class, diversity, and tolerance? The answer to this question is largely no. First, actual tolerance has only been measured in a few studies to date (see Reese and Zalewski, 2015 for an exception). Diversity appears positively related to the same-sex and creative index but is not related to high-tech occupations. Nor are high-tech occupations correlated with higher scores on the gay/creative index. This last finding actually makes considerable sense based on Bourdieu's original social space theories that argued that artistic producers were likely to have high cultural but low economic capital. Conversely, industrial employers had the opposite characteristics. Thus, economic capital was unlikely to accrue in the same social space as cultural capital (Bourdieu, 1984; Ley, 2003).

Finally, are creative class, diversity, and high-tech employment related to economic growth? The answer again appears to be mostly no. The presence of same-sex households and residents in creative occupations is positively correlated with more highly ranked downtowns and overall economic health in both 1996 and 2001. However, high-tech employment is unrelated to overall economic health. And there is no relationship between improved economic health and any of the creative class indicators. Thus, while higher numbers of same-sex households and creative and diverse residents are correlated with health at static points in time, none of the attributes are related to actual economic improvement. While those cities that were healthier in 1996 stayed healthy, at least relatively speaking, in 2001, increases or decreases in health are unrelated to static health just as they are unrelated to creative class, diversity, and high-tech industries.

What, then, does this suggest for local officials trying to stimulate economic growth, particularly for those who have begun to jump on the

Figure 5.8 Estimated relationships

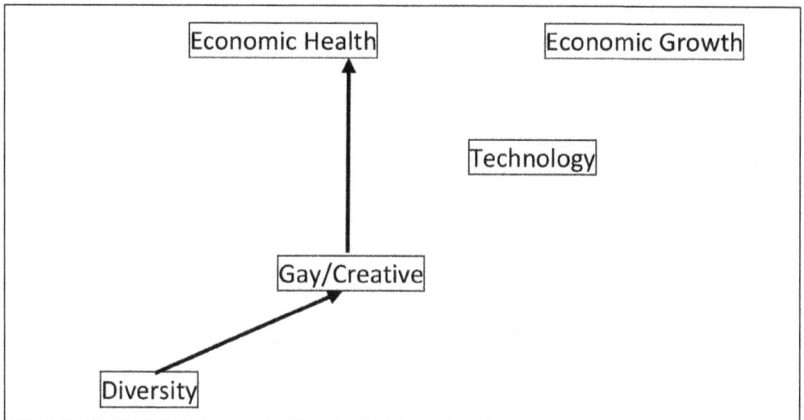

creative class bandwagon? Are economic development strategies based on cultivating the creative class the best means of improving urban areas? The analysis of midsize Canadian urban areas presented here suggests that they are not. Indeed, there appears to be little connection between the various creativity measures and generally accepted metrics of economic well-being. Figure 5.8 summarizes the relationships (or lack of) that were found in our analysis. It is not just the causal chain that is imperceptible; it was not possible to find even a respectable level of correlation. Thus, while Florida's arguments have presumed that attracting creative class individuals will lead to economic prosperity and growth, it is just as likely that the creative class is drawn to prosperous urban areas (indeed, even Florida [2002a] admits that his findings should not imply "direct causal and mechanistic relationships"). Still, before the causal direction can be established, the essential correlations must consistently be present.

Clearly, further careful research is needed. The analysis in this chapter needs to be expanded in several ways to provide more viable answers. First, a number of other city traits could well be related to both creative class and economic growth. Just because the percentage of college graduates and university employees do not correlate with economic health and creative class in midsize Canadian urban areas does not mean that education is unimportant. Perhaps resources devoted to, or student success in, local schools are critical. Perhaps the nature or size of a local university is more important than gross numbers of employees. Previous research has indicated that the percentage of college graduates was far more important than other creative class indicators in linking to high-technology development (Clark, 2011). Some observers have turned creative class on its head to suggest that what governments need to do is enhance education to make citizens "better consumers of art" rather than providing supply-side incentives (Luciani, 2006: 3). Research should also be expanded to explore the impact of good city services, generally differentiating between amenities such as museums, golf courses, and canoe liveries and the basic bread and butter services—schools, public safety, and transportation—that impact quality of life most directly. Indeed, research has suggested that schools and public safety are particularly important to growth (Cullen and Levitt, 1999; Glaeser et al., 2001; Reese and Ye, 2011).

The overall economic pattern over the five-year period between 1996 and 2001 was one of stability; very few cities made significant gains or losses in economic health. However, six cities deviated from this pattern. Three—Red Deer, Fredericton, and Sudbury—made relatively large gains in health, while three others—Moncton, Thunder Bay, and Nanaimo—experienced sharp economic declines. In some cases, cities in the two groups (Moncton and Fredericton, for example) are in the same geographic area and share a regional economy. So what is going on in these cities that made some successful and some apparent economic failures? More case study research is needed to explore these exceptional cases. Most importantly, do the two groups (gainers and losers) have significantly different strategic approaches toward economic development? Are they offering different policies or incentives? Are some cities focusing on creative class attraction and are they the more successful cases? These are critical questions for local policy makers. For significant losers such as Nanaimo, the relationships between the creative class and the "underclass" are clearly pertinent (Morgan and Ren, 2012). Little creative class research focuses on what cities should be doing in addition to attracting highly educated and creative individuals. What about the less fortunate? "The formulation of specific policies to ameliorate those parts of urban space that continue to lie outside the more privileged foci of production, work, and social life must . . . be a high priority in any effort to build thorough-going creative cities" (Scott, 2006: 12).

All communities do not have the same ambitions, do not want to be the same when they grow up, do not define economic development success in the same way. It is only when all communities are judged by a single measure of success (number of coffee shops or clubs, graduate degrees or high-tech startup businesses) that they can be classified as successful or hopeless, full of promise or forlorn. But if communities are judged by their own objectives, a much more complex assessment is necessary. Is a community attracting a call center that will employ several hundred residents inevitably less successful than a community that funds a program of street art? Is a relatively pedestrian bedroom suburb with commercial strips drawn from generica but with strong schools, good infrastructure, and stable housing stock inherently less successful than a trendier, more urbanized area with martini bars and independent movie houses? As is often the case, the answer to these questions is, most likely, "That depends." Neither empirical research nor creative class devotees have provided more definitive answers. And without such answers and a consideration of local characteristics and growth within the context of local goals, it is irresponsible to promote any one "silver bullet" to local officials.

While this analysis raises some interesting points, it hardly provides sufficient basis for generalizing the findings to render a definitive judgment on creative class theories. The research is limited to a small number of cities, is mostly cross-sectional, and embodies a number of subjective judgments, including the selection of specific variables. While such questions can be raised with respect to any research design, they seem to be particularly important here, or in any study that seeks to identify public policy levers that have practical application. Nevertheless, the findings seem to make some contribution to the debate over these policies.

Would the selection of a different set of cities have produced different results? Possibly. Larger cities within the sample seem to have different characteristics; the same is true for more isolated urban areas. But even if findings cannot be broadly generalized, they are nevertheless representative of a set of urban areas with an aggregate population of almost five million.

Would the findings be the same for comparably sized US urban areas? Here, the possibility of different results is even more likely. The racial polarization in many US urban areas would likely have a substantial effect on the diversity measures. The results, however, might be a decrease in the importance of diversity or, at the very least, indicate a need for considering race and ethnicity separately.

Would a different or longer time period yield different results? Again, possibly. The latter half of the 1990s was generally a prosperous time in Canada, although there were notable regional differences. The first half of the next decade followed similar trends. Testing these relationships in periods of economic decline could yield different results. Utilizing a longer time period would allow further tests of the predictive value of the various measurement schemes.

Would different definitions of individual variables improve the results? For example, would a more comprehensive definition of the gay population yield different results? Probably, but it is not clear that the differences would be substantial or important. Similarly, including more or different variables to define creative class occupations or economic health would likely yield different, but not necessarily more useful, results.

Do creative class strategies have any value to economic development programs aimed at increasing community wide economic health? Here the answer is more difficult. The relationship between individual creative class variables was found to be weak, at best. That is not to say, however, that they might not be useful. Supporting the visual and performing arts (thus increasing opportunities in relevant occupations) can contribute to the quality of life. Enactment of ordinances extending employment benefits to same-sex common law couples may be a better indication of tolerant attitudes than statistical measures of diversity. Neither of these measures (or, for that matter, any of the other measures tested) seem to be instrumental variables related to economic growth. They may make a community a better place to live (a worthwhile objective in and of itself), but they are not a guarantee of economic expansion.

APPENDIX: CRITERIA FOR CLASSIFYING
LOCAL ESTABLISHMENTS

Coffee shops: Coffee shops include only those places where the entire emphasis is on either coffee or bagels. Excluded were most places that had menus and servers. Chain coffeehouses most often included Coffee Time, Second Cup, Starbucks, Tim Hortons, Williams Coffee Pub Serious Coffee, Coffee Time Donuts, and Great Canadian Bagel.

Local independent restaurants: The website foodinc.ca was used as the base for this category. It lists restaurants for all major Canadian cities, making comparisons across different cities more standardized and reliable. Still, this system is by no means perfect because the public can add restaurants to the site as they choose. As a result, a passionate resident of a small town might have listed every single restaurant located there, while few people may have listed restaurants for a midsize urban areas (so there would be an under-representation of the number of restaurants in the medium-sized town). Still, this website provided at least some form of standardization and was more reliable when one makes comparisons as opposed to counting restaurants from different websites for each city individually. However, the total number listed for a city on foodinc.ca was not used for the local/independent restaurant count. This is because the list includes chain restaurants, vegetarian/health restaurants, and some coffee shops and bars/clubs—all of which were already categorized. To maintain category exclusivity, these "restaurants" were subtracted from the total.

Chain bookstores most typically included Chapters Bookstore, Coles Bookstore, and Gospel Lighthouse Bookstore.

Chain movie houses most typically included Galaxy Cinemas and Landmark Avalon Cinemas.

6

Immigrants and Prosperity in Midsize Canadian Cities

Canada prides itself at home and abroad as a country made up of a cultural mosaic rather than a cultural melting pot. The mosaic is based on our belief that Canada as a whole becomes stronger by having immigrants bring with them their cultural diversity for all Canadians to learn from. The cultural melting pot as adopted in the United States tells immigrants that no matter who they have been in the past, upon landing on American shores, they are Americans and are expected to adopt and follow the American way.

Levine and Serbeh-Dunn, 1999

In cities across North America, immigrants have long played an important role in community prosperity and growth. Along with domestic migrants, the foreign-born population has accounted for most of the population growth in both large and small metropolitan areas. Communities with diverse populations are thought to have an advantage over more homogeneous ones, regardless of the characteristics of the immigrant populations, such as education or creativity.

Although the potential contributions of foreign-born residents are widely acknowledged, the specific causal connections often remain vague. Some of the structural effects clouding the connections between immigration and growth include the presence of enclave economies where businesses thrive by catering to particular ethnic groups or narrow economic niches. Such situations may initially help immigrant businesses grow but then result in marginalization and limited long-range growth (Malecki, 1997; Hackler and Mayer, 2008; Wang, 2015). Indeed, immigrants residing in "own-group" concentrations tend to reap an earnings benefit initially, but continued residence in such places seems to be disadvantageous over time (Musterd et al., 2008). Research specifically focused on Canada, however, suggests that most areas of immigration are socially and economic heterogeneous (Hiebert et al., 2007).

The literature is not uniformly positive about the contributions of diversity to economic health, however; any connections between them may well be dependent on particular environmental factors. For example, negative outcomes could result from diversity, including divisions and conflicts creating lower levels of trust, less social capital, reductions in wages among the native born, and fewer public goods produced because groups either cannot agree or the majority does not want to support benefits for the minority (Knack, 2002; Alesina and La Ferrera, 2005; Lee, 2011; Longhi et al., 2010). Research focusing on Canadian gateway cities suggests that, at least for Toronto and Vancouver, increases in the immigrant population is pushing native-born residents with less education out of the central city (Hou and Bourne, 2006).

The literature is also not without contention regarding the precise mechanisms and causality of connections between foreign born and economic health. For example, it remains unclear whether diverse places allow immigrants to prosper or if the connections between foreign-born and growth are dependent on, and the result of, overall population growth in areas with more immigrants (Hackler and Mayer, 2008). Lines of causality are an issue because research indicates that immigrants are drawn to areas that are already growing and prospering. Canadian narratives, however, tend to focus more on immigration leading to growth (Abu-Laban and Garber, 2005).

Scholars have also found that immigration alone is not sufficient to create economic growth. Supportive public policies are required to foster small business growth, including start-up funding, "economic gardening," programs facilitating market access, human capital development, minority business procurement requirements, and technical assistance (Bates, 2006; Hackler and Mayer, 2008; Moon et al., 2014).

Many immigrants face barriers that make their integration in new locations problematic—poor housing, lower quality schools, and underemployment, for example.

Moreover, the assumption that there is a direct connection between immigrants and economic prosperity has not been substantiated. Indeed, the most pressing concerns of migrants, based on a survey of migrant civic groups, are language barriers, substandard employment, health and social services, immigration and citizenship issues, and affordable housing (Theodore and Martin, 2007: 273; Lichter, 2012). Investment in human capital, social policies, and the presence of community organizations and nonprofits providing immigrant services have been found to be critical to their success both economically and politically (Musterd and Salet, 2003; Lin, 1998).

Finally, immigrants will not necessarily benefit from local or regional growth (Theodore and Martin, 2007; Smith, 2006). The positive effects of diversity may not produce equal benefits for all groups across a city (Fainstein, 2005; Hackler and Mayer, 2008). And contextual factors in the metropolitan labor market can impact the success of immigrant business owners, particularly Hispanics and women (Wang, 2015). Different ethnic groups exhibit varying rates of entrepreneurship that will affect community outcomes (Baycan-Levent and Nijkamp, 2009). General ethnic diversity may not be as important to economic prosperity as the proportion of foreign born specifically, and diversity within the foreign-born population appears particularly strongly related to growth (Rupasingha et al., 2002; Lee, 2011).

PATTERNS OF MIGRATION

In an oft-cited report on immigration in the United States, Singer (2004) identified different types of cities: former gateways that were immigrant centers in the past but where immigration has slowed (Cleveland, Boston, Detroit); continuous gateways that have had steady and significant immigration over time (New York, Chicago); post–World War II gateways that received increased immigration after the war (Los Angeles, Miami);

emerging gateways that have had the fastest immigrant growth over the past twenty years (Washington, DC, Dallas, Atlanta); and pre-emerging gateways that have seen increased immigration in the 1990s (Salt Lake City, Raleigh-Durham). These latter two categories have experienced increases in both immigrants and native-born residents and have higher rates of job growth; that is, increases in the foreign born are not accompanied by stabilization of native populations as has often been the case in immigrant gateways in the past.

While it is important to note that Canadian immigrant gateways such as Toronto, Vancouver, and Ottawa still receive large numbers of new immigrants, changing trends are clearly evident, as immigrants expand their cities of location around the country and down into lower tiers of cities (Martin and Holloway, 2005). Settlement of new immigrants beyond traditional gateways is a trend seen in other western countries, the United Kingdom, for example (Robinson, 2010). It has been suggested that location patterns away from the largest metropolitan areas are increasingly driven by housing, cost of living, job access, schools, and the location of friends and relatives (Hobson, 2002; Sheridan and Cohn, 2001). Immigrants are locating and relocating in areas that have good global connections but lower costs of living and less poverty than many of the traditional gateway cities (Baird et al., 2008). Thus, economic considerations may be becoming more important in the location decisions of immigrants than social choices (Scott et al., 2005). More highly educated immigrants are particularly likely to select places other than gateways (Hempstead, 2005). Rural areas are also seeing increasing immigration (Sanez et al., 2003).

"Between 1991 and 2000, Canada admitted 2.2 million immigrants, the highest intake of newcomers in any decade in the past one hundred years, and one of the highest rates in the Western world" (Hou and Bourne, 2006: 1506). Scholars have noted that Canadian immigration and multiculturalism have moved through several stages over time: demographic multiculturalism (a recognition that the ethnic composition of the country is diversifying); symbolic multiculturalism (support for visible demonstrations of cultural diversity such as ethnic festivals and events); and structural multiculturalism (integration of immigrants socially and politically through equality protections) (Kobayashi, 1993; Ley, 2007).

Historically in Canada, immigrants and visible minorities were more likely than others to locate in central cities; 63 percent of the white-collar immigrant workforce remains in the three largest Census Metropolitan Areas (CMAs), while only 30 percent of other Canadians reside there. The tendency for immigrants to congregate in the largest cities increased between 1996 and 2001, suggesting that immigrants are actually becoming more centralized over time in Canada, as opposed to recent US data indicating dispersion beyond gateway cities (Moos and Skaburskis, 2010). Indeed, all of the recent population growth in the Montreal CMA is due to immigration, and over 75 percent of growth in Toronto and 50 percent in Vancouver is due to immigration (McIssac, 2003; Bourne, 2007).

Concerns about low population increase and lack of skilled labor in some areas of Canada led to a federal plan for dispersing immigrants to spread economic growth (Abu-Laban and Garber, 2005). Citizenship and Immigration Minister Denis Coderre consciously encouraged settlement in different regions; Manitoba and Winnipeg appeared particularly receptive. Those efforts have had little effect on regionalization of immigrants, however; the current provincial efforts under the Provincial Nominee Program have had more impact.[1] Scholars have suggested that such policies are evidence of different national approaches to immigration in the United States and Canada; in the former location decisions are left to individuals and cities have to address resulting policy issues. In Canada, immigration is more of a national policy issue (Abu-Laban and Garber, 2005). As multiculturalism was incorporated into the Canadian constitution in the Charter of Rights and Freedoms in 1982, the mosaic concept (as opposed to a melting pot) became a matter of national policy

---

1. Immigrants who have the skills, education, and work experience to make an immediate economic contribution can be nominated for immigration by a specific province or territory. Nominated individuals (and their families) are selected for permanent residence status based on a pre-approved job offer in the province.

(Lipset, 1990). The federal Department of Canadian Heritage is charged with protecting and promoting "cultural pluralism" or "multiculturalism" in Canada, and its mission statement emphasizes equality along with maintaining identity and accepting diversity (Ley, 2007).

Despite arguments positing beneficial connections between the presence of immigrants and economic vitality, debate about the most desirable level of immigration is apparent in Canada (Ley, 2008). Media reports point to recent efforts to limit immigration—increasing the difficulty of the citizenship test and giving priority to more educated and skilled individuals—perhaps in reaction to open-door policies of the past when people were needed to fill space and build the economy (Immigration in Canada, 2010; Canadian Broadcasting Corporation, 2010, 2011). Concerns relative to immigration have been raised about security, housing shortages and costs, employment competition, challenges to building a Canadian national identity, and fear among some immigrant communities of loss of cultural heritage (Ley, 2007). But many still believe that immigration drives innovation, and Canadian public opinion surveys suggest that current levels of immigration are "about right" (*Immigration to Canada*, 2010), with three out of four survey respondents endorsing immigration (Hiebert, 2006; Ley, 2007). As of 2006, 20 percent of the Canadian population was foreign-born, with the top ten sources of immigrants being China, India, the Philippines, Pakistan, the United States, South Korea, Romania, Iran, the United Kingdom, and Colombia (Statistics Canada, 2006).

Although Canadian gateway cities continue to be important, the 2001 census indicated that the foreign born were increasingly locating in suburban municipalities outside Toronto, as well as in other smaller cities in Ontario—Hamilton in particular (Carey, 2003; Abu-Laban and Garber, 2005), and in communities outside Montreal (Hou and Bourne, 2006). A 2007 study by Hiebert and colleagues indicates that immigrants are increasingly locating in suburbs, creating more "socially variegated" communities (2007: 7). More recently, newcomers have been moving to other provinces besides Ontario, with a corresponding decrease in federal funding for immigrant settlement programs there;

Figure 6.1 Victoria, BC, Chinatown

even Toronto is settling fewer immigrants (Canadian Broadcasting Corporation, 2010).

Lack of settlement services and educational resources have been suggested as reasons why immigrants are not as likely to locate outside of central cities (Carey, 2003). Yet Ley (2007) argues that such services are a "work in progress" and that such supports are generally effective. Thus, greater dispersion of federal funding may help attract foreign-born residents to second tier and smaller cities. The combination of support programs, emphasis on multiculturalism, and generally supportive citizen attitudes toward immigration present a different picture than the melting pot in the United States and may contribute to the conclusion that "issues of social inclusion in Canada" are not "inherently linked to residential behavior" (Hiebert et al., 2007: 6).

While the literature just discussed raises some questions about the nature and effects of the presence of foreign-born residents, the preponderance of research suggests positive associations between immigrants and local economic prosperity. Further, much research suggests that diversity of *any* kind can foster economic growth. Trends suggesting the dispersion of immigrants beyond traditional gateway cities argue for more exploration of the connections between diversity, immigration, and local economic health in smaller cities.

METHODOLOGY

Data Sources

Data from the Canadian census (1996, 2001, and 2006) describing demographic characteristics of these midsize metropolitan areas, supplemented by data from Industry Canada on employment and income, provide the basis of the analysis in the chapter. In particular, measures of talent (educational attainment, occupational mix) and diversity (immigration, racial/ ethnic mix, lifestyle) are considered. Trends in these dimensions are compared to standard measures of economic prosperity such as employment and income (Moss, 1997). The issue of cause is important at this point. The analysis explores trends in immigration over time. For this purpose, immigration data from the three different census years are examined. The other purpose of the analysis it to examine the relative relationships between immigration, other types of diversity, and other community traits (described below) and economic health. For this part of the analysis prior year, census data (2001) are compared to later (2006) economic data. This approach has been used in previous work aimed at assessing initial levels of variables such as diversity with later economic conditions (Shearmur and Polese, 2005). Without definitively establishing causal ordering, it does consider relationships between past diversity levels and future economic health. Thus, the time ordering necessary to establish cause is incorporated into the analysis. Non-spuriousness cannot be ruled out, even with the inclusion of control variables; thus the findings suggest that particular past traits are related to economic health in the future but not with certainty that they cause it.

In order to provide a set of measures that are reasonably comparable, a location quotient was calculated for most of the variables. The location quotients compare the local value (expressed as a percent) with the corresponding provincial value. If the local value is identical to the provincial value, the location quotient is unity. Location quotient values greater

Table 6.1 Components of Diversity

Population diversity: Simpson's Diversity Index based on Canadian-born and immigrants from Western Europe, Eastern Europe, United States, Africa, Middle East, South America, East Asia, Southeast Asia, South Asia, Oceania
Immigrant diversity: Simpson's Diversity Index based on immigrants from Western Europe, Eastern Europe, United States, Africa, Middle East, South America, East Asia, Southeast Asia, South Asia, Oceania
Percent immigrated from Western Europe, Eastern Europe, United States, Africa, Middle East, South America, East Asia, Southeast Asia, South Asia, Oceania
Percent non-Christian
Percent visible minority
Percent composition of the visible minority population
Percent same-sex couples
Percent speaking English, French, other languages

than 1.0 indicate the locality has an above average concentration of the particular variable, while values less than 1.0 occur when the locality is below average. The calculated location quotients generally range between 0.5 and 2.0.

Operationalization of Variables

Diversity: The operationalization of diversity is at best a subjective enterprise. Based on previous research and data available in the census, Table 6.1 lists the variables used to measure diversity. Two of the indicators in this table—general diversity and immigrant diversity—are based on the Simpson's Diversity Index, calculated using each of the three waves of census data.[2] The Simpson Diversity Index ranges between 0 and 1, with higher values indicating greater diversity; specifically, the index represents the probability

---

2. www.tiem.utk.edu/~gross/bioed/bealsmodules/simpsonDI.html The formula for Simpson's Index of Diversity is:

$$D = \frac{\sum N(n-1)}{N(N-1)}$$

that two individuals randomly selected from a sample will belong to different groups. In the case of country of origin (*immigrant diversity*), the number of possible categories or groups is ten, corresponding to the regions indicated in the table. For *population diversity*, the maximum number of possible groups is eleven: each immigrant group plus non-immigrants.

Economic Prosperity: This is measured by the same index of census variables used in previous chapters and that has been used in a number of other studies to represent the economic health or well-being of a city's population (Rubin and Rubin, 1987; Sharp, 1991; Fleischman et al, 1992; Wolman, 1996; Moss, 1997; Reese and Rosenfeld, 2002; Sands and Reese, 2008).

Employment Base: In addition to the relationship between immigration, diversity, and economic health, other elements of creative class arguments are also considered here. These include the nature of the employment base (talent) and the physical amenities purported to be essential to attract the creative class. Indicators used to measure the nature of the employment base allow an assessment of the relative relationship between employment or skill diversity and economic health. The measures used here represent industry rather than occupation. This was done to facilitate comparisons with other creative class research using Canadian data (Gertler et al., 2002). Research on Canadian cities suggests that there is no systematic bias in using industry rather than occupation data (Sands, 2005).

The creative class index is the same one used in the previous chapter and combines education with industry employment measures based on empirical analysis indicating they are part of the same underlying concept. The index again corresponds to previous work on Canadian cities and creative class employment (Gertler et al., 2002; Sands and Reese, 2008). The individual components of the other operational measures are identified in Table 6.2.

Amenities: Indicators of physical amenities represent the general quality of the local built environment and the amenities offered. These are included because of the emphasis in much of the creative class work on "place quality" in drawing both skilled and diverse residents. The downtown quality indicator is the same as the one introduced in Chapter 4.

Table 6.2 Components of Operational Measures

Economic Health	Employment Base	Physical Amenities
Population	Trade	Downtown Quality
Population Change	FIRE	Unique Local Amenities
Median personal income	Business services	Chain/Generic Amenities
Median family income	Professional services	
Average home values	Manufacturing	
Unemployment	Natural resources	
Female labor force participation	University employment	
Percent on public assistance	Creative class index	

This, too, is related to the argument that creative class individuals will be drawn to urban areas that contain particular amenities attractive to them because they serve their creative impulses and make the community more distinctive. The unique and local and chain amenity indexes described in the previous chapter are again used here.

ANALYSIS

The data analysis is organized around three primary research questions, as noted below.

- Is there a measurable relationship between diversity (as indicated by foreign-born residents) and community prosperity? How does the relationship compare to that of other correlates of economic health?

Table 6.3 provides correlations between the 2006 Economic Health Index and all of the measures of diversity over time, along with measures of employment, demographic, and physical quality variables. Because previous research has indicated significant differences between cities in

Table 6.3 Correlations of Diversity Measures with 2006 Economic Health

Variable	Correlation		Variable	Correlation	
	All Midsize	Quebec Excluded		All Midsize	Quebec Excluded
Health 01	.92**	.88**	East Asia 06	.59**	.44*
Health 96	.90**	.83**	Southeast Asia 06	.65**	.58**
Pop diversity 96	.64**	.42*	South Asia 06	.15	.01
Pop diversity 01	.61**	.39*	Oceania 06	.32*	.09
Pop diversity 06	.61**	.40*	Central America 01	.67**	.64**
Immigrant diversity 96	-.002	.38*	Western Europe 01	.51**	.22
Immigrant diversity 01	.12	.42**	Eastern Europe 01	.46**	.26
Immigrant diversity 06	.21	.49**	US 01	.32*	-.09
Central America 06	.47**	.17	Africa 01	.62**	.55**
Western Europe 06	.46**	.27	Middle East 01	.37*	.33
Eastern Europe 06	.46**	.27	East Asia 01	.61**	.49**
US 06	.38**	-.02	Southeast Asia 01	.61**	.52**
Africa 06	.49**	.59**	South Asia 01	.15	.01
Middle East 06	.41**	.37**	Oceania 01	.31*	.07
Central America 96	.66**	.63**	Downtown Quality	.31*	.23
Western Europe 96	.55**	.28	Creative Class 01	.53**	.38*

Table 6.3 Correlations of Diversity Measures with 2006 Economic Health (*continued*)

Variable	Correlation		Variable	Correlation	
	All Midsize	Quebec Excluded		All Midsize	Quebec Excluded
Eastern Europe 96	.47**	.25	Unique Amenities	.43**	.33
US 96	.38*	.01	Generic Amenities	.53**	.38*
Africa 96	.64**	.64**	University degrees 01	.26	.30
Middle East 96	.42**	.36*	Non-Christian 01	.39**	.19
East Asia 96	.61**	.46**	English 01	.63**	.54**
Southeast Asia 96	.61**	.52**	French 01	-.50**	-.14
South Asia 96	.18	.03	Other Language 01	.53**	.47**
Oceania 96	.29	.07	Same sex 01	.18	.15
Resources 01	.15	.11	Trade 01	.15	.08
Manufacturing 01	-.26	.003	FIRE 01	.31*	.42*
Prof services 01	.45**	.24	Business 01	.41**	.11
Health Education 01	-.10	-.18	Population 96	.46**	.47**
Population 01	.49**	.50**	Population 06	.55**	.55**
University employ 01	.25	.19	Visible Minority 01	.62**	.78**
VM Chinese 96	.59**	.44*	VM Chinese 01	.61**	.49**

Table 6.3 Correlations of Diversity Measures with 2006 Economic Health (*continued*)

Variable	Correlation		Variable	Correlation	
	All Midsize	Quebec Excluded		All Midsize	Quebec Excluded
VM S. Asian 96	.25	.08	VM S. Asian 01	.23	.08
VM Black 96	.50**	.48**	VM Black 01	.52**	51**
VM Filipino 96	.60**	.46**	VM Filipino 01	.64**	54**
VM Hispanic 96	.48**	.44*	VM Hispanic 01	.57**	59**
VM SE. Asian 96	.47**	.36*	VM SE. Asian 01	.45**	.33
VM Arabic 96	.34*	.30	VM Arabic 01	.34*	.32
VM Korean 96	.43**	.21	VM Korean 01	.50**	.35*
VM Japanese 96	.12	-.06	VM Japanese 01	.18	-.02
VM Chinese 06	.65**	.55**	VM SE. Asian 06	.51**	.41*
VM S. Asian 06	.20	.06	VM Arabic 06	.25	.24
VM Black 06	.56**	.54**	VM Korean 06	.30	.10
VM Filipino 06	.67**	.61**	VM Japanese 06	.24	.02
VM Hispanic 06	.42**	59**			

*Significant at the .05 level
**Significant at the .01 level

Quebec and those in the rest of Canada on many traits, including economic health (Reese et al., 2010), the table provides the correlations for
all forty-two cities first in each cell, followed by a coefficient excluding
the nine cities in Quebec.

Change in local economic health (as measured by differences between index scores in 1996 and 2006) was also considered. None of
the immigration and diversity variables were significantly correlated
with health change; thus, it was excluded from further analyses. This
result is similar to previous research indicating that no variables commonly used to measure creative class, high-tech employment, and diversity are related to economic growth or improvement in residential
economic health (Sands and Reese, 2008; Reese et al., 2010). While this
may suggest that there is no causal relationship between diversity and
economic health, such a conclusion would be premature. First, as previously noted, other econometric analyses have indicated that diversity
is related to economic expansion (Ottaviano and Peri, 2005). Second,
change in the health index over time is measuring improvements (or decreases) in the prosperity of residents, but not necessarily growth in the
larger local economy that would potentially include property valuation
increases, tax base improvements, industrial expansion, business starts,
and the like.

Clearly, many aspects of diversity are significantly and positively
correlated with economic health; moreover, these relationships have remained stable over the time period included. Overall diversity of the
population is significantly correlated with economic health, although
the diversity among immigrant populations is significantly correlated
only when the Quebec cities are removed. This is likely the case because
the Quebec cities have low numbers of immigrants from only a limited
number of regions (predominantly French-speaking Africa, Southeast
Asia, and France) and local economies in Quebec are relatively poor. In
2006, immigration from all regions except South Asia and Oceania is
significantly and positively correlated with economic health for all cities.
In earlier census years, immigration from most of the world regions is
significantly correlated with the exception of the United States (1996,
2001) and the Middle East (2001).

Figure 6.2 Drummondville, QC, *Mondial des Cultures* (World of Cultures) Festival

The results are considerably different when the midsize cities in Quebec are removed from the analysis. The only regions of immigrant origin that are significantly correlated in all three years are Africa and Southeast Asia. There is a significant correlation with health and Central American immigrants in 1996 and 2001. Immigration from the Middle East is a significant correlate in 2006, while East Asian immigrants are significant only in 1996.

Other measures of diversity are also correlated with economic health.[3] Religious diversity (the percent of the population that is non-Christian) is significantly and positively associated with prosperity. The percent of English speakers and those speaking "other" languages are positively correlated with health, while the percentage of francophones is negatively correlated. When the Quebec cities are removed, the latter relationship

---

3. For all the diversity indicators except immigration, only the location quotients from the 2001 census are used. This was done primarily to simplify the analysis and presentation of data. It also limits problems with multicollinearity later in the analysis when regression is used. For the amenity (2009), downtown quality (2003), and same sex variables (2001) there is only a single data point.

disappears. The presence of visible minorities is significantly and positively associated with economic health, but there is no correlation between percent same sex households and health, the only diversity measure to be completely unrelated to economic health.

A number of other demographic and physical features are also correlated with economic health. Cities with greater economic health have more highly rated downtowns (when cities in Quebec are included) and more generic and unique local amenities. This conforms to previous research indicating that unique local restaurants, bookstores, and entertainment tend to be co-located with more generic ones, rather than posing exclusive alternatives (Reese et al., 2010), possibly because of the expansion of chain retailing into smaller markets in Canada (Gomez-Insausti, 2006). Employment in professional services, Finance, Insurance and Real Estate, and business services is significantly and positively correlated with economic health. Larger populations are consistently and positively correlated with prosperity. Finally, it should be noted that past economic health—in 1996 and 2001—is positively correlated with health in 2006, suggesting a high element of path dependency to economic health, as was found in previous analysis.

- Are higher levels of immigration from particular areas of the world more consistently related to local economic health than others? Are there particular groupings or co-locations of immigrant groups that are related to economic health?

The correlation analysis just presented would suggest that the answer to this question is no; generally, immigration from any region is associated with economic health. For cities not in the province of Quebec, immigration from Africa, the Middle East, East Asia, and Southeast Asia appears particularly important.

However, it is possible that specific configurations or groupings of foreign born are more important than the location of single groups. Past research emphasizing the importance of ethnic enclaves suggests that co-location may be important in economic success. Appendix B presents the results of a factor analysis of the ten regions of origin for each

Figure 6.3 Windsor, ON, ethnic enclave

of the three census periods. The results suggest that there are identifiable immigrant profiles or groupings in cities. In both 1996 and 2001, there were two immigrant profiles in midsize Canadian cities. The first profile represents cities with higher levels of immigrants from less industrialized regions: Central America, Eastern Europe, Africa, the Middle East, and Southeast Asia. The second profile represents cities with more immigrants from Western Europe, the United States, East and South Asia, and Oceania. By 2006, these profiles changed somewhat and a third immigrant complex appears, suggesting a greater dispersion or mixing of immigrant groups. The distinctions among the three groups are perhaps more geographic than economic. The Asia/Africa profile includes immigrants from Africa, Southeast Asia, and South Asia. Foreign-born immigrants from Europe and the Middle East are co-locating. The third profile is composed of cities with higher percentages of immigrants from the Americas, East Asia, and Oceania.

Each of the immigrant profile factors is positively and significantly correlated with economic health in 1996, 2001, and 2006 (Table 6.4). None, however, are related to economic growth between 1996 and 2006. Similar results are also obtained when urban areas in Quebec are omitted.

Table 6.4 Correlation of Immigrant Factors and Economic Health

1996		2001		2006	
Less industrial	.68**	Less industrial	.66**	Pacific	.50**
More industrial	.52**	More industrial	.50**	Europe	.48**
				Africa/Asia	.57**

- What types of diversity appear most strongly related to economic growth: sexual preference, race, ethnicity, language, or religion? What are the relative relationships of diversity and other demographic and physical features to local economic health?

The forgoing analysis does not address the relative correlations between measures of diversity and economic health. Regression analysis was conducted with the Economic Health Index in 2006 as the dependent variable; the independent variables included all the indicators that were significantly correlated with health in bivariate analyses. Because of the multicollinearity among the variables, factor analysis was used to create summary measures for related variables. The variables comprising each index are as follows:

- **White-collar employment** includes professional services, FIRE, and business service employment
- **Ethnic/visible minority index** includes measures of the Black and Arab population
- **Other languages** excludes speakers of Canada's official languages, French and English

The results of the regression analysis are presented in Table 6.5. To reduce multicollinearity, only data from the 2001 census are used. Thus, the regression represents relationships between demographics in the past (2001) and later economic health (2006). All together the variables in the equation predict 59 percent of the variation in economic health, although only two variables are significantly correlated to health at the .05 level in multiple regression analysis; another remains correlated at the .10 level.

Table 6.5 Economic Health 2006 Full Regression Model

Variable	b	Beta	Error	Significance
White collar employment	.37	.37	.14	.01
Population diversity 01	7.27	.79	3.45	.04
Immigrant diversity 01	3.64	.25	2.38	.14
Downtown quality	.16	.17	.13	.26
Population 01	-1.235E-6	-.13	.00	.64
Locally unique amenities	-.01	-.02	.22	.95
Ethnicity/visible minority Index	.003	.22	.003	.99
Other language 01	-2.20	-.14	5.23	.68
Constant	-3.06		2.08	.15
R square = .59				

The best predictor of economic health in 2006 is the level of diversity within the general population in 2001. Higher levels of employment in white-collar professions in 2001 also remain a significant predictor of economic health in 2006 in multiple regression. As suggested in research by Lee (2010), greater diversity (represented here by the visible minority index) is not as important to economic prosperity as diversity within the immigrant population.

DISCUSSION

Several conclusions can be drawn from the analyses presented here. The most important is that the presence of diversity in the local population—in terms of immigration status, race, language, and religion—is positively associated with higher levels of economic health in midsize Canadian urban areas. Immigrants from Africa, the Middle East, East Asia, and Southeast Asia appear to be particularly strongly associated with prosperity measures. In multiple regression analysis, holding a number of other economic and demographic traits constant, the most important correlate of economic health is diversity within the general population.

To explore the potential dynamics of this relationship more closely, Table 6.6 presents selected characteristics of the ten cities with the

Table 6.6 Top Ten Cities on the Total Diversity Index

	Rank	Health	Location	Manufacturing	Population	University	Creative Index
Windsor	1	.54	Border-Detroit	1.71	323,342	1.13	-.33
Abbotsford	2	.01	Vancouver	1.04	159,020	.45	-.65
Kitchener	3	1.69	Toronto	Na	451,253	2.19	.95
Guelph	4	1.32	Toronto	1.51	127,009	5.31	.47
London	5	.95	Independent	1.09	457,720	2.12	.76
Victoria	6	1.47	West Coast	.49	330.088	2.19	3.83
St. Catharines-Niagara	7	.11	Border-Buffalo	1.17	390,317	.87	.27
Oshawa	8	1.81	Toronto	1.26	330,594	.20	.36
Nanaimo	9	-.77	Vancouver	.69	92,361	1.22	.65
Kelowna	10	.10	Isolated	.91	162,276	.18	1.11

highest levels of population diversity in 2006. Several general patterns stand out. First, geographically, these diverse cities tend to be either on the coast, proximate to the US border, or within commuting distance of a major city. Not surprisingly, they are located in the populous provinces of Ontario and British Columbia, but not Quebec.[4] Only one of the cities—Kelowna—is relatively isolated. With the exception of Nanaimo they are in the higher population range of the midsize cities; indeed population size in 1996 is significantly correlated with diversity in 2006. Nanaimo is also the only city among the top ten with a negative correlation between diversity and economic health. With a couple of exceptions the cities have relatively high levels of university and manufacturing employment.

In general, correlation analysis between past economic health (1996) and later diversity indicates that diversity is higher in places that have

---

4. In general, the Ontario cities have higher health scores than the province as a whole (at .71), while those in British Columbia are lower than throughout the province (-.71).

been and continue to be prosperous. Thus, it is very hard to disentangle whether immigrants are attracted to healthy places or whether they contribute to economic health (indeed, the relationship is likely to be non-recursive). But given previous research indicating that diversity actually causes health (Ottaviano and Peri, 2005) and the fact that past diversity is strongly related to future health, it is not unreasonable to conclude that places that were more diverse at earlier points in time will have greater economic health in later ones.

The last column in the table shows scores on the creative class index that includes employment in design, computer services, scientific services, arts companies, and independent artists, and the percentage of same-sex households. Higher scores on the index are positively and significantly correlated with population diversity. The top ten cities here illustrate this trend with most being high on the index, particularly Victoria and Kelowna. The latter may suggest why that city, although quite isolated, still has a very diverse population. Nanaimo's relatively high score, as well as its proximity to Victoria and Vancouver, may also relate to its diverse population. Overall, these results suggest that diversity is related to population size, greater economic health (those with higher incomes and less unemployment), creativity, and geographic location near larger urban nodes or on borders. Thus, while immigrants to Canada may be dispersing from their historic preference for the three gateway cities, they are not going far into the hinterlands.

Given the importance of population diversity, it is also interesting to note that only fifteen cities actually experienced an increase in population diversity between 1996 and 2006. And there is very little overlap between those increasing in diversity and the top ten most diverse cities; indeed, Windsor, Abbotsford, and Kitchener are the only cities on both lists (Table 6.7). Rather, diversity was more likely to increase in urban areas where the initial proportion of foreign born was low. These increasingly diverse cities evidence few consistent patterns in economic health (although as a group they are less healthy than the high diversity cities), creativity, or population size. These cities are much more likely to be in Quebec and are more isolated than the previous set of cities. They also tend to have higher than average employment in manufacturing. In the

Table 6.7 Cities with Increasing Diversity, 1996–2006*

	Rank	Health	Location	Manufacturing	Population	University	Creative Index
Windsor ON	1	.54	Border-Detroit	1.71	323,342	1.13	-.33
Abbotsford BC	2	.01	Vancouver	1.04	159,020	.45	-.65
Cornwall ON	3	-1.69	Toronto-Border	1.49	58,485	na	na
Saint-Hyacinthe QC	4	-.85	Isolated	1.40	55,823	.78	-1.20
Granby QC	5	-.45	Isolated	1.95	68.352	.19	.04
Barrie ON	6	1.23	Toronto	1.24	177,061	.12	.04
Sherbrook QC	7	-.70	Isolated	1.28	186,952	2.64	.26
Drummondville QC	8	-1.26	Isolated	1.77	78,108	.21	-.06
Kitchener ON	9	1.69	Toronto	Na	451,253	2.19	.95
Fredericton NB	10	.07	Capital	.51	85,688	3.56	.52
Trois-Rivières QC	11	-1.51	Isolated	1.17	141,529	1.30	-.82
Saguenay QC	12	-1.39	Isolated	1.15	143,692	1.12	-.84
Halifax NS	13	.87	East Coast	.57	372,858	2.43	2.19
Belleville ON	14	-.48	Isolated	1.09	91,518	.17	-.20
Saint-Jean-sur-Richelieu QC	15	-.15	Montreal	1.33	87,492	.30	-.60

case of the Quebec cities, increasing diversity often occurs among immigrants from Africa, South America, and the United States.

Table 6.8 is drawn from census projections for the largest of the midsize CMAs in Canada and thus does not include all of the midsize cities in this study. However, there is sufficient overlap to conclude that cities with the highest levels of population diversity are projected to experience increases in their foreign-born population over the next twenty-five years. Two other trends are worth noting. First, it is clear that foreign-born individuals will continue to locate outside the traditional gateway cities

Table 6.8 Foreign-Born Population Projections

	Foreign Born % 2006	Foreign Born % 2031	Change 2006–31	Foreign Born Share of Increase
Abbotsford	23.8	28.5	4.7	44.0%
Barrie	13.0	12.6	-0.4	11.3%
Brantford	12.6	12.8	0.2	13.8%
Greater Sudbury	6.7	5.3	-1.4	-33.3%
Guelph	20.5	24.8	4.3	42.4%
Halifax	7.3	11.0	3.7	52.9%
Kelowna	14.4	13.7	-0.7	11.5%
Kingston	12.7	14.0	1.3	28.6%
Kitchener	23.0	28.0	5.0	45.9%
London	19.3	22.7	3.4	43.6%
Moncton	3.1	5.3	2.2	150.0%
Oshawa	16.3	18.7	2.4	25.9%
Peterborough	9.1	10.9	1.8	42.9%
Regina	7.6	9.5	1.9	38.5%
St. Catharines-Niagara	18.3	18.7	0.4	24.1%
Saint John	4.0	6.0	2.0	-25.0%
St. John's	2.7	3.7	1.0	33.3%
Saskatoon	7.6	10.3	2.7	37.5%
Saguenay	1.3	2.2	0.9	-5.6%
Sherbrooke	5.9	11.3	5.4	80.0%
Thunder Bay	10.2	8.4	-1.8	-50.0%
Trois-Rivières	2.1	4.8	2.7	133.3%
Victoria	16.2	19.7	3.5	37.3%
Windsor	23.2	28.4	5.2	40.7%

Source: Statistics Canada, *Projections of the Diversity of the Canadian Population 2006 to 2031*, Ministry of Industry, 2010

of Toronto, Vancouver, and Montreal. In terms of relative percentages of population that is foreign born, St. John's, Halifax, and Sherbrooke are projected to enjoy significant increases. The last column in the table indicates the percent of projected population increase due to increases in the foreign-born population. The relatively isolated cities of Moncton, Trois-Rivières, and Sherbrooke have high levels of growth due exclusively to increases in immigrants, as does the larger city of Halifax. Percentages over 100 indicate that the growth of immigrants is projected to occur along with a reduction in the non-immigrant population. For all the cities in the table there is a 38 percent increase in population due exclusively to foreign-born individuals.

SUMMARY AND POLICY IMPLICATIONS

Revisiting the research questions guiding the forgoing analysis provides a cogent summary of the findings. First, is there a measurable relationship between diversity as indicated by foreign-born residents and community health? How does the relationship compare to that of other correlates of economic health? Findings indicate that there is a significant relationship between immigration and health. Several aspects of diversity—language, visible minority status, and religion—are also related to economic health. Only the correlation with foreign-born residents remains significant in multiple regression, however.

The second set of questions were as follows: Are higher levels of immigration from particular areas of the world more consistently related to local economic health than others? Are there particular groupings or co-location of immigrant groups that are related to economic health? The data for midsize Canadian cities indicate that immigrant levels from different countries have slightly different relationships to economic health. Immigration from Africa, the Middle East, East Asia, and Southeast Asia is most strongly related to health. However, any type of immigration is related to economic health, particularly when cities outside Quebec are considered.

Third, what types of diversity appear most strongly related to economic growth: sexual preference, race, ethnicity, language, or religion?

What are the relative relationships of diversity and other demographic and physical features to local economic health? The data indicate that immigration is the diversity variable most consistently related to economic health. Sexual preference in particular is unrelated to economic health, and visible minority status is less important than diversity among immigrants. Again, only the correlation with foreign-born residents remains significant in multiple regression.

The extent that population growth is dependent on immigration and the clear dispersion of immigrants to midsize communities in Canada argues for greater attention to public policies that facilitate these trends (Hiebert, 2000; Teixeira et al., 2005; Hiebert et al., 2007). The analysis presented here showing increasing dispersion and mixing of immigrant groups supports and extends earlier work. While the Canadian national government has a history of pursuing immigration as an economic development strategy using such policies as points-based factors (such as education, language skills, and work experience) and business migration programs (targeting immigrants most likely to start new businesses based on net worth and business management experience), local-level initiatives can augment these programs and may warrant greater consideration.[5]

While research has documented the challenges faced by many immigrants in Canada, including a greater tendency toward lower incomes, weaker labor market attachment, and language and cultural barriers, as well as insufficient access to business financing (see for example Murdie, 1997; Smith, 2004; Picot, 2004; Hiebert et al., 2007; Teixeira et al., 2005), most areas of immigrant concentration appear to have mixed income profiles and relatively high diversity in skills, education, and resources (Teixeira et al., 2005; Hiebert et al., 2007). Barriers to business development appear lower in Canada than in the United States or Europe, however (Jones et al., 2000; Teixeira, 2001). Thus, local policies focused on immigrant integration and support are desirable because of increasing need among immigrants, do not appear to lead to persistent pockets of

---

5. See www.workpermit.com/canada/individual/skilled.htm and blog.visabureau.com/post/canada-business-migration-and-the-investor-immigrant-irogram.aspx for descriptions of these programs.

poverty in the communities with higher levels of immigrant settlement, and should allow communities to reap the greatest economic growth benefits from a well-integrated and prosperous foreign-born population.

From a policy perspective, the findings here indicate that greater diversity among residents, particularly within the immigrant base in earlier years, is significantly correlated with future economic health, even controlling for other demographic and employment factors. While this does not conclusively prove that immigrants cause economic prosperity, it is clear that communities with higher diversity have stronger economic health. This implies that local government officials would do well to consider immigration and diversity as potentially important to economic development efforts. The findings here suggest an expansion of the types of local government policies traditionally considered to foster economic development. Beyond business development, attraction, retention, enhancement of amenities, and land development, economic development may well entail the attraction and support of particular types of residents. While other research has suggested that focusing on families may be a productive way to foster economic health (Reese, 2012; Reese and Ye, 2011), the analysis here also suggests that immigrants make important contributions to local economic health.

It is useful to reiterate some of the variables *not* correlated with economic health in multiple regression, including creative employment, most other aspects of the employment base, same-sex couples, downtown quality, and place-specific amenities. These are central aspects of Florida's creative class argument, and their lack of correlation with economic health, particularly when controlling for immigration, suggests that local officials should consider carefully the potential benefits of focusing on many aspects of the creative class economic development strategy. This finding is consistent with several pieces of research that also raise significant questions about the effectiveness of economic development policies directed at attracting the creative class (see, for example, Sands and Reese, 2008; Donegan et al., 2008; Hoyman and Faricy, 2010; Reese and Ye, 2011).

It appears that local economic development policies might more effectively focus on diversity generally and on immigrants specifically. Conceptually there are two general strategies or forms for such policies to take: a focus on the settlement or integration of immigrants into local society more generally, and more specific efforts to enhance labor force participation and encourage entrepreneurialism. Research has begun to identify areas where immigrant support policies should be considered by local governments: language programs; health and social service supports; immigration and citizenship assistance; and affordable housing (Bates, 2006; Theodore and Martin, 2007; Hackler and Mayer, 2008; Gross, 2010). These all present general supports to immigrants as they resettle in their new communities and are largely motivated by basic humanitarian concerns.

Considering immigration as a more focused economic development policy would entail a slightly different set of local programs directed at training, employment, and credentialing assistance on the one hand and entrepreneurialism supports, most prominently including access to business financing, on the other (van Delft et al., 2000; Teixeira et al., 2005; Moon et al., 2014). A recent study on the entrepreneurial success of visible minority immigrants in Toronto has suggested several primary barriers to business development: lack of recognition of foreign educational and professional credentials; weak language abilities; lack of information; and inadequate access to capital (Teixeira et al., 2005). Local governments could focus on a number of public efforts to address settlement and economic integration barriers.

General policies to support the *settlement of immigrants* might include:

- one-stop general information centers to provide assistance and information on educational and training options
- provincial and local processes and procedures both for economic and political integration
- informational materials in appropriate languages
- citizenship assistance
- housing assistance
- health care counseling

Policies to support the *economic integration* of immigrants might include:

- programs to help immigrants gain Canadian credentials
- one-stop business shops to assist with local ordinances and information on funding
- support for mentoring programs to foster networks among immigrant entrepreneurs and provide technical assistance
- working with financial institutions to foster immigrant capital programs such as micro loans or revolving loan programs
- reductions in local red tape in starting and locating businesses
- minority procurement programs

And there is no requirement that local governments pursue these policies on their own. Cooperating with existing immigrant support or ethnic groups or other community or nonprofit organizations is a way to design culturally appropriate programs, access ethnic communities, and provide services in a cost effective manner (van Delft et al., 2000; Theodore and Martin, 2007).

The findings here also suggest that particular immigrant groups—from Africa, the Middle East, East Asia, and Southeast Asia—are more consistently correlated with economic health. Thus local officials may want to target programs to these groups. The fact that these countries of origin include immigrants from visible minority groups also supports the need for targeted policies since other research has indicated higher barriers to their success (Henry, 1994; Teixeira et al., 2005).

Further research explicitly identifying and evaluating such policies would be an important contribution to the public policy literature on local economic development. In short, policies that ease immigrant transitions are good for the foreign born, but also are likely to be good for local economies.

7

City Center Management Organizations

> Downtown is the economic engine that pulls the city train.
> Downtowns provide many dollars of tax revenues for each dollar
> of service consumed. Great downtowns and great business dis-
> tricts are built on potent, well-crafted, broadly understood and
> supported visions.
>
> Feehan, 2006: 30

Across North America, cities large and small are facing financial
problems that range from serious to crisis. Local revenue sources,
as well as intergovernmental transfers, are stagnant or declining while
the costs of maintaining essential public services continue to increase.
Local ratepayers are reluctant to approve tax increases and indeed, in
many instances, voters have enacted limits on such increases. For many
municipalities, the result is a combination of diminished services and
deferred maintenance. Cities ranging in size from Toronto and Chicago
to Highland Park, Michigan, and Cornwall, Ontario have been forced
to adopt cost-cutting measures. The inevitable result is a decline in the
quality of public services and, ultimately, the overall quality of life in
these communities.

In the face of widespread public sector fiscal problems, it has become
increasingly common for private interests to undertake the provision of
what have traditionally been public services. Cooperatives and condominium associations typically provide their residents with some "public"
services, services that are usually the responsibility of municipal governments. Single-family residential areas may assess themselves to provide for
private security to complement municipal services or to support private

recreational programs, available only to resident members. Such arrangements are most common in higher income neighborhoods, and are most obvious in so-called gated communities (Blakely and Snyder, 1997).

Business districts have also adopted programs to enhance provision of public services, particularly as they relate to an area's appearance, security, and economic viability. This chapter examines the common models of commercial business district organizations in the wake of recent recessionary pressures and compares three different organizational models: business improvement areas (BIAs), downtown development authorities (DDAs), and Main Streets. Commercial district management organizations (CDOs)—whether Main Street, BIA, or DDA—are, and will likely remain, major tools for revitalization of both city centers and neighborhood commercial districts.

Research on commercial district organizations has focused on three major themes: theoretical works discussing the implications and nature of the district organization as a public-private partnership; enumeration of the activities and services of business district associations; and assessments of their efficiency and effectiveness (Stokes, 2007). Overall, this research has tended to be static and cross-sectional; the current literature does not address the key criterion of economic restructuring, let alone potential changes in district organizational structure, financing, and activities in the wake of increasing economic stress in cities and to their constituent business base. Thus, it is particularly important to ensure a better understanding of the potential contribution of commercial district organizations to the economic well-being of communities and neighborhoods in these changing and increasingly stressful economic times. The following are the key questions addressed in this chapter:

- Have CDOs had significant impacts on their neighborhoods and communities?
- Are there particular attributes (size, location, community economy, governing structure, types of businesses) that characterize successful CDOs?
- Are the different models of CDOs (Main Streets, BIA, DDA) equally effective?

- Have CDOs responded adequately to contextual changes and new economic realities?

ORGANIZATIONAL MODELS

Main Street

Many local business districts have adopted the Main Street model, which emphasizes organization, design, promotion, and economic restructuring. Originated by the United States Department of the Interior's National Trust for Historic Preservation, the Main Street model was first applied to small towns in rural America. These city centers were the literal Main Streets of their communities, where not only retail commercial activity was concentrated, but also where government and professional offices were located. The significance today of these commercial streets, however, is often enhanced by the presence of historic buildings. The construction of highway bypasses and peripheral shopping developments drew customers away from these city centers. The combination of the Interstate Highway system and "big box" retailers like Wal-Mart has resulted in the devastation of many small town economies.

The Canadian Main Street initiative began in 1980 as a pilot project by Heritage Canada the National Trust in seven communities across Canada (Heritage Canada, 2014). In addition to the basic activities included in the US Main Street model, the Canadian Main Street program emphasizes the conservation of heritage buildings. The Heritage Canada Foundation subsequently received funding from the Government of Canada to extend the efforts to additional cities (Plaine, 2007). Although federal government funding has been limited, the Main Street program continues to be active, primarily in Alberta and Quebec. In the latter province, a separate entity, *La foundation Rues principals*, provides advice to communities on a fee-for-services basis (Plaine, 2007).

The Main Street model focuses on the organization of local businesses (typically retail and personal services) so that they are able to act more like their primary new competition, shopping malls, and big box retail outlets. In many instances, grant funds have been used to support the hiring of a Main Street manager who is responsible for soliciting the participation of member businesses (as well as for securing additional funding) in program activities. The Main Street model is sufficiently flexible that it can be limited to relatively simple and inexpensive activities (coordinating store hours and scheduling sales dates) or incorporate larger scale activities, such as provision of parking. The effectiveness of some of the early Main Street efforts has led to the adaptation of the model to neighborhood shopping streets in larger cities.

As a voluntary organization, Main Street programs are limited by the lack of a dedicated source of funding. Some Main Street districts sustain their ongoing operations by voluntary contributions from their merchant members and property owners (in some instances the majority of funding comes from one or two large contributors). Foundation or other grants may be used to support specific activities, such as streetscapes or façade improvements.

Business Improvement Areas

The financial limitations of the Main Street model have been addressed by the creation of more formal organizational structures under state or provincial enabling legislation. One of these is the *Business Improvement Area*. As specified in statutes, these organizations may be called Business Improvement Districts (United States), Business Improvement Areas (English Canada) or *Sociétés de développement commercial* (French Canada).[1] (Main Street programs continue to exist as separate entities in each of these jurisdictions.) The nature of the legislation varies but typically includes criteria for the establishment of districts, membership eligibility, and methods for assessing district levies, eligible activities and organizational governance. Thus, Business Improvement Areas are both spatial— they operate in a specific area of the city—and organizational entities.

A BIA, unlike a shopping mall, is more organic, composed of an often eclectic mix of independent merchants and multiple property owners,

---

1. The enabling legislation also specifies the nomenclature, such as Business Improvement Districts, Zones, or Areas; here, we will use the terms interchangeably for equivalent entities.

Figure 7.1 Oxford, MI, Main Street

within specific boundaries (BIAs have also been referred to as "malls without walls" [Lippert 2010]). As a result, the parameters with respect to membership, annual and special assessments, and eligible activities established by the BIA enabling legislation effectively define the potential of the BIA. And there appear to be significant variations among jurisdictions in the organizational structure and legal powers of business improvement organizations (Morcol and Wolf, 2010). Enabling statutes are also important in ensuring that these essentially private organizations act in a manner that is consistent with the public interest, although, again, there is extensive variation in that respect. For example, state enabling statutes in the United States require agreement by as few as 20 percent or as many as 75 percent of the proposed members to establish a BID (Billings and Leland, 2009).

Business Improvement Areas may undertake a wide range of activities, often well beyond those typical of voluntary merchant associations. The most common activities relate to promotion, environmental maintenance (litter control, landscape maintenance) and public safety. The BIA may also implement improvements to public spaces (street furniture, banners, and lighting), market research and event coordination (for example, concerts and other activities to attract visitors). However, even

Figure 7.2 Saint-Hyacinthe, QC, Business Improvement Association

given the variation in activities there is general consensus that BIAs have: a geographically defined area with extra taxes and services; a means of limiting those services to the area so that few spillovers occur; approval from city or higher-level governments; and a governing board typically composed largely of business owners (Billings and Leland, 2009: 110).

Downtown Development Authorities

Downtown Development Authorities are another commercial district model, particularly prevalent in the United States. Typically they involve the use of tax increment financing (TIF), as opposed to relying on voluntary assessments as with BIAs. Tax increment financing is often an attractive tool because it allows municipalities to undertake important and costly improvements (particularly when bond financing is required) without levying new taxes.[2] Once a TIF district has been established, any subsequent growth in aggregate property tax revenues, both as a result of new construction or rising values of existing properties, is "captured" by the

---

2. TIF revenue bonds are generally not backed by the full faith and credit of the municipality and, in some states, are outside municipal debt limits.

Figure 7.3 Plymouth, MI, Downtown Development Authority

district and used for investments within. The property tax rates are the same within the tax increment finance district as elsewhere in the community; the incentive for being included in the district is that taxes paid result directly in public investments in the district. Tax increment finance districts can take a number of different forms (Weber, 2003; Sands et al.,

Table 7.1 Types of Commercial District Organizations

	Business Improvement Areas	Downtown Development Authorities	Rues Principals / Main Street
Primary Focus	Clean & Safe	Capital Improvements	Design, Organize, Promote, Restructure
Authority	Statute	Statute	Voluntary
Participants	Businesses, incl. Tenants	Property Owners	Primarily Retail Businesses
Time Line	Long	Long	Indefinite
Primary Funding	Millage	Tax Capture*	Grants
Added Cost	Yes	No*	Possibly

*Michigan DDAs are allowed to levy a millage; however, few actually do.

2007). They may provide the basis for bond financing of a specific public improvement, such as a water or sewer line or be used to meet the cost of remediation of brownfield sites. Downtown Development Authorities may use revenue from TIF districts for a range of activities, including ongoing operating expenses, infrastructure improvements (parking decks and street improvements for example), and subsidies to firms or community events.

The fundamental differences between the three organizational models are summarized in Table 7.1. DDAs in particular tend to focus on larger capital improvement projects funded by revenue bonds that are paid off utilizing the captured value resulting from increases in the tax base of the DDA. BIAs involve an added assessment on businesses and tend to focus on safety and general attractiveness of the area. Main Streets are voluntary and generally rely on grants for funding. Hence their activities tend to be limited to organization and promotion.

LITERATURE REVIEW

Commercial district organizations are common in municipalities across Canada and the United States. BIAs are quite popular; virtually every province has enacted BIA legislation. Almost 200 have been established in Ontario alone. There are some 55 BIAs in British Columbia, as well as more than a dozen in Atlantic Canada and in the Montreal Urban Community. Further, the BIA or BID concept has been applied globally with increasing frequency, from Canada and the United States to Eastern and Western Europe, the Caribbean, and South Africa (Hoyt, 2006; Ward, 2006; Morcol and Wolf, 2010; Ruffin, 2010). While some scholars have claimed that the concept for the BIA originated in Canada (Ward, 2006), the variety of "names" for self-imposed financing mechanisms in business areas (public improvement districts, neighborhood improvement districts, and city improvement districts are examples) makes it hard to identify an origin with certainty (Hoyt, 2003; Ward, 2006).

A wide array of common commercial district services are provided by CDOs, ranging from maintenance, appearance, and promotion to public safety, hospitality, and tourism, as well as capital improvements (Huey et al., 2005; Lippert, 2007; Lippert and Sleiman, 2012). In the area of service provision alone, it has been noted that BIAs specifically are involved in as many as nine different types: capital projects, marketing, economic development, maintenance, parking/transportation, public policy advocacy, regulation of public space, security, and even social services (MacDonald, 1996: 42; Lewis, 2010), although making sure the areas are "clean and safe" seems to be the most prevalent activity (Lewis, 2010). Ambassador Programs cross the boundaries between many of these activities as they incorporate individuals who clean streets, distribute promotional material, assist visitors, and provide references to social agencies and information to the police (Lippert and Sleiman, 2012). Some scholars have also found BIAs in lower income areas to move beyond marketing services to provide technical support for new business owners (Gross, 2005).

Commercial district organizations generally provide both tangible and intangible benefits. While public safety, planters, banners and promotional materials are concrete evidence of a business district organization, enhanced feelings of safety and a delineated physical space are psychologically reassuring to shoppers (Gross, 2005) and create an esprit de corps among business owners that facilitates cooperative endeavors (Lewis, 2010) and may attract more businesses to the area thus serving an economic development function.

Downtown Development Districts that rely on tax increment financing are similarly popular in the United States. Initially employed to offset declining federal assistance for urban redevelopment projects, tax increment finance districts are now common (Goshorn, 1999: 924). Most states enabled local governments to use TIF authorities by the turn of the century (Johnson and Mann, 2001); the majority allow the use of TIF districts for either commercial or industrial projects, and thirty states allow tax increment financing for residential uses. Tax increment financing is also increasingly used to fund brownfield remediation. Over time, TIF has become one of the most popular economic development tools, with steadily increasing use since the 1970s (Forgey, 1993). In part, its popularity lies in the presumptive benefits: municipalities do not have to increase property taxes to pay for desired improvements; for business owners in the TIF districts, higher levels of services can be provided without requiring them to pay higher taxes. For TIF districts that are allowed to use bond financing, the installation time of capital improvements can be greatly accelerated.[3] They can also aid redevelopment in targeted areas of blight or financial need (Weber, 2003; Sands et al., 2007).

Although BIAs and DDAs have existed for decades, systematic evaluations have reached mixed conclusions on their impacts. Some studies have found that BIAs are associated with reduced crime rates and increases in the value of property; they have also been found to be efficient providers of services (Ross and Levine, 2001; Symes and Steel, 2003; Hoyt, 2006; Lewis, 2010), in some cases more effectively than local governments (Traub, 1996). The services provided by the BIAs appear to be complementary to, rather than competitive with, city services and solve the free-rider problems experienced by more generalized business organizations such as Chambers of Commerce (Billings and Leland, 2009).

---

3. Although TIF revenue bonds have generally been considered good investments, recently declining property values have resulted in revenue shortfalls for some TIF districts.

However, a large body of research has raised concerns about BIA's tendency to favor business over residential needs and divert revenue from the general fund, their potential to create a two-tiered system of service quality, and their inherently undemocratic (read private) nature (Briffault, 1999; Ross and Levine, 2001; Loukaitou-Sideris et al., 2004; Lewis, 2010). And while they can be entrepreneurial and innovative, many are more focused on political issues or managerial tasks (Mitchell, 2001) limiting their service activities.

Regarding DDAs, most criticisms revolved around the tax increment funding mechanism, raising concerns similar to those directed at BIAs. Criticisms of tax increment financing for downtown development include the following:

- Even when property values rise and TIF revenues grow, the funds are not available to support general services. Thus, municipalities may need to raise citywide tax rates to ensure that necessary services are provided outside of the district or decrease services. This raises equity issues as potential public revenues are diverted to business districts (Weber, 2003; Sands et al., 2007).
- The tax increment finance district may divert substantial revenues from local school or park districts. Such jurisdictions may also be required to provide additional services as a result of development in the TIF (Lehnen and Johnson, 2001; Weber, 2003).
- A concern that designation is used arbitrarily, without meeting rigorous standards for the allocation of tax revenues; in particular, some state enabling legislation limits TIF use to blight elimination or requires a determination of necessity; the proposed project would not proceed without ("but for") the TIF designation. Flexible standards in the definition of blight can result in private subsidies rather than true economic development (Luce, 2003).
- TIF can be problematic if sunset provisions are not included, TIF districts are often governed by boards that lack transparency and accountability, and TIF is only likely to be effective when new development does in fact occur or where property values are

increasing, thus the original designation should be done carefully (Sands et al., 2007).

Unlike tax increment financing districts, a BIA may not have sufficient revenue to fund major capital improvements, such as parking decks. BIAs are generally funded by an additional levy on property owners or business establishments within the district. Thus, BIAs in particular are a "tax enhancement strategy" (Gross, 2005). They turn policies such as locational tax incentives on their head as the private sector is, in essence, agreeing to pay increased taxes because they are dedicated to a specific business area (Kantor and Savitch, 1998). Because this effectively adds to the property tax burden of the businesses, the actual amount of the BIA levy tends to be relatively small, limiting the activities of the BIA. Indeed, research has suggested that the activities of BIAs are significantly correlated with their size and resources (Gross, 2005). For example, larger BIAs are more likely to engage in capital improvements while smaller ones are more limited to maintenance and promotion. Moreover, BIAs in areas with higher incomes have enhanced organizational capabilities and human resources to go along with their generally larger budgets (Gross, 2005). Indeed, BIAs appear more likely to form in areas with higher property values and at least some economic growth (Meltzer, 2011).

These mixed results emanate from several realities. Measuring success of CDOs is, of course, particularly difficult because it requires identifying the unique contribution of the organization to the success of a business district. There is no available counterfactual—what would have happened to the business district if the CDO did not exist. Further, because CDOs tend to work collaboratively with local governments and other business groups such as Chambers of Commerce, it is difficult to isolate the unique impacts of the CDO (Mitchell, 2008).

As this review of the literature shows, there is a dearth of research examining the roles of commercial district organizations in, and their reactions to, changes in the local economy. And no work has explicitly compared the different district structural options. Research since the Great Recession has not explicitly focused on potential changes in both the nature of CDO members and the activities of the organization. Turner

(2002: 533) suggested that the nature of larger city downtowns has been changing from places of consumption and commerce serving local residents to places "designed more like amusement parks for tourists." She argues that downtown changes as of the early 2000s included a shift from public to private space; more brand-name and fewer local stores; increasing loft and town home housing; and emphasis on middle- and high-income consumers. But, in some cases, she also found efforts at a broader governance structure for local commercial district organizations. Again, two major questions remain unanswered—have such changes continued in the wake of the Great Recession, and are these processes only applicable to large cities or those with particular types of downtowns? In short, many interesting questions remain unanswered, most prominently whether the goals and activities of CDOs have changed as local economies have and whether more adaptable CDOs experience better outcomes.

METHODOLOGY

This chapter is based on a survey of all Business Improvement Associations (or equivalent) in Ontario (N=263) and Downtown Development Authorities in Michigan (N=382) conducted in 2013. Because there are no complete lists of commercial district organizations, the population was identified through web searches, examination of websites, commercial district associations, and lists of commercial districts in specific cities. While it is possible that some CDOs are missing, there is confidence that most have been accounted for. Because a primary question of interest is which form of CDO appears most effective, comparisons between BIAs (used primarily in Canada) and DDAs (more typically used in the United States) are required. A single state (Michigan) is examined due to the cost and complexity of data collection. Because of limited numbers of BIAs in midsize cities, this analysis includes CDOs in cities of all sizes across Canada.

Approximately 120 of the 379 active DDAs in Michigan provided responses to the survey. The overall response rate of 32 percent is typical for this type of survey. There is good geographic representation, that is, by rural/urban location and area of the state. DDAs in Michigan's

Map 7.1 Michigan DDA survey respondents

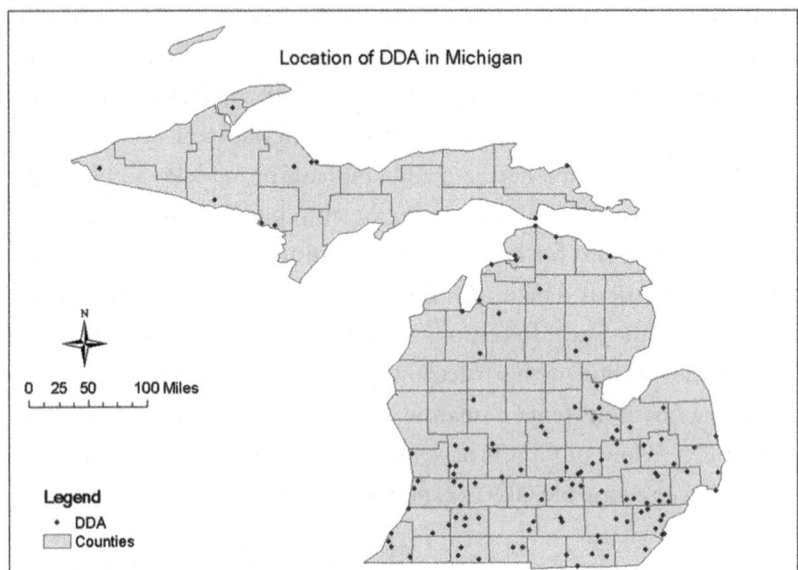

largest cities, those with population's over 50,000, are somewhat under-represented (Map 7.1).

A total of 84 responses were received from the 299 BIAs in Canada, a response rate of 28.1 percent. With one exception (Prince Albert, SK) all of the responses came from organizations in Ontario or British Columbia. Responses came from the largest cities in these provinces as well as from smaller communities in more rural areas (see Map 7.2).

Respondent Profile

The BIA population includes two distinct types of commercial districts, city centers and neighborhood BIAs. Most of the city center BIAs that responded are located in smaller municipalities. Neighborhood shopping districts represented the majority of BIA respondents (Table 7.2). The larger cities in Ontario and British Columbia—Toronto (16), Hamilton (8), Windsor (3), Ottawa (3), and Vancouver (4)—account for almost two-thirds of neighborhood commercial district respondents. Response data are reported separately for these two types of BIA, although the differences between them are frequently not significant.

Map 7.2 Ontario BIA survey respondents

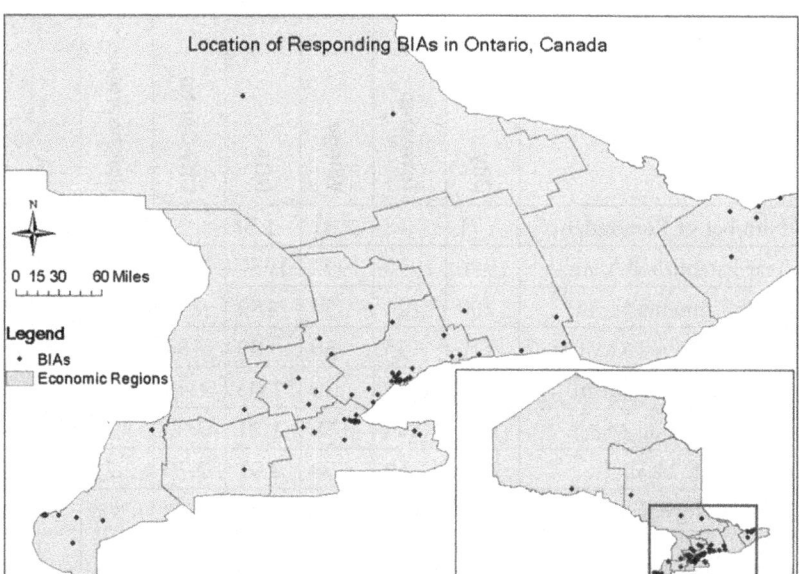

The Michigan responses came from three distinct types of municipalities: cities, townships, and villages. Each of these categories of municipality has different powers and responsibilities. Michigan cities range in population size from less than 500 to about 700,000. Villages have much less authority and are generally small, with an average population of about 1,000. Townships generally provide limited public services to rural areas, although townships in suburban locations (most of those responding to the survey) have larger populations and provide more services. Cities and villages are well represented in the survey but townships are not.

Table 7.2 provides a profile of the Downtown Development Authorities that responded to the survey. The oldest DDA in the survey was established in 1971, the newest in 2009. The average age is twenty-two years. About half were created between 1984 and 1994. The average number of establishments in these DDAs is 152. The median number of businesses is 89; the range is from 3 to 1,500. The number of establishments per DDA was highest in cities and lowest in villages.

Table 7.2 Profile of Respondents

	City	Township	Village	DDA	City Center	Neighborhood	BIA
Number of Respondents	71	18	31	**120**	32	52	**84**
Year Established Median	1986	1992	1992	**1987**	1982	1987	**1985**
Establishments Mean	200	124	50	**152**	279	313	**300**
Establishments Median	110	55	36	**89**	180	223	**200**
Full-Time Staff Mean	1.13	0.63	1.0	**1.03**	1.44	1.16	**1.22**
Part-Time Staff Mean	1.42	0.84	0.58	**1.21**	2.00	1.35	**1.48**
Total Staff Mean	2.21	1.40	1.58	**2.01**	2.70	2.25	**2.49**
No Employees	38%	50%	53%	**43%**	17%	28%	**24%**
Volunteers	22.9	15.5	9.2	**21.1**	9.9	8.8	**9.2**

The DDAs surveyed generally employ very limited staff. Most (68 percent) have no full-time staff; only seven reported having two or more full-time staff. The most common arrangement is to utilize part-time staff. About 56 percent of the DDAs have only part-time employees; three-quarters of these rely exclusively on part-time employees. In many cases, the DDA staff are full-time municipal employees, such as the city manager or community development director, who devote some time to managing the DDA. Close to 40 percent of the respondents reported utilizing volunteers, with the reported number of volunteers ranging up to 300. Seventeen DDAs rely exclusively on volunteers, in many cases limited to their board members.

The BIAs responding to the survey were slightly older than the DDAs, with a median age of twenty-four years. They are typically larger than the DDAs, perhaps because tenants are included as well as property owners. The neighborhood BIAs have more members than do the city center districts.

The BIAs surveyed indicated that they typically had more paid staff than the DDAs. While the differences are just a fraction of a person in both

Table 7.3 Moderate to High Concentrations of Establishments

		No Dominant	Entertainment	Retail	Office	Culture/Tourism
DDA	City	30%	64%	31%	30%	6%
	Township	37%	56%	6%	19%	0%
	Village	35%	61%	16%	13%	16%
	TOTAL	**33%**	**63%**	**24%**	**24%**	**8%**
BIA	City Center	10%	83%	50%	47%	27%
	Neighborhood	12%	72%	35%	52%	15%
	TOTAL	**12%**	**78%**	**41%**	**50%**	**19%**

the full and part-time employee categories, more than three-quarters of the BIAs have some paid staff, compared to only about half of the DDAs.

Types of Businesses Included in the Districts

Both DDAs and BIAs include a wide range of business types. The survey listed ten broad categories of business establishments, which can be grouped in four general categories: retail, entertainment, shopping, and culture/tourism. Two-thirds of the BIAs responding, and three-quarters of the DDAs, reported that they had a moderate to high proportion of businesses in one or more of these categories (Table 7.3). The most common concentration was the entertainment category, which includes restaurants, bars, and clubs; 56 to 83 percent of respondents reported this specialization. The Canadian BIAs were about twice as likely to report a concentration of businesses in the other three categories. With the exception of township DDAs, the subgroups have similar proportions of businesses in each of the four categories. Township DDAs were less likely to have high concentrations of retail and culture/tourism establishments.

Both DDAs and BIAs reported that their business base was relatively stable (Table 7.4); 71 percent of all DDA respondents indicated

Table 7.4 Trends in Number of Businesses by Type

	BIAs		DDAs	
	Stable	**Increasing**	**Stable**	**Increasing**
Food Stores	57%	32%	67%	22%
Entertainment	34%	63%	51%	41%
Retail	68%	16%	57%	23%
FIRE	77%	16%	85%	15%
Personal Services	67%	24%	68%	28%
Medical	75%	24%	71%	20%
Office	82%	13%	82%	14%
Arts/Media	59%	31%	82%	15%
Culture	48%	30%	72%	26%
Tourism	59%	36%	78%	21%

that the number of businesses in each category had remained stable over the previous five years, roughly 2007–2012. Some 63 percent of BIAs reported that the number of businesses was stable; however, 29 percent reported increases. Almost one-quarter (23 percent) of the

Figure 7.4 Grand Haven, MI, DDA tourism

DDAs reported that the number of businesses in each category had actually increased.

Declines were reported to have occurred in an average of just seven to eight percent of the districts. The BIAs were more likely to report increases, particularly for entertainment establishments, than the DDAs. Both types of organizations reported declines of more than ten percent in general retail stores. BIAs saw the number of Food Stores and Arts/Media establishments decline by more than ten percent.

Sources of Funding

Table 7.5 indicates the primary funding sources for both types of CDO. Member contributions are a moderate or high source of funding for 88 percent of BIAs. For the DDAs, 69 percent reported that the majority of their funding came from TIF revenue. Over three-quarters of the DDAs indicated that they received no funds from member contributions; none of the BIAs reported TIF revenue. Revenue from other sources, such as operations and grants, was important for only a small proportion of the respondents.

Over the past five years, revenues from most sources have remained stable or increased, particularly for BIAs. Two percent of BIA respondents reported a decrease in income from members and three percent had less grant income. Revenue trends for DDAs are somewhat more negative, with one of every five DDAs reporting a decline in TIF revenue; 5 to 8 percent of respondents indicated declining

Table 7.5 Sources of Funding

	DDA		BIA	
	None	Moderate or High	None	Moderate or High
Members	78%	12%	3%	88%
Operations	30%	5%	32%	11%
Grants	60%	9%	54%	3%
Other*	34%	61%	57%	23%

*For DDA, "Other" includes TIF; for BIA, rental income, parking, and gifts

Figure 7.5 Granby, QC, BIA event

revenues in the other categories. Revenue from operations had the largest increase, 44 and 28 percent for BIAs and DDAs, respectively. The Great Recession of the last decade was more severe in the United States, contributing to the decline in the primary source of revenue for DDAs. Although most DDAs have managed to increase funding from other sources, BIAs appear to be much more aggressive in diversifying their revenue sources.

Primary Activities

Respondents were asked to indicate the level of expenditures that they devoted to six different categories of activities (Table 7.6). The BIAs focused their efforts on three areas: operational costs, events, and area appearance, each of which represented at least one-third of the annual budget for two of every five BIAs. Surprisingly, a substantial portion of the BIAs indicated relatively low levels of spending on public safety and cleanup. When asked how much time they spent on safety issues, however, over one-third of the BIAs indicated that they spent at least a moderate amount of time on this activity. The respondents indicated that over the past five years expenditures in each category had remained stable

Table 7.6 Level of Expenditures by Activity

	Spending as Share of Budget			
BIA	**None**	**Less than 1/3**	**1/3 to 2/3**	**2/3 or more**
Operations	5%	57%	28%	10%
Capital Improvements	35%	50%	14%	2%
Cleanup	29%	64%	6%	2%
Safety	59%	33%	6%	2%
Appearance	3%	51%	39%	8%
Events	4%	44%	36%	16%
DDA				
Operations	16%	62%	17%	5%
Capital Improvements	18%	43%	31%	9%
Cleanup	46%	49%	5%	1%
Safety	75%	22%	2%	1%
Appearance	15%	68%	14%	2%
Events	26%	58%	14%	3%

or increased, with increased spending occurring most frequently on area appearance, events, and capital improvements.

DDAs were likely to spend relatively large proportions of their budget on capital improvements in the district (40 percent of DDAs), followed by operations (22 percent). Area appearance and events were major expenditure items for one of every six DDAs. Three of four DDAs reported no direct spending on public safety; almost half (46 percent) spent nothing on cleanup activities. Although a majority of the DDAs reported that expenditures in each category had been stable or increased over the past five years, DDAs were much more likely than BIAs to report declines in spending. The proportion of DDAs reporting spending declines was in excess of 10 percent for every activity except public safety, a service that relatively few of the respondents provided. More respondents reported decreases than increases in their expenditures on operations, area appearance, and cleanup; the net declines were 11, 10, and 5 percent, respectively.

Figure 7.6 Brantford, ON, BIA safety

Changes in spending levels were rarely associated with formal changes in organizational priorities. DDAs reporting a change in priorities were more likely to increase their spending on area appearance. On the other hand, BIAs that revised their priorities tended to decrease their spending on operation of the organization. None of the other changes in spending has a statistically significant association with changes in priorities.

SELF-ASSESSMENT OF SUCCESS

Respondents were asked to indicate whether they had been successful in achieving their goals and objectives. None of the CDOs reported that they had been completely successful and only eight (two BIAs and six DDAs) indicated that they had had no success at all. Just over half of the BIAs (51 percent) reported moderate success, compared to 43 percent of the DDAs.

In general, there are few attributes that have a significant correlation with this self-assessment of success.[4] There were no significant

---

4. The limited range of responses contributes to the lack of significance.

correlations between success and geographic location (city center or neighborhood), types of businesses, funding sources, staff size, and organizational priorities.

The relatively few items that did produce significant correlations with success are primarily associated with expenditure levels—specifically what were the dominant expenditure categories. The success of DDAs was positively and significantly associated with high levels of spending on capital improvements (r^2 = .201, sig. = .042) and organizational operations (r^2 = .215, sig. = .030). BIA success, on the other hand, was positively and significantly related to expenditures on cleanup (r^2 = .334, sig. = .008) and public safety (r^2 = .354, sig. = .008). In effect, the CDOs were more likely to consider themselves successful if they invested heavily in the primary activities for their organizational type.

The only other significant correlate with success was found in the BIA data. There was a strong negative correlation (r^2 =-.380, sig. = .005) between estimate of success and changes in priority. BIAs were more likely to change their priorities if they did not feel they had been particularly successful.

Effectiveness

When asked to name their most effective activities, the BIAs were most likely to indicate the events that they sponsored (Table 7.7), followed by services to members. Less than five percent of the BIAs indicated effectiveness in providing capital improvements. For the DDAs, appearance improvements and capital improvement projects were their most effective areas. Services to members was another area in which DDAs claimed to be effective.

Ineffectiveness

Commercial development organizations in both countries were most likely to indicate that they were ineffective in providing services to members, with almost half of the respondents in each group listing this as a problem area. Note that for the DDA respondents, member services were highly ranked for both effectiveness and ineffectiveness. DDAs also felt that they were ineffective in capital improvement projects, perhaps

Table 7.7 Effective and Ineffective Activities

	Canada		United States	
Effective	**% of First Responses**	**% of All Responses**	**% of First Responses**	**% of All Responses**
Appearance	16%	18%	37%	30%
Marketing	10%	19%	4%	12%
Capital Projects	3%	4%	24%	22%
Events	54%	36%	14%	14%
Member Services	17%	22%	21%	23%
	Canada		United States	
Ineffective	**% of First Responses**	**% of All Responses**	**% of First Responses**	**% of All Responses**
Appearance	11%	10%	6%	5%
Marketing	9%	10%	13%	10%
Capital Projects	13%	14%	20%	23%
Events	22%	20%	10%	9%
Member Services	44%	48%	51%	53%

their most important activity area. Similarly, for events, BIAs reported that they encountered more problems even though more than half of the respondents indicated it was their primary area of effectiveness.

Obstacles

DDAs and BIAs reported different obstacles to their successful operations (Table 7.8). For BIAs, almost one-third of the respondents indicated that their efforts were hampered by insufficient member participation; lack of adequate funding was the second most frequently mentioned obstacle. In the responses from the DDAs, the ranking of these items were reversed. Twelve percent of the DDAs indicated that the poor performance of the local economy had been an obstacle. The adequacy of available infrastructure was cited as an obstacle by one of every six BIAs.

Table 7.8 Most Frequent Obstacles to Success

	BIAs	DDAs
Funding	22%	35%
Participation	33%	20%
Organizational	9%	11%
Infrastructure	16%	7%
Local Economy	1%	12%

CHANGES IN DISTRICT PRIORITIES

Three out of five DDAs indicated that they have a diverse set of goals; that is, their top five objectives represented five different categories. Almost one-quarter of the respondents indicated that physical improvements were their top priority; in two instances all five of their most important objectives related to physical improvements. Business development, the retention or attraction of businesses to downtown, was the top priority of about 10 percent of DDAs. Improving the appearance of downtown was a priority for five respondents, as were a variety of organizational objectives.

Respondents were asked to write in their top five priorities, in order of importance. The results are summarized in Table 7.9. By far the most common category was the provision of physical improvements, such as street lighting, banners, benches, and other infrastructure improvements. Capital improvement projects were the most commonly mentioned activity in each of the four top categories. Well behind were business development, DDA operations (including finance issues), and events and marketing. Business development was often the number one priority of the DDA; events and marketing were given somewhat lower priority, generally second to fourth. It is interesting to note that very few of the DDAs reported priorities related to quality of life—such as sustainability and safety. When these topics were cited, it was most often at a lower-priority ranking. Thus, in comparison to the forced-choice question about activities the DDA spent revenues on, goals were much more likely to continue to be focused on capital improvements when respondents were allowed to identify their own goals and priorities.

Table 7.9 Priority Objectives of DDAs

	BIA		DDA	
	% of First Responses	**% of All Responses**	**% of First Responses**	**% of All Responses**
Appearance	12%	12%	15%	12%
Business Development	42%	33%	23%	33%
Capital Improvements	10%	16%	31%	16%
Events	7%	10%	1%	10%
Organizational	28%	27%	31%	27%
Quality of Life	1%	2%	0%	2%

Cities, and their commercial districts, may be more resilient to economic crises if they are able to be adaptable to changing economic conditions. Among respondents, BIAs were slightly more likely (63 versus 59 percent) to report that they had revised their priorities in the past five years (Table 7.10). The reasons for these changes, however, differed considerably. DDAs indicated that they had changed their priorities because of changes in the local economy (Table 7.10). This reason was cited much more frequently than any other factor.

On the other hand, BIAs revised their priorities primarily as a result of a board initiative. This result is consistent with the grass-roots nature

Table 7.10 Factors Affecting Changes in Priorities

	BIA		DDA	
	Moderate Effect	**Significant Effect**	**Moderate Effect**	**Significant Effect**
Local Economy	37%	32%	32%	46%
Competition	38%	13%	26%	3%
Membership	30%	19%	17%	7%
Target Market	29%	15%	18%	10%
Board Initiative	40%	41%	37%	27%

of the BIA boards. Other reasons for changing priorities (changing membership, competition) were mentioned much more frequently by BIA respondents than DDA respondents.

SUMMARY

Many of the observed differences between Business Improvement Associations and Downtown Development Authorities are related to their governance structures and their primary funding sources. DDA directors are usually appointed by the municipality that created the DDA. In most instances, not all board members are property or business owners in the district. For those DDAs created for the primary (or sole) purpose of issuing TIF bonds to finance capital improvements, staffing of the DDA often consists of local government officials who manage DDA operations on a part time basis.

While not all DDAs have a significant income stream from the incremental growth in the tax base, most authorities can count on steadily increasing revenues. Even when the DDA's primary function is financing capital improvements with revenue bonds, continued growth of the tax base will generate increasing annual revenues. The surplus over and above the amounts required for bond payments becomes available for other activities. While this revenue source allows DDAs to undertake more ambitious infrastructure projects than BIAs, the funding source is more reliant on the larger economy. Thus, there is a tendency for BIAs to report greater growth (or less loss) of businesses in recessionary times.

Although Business Improvement Areas are also created by local governments, their boards are usually elected by the membership, which includes both property owners and business tenants. The majority of the board members must have an interest in the BIA. The board is responsible for hiring staff, setting the budget, and providing overall policy direction for BIA activities. BIAs are funded by an additional tax levy on property within the district.[5] Because this additional tax must be

---

5. Although the BIA levy is added to the property tax bill, businesses who lease their premises contribute through their rental payments.

approved annually by the membership, BIA budgets are more limited and subject to change from year to year, making bond financed projects more difficult.

Despite these differences, both DDAs and BIAs typically have similar operational profiles. They both undertake marketing campaigns, customer recruiting events, beautification projects, and member services. Public safety is a surprisingly low priority for both types of organizations. Business development activities are a higher priority among BIAs, while capital improvements are the highest priority for DDAs.

A mature DDA may face the "problem" of determining how the available funds should be spent; BIAs must find funds for the projects that they wish to undertake. This difference seems to have contributed to the BIAs' more aggressive attempts to diversify their revenue sources. The BIA boards are also more likely to take the initiative in adjusting their priorities and programs in the face of changing circumstances. The DDAs, on the other hand, seem more cautious, changing mostly in response to changes in the local economy.

It is impossible to say whether Canadian cities' reliance on the BIA as opposed to the DDA form of downtown development authority is better or worse than the comparative US use of DDA. However, the BIA structure appears to give members a greater voice or role in decision making and boards are more responsive to members. Because they do not use TIF revenue, BIAs must diversify their income sources. This limits the types and volume of activities they can perform but appears to make them more resistant to economic downturns and better able to change course when needed.

8

New Urbanism

Part of a broader trend toward the restoration of community and concern for a more sustainable environment, the New Urbanism addresses many of the crucial issues of our time: the decline of America's cities, the rebuilding of its crumbling infrastructure, housing affordability, crime, and traffic congestion.

Katz, 1994

Comprehensive master plans include more than just land use and circulation; they also address planning for the local economy. The primary focus of local economic development strategies has typically been on employment centers—industrial estates, office parks, and city centers. More recently, however, there has been increasing recognition that community prosperity is also a function of the quality of life offered to its residents. The suburban model of the last half of the twentieth century, while still dominant, is no longer universally accepted as the only, or the best, development paradigm. Providing alternative forms, such as densification of urban neighborhoods, transit-oriented development, and the New Urbanism, is seen as essential to attracting and retaining the growing segment of the population that rejects low density, single-use, auto-dependent, post–World War II suburban development.

There are considerable similarities between New Urbanism and creative class economic development strategies. Both advocate creation of a context in which individuals and communities can flourish, rather than a direct focus on jobs or income. New Urbanism advocates more attention to the quality of urban design and physical forms that encourage interpersonal relations. Such an environment will make communities more desirable and more prosperous.

In this chapter, we consider the following questions:

- In what ways does the New Urban development paradigm differ from the suburban model that has prevailed across North America since the 1950s?
- What aspects of the New Urban model are most important to potential residents?
- Can a New Urbanist project be successful if it incorporates only some of the principles of New Urbanism?
- What are the obstacles to the widespread adoption of the New Urbanist model?

The predominant urban form of metropolitan areas throughout North America at the beginning of the twenty-first century is low density and poly-nuclear. Metropolitan areas have become characteristically sub-urban rather than urban. Most of the buildings—the residential subdivisions, shopping centers, offices, and factories—in metropolitan North America have been built within the past fifty years (Jackson, 1985; Rusk 1993; Teaford, 1993). These postwar developments have been shaped by private enterprise working within public planning and development controls (Church et al., 1997; Kuntsler, 1993; Li, 1996). Market forces and formulaic public regulations have contributed to the considerable similarity in the appearance and form of urban areas across North America (Knack, 1989; Sewell, 1993).

The main paradigm in the latter half of the twentieth century for North American suburban development has been influenced by the principles of British Garden Cities, adapted to a society shaped by single-family detached housing and the private automobile (Carver, 1962; Howard, 1965 [1902]). The Garden City model, later widely adopted by the British New Town movement, implied a reduction of densities (at least relative to the prevailing urban standards), a specialization of land uses, and the presence of diverse activities to assure a high degree of self-sufficiency. The model called for a well-defined center and the use of a green belt to demarcate the community.

As applied throughout North America, these planning principles evolved into neighborhoods of single-family homes on large lots, set in curvilinear or cul-de-sac street patterns (Christensen, 1986; Southworth and Ben-Joseph, 1995). Commercial developments, typically located along arterial highways, are separated from the neighborhoods they serve by widening expanses of parking (Kuntsler, 1993). Suburban employment centers—especially office and business parks—are similarly low density, primarily one or two story buildings surrounded by ample, free parking and extensive landscaping.

This suburban development paradigm has been mapped out in the publications of the Urban Land Institute, the Urban Development Institute, and other trade associations, and perpetuated by local zoning codes.[1] The federal and state/provincial governments in both the United States and Canada have also encouraged these development forms through infrastructure funding, mortgage support, and the publication of model ordinances and policy guides (Department of Housing and Urban Development, 2000; Ministry of Municipal Affairs, 1993; NAHB Research Center, 1993; Tomalty, 1997).

The Garden City–based suburban development model has had both positive and negative effects on the urban pattern (Jackson, 1985; Teaford, 1993). The standardization and uniformity of the products facilitated the construction of millions of new homes and tens of millions of square feet of non-residential development in a relatively short time period (Mayer, 1978; Sands, 1982). This form of development is well understood and predictable; both local governments and private developers are comfortable with it. The standardization is also seen as favorable to property values (Carver, 1962; Spurr, 1976).

On the other hand, the suburban model is best suited for automobile-oriented, low-density, and functionally specialized developments; thus,

---

1. See, for example, the Urban Land Institute's *Development Handbook* series (2000-2008), which provides models for residential, multifamily, retail, mixed use, business park and industrial development.

it is wasteful of land, energy, and infrastructure (Kelbaugh, 1999; Kuntsler, 1993). As suburban developments of the 1980s and 1990s became increasingly specialized and low density, their resemblance to the original Garden City prototype diminished. Moreover, as the suburban model supplanted more urban forms of development, many central cities—with their higher densities and limited parking—have fallen out of fashion (Teaford, 1993). Even some older suburbs experienced functional obsolescence long before their physical decay (Orfield, 1998).

In the last decade of the twentieth century, however, attention began to be drawn to models of development that are more urban, not only for central city redevelopment projects, but also for greenfield developments in the suburbs (Berridge Lewinberg Greenberg Ltd., 1991; Sutro, 1990). The New Urbanist town planning movement has been offered as an alternative to the present patterns of sprawling metropolitan growth (Bookout, 1992; Cuomo, 1997; Katz, 1994; Moore and Siskin, 1985). It advocates for greater diversity at the neighborhood level, a de-emphasis on the private automobile, an increased importance of public spaces, and the fostering of a greater sense of community.

Unlike the Garden City model, elements of which quickly spread to mass market development projects, the New Urbanist model has, thus far, continued to be the exception rather than the rule; the number of New Urbanist projects across North America is in the hundreds, mostly medium and small-scale projects (*New Urban Projects*, 2002). Often these developments incorporate only some of the key features of the New Urban paradigm. Such developments may serve a niche market, appealing to a limited, but still important, segment of the total demand. It seems improbable, however, that, forty years from now, the periphery of any North American urban area will be dominated by high-density New Urbanist neighborhoods.

These contrasting planning paradigms bear the mark of the distinct planning periods to which they belong. To understand differences in their respective scope and impact, the two models must be seen within the context of the evolution of planning and urban development over the last fifty years. The post–World War II suburban development model addressed the need for high volumes of new development to erase the deficits of the Great Depression and the war years. It produced a lower density urban form adapted to the automobile and overall rising levels of consumption. The New Urbanist movement is part of a widespread but not universal (Talen, 2001) reaction against postwar suburbanization, especially its car orientation, specialized land use, and low densities. But the entrenchment of the suburban form limits the potential influence of this reaction. The existing low-density suburban configuration limits alternative transportation modes, such as public transit, bicycles, and walking. The high levels of car dependency in many suburbs make it difficult to return to the prewar urban pattern.

Individual values and preferences have also been shaped by the location patterns that are part of the dominant suburban development paradigm. Whatever the merits of the corner store, both habit and economics are likely to favor large car-oriented facilities that can offer wider choice and lower prices. Thus, New Urbanist communities are likely to continue to encounter difficulties in filling street-level retail space. The suburban landscape has evolved around a transportation-land use dynamic that encourages automobile use, low density, and land use specialization.

Both of these development concepts have found expression in the master planned communities in the Greater Toronto Area (GTA), which helped to absorb development pressures (Pressman, 1976). These large master planned communities, covering thousands of acres, allowed for the inclusion of a number of planning innovations, making them "planning show cases." They have had a significant influence on private planners' designs for new development projects and in the public sector's development of new regulations and codes (Bousefield, 1992).

GREATER TORONTO AREA

In 1951, Toronto was the second city in Canada, with a population of some 600,000. Its suburbs, with a population of about the same size, included a dozen local government units, many of which exercised their own planning and development controls (Harris, 1996; White, 2016). Toronto today is one of the five largest cities in North America, with a population of 2.6 million. It is the financial and business leader in Canada, in addition to being the country's leading manufacturing center (Greater Toronto Area Task Force, 1996; Tomalty, 1997; Simmons and McCann, 2000). The metropolitan region (the GTA) has reached a population of 6.1 million as of 2011 and covers about 2,300 square miles.

Strong development controls and the creation of an innovative metropolitan government have been instrumental in accommodating this growth (Sewell, 1993; Tomalty, 1997). Since 1953, the Toronto region has undergone a number of municipal consolidations and government reorganizations, assuring the availability of planning expertise and sufficient financial resources to support development in peripheral localities (Tomalty, 1997). Currently, the City of Toronto and four regional municipalities provide planning and development controls throughout the Toronto metropolitan region. While the need for improved coordination among the regional entities has been suggested, this system has largely been successful in preventing haphazard development (Miller, 1997; Greater Toronto Area Task Force, 1996).

GARDEN CITY PARADIGM

Canadian planning has been influenced by British planning thought and by the British planners who immigrated to Canada, particularly in the periods following the world wars (Carver, 1962; Hodge, 1998; Sewell, 1993). These planning professionals brought with them a development model that emphasized single-family homes, ample green space, segregated land uses, and distinct neighborhoods. Even in large-scale mixed use developments, the separation of land uses was mandated. Canadian planners also sought to accommodate the increasingly popular private automobile (Miller, 1997) by construction of arterial roads and expressways; public transit was also an important component of Toronto's planning (White, 2016).

Early applications of these principles can be seen in the Town of Ajax, to the east of Toronto, and in the Thorncrest Village development in the Town of Etobicoke, west of the city (Barker, 1951; City of Toronto Archives, 1998; Faludi, 1950a, 1950b; White, 2016). The province of Ontario planned the former, while the latter was privately initiated.

Both included home ownership for middle-income households in a low-density, clearly suburban, environment. Curvilinear street patterns set these new neighborhoods off from the nearby older urban areas.

Don Mills

One of the best-known North American examples of a privately master planned new community is Don Mills, located between Eglinton and York Mills roads, just west of the Don Valley Parkway. Begun in 1953, and largely completed by 1960, Don Mills provides a mixture of land uses including residential, commercial, and industrial.[2] Although relatively close to downtown Toronto (less than eight miles), Don Mills has distinct boundaries, formed by ravines, rail lines, and industrial development. The community has a recognizable image, despite being contained wholly within the municipality of North York at its inception (and now as a part of the City of Toronto) (*Don Mills, the Planned Industrial Community*, 1961; *Don Mills: Nearly a New Town*, 1961).

The urban structure of Don Mills is established by its hierarchical circulation system. A boulevarded loop road defines the town center. To improve traffic flow, direct vehicle access to major streets (Lawrence Avenue, Don Mills Road and the loop itself) is limited (Oldham, 1960). No homes face directly on these roads; the number of commercial drives is restricted as well. Residential development along the minor collectors includes semidetached and row house units. Single-family homes are primarily located on loop roads and cul-de-sacs.

Pedestrian circulation is also accommodated in a hierarchical fashion. Major roads, those that are part of the citywide grid as well as the ring road, are provided with wide sidewalks on both sides of the street. Collector roads have a somewhat narrower sidewalk only on one side of the street. Residential streets are not provided with sidewalks, however. Rear lanes are absent and detached garages prohibited (Oldham, 1960). There is a pedestrian path system that runs along the back of some houses, linking them to school sites and recreation areas, as well as to the

---

2. Industrial development continued into the 1960s; a small amount of infill residential development has occurred in recent years.

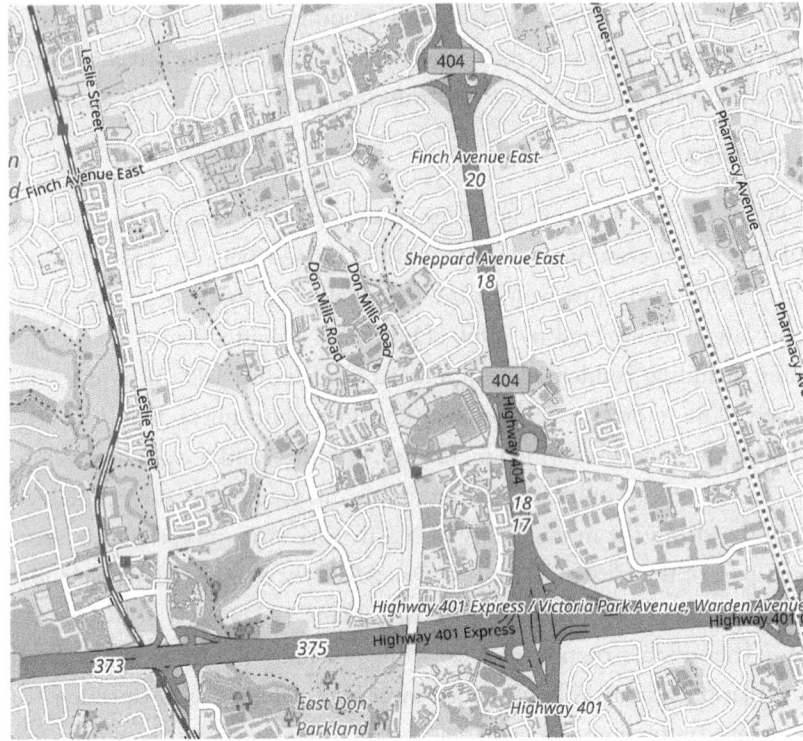

Map 8.1 Don Mills

community center. Grade separations between the paths and major roads
are used to promote pedestrian safety.

The single-family homes are a mixture of bungalows, split-levels, and
two-story units. Lot frontages typically range from 46 to 66 feet; some
lots are 100 feet wide. This was considerably wider than typical frontages
in the nearby north Toronto neighborhoods built in the interwar and
early postwar period, where lot frontages are in the 30 to 35 foot range
(Harris, 1996). The surface of single-family home lots ranges from 5,400
to 12,000 square feet, with most of these approximating 8,000 square
feet. Don Mills includes a much higher proportion of multifamily housing (both rental apartments and condominium units), almost 60 percent
of the total, than was typical of the era (Pressman, 1976). Multifamily
housing is clustered around the core so that there is a clear decline in residential density as one moves away from the core.

The commercial center initially contained 120 stores, including a large super market and a department store, as well as a number of public uses (ice arena, post office, police station, and library). A total of 4,500 parking spaces were provided (*Business Builds a City,* 1954). There is only one other retail commercial area in Don Mills, a small neighborhood plaza intended to serve the relatively isolated northwest part of the community (Oldham, 1960).

The curvilinear street patterns, specialized land uses, the presence of a multi-use center, a readily observed density gradient, an abundance of green space, and efforts to set clear boundaries between Don Mills and surrounding areas warrant the perception of this district as an emanation of the Garden City Model.

Other Communities Planned on the Garden City Model

Don Mills was a model for many of the suburban developments that followed in the 1950s and 1960s (*Don Mills, the Planned Industrial Community,* 1961; Oldham 1960; Sewell 1993). Planning principles showcased in Don Mills—from the non-orthogonal street pattern, through the orientation of houses and their lots to the streets, to the variety of housing types—quickly spread to other suburban developments. Local planning standards were also revised to incorporate these principles, indeed, often making them mandatory rather than innovations. Much larger-scale, privately master planned developments in Brampton and Mississauga were initiated in the late 1950s and the 1960s (Table 8.1). These new communities (planned for populations between 75,000 and 165,000 at build out) incorporated many of the design features of Don Mills, including hierarchical structures for circulation, retail, and residential densities (Bureau of Municipal Research, 1973; Lorimer, 1978). Consistent with the Garden City model, these communities were designed to be largely self-sufficient, with a mixture of housing types (and thus of income groups as well), a full range of retail, and plentiful industrial, service, and office employment.

Master planned communities such as Bramalea, Erin Mills, and Meadowvale differed from Don Mills in a number of important ways, however. They offered a greater variety of land uses, including highway oriented

Table 8.1 Garden City/Suburban Master Planned Communities

	Don Mills	Bramalea	Erin Mills	Meadowvale
First construction	1954	1959	1969	1970
Land area (acres)	2,063	8,191	7,000	2,915
Population targets	27,980	165,500	154,000	75,000
Housing Units	8,121	31,203	NA	21,623
Units/acre	3.9	3.8	NA	7.4

Source: Pressman (1975)

commercial and various forms of affordable housing. Because of their larger size (and the correspondingly longer development period), the original plans for these communities were much less detailed than was the case for Don Mills, anticipating the necessity of adapting to the inevitable market changes. As development costs rose over time, residential densities increased; much of this increase was achieved by the reduction of single-family lot sizes, as opposed to increased proportions of multifamily housing.

NEW URBANIST PARADIGM

Despite changing tastes and market conditions, and the compromises necessitated by increasing development costs, the paradigm for suburban development in the early 1990s differed little from that of the early 1960s. New developments in the Toronto suburbs of Vaughan or Mississauga continued to be more clearly derived from the Don Mills model than from the pre–World War II development in Toronto and its older suburbs.

Two factors converged in the 1990s to advance a new model for suburban development in the GTA. One was the growing concern over low-density sprawl within the metropolitan region, expressed with particular force by the provincial government over the 1985–1995 period (before the laissez-faire oriented Conservative Party assumed power). Over these years, the province compelled suburban regional governments to raise the density of their new developments (see, for example, Ministry of Municipal Affairs and Housing, 1995).

The second factor was the emergence of a clearly articulated alternative development model, the New Urban or Neotraditional town planning concept. As articulated by American architects Andres Duany, Elizabeth Plater-Zyberk, and Peter Calthorpe (Katz, 1994; Kelbaugh, 1999; Kunstler, 1993; Talen, 2005), New Urbanism offered an alternative to suburban sprawl (Sutro, 1990; Brown and Cropper, 2001).[3] New Urbanist planning principles advocate a more urban paradigm, one that reduces reliance on private transportation, raises densities, achieves a more finely grained mixture of land uses, celebrates vernacular architectural styles, and brings greater attention to design quality (Berridge Lewinberg Greenberg Ltd 1991; Bookout, 1992, Talen, 2002).

New Urbanism has been promoted as a model for development that not only looks better but one that also functions better than the typical postwar suburb (Steuteville and Langdon, 2003). Proponents of New Urbanism argue that the physical form of New Urban communities facilitates a higher level of social interaction contributing to a sense of community that is missing from the suburbs where a majority of North Americans live (Katz, 1994). New Urbanism represents a template for building better suburbs, as well as for renewing central cities (Duany, 2000). Such developments have been encouraged by senior levels of government in both Canada and the United States (Ministry of Urban Affairs and Housing, 2006; Department of Housing and Urban Development, 2000).

The New Urban model draws on several diverse themes. Its emphasis on the public realm and the creation of a sense of place (Talen, 2000) addresses the widespread alienation and anomie often seen as prevalent in American suburbs (Oldemberg, 1991; Putnam, 2000; Brindley, 2003). New Urbanism advocates preservation of important elements of the natural and built environment, heritage properties in particular (Congress for the New Urbanism, 2004). The fine-grained mixture of land uses that facilitates non-motorized transportation and public transit supports both health and environmental values (Calthorpe, 1993; Frumkin et al., 2004).

The implementation of the New Urban model has, however, focused on housing and the immediately attendant land uses such as schools and

---

3. A similar claim was made for Don Mills (see Hancock, 1965).

neighborhood-level retail. If in Toronto the Garden City model drew its inspiration from the suburbs and attempted in the 1950s, 1960s, and 1970s to improve on this form, the New Urbanist model looks back to the prewar town or city to design an urban form that breaks from the prevailing suburban pattern. A key tenet of New Urbanism is to make higher densities more palatable for suburbanites.

Cornell

Cornell provides an example of a New Urbanist inspired master planned community. It is located in the town of Markham, a short distance north of the City of Toronto (formerly Metro) boundary. The land for Cornell was originally part of a 1970s Ontario land assembly project (Hertel, 1999; Ministry of Housing, 1974). The site was not developed as planned and in the mid-1990s part of it was eventually made available for private development. The residual of the land assembly (east of Cornell) has been designated as a nature preserve and incorporated in the regional greenbelt, providing a permanent definition of the community along its eastern and southern boundaries. Most of the site was optioned to a single, private owner upon completion of the preliminary planning (Hertel, 1999).[4]

The plan for Cornell called for a new mixed-use community with a target population of about 28,000 persons on a 2,000-acre site. The development guidelines were prepared by Duany/Plater-Zyberk for the province of Ontario (Duany, Plater-Zyberk and Speck, 2000). These standards, with some modifications, were adopted in the Markham Secondary Plan for Cornell (Markham, 1995). Residents are provided with a number of neighborhood-level amenities, including commercial developments, transit stops, and public facilities (parks, plazas, and schools). They are encouraged to walk to these facilities, both by the provision of sidewalks on both sides of all streets and by limitations on off-street parking facilities.

Cornell's road structure differs from that of most other Markham neighborhoods. While the street pattern in the adjacent subdivisions

---

4. Eighty-five percent of the Cornell site is in single ownership. The remaining parcels, held by a small number of property owners, have been incorporated in the Cornell development plan, with the same standards being applied.

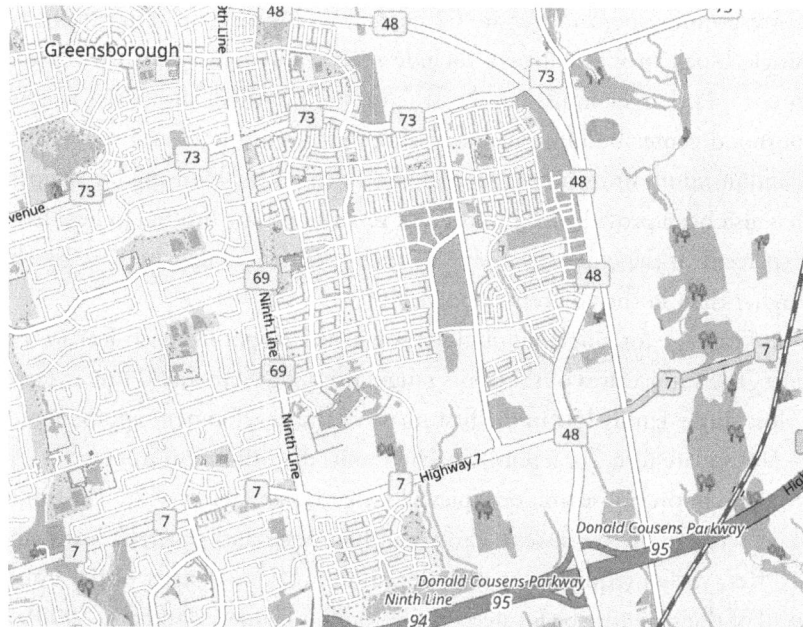

Map 8.2 Cornell

consists primarily of cul-de-sacs and loop roads, Cornell's internal street pattern is rectilinear. Map 8.2 illustrates the differences between the relatively dense, orthogonal streets of Cornell and the more widely spaced, curvilinear streets in the adjacent area of Markham. The first phase of the development included minor collector roads, residential streets, and lanes (Ministry of Municipal Affairs and Housing, 1997). Although street connectivity is an import component of New Urbanist planning, regulations that limit the number and spacing of intersections between arterial roads and local streets have made it difficult to fully integrate Cornell with adjacent areas of Markham.

The first phase of development, consisting of residential and neighborhood commercial uses, was strongly oriented to the street. Front yard setbacks are shallow in the residential areas and, because access to garages is through back lanes, the streetscape presents a continuous building line. As a result, the streetscapes project a strong urban image. Cornell contains a variety of housing types, but single-family detached (47 percent) and row houses (31 percent) predominate; in Markham as a whole, the corresponding percentages are 62 percent and 4 percent, respectively. A single block in Cornell may include several different residential structure types. Larger multi-family structures are limited; the initial neighborhood center building included shops at ground level and residential condominium units on the second and third floors. Housing for seniors has also been provided. Purpose-built rental units are limited to less than 7 percent of the current supply.[5] Cornell's residential densities are much higher than in the adjacent subdivisions.

Frontage for single-family lots in Cornell ranges from 26 feet to 39 feet. The surface area of these lots ranges from 2,900 to 4,800 square feet. Most single-family lots in the first phase of the development approximate 3,500 square feet. For a semi-detached unit, the minimum frontage is 23 feet. Each row house unit occupies a lot that is just 19 feet wide. The front yard setbacks are consistent across building types and generally less than 10 feet, with a requirement that a minimum of one-quarter of the front wall of the structure be located on the "build to" line (Markham, 1995).

Eventually Cornell may provide 375,000 square feet of retail in the central core Main Street area. In addition, approximately 15,000 square feet of retail will be sited in each of several planned neighborhood centers. The initial neighborhood center included a coffee shop, convenience store, chiropractor, dentist, barber/beauty shop, bank, and dry cleaner, along with several unoccupied storefronts. Over time, the neighborhood center has primarily become the location for medical offices. A limited amount of office and commercial services are provided on the collector roads. Off-street parking for commercial uses is limited.

DISCUSSION

Privately master planned communities in the GTA have helped facilitate the rapid growth of the metropolitan area since the mid-1950s by providing an efficient development vehicle. These large-scale projects enabled

---

5. Although the original concept called for rental units to be developed over the detached garages, most owners thus far utilize this space for a home office, or other non-residential use.

local communities, such as Mississauga, to respond to growth pressures much more easily than if the developments had been undertaken piecemeal. The Garden City model master planned communities have also had a significant impact on the planning fashions that have prevailed in residential developments outside these privately planned projects.

The impact of the early privately master planned communities can most clearly be seen in the design of residential areas. Don Mills's approach to minimizing vehicle traffic on residential streets was soon copied by other developers. The Garden City type street layout became so common that the proposed design guidelines for the re-urbanization of Toronto (Berridge Lewinberg Greenberg Ltd., 1991) used the Don Mills street pattern as an example of designs that should be avoided (Bousefield, 1992).

The New Urbanist model, however, has been adopted only sparingly thus far. Two of the touchstones of New Urbanist residential developments, rectilinear street patterns and rear lanes, can be found in some newer suburban developments. With the exception of the Town of Markham, most suburban Toronto municipalities have been slow in changing their development regulations so as to permit, let alone require, that future development conform to the New Urbanist model. Provincial interest in encouraging higher density suburban development has also waned.

Neither paradigm seems to have had much of an impact on models of commercial development. Retail components of these planned communities fall within the well-known categories: regional mall, local mall, neighborhood plazas, and big box stores, with few, if any, innovations in their design. With the exception of the neighborhood center in Cornell, the commercial facilities have limited connectivity to adjacent districts. The Uptown Core development in Oakville, despite its New Urbanist framework, currently offers a retail layout that is consistent with suburban norms and lacking coherence as a focus for the community. The sole observed effort at integrating retail within the texture of a New Urbanist neighborhood—Cornell—is modest, and its economic viability remains uncertain.

There has, however, been a change in retail commercial developments, moving them to a more traditional model. For example, the commercial center of Don Mills was initially an enclosed mall with a department store as an anchor tenant (Figure 8.1). The site was developed

Figure 8.1 Don Mills Shopping Center, 1999

with a jumble of buildings isolated from the community, and each other, by large expanses of parking lot.

The retail development struggled, particularly after the Eaton's department store closed. The center was demolished and in 2009 reopened as an open-air lifestyle center. The Shops at Don Mills no longer have an anchor tenant but now include some seventy high-end retail shops and restaurants. A grid street pattern has been introduced. The large surface parking lots have been replaced by on-street parking in front of the stores and a multilevel parking structure (Figure 8.2). In addition, high-rise residential buildings are being developed within the core. The result is a mixed-use, pedestrian-oriented neighborhood commercial district.

Master planning, whether public or private, inspired by the Garden City or New Urbanist models has had only limited success in effectively integrating land uses. While *suburban activity centers* and *village centers* have become standard items in the planners' tool kit (Chapin and Kaiser, 1979), their physical manifestations seldom achieve the coherence and mixture of uses suggested by planning documents. Land use within master planned communities remains functionally specialized, perhaps as much as in other suburban areas.

Figure 8.2 Shops at Don Mills 2016

The planning principles embodied by Cornell and some of the other master planned communities of the late 1990s do, however, represent a potentially important departure from general suburban development patterns. Cornell has a much different look and feel. Even the most casual observer will note the differences: higher densities, a much more intimate ambiance, more finely grained land uses, and more formal design elements. While these physical features are intended to foster certain social values such as neighborliness and a strong sense of community, it is too difficult to judge whether the development will be effective in this regard.

Similarities and differences between the Garden City and the New Urbanist paradigms are highlighted in Tables 8.2 and 8.3, which compare objectives and attributes of Don Mills and Cornell. Table 8.2 shows that the size, number of neighborhoods, and population projection of the two districts are broadly similar. Like Don Mills forty-five years earlier, Cornell has been developed at the edge of the urbanized perimeter, and the two areas are, in part, shaped by surrounding greenbelts. Both districts benefited from single land ownership at the onset of their development. Strict development controls—provided by the developer in the case of Don Mills and by the tailor-made zoning bylaws in the case of

Table 8.2 Comparison of Don Mills and Cornell: Similarities

	Don Mills	Cornell
Acreage, gross	2,058	2,421
Acreage, net	1,704	1,544
Relation to urban area	Adjacent	Adjacent
Greenbelt	Yes	Yes
Population projection	27,980	27,300
Number of neighborhoods	5	4
Innovative street pattern	Yes	Yes
Architectural controls	Yes	Yes
Major shopping center	Yes	Yes (proposed)
Single land ownership	Yes	Yes
Expressway access	Yes	Yes

Sources: Pressman, 1976; Law Development, 1998.

Cornell—are integral to both communities. Both areas post (or posted) innovative street patterning: Don Mills was one of the first large-scale developments to adopt a curvilinear pattern and Cornell is one of a very few recent suburban districts to opt for a rectilinear street pattern with rear lanes. Finally, the two areas benefit from present or anticipated expressway access.

As indicated in Table 8.3, there are also considerable differences between the two, which in large part mirror the differences between the Garden City and New Urbanist models. As expected, the street patterns of the two neighborhoods differ considerably. In Cornell, comfortable walking distances serve to determine the location of facilities. Front setbacks require buildings to be close to sidewalks, fostering a reassuring sense of enclosure for pedestrians. In contrast, in Don Mills setbacks are both deep and varied; indeed, sidewalks are not provided in cul-de-sacs in this community and sidewalks are provided on only one side of many of the streets.

Whereas in Don Mills relatively high densities result from a high proportion of multi-family dwellings, Cornell relies on narrow lot frontages to achieve a similar result. There is much more architectural convergence in Cornell, where all buildings adopt historical styles and must be sanctioned

Table 8.3 Comparison of Don Mills and Cornell: Differences

	Don Mills	Cornell
Inspiration	Better organized suburb with specialized land use	Mixed residential, traditional style architecture
Street Pattern	Curvilinear, discontinuous	Orthogonal
Road Widths	Arterials 77 feet Boulevard 56 feet Residential 28	Boulevard 49 feet Collector 36 feet Residential 28 feet Lanes 16.5–19.5 feet
Pedestrian Environment	Sidewalks, paths	Sidewalks
Single family lot sizes	5,400 to 12,000 square feet	2,900 to 4,800 square feet
Front setback	16 feet	5–7 feet
Schools	8	12 (proposed)
Community centers	1	3 (proposed)
Neighborhood commercial centers	1	4 (proposed)
Build out time	8 years from 1953	20 years from 1995

Sources: Pressman, 1976; Law Development, 1998.

by a control architect. In contrast, the reliance on a large number of builders in Don Mills was motivated by a desire to assure architectural diversity.

The New Urbanist neighborhoods in Cornell have been successful in the market (Hertel, 1999). This acceptance may be attributed to a number of factors in addition to the merits of the planning principles. The property market in the Toronto area has been extremely strong, particularly for single-family homes. A new home in Cornell is seen as offering relatively good value for the money; the average home price of $631,000 in Cornell is $137,000 less than the average of $768,000 for all homes in Markham (Toronto Real Estate Board, 2015).

Despite the market acceptance of Cornell, it seems unlikely, however, that the New Urbanist development model will supplant the prevailing form of suburban development. This conclusion reflects the concerns of the diverse participants in the development process:

- Developers and residential builders in the GTA, as elsewhere, appear to have only a limited commitment to the canons of New Urbanism (McDougall, 2000; Bookout, 1992). Building costs in New Urbanist neighborhoods are reported to be higher because of the tight sites, requirements for lanes and detached garages, as well as the more demanding utility and street standards. Alternate forms of development, such as wide/shallow lots, are capable of providing similar densities at lower cost and thus continue to be favored by some developers.
- Developers also question the long-term viability of the neighborhood level amenities, including both civic and neighborhood commercial facilities; thus important components of the New Urbanist model seem questionable. As has been the case with earlier efforts to implement the neighborhood unit model articulated by Clarence Perry, modern lifestyles will likely prove to be at odds with the more limited options that can be offered within walking distance of one's home. While great admiration may be expressed for corner stores and neighborhood main street retail, economic realities suggest that required sales volumes will be difficult to sustain.
- Provincial and state governments in both Canada and the United States have embraced many aspects of the New Urbanist model (Fulton, 1996; Lee, 2000; Weissman, 2000). A number of state legislatures in the United States have adopted enabling legislation that permits New Urbanist developments, but only if approved by local governments (Burchell, Listokin, and Calley, 2000). Some elements of "Smart Growth" legislation are similar to the principles of New Urbanism (Nationwide Overhaul of Land Use Laws, 2001).
- Only a small proportion of the Toronto-area municipalities appear to be fully committed to the New Urban model. The Town of Markham is a leader in its commitment to some of the concepts of New Urbanist planning. Local officials there, however, are also willing to consider hybrid and alternate development forms to

achieve the desired densities (Markham, n.d.). A prerequisite to the spread of New Urbanist developments is the adoption of new forms of development controls, which thus far has not occurred (Bousefield, 1992; Weissman, 2000).

- Obstacles also exist within the financial community (Gyourko and Rybczynski, 2000; Leinberger and Davis, 1999). The scale and complexity of many New Urbanist developments creates the perception of risk, or at least uncertainty, in the minds of lenders. Despite the track record of market acceptance of the existing New Urbanist developments, lenders and investors remain skeptical of the viability of such key elements as higher residential densities, mixed-use structures and integral neighborhood commercial.

- Despite survey research that indicates favorable public attitudes toward the principles of New Urbanism (Talen, 2001), the demand for Cornell and other New Urbanist communities may be confined to niche markets. New Urban developments seem to be most successful when they represent only a small proportion of a large and vigorous market. The development pace in Cornell has, in fact, been much slower than that of Don Mills four decades earlier.

- A key feature of New Urban developments is a reduced emphasis on automobiles. Moving garages to rear lanes, reducing off-street public parking, and more finely grained land uses are some of the more visible manifestations of this objective. Yet North Americans value the freedom, flexibility, and choice offered by private transportation, and disdain long walks from a remote parking lot, let alone to the store. In areas where public transit is minimal, it will be difficult to realize the New Urban ideal of a circulation system that does not rely heavily on the automobile.

RESIDENT SATISFACTION IN NEW URBAN COMMUNITIES

Opinion surveys and market research suggest that a substantial proportion of the North American population would actually prefer to live in a community with the characteristics of a New Urban Development (Katz,

1994; Morrow-Jones et al., 2005). Despite expressed preferences for (or at least interest in) many of the ideals of New Urbanism, the suburban model continues to dominate. In part, this is the result of municipal development regulations that make it difficult, if not impossible, to develop communities that follow the principles of New Urbanism (Gyourko and Rybczynski, 2000; Levine, 1998). Few developers are willing to invest the time and money to make changes in local development regulations necessary to accommodate New Urban developments.

Many local governments, however, have been reticent to fully embrace the New Urbanist concepts. Partly in response to market pressures, development regulations have evolved to eliminate alleys (lanes), sidewalks, and other requirements that add to housing development costs and ongoing public maintenance costs. The cooperation of other public agencies is often difficult to attain. Independent school authorities may be reluctant to build additional schools, let alone ones that are consistent with New Urban design criteria. Public transit operators cannot provide extensive and frequent service to New Urban communities until economic standards can be met, with the result that the initial residents must rely on automobiles. The fire department wants wider streets for its equipment. Finally, the traffic engineers are skeptical of a restricted road hierarchy since the area does not fit into a surrounding pattern of grid streets.

This skepticism is not limited to the public sector. Landowners generally have only limited interest in cutting edge planning innovations if their adoption means slower sales; they are more likely to be concerned with obtaining a rapid and substantial return on their investment. While not necessarily opposed to the New Urbanist concepts of building place and community, they simply prefer developments that have the broadest market appeal. Much the same is true of the homebuilders.

Although plans may have impeccable New Urbanist credentials, in the course of implementation, developments may become "hybrids"; while some New Urbanist concepts remain, others may be seriously compromised. How do residents of New Urban developments in Canada assess the reality of living in a community that incorporates New Urban ideals? Households residing in communities with New Urban characteristics have already accepted community density. Their attitudes toward other aspects of the development may assist local policy makers and developers in designing both development regulations and specific projects.

Case Studies

In the balance of this chapter, we consider how satisfied residents of New Urban developments are with their housing choice. Bois Franc is located in Ville St-Laurent, a Montreal suburb; Cornell, as noted, is in Markham, on the fringe of the city of Toronto. The two case study communities are described in more detail below.

Bois Franc, St-Laurent Quebec. Bois Franc is a large infill development in the borough of St-Laurent, well within the perimeter of the Montreal Urban Community, less than eight miles (thirteen kilometers) from the Montreal city center (Map 8.3). The site is a former airfield being developed by the real estate arm of the Bombardier Company, a large industrial firm. Plans for the site include light industrial and warehouse uses oriented toward the nearby airport, a commercial area, and an eighteen-hole championship golf course along with about 8,000 residential units (Duany, Plater-Zyberk and Speck, 2000). Open space, including the golf course and water features, will occupy about one-sixth of the site.

Most of the planned residential development consists of multifamily housing, including owner-occupied garden apartments and row houses; the proportion of rental apartments, currently about 12 percent, is well below the city-wide average of 64 percent. About 30 percent of the planned housing units were completed in the first dozen years after the project began in 1994 (Bois Franc, 2006). In 2011, just over 4,600 housing units had been completed in Bois Franc, predominantly row houses (38 percent) and low-rise apartments (36 percent). Both of these figures are well above the corresponding averages of 3 percent and 27 percent for the city of Montreal. Single-family detached units comprise 15 percent of the Bois Franc units.

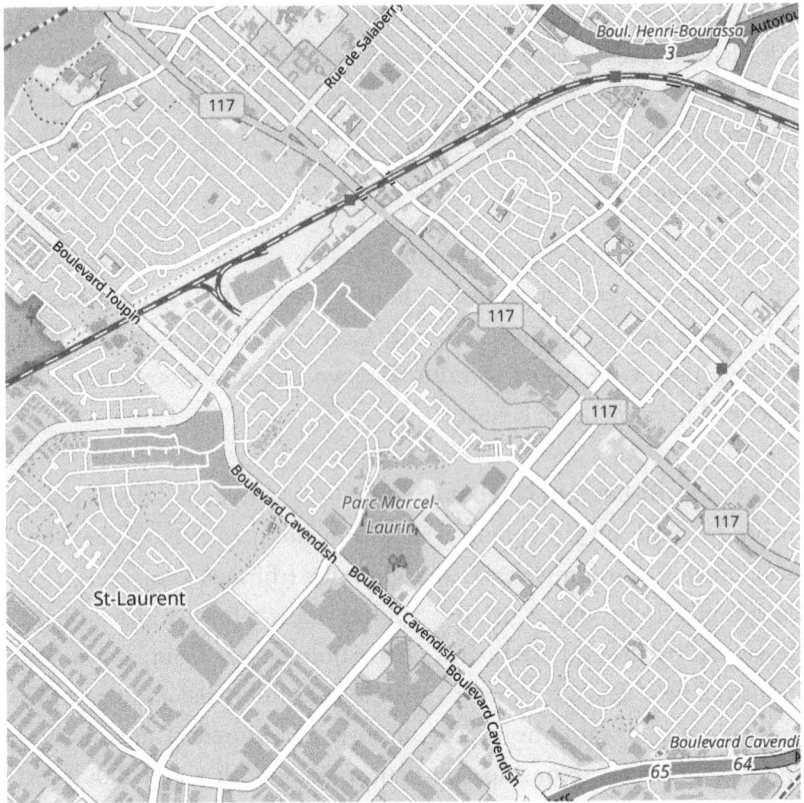

Map 8.3 Bois Franc

Bois Franc is distinct from the overall city and the Montreal CMA in several respects (Table 8.4). Its residents are less likely to be elderly but more likely to be a member of a visible minority or hold a university degree. Bois Franc households are larger and more likely to have children at home than either Montreal as a whole or Montreal CMA. The average household income in Bois Franc is double that of the city of Montreal. Bois Franc has a much higher homeownership rate than the larger areas; home values are about 35 percent above the city and metropolitan averages. Ten years earlier the household income and home values in Bois Franc were closer to those of Montreal as a whole and the metropolitan area as well.

Table 8.4 Community Characteristics, 2011

	Bois Franc	Montreal	Montreal CMA	Cornell	Markham	Toronto CMA
Population	12,377	1,649,519	3,824,221	11,968	301,790	5,583,014
Aged 65+	9%	12%	15%	4%	10%	13%
Visible Minorities	35%	31%	20%	69%	72%	47%
University Degree	58%	28%	24%	34%	33%	30%
Households	4,617	759,946	1,613,260	3,548	90,534	1,989,705
Average HH Size	2.68	2.17	2.37	3.37	3.33	2.81
HH with children	50%	38%	39%	67%	66%	51%
Average HH Income	$126,400	$57,700	$70,300	$100,600	$109,000	$95,300
Homeowners	88%	36%	55%	93%	89%	68%
Average Home Value	$503,300	$373,500	$320,700	$452,200	$547,600	$495,400

Source: Statistics Canada, 2011

Figure 8.3 Bois Franc streetscapes

Bois Franc has been developed in a local housing market that has experienced relatively slow growth in recent years. New housing starts within the Montreal Urban Community average about 12,000 units a year and have been dominated by multifamily housing; high-rise condominiums in the city center and attached housing developments on infill parcels predominate. Most of the new single-family development currently being built is located far from the core.

Cornell, Markham, Ontario. Cornell Village is located in the city of Markham, about 16 miles (27 kilometers) northeast of downtown Toronto. Markham has experienced rapid growth in its (predominantly single-family) housing stock, as well as its employment base and commercial development. A number of technology firms have located their headquarters in Markham, providing the basis for Markham's designation as the high-tech capital of Canada. Household incomes in Markham are above the metropolitan average. Most households have children living at home and average household size is well above the mean for Toronto.

From a population of 56,000 in 1976, Markham grew to 154,000 residents in 1991, and then doubled its population to 302,000 in 2011. An additional 40,000 people have moved to Markham since the 2011 census. This sustained high growth prompted the adoption of development regulations that would ensure contiguous development and that followed the New Urban principles of higher density, mixed uses, alternate modes of transit, and high-quality design standards (Carlson, 2006). The intent was to slow land development and reduce infrastructure costs by encouraging more compact developments, while still preserving a high quality of life for residents (see also Valpy, 2007). Markham is the site of a number of residential developments that follow New Urban criteria (Skaburskis, 2006). Cornell is one of the largest of these and perhaps the most consciously New Urban.

The original design by Duany/Plater-Zyberk has been modified somewhat to meet local standards but maintains a structure in which each neighborhood offers a variety of land uses and housing types (Markham, 1995). The developers have sought to ensure that neighborhood commercial facilities, schools, and recreational amenities are built concurrently with increases in the residential stock in each neighborhood. The street pattern is orthogonal with a clear hierarchy; wider collector roads are used to define the neighborhoods. Much of the development in Cornell consists of single-family homes, with duplexes and row houses mixed in; some collector streets offer residential units over storefronts.

Figure 8.4 Cornell streetscapes

Cornell's residential densities are only slightly higher than in other parts of Markham; the use of detached garages accessed by rear lanes substantially changes the streetscape, however (Skaburskis, 2006).

Overall, the profile of Cornell residents is similar to that of Markham as a whole, but differs considerably from that of the Toronto metropolitan area (see Table 8.4). Cornell includes higher proportions of both university graduates and visible minorities than the rest of Markham. Average household size is also higher in Cornell, with households considerably more likely to include children. Average household income is slightly less than that of Markham but somewhat above the metropolitan figure. Home values are less than the Markham-wide average and noticeably below the Toronto CMA average.

Resident Survey

A mail survey was sent to a systematic sample of residents of these two New Urban communities in 2003 to assess their preferences and levels of satisfaction with their neighborhood. The survey was prepared in both French and English and mailed to a total of about 250 addresses. Recipients were asked to complete the survey and return it in a postage-paid envelope. One reminder postcard was sent. The resulting response rate was about 30 percent overall. The number of responses from Bois Franc residents was slightly higher than from Cornell residents.

Recipients were first asked a series of questions about the relative importance of home and neighborhood features. A five-point scale ranging from Very Important to Not Very Important was used for each measure. The list included general considerations (home size and price), as well as questions about distinctively New Urban attributes, such as pedestrian friendliness of the environment, diversity of housing, community facilities, and design features.

Ninety percent of the respondents had occupied their home for at least eighteen months. The survey asked them to indicate their satisfaction level (again, on a five-point scale) with a list of specific home and neighborhood attributes. Respondents also rated their house and neighborhood on a ten-point scale. In addition to household demographic data, the survey asked for information on whether they had looked anywhere else before buying their current house.

The characteristics of the survey respondents are summarized in Table 8.5. There are few significant differences between the Bois Franc and Cornell samples. They are comparable with respect to average household size and proportion of households with children. Respondents in both

Table 8.5 Profile of Respondents

	Bois Franc	Cornell	Sig.
Average Household Size	3.13	3.14	.962
Households with Children	57%	58%	.659
Head Age 45+	33%	50%	.391
University Degree	55%	80%	.012
Professional Occupation	85%	84%	.892

N=81

locations were equally likely to work in a professional occupation. Bois Franc respondents were somewhat younger, with only about one-third of the householders over the age of forty-five, compared to over half in the Cornell sample; the difference is not statistically significant, however. The only significant difference is the proportion of householders with a university degree, with a much higher proportion of Cornell respondents in this category. All of the respondents were homeowners; both developments had only limited rental housing available at the time of the survey.

Over 90 percent of respondents were the first occupants of their unit and had lived in their home for an average of about four years. More than 80 percent of the households in both samples reported that they had looked at other housing before deciding to purchase their current home. About half of the Bois Franc households shopped for homes in other St-Laurent neighborhoods or other municipalities. Three-quarters of the Cornell respondents had looked at homes in other Markham neighborhoods, while just one-third had shopped in other municipalities.

Respondents were asked to rank on a scale of one (not very important) to five (very important) the relative importance of some twenty attributes of their current housing unit and neighborhood. The attributes with the highest rankings for each sample are listed in Table 8.6. Neighborhood appearance received the highest ratings of any attribute in Bois Franc and was the second most important in the Cornell sample. Housing cost was the highest ranked feature for Cornell residents, significantly higher than in Bois Franc. Several other highly ranked attributes relate to elements of the public realm. Again, few of these differences are statistically

Table 8.6 Important Features of Home and Neighborhood

	Bois Franc	Cornell	Sig.
Neighborhood Appearance	4.58	4.42	.355
Home Cost	4.33	4.61	.067
Housing Styles	4.15	4.08	.735
Size of Home	4.20	3.97	.229
Sidewalks	4.03	4.14	.588
Landscaping	4.05	4.00	.821
Friendly Neighbors	3.60	4.47	.000
Live in Neighborhood	3.63	4.22	.002

N=81

significant. Cornell residents, however, were more likely to consider New Urban touchstones, such as friendly neighbors and living in a neighborhood, to be among the most important considerations.

An exploratory factor analysis was used to reduce the twenty variables to six factors, which together explained over 68 percent of the variance in housing preferences (Appendix B). Four of the resulting factors (diversity, public realm, child friendly, and accessibility) describe attributes of the neighborhood. The other two factors include characteristics of the individual dwelling. Size and cost of the dwelling unit composed one factor; the other included the front and rear yard sizes.

The average importance index scores were calculated by averaging the ratings of individual attributes; the resulting scale ranges from one (least important) to five (most important) (see Table 8.7). Overall, housing unit characteristics (size and price) were most important, while the yard size was the least important. The public realm factor—which includes neighborhood appearance, housing styles, housing variety, landscaping, and traffic—received the next highest ranking, followed by the child friendly factor (recreation, schools, playgrounds, and sidewalks). With the exception of the diversity factor (housing type and housing price variety, living in a neighborhood, friendly neighbors), which was more important to Cornell residents, there is no significant difference between the average scores for the Bois Franc and Cornell respondents.

Table 8.7 Importance Factor Average Scores

Factor	Bois Franc	Cornell	Sig.
Diversity	3.22	3.87	.000
Public Realm	3.78	3.95	.249
Child Friendly	3.70	3.69	.310
Accessibility	3.04	3.09	.809
House	4.26	4.29	.477
Yard	2.50	2.26	.477

N=81

In addition to ranking the importance of these housing and neighborhood characteristics, respondents were asked to indicate their preferences for three specific neighborhood characteristics:

- a mix of single-family and multifamily housing, or all single family homes
- a mix of housing and commercial uses, or only housing
- small home sites with abundant community spaces throughout the neighborhood, rather than large lots and limited public green space

Preferences for a mix of housing types and land uses, along with small lots with shared green spaces, reflect New Urban characteristics.

Bois Franc respondents indicated a preference for a neighborhood with only single-family housing and no commercial activities (Table 8.8). They also favored large lots over small lots and community parks. These expressed preferences not only differ from New Urbanist ideals, but they also differ from the community in which the respondents had actually purchased their homes. At the time of the survey, Bois Franc consisted primarily of multifamily housing (with some single-family homes on small lots) and lacked retail facilities within its boundaries.

Cornell residents, on the other hand, moved to a development that was much more consistent with their preferences, one clearly more representative of New Urban ideals. Between two-thirds and three-quarters of

Table 8.8 Preference for New Urban Attributes

	Bois Franc	Cornell	Sig.
Single/Multi Family Mix	39%	67%	.021
Residential/Commercial Mix	30%	75%	.000
Small Lots, Common Green Space	15%	36%	.089

N=80

the Cornell survey respondents indicated a preference for mixed housing types and land uses within their neighborhood. These results are significantly different than the Bois Franc responses. A majority of Cornell respondents favored larger individual lots, rather than small lots and common green space, even though their neighborhood actually offered small lots and community green spaces. The difference between the two subsamples on this question is significant only at the .10 level.

For the Bois Franc respondents, the incongruity between their expressed preferences for conventional suburban development and their actual housing choice may be related to local housing market conditions. In the Montreal metropolitan area, it is difficult to find ground-oriented, new, homes in close proximity to the city center. New residential construction close to the Montreal city center has been in multifamily, mid-to high-rise structures. Cornell respondents, on the other hand, had a range of housing choices available to them in the town of Markham. Some of these other new home choices provided similar lot sizes but with front garages.

Satisfaction Measures

Respondents were asked to rate their satisfaction with a list of specific attributes of their new home and neighborhood (Table 8.9). Neighborhood appearance received the highest average satisfaction rating, ranking first in Cornell and second in Bois Franc. Walkability was the top ranked attribute among Bois Franc residents. With this one exception, Cornell residents gave higher average ratings to each of the attributes than did the Bois Franc residents. For most (nine of fourteen) items, the difference between mean scores is statistically significant. Bois Franc residents were

CHAPTER 8

Table 8.9 House and Neighborhood Satisfaction Ratings

	Bois Franc	Cornell	Sig.
House Size	3.03	3.40	.049
Yard	2.61	2.90	.269
Neighborhood Appearance	3.33	3.75	.003
Parks	2.89	3.52	.011
Privacy	2.81	3.38	.009
Open Space	2.78	3.15	.103
Trails	1.72	2.67	.002
Shopping	2.05	2.87	.001
Schools	2.86	2.90	.886
Parking	2.11	2.93	.005
Congestion	2.50	3.13	.005
Public Transit	2.58	2.65	.769
Vehicle Traffic	2.50	3.16	.002
Walkability	3.50	3.28	.181

N=80

least satisfied with trails, not surprising since these were not part of the development at the time of the survey. They also were significantly less satisfied with the attributes related to automobiles (traffic, parking, congestion); parking problems in particular became a major issue (CBC, 2004).

A factor analysis of these responses produced five factors, which together explained just over 70 percent of the variation in neighborhood satisfaction (see Appendix B.). Each of the variables loaded on one of the factors, with the exception of public transportation, which did not load significantly on any factor. For Cornell respondents, satisfaction ratings are highest for urban design and walkability factors, both important New Urban touchstones (Table 8.10). Bois Franc residents reported lower satisfaction levels for all factors, with the exception of the walkability factor, which had the highest overall rating for Bois Franc residents. The differences are significant for the urban design, traffic, and accessibility factors.

Differences between the two samples with respect to the respondents' satisfaction with urban design and traffic were highly significant. There

Table 8.10 Satisfaction Factors

	Bois Franc	Cornell	Sig.
Urban Design	2.66	3.27	.000
Traffic	2.42	2.96	.000
Access	2.44	2.78	.042
Walkability	3.50	3.28	.181
Own House	2.82	3.15	.107

N=81

is a significant difference in the access factor scores as well. In all three instances, the Cornell residents expressed a higher degree of satisfaction. Because parking is included in the traffic factor, the lower satisfaction levels in Bois Franc are not unanticipated (CBC, 2004).

Respondents also provided a summary evaluation of both their new home and neighborhood, on a scale of one to ten, with ten being the most favorable rating. Most respondents appear to be quite satisfied with their houses. Less than 20 percent of all respondents gave their dwelling a rating score lower than eight. Cornell residents were somewhat more likely to provide higher ratings for their homes, but the difference is not significant (p=.957).

Respondents were even more positive about their new neighborhood. Over 92 percent of all responses indicated a level of satisfaction of eight or higher. Bois Franc respondents reported the same level of neighborhood satisfaction as did the Cornell sample, about 8.5 in both instances. Residents of both Bois Franc and Cornell generally expressed greater satisfaction with their neighborhood than with their house,

The summary satisfaction rating was regressed against the satisfaction measures to identify the elements making the largest contributions to the overall satisfaction level. A stepwise regression that included the individual neighborhood satisfaction measures, demographic data, and New Urban preferences was used. The summary measure of satisfaction with the respondent's house was also included, but not the individual variables related to house or yard. The regression results for all respondents and for the two sub-samples explain more than half of the variance

Table 8.11 Neighborhood Satisfaction Rating: Regression Results

		Standardized Beta	t	Sig.
All Responses	Constant		12.957	.000
	Parks	.270	2.956	.005
	Walkability	.371	4.540	.000
	Trails	.228	2.387	.021
	Parking	.335	3.777	.000
	Vehicle Traffic	-.319	-3.343	.002
	Public Transportation	.282	3.243	.002
	House Rating	.215	2.511	.015
Bois Franc	Constant		5.094	.000
	Parks	.432	3.220	.003
	House Rating	.348	2.590	.016
	Shopping	.263	2.132	.043
Cornell	Constant		19.510	.000
	Trails	.707	4.994	.000
	Public Transit	.598	4.262	.000
	Walkability	.519	3.362	.001
	Small Lot Preference	-.330	-2.298	.031

in the overall neighborhood rating (Table 8.11; see also Appendix B). Each of the variables in Table 8.11 was significant (p=.05); they are listed in the order in which they entered the regression equation. None of the demographic measures made a significant contribution; nor did either of the other two preferences for New Urban features such as mixed land use and mixed housing structure types.

For the combined sub-samples, the top three attributes relate to aspects of community green space, suggesting that residents do make an implicit trade-off between public and private outdoor space. The next three attributes relate to transportation. Finally, being satisfied with one's own home helped to explain neighborhood level satisfaction.

The regression analyses for the two subsamples identified shorter lists of statistically significant explanatory variables. It is interesting to

Table 8.12 Correlations between Importance and Satisfaction Ratings

	Correlation	sig.
Neighborhood Appearance	.180	.115
Community Open Space	.090	.434
Playgrounds	.112	.330
Jogging/Bike Trails	-.086	.458
Shopping	-.030	.797
Schools	-.094	.412
Vehicle Traffic	.152	.184
Public Transit	-.036	.754

note that, although most of the significant variables in the individual regression equations are also significant in the pooled analysis, there is no overlap between the significant variables in the two subsamples. The Bois Franc regression introduces a significant variable, access to shopping, which was not significant in the regression using the combined data. Although there were no on-site commercial developments in Bois Franc at the time of the survey, it would seem that Bois Franc residents were satisfied with their access to a variety of shopping opportunities in close proximity to their homes (but not actually in the development). For Cornell residents, preference for smaller lots with community green space was negatively related to neighborhood satisfaction.

Finally, Table 8.12 reports the correlations between the neighborhood attributes that respondents considered to be important when looking for a new home and their reported satisfaction with the same measures in their current neighborhood. The correlations are low and neighborhood appearance approaches statistical significance. About half of the measures yielded negative correlations, indicating that higher importance ratings were associated with relatively low satisfaction ratings.

DISCUSSION

Like most previous surveys of New Urban developments, these results confirm that residents of New Urban developments are generally quite satisfied with their housing and neighborhood choice. This is the case whether the traditional neighborhood development is a unique offering in the local market (Bois Franc) or is one of many choices of both conventional and New Urban subdivisions (Cornell). Survey respondents were at least as pleased with their neighborhoods as they were with their homes.

Respondents indicated that they attached considerable importance to some of the neighborhood characteristics that are the touchstones of New Urbanism—variety in housing types, a pedestrian friendly environment, and accessibility to commercial facilities. This is an expected result since the respondents are a subset of the general population that, usually after some comparison-shopping, also elected to move to a development that incorporates many of these features. It would indeed be surprising if respondents did not attach importance to these attributes.

These New Urban community residents also expressed high levels of satisfaction with their new neighborhood. After an average length of residence of four years, respondents should be in a good position to meaningfully evaluate whether their new neighborhoods were adequate in meeting their preferences. Although Cornell residents generally report higher levels of satisfaction, the differences are not significant in most instances. Bois Franc residents reported lower levels of satisfaction with neighborhood appearance, open space, and attributes related to vehicle traffic, parking, and congestion.

The lack of differences is noteworthy because the two developments differ considerably in their faithfulness to New Urban principles. Bois Franc is much more of a New Urban "hybrid" than Cornell, offering less variety in terms of housing price and structure type, limited commercial facilities, a relatively low proportion of green space (not all of which is public), and an almost total lack of public buildings within the community.

Cornell, on the other hand, is quite self-consciously New Urban and clear efforts have been made to ensure that New Urban criteria are maintained. Most of the housing there consists of single-family homes and row houses, both of which directly relate to the street and the public realm. Land uses are mixed on the neighborhood level and the development of public buildings and open space is coordinated with the residential development.

These results suggest that developers need not provide all of the New Urban elements to have a successful project. Limited availability of public transportation and jogging trails, for example, seem to have little effect on overall levels of satisfaction. Provision of neighborhood shops and cafés concurrently with the initial residential development, as in Cornell, is expensive and difficult to sustain. Bois Franc residents were just as satisfied with their neighborhood, even though these features were not available within the development at the time of the survey.

It is likely that residents of the two developments viewed the availability of neighborhood commercial opportunities differently. Although commercial facilities were available in Cornell, they were quite limited and were unlikely to meet the needs of residents. Since outside commercial facilities in the vicinity of Cornell are limited, Cornell residents faced less than optimal commercial options. Even though initially Bois Franc lacked commercial development, residents there had ample options available in the surrounding neighborhoods. Thus, they were able to meet their commercial needs more easily.

The lessons for local policy makers are similar—mandating the principles of New Urbanism is not the only way to provide an alternative to the typical suburban development paradigm. Models that depart from the strict canons of New Urbanism may be successful, so long as they provide high quality urban design, an attractive public realm, and walkable neighborhoods. Some of the public's apparent aversion to small lots, for example, can be mitigated by careful attention to neighborhood appearance and a pedestrian friendly environment. Indeed, walkability and open space appear to be related to economic prosperity (Peach and Petach, 2016), suggesting that even a modest application of New Urbanist residential design can contribute to the economic sustainability of the larger community.

9

Casino Gambling

Many states legalized gambling in the early 1990s with the hope that casinos would create jobs, attract tourist spending, increase state tax revenues, and revitalize local economies.

Walker, 1999

The prosperity of midsize cities is often limited by circumstances. By definition, their size means that they provide a relatively small market for goods and services. Moreover, they may only offer a limited labor pool, especially the highly specialized and skilled talent necessary to attract new businesses. The location of some midsize cities was often determined by the availability of natural resources and thus may not be well suited as a location of New Economy enterprises. Because of these limitations, there is a tendency for midsize cities to pursue economic development strategies that are borrowed from other places, whether or not they are actually an appropriate choice for the new location. This chapter considers one of these borrowed strategies, casino gambling.

Today there are almost 1,900 gambling locations in the United States and Canada, ranging from large casino/hotel complexes through "charity" casinos and bingo parlors to slot machines at racetracks (Casino City, 2014). Some type of government sanctioned gambling exists in every state and province. In 1970, casinos and lotteries were prohibited almost everywhere in both Canada and the United States. Horseracing and bingo were the most common forms of gambling allowed at that time. A quarter-century later, forty-six states and all provinces had authorized some form of casino gambling.

The growth in legal gambling is all the more remarkable because there is staunch opposition to virtually every form of gambling. Gambling is seen as addictive, with problem gamblers at risk of losing not just their money but also their families, homes, and jobs (Morse and Goss, 2009; Mallach, 2010). Others believe that casino gambling attracts criminal activities, including racketeering and prostitution. And for many, gambling is morally wrong and should not be a state-sanctioned activity.

In part, casino gaming spread because provincial/state and local jurisdictions felt compelled to join the game as well, to avoid losing out to other communities. Most new casino facilities have done well, suggesting that the market was without practical limits. And once governments became accustomed to the revenue streams generated by legal gambling, the odds against returning this jinni to its bottle increased.

Casino gambling has provided much needed new sources of public revenue (Navin and Sullivan, 2007). For many state/provincial and local governments, casino gambling has considerable allure as a painless means of raising revenue. Like excise taxes on tobacco and alcohol and other "sin" taxes, the burden of gambling taxes is borne by only a portion of the total population. Participation in gambling is seen as voluntary; as a result, any taxes can easily be avoided, either by not gambling or by not winning.

In addition to generating public revenues, proponents suggest that casinos may provide other economic development benefits for the host communities. Casinos provide employment opportunities, including jobs, requiring a variety of skill levels at different wage rates. They also may purchase supplies and services from local companies. Casinos are often expected to generate economic spinoffs, as tourists and others spend money in neighborhood retail, restaurant, and entertainment establishments.[1]

But all of these a priori claims and anticipated benefits are based on assumptions and projections that may not prove to be accurate. As is often the case with new public policy initiatives, casino development has proceeded with very little evaluation of the likely costs and benefits. Some observers consider the results produced by various studies as

---

1. Casinos have historically attracted a substantial proportion of customers from outside the local market.

biased, offering only a narrow perspective on the likely consequences (Goodman, 1994).

Whether or not casinos represent good public policy choices, it is worth considering the evidence provided by existing casinos to improve future public policy choices. It may not be possible to correct past mistakes, but understanding what has gone before may help prevent similar errors being made in the future. Moreover, there are increasing indications that the casino gambling market is neither infinite nor totally immune from economic fluctuations. Consequently, decisions about allowing new casinos are becoming increasingly risky in many markets (Navin and Sullivan, 2007; Rossback et al., 2014).

The purpose of this chapter is to contribute to a policy framework for evaluating proposals for new gaming facilities that will lead to decisions and agreements favorable to the public interest, particularly for the local government jurisdiction in which the gaming facility would be located. The emphasis here is on costs and benefits, especially those that can readily be expressed in dollar values. There is no single correct answer regarding casino gambling; rather, our objective is to identify the factors that are relevant to policy makers' deliberations on casino proposals and agreements.

As with most studies, our approach is not free of bias. But our bias is not either for or against casino gambling or any other form of gambling; rather, it favors helping public policy makers maximize the net public benefits when they sanction new gambling enterprises. We are not concerned with whether casino gambling is (morally) good or bad; whether it is better or worse than other forms of government-sanctioned wagering (horse racing, lotteries, bingo); or whether the social costs exceed public benefits. These normative issues are important and consequential. But this study focuses on the community and economic development impacts resulting from casino gambling, based on case studies in Ontario and Michigan. Specifically, we examine three issues:

- Do new casino developments, particularly those located in urban areas, have adverse impacts on traffic flow?
- Do new casino developments generate "spillovers," inducing additional investments and economic activity in the surrounding areas?

- Does casino development provide significant fiscal benefits to the host community?

A factual assessment of these issues may provide governments dealing with requests for new casino development with more evidence-based insight into what they can expect.

The chapter is organized as follows. First we briefly describe how casino gambling developed in the two jurisdictions, including the types of casino establishments that are allowed, their ownership structure, and their locations. The next two sections consider the traffic impacts of urban casinos and the land use and economic development impacts of casinos on surrounding areas. The final section considers the fiscal benefits to state/provincial and local governments. The chapter closes with a summary of the findings and some guidance, particularly for municipalities, for governments faced with decisions on allowing new casinos.

BACKGROUND ON CASINO DEVELOPMENT

This study focuses on casino gambling in the province of Ontario and the state of Michigan. There are a number of differences between these two jurisdictions (see Table 9.1); most of the economic indicators (unemployment rate, household income, and housing values) favor Ontario. While Ontario's population continues to increase, Michigan's has changed little over the last thirty years. There are similarities between the two jurisdictions with respect to median age, university graduates, and homeownership. In addition, there are important differences in government structure and approaches to gambling activity. These contextual differences have a significant effect on the community impacts of the casinos in each jurisdiction.

Both Ontario and Michigan allowed pari-mutuel wagering at horse racing tracks and government-run lotteries before casino gambling was authorized. Ontario also licensed commercial bingo parlors; bingo in Michigan was generally confined to specially licensed charity events. The two jurisdictions offer interesting contrasts with respect to their approaches to casino gambling.

Table 9.1 Ontario and Michigan Profiles, 2011

	Ontario	Michigan
Population	12,651,795	9,920,621
Median Age	40.4	38.5
University Graduates	23.4%	25.3%
Median Household Income	$66,358	$48,669
Manufacturing Employment	10.2%	17.3%
Unemployment Rate	8.3%	12.3%
Median Home Value	$300,862	$137,300
Homeownership	71.0%	73.5%

Sources: Statistics Canada, 2011; American Community Survey, 2011

Ontario

The province of Ontario is home to twenty-seven casino facilities, about one-fifth of the Canadian total (Casino City, 2014). Ontario has three categories of casinos, most of which are owned and operated by Ontario Lottery and Gaming (OLG), a Crown Corporation (Table 9.2). The largest facilities are the four resort casinos (three of which are located in midsize metropolitan areas) that are operated on behalf of OLG by professional management companies. When these casinos were first authorized, in 1990, "temporary" facilities were built in Niagara Falls, Windsor, and Rama (just outside Orillia). The latter is located on a First Nation reserve and is operated by OLG for the band.

In addition, there are seven "charity casinos" (three in midsize urban areas), two of which are owned by First Nation bands. Charity casinos, with the exception of the First Nation's casinos in Kenora and Scugog, are located in border communities or relatively close to the United States or another province.[2] These locations allow Ontario to more easily tap the markets in Michigan, New York, Manitoba, and Quebec.

OLG also provides slot machines at sixteen horse racing tracks. These facilities were created in response to requests from the horse industry

---

2. The charity casinos are spread across the province; the distance between the Thousand Islands Casino and the Kenora Casino is almost 2,100 kilometers (1,275 miles).

Table 9.2 Ontario Casinos

Name	Type	Location	Opened	Slot Machines	Table Games
Brantford Charity	Charity	Brantford	1999	514	69
Casino Sault Ste. Marie	Charity	Sault Ste. Marie	1999	450	21
Golden Eagle	Charity	Kenora	2009	435	9
Great Blue Heron	Charity	Scugog	2000	545	60
Pt. Edward Charity	Charity	Pt. Edward	2000	442	37
Thousand Island	Charity	Gananoque	2002	520	18
Thunder Bay	Charity	Thunder Bay	2000	452	17
Ajax Downs	Race track	Ajax	2006	250	0
Clinton Raceway	Race track	Central Huron	2000	108	0
Dresden Raceway	Race track	Chatham Kent	2001	108	0
Flamboro Downs	Race track	Hamilton	2000	791	0
Ft. Erie Race Track	Race track	Ft. Erie	1999	1111	0
Georgian Downs	Race track	Innisfil	2001	455	0
Grand River Race	Race track	Centre Wellington	2003	240	0
Hanover Raceway	Race track	Hanover	2001	125	0
Hiawatha Horse	Race track	Sarnia	1999	454	0
Kawartha Downs	Race track	Cavan Millbrook	1999	450	0
Mohawk Racetrack	Race track	Milton	1999	852	0

Table 9.2 Ontario Casinos (*continued*)

Name	Type	Location	Opened	Slot Machines	Table Games
Rideau Carlton	Race track	Ottawa	2000	1250	0
Sudbury Downs	Race track	Sudbury	1999	343	0
Western Fair Race	Race track	London	1999	750	0
Windsor Raceway	Race track	Windsor	1998	750	0
Woodbine Race	Race track	Toronto	2000	1947	0
Woodstock Races	Race track	Woodstock	2001	180	0
Casino Niagara	Resort	Niagara Falls	1996	2400	79
Casino Rama	Resort	Rama Orilla	1996	2500	110
Casino Windsor	Resort	Windsor	1994	3300	83
Niagara Fallsview	Resort	Niagara Falls	2004	3000	100

Source: OLG

for ways to supplement their racing income, which had been dwindling in recent years, partly as a result of competition from other province-sanctioned gambling opportunities. These facilities are primarily located in southern Ontario communities, including Toronto, London, Windsor, Sarnia, Hamilton, and Ajax. The gross wagering receipts for the racetrack slots are allocated to the racetrack, the horse racing industry, and the OLG; the exact allocation formula varies among the tracks. The OLG facilities provide a total of almost 23,000 slot machines and 638 table games (cards, roulette, and dice).

Michigan

In 2010, the state of Michigan had twenty-five casinos (Michigan Gaming Control Board, 2013); all but three of the existing facilities are owned

by Native American (First Nations) people and are often referred to as
tribal casinos. They are generally exempt from most state laws and regulations, as well as from local statutes, because the recognized Native
American bands are considered sovereign. Eight of the twelve recognized
Indian tribes in Michigan operate casinos on reservations or other tribally
owned land. The tribal casinos are regulated by treaties with the federal
government and compacts with the state of Michigan.[3] The Michigan
compacts were approved in 1994 and 1998.[4]

The first tribal casinos were located in northern Michigan on traditional tribal lands. More recently, tribal casinos have opened in the southern part of the state; some are relatively large facilities that include hotels,
entertainment venues, and other amenities. The largest tribal casinos are
located just outside of Mt. Pleasant in central Michigan and in southwest
Michigan (Table 9.3). The FireKeepers Casino in Battle Creek is the only
Michigan tribal casino with an urban location; all others are in rural areas.

Michigan also has three commercial casinos that were authorized
in 1999 by a statewide referendum that allowed the city of Detroit to
license three casinos. There was considerable interest in obtaining these
licenses, including from national firms. After opening in temporary facilities in 1999 and 2000, these casinos have moved into permanent
facilities that increased their gaming areas and added hotels and restaurants. Operators were granted a license based on terms that included
a substantial tax (initially 18 percent) on gross gaming revenues, providing new facilities that include at least 400 hotel rooms and quotas
for hiring Detroit residents. Together, these three casinos represent the
fifth largest gambling center in the United States, based on revenues.
Although the total number of gambling casinos is higher in Ontario
than in Michigan, on a per capita basis the Michigan market is more
saturated. The Ontario gambling facilities have fewer slot machines and
table games than the Michigan casinos.

---

3. The compacts provide a state pledge to limit approval of additional
competitive casinos in return for payments based on revenues.

4. The Saginaw Chippewa Tribe operated a bingo hall and card room on
reservation land east of Mt. Pleasant in the 1980s, well before the first compact
was signed.

Table 9.3 Michigan Casinos

Name	Location	Opened	Slot Machines	Table Games
Greektown Casino	Detroit	2000	2400	90
MGM Grand Detroit	Detroit	1999	4129	113
Motor City Casino	Detroit	1999	2200	59
Bay Mills Resort	Brimley	1993	700	100
Chip In's Island Resort	Harris	1985	250	70
FireKeepers	Battle Creek	2009	2900	24
Four Winds Casino	New Buffalo	2007	3900	28
Gun Lake	Wayland	2011	1600	17
Kewadin Casino	Sault Ste. Marie	1993	800	40
Kewadin Casino	Christmas	1993	250	14
Kewadin Casino	Hessel	1993	150	22
Kewadin Casino	Manistique	1993	250	4
Kewadin Shores	St. Ignace	1993	750	19
King's Club	Brimley	1993	260	0
Lac Vieux Desert Casino	Watersmeet	1993	650	16
Leelanau Sands	Suttons Bay	1993	400	7
Little River Casino	Manistee	1998	1500	11
Odawa Casino	Petoskey	1998	1200	8
Ojibwa Casino	Marquette	1998	300	9
Ojibwa Casino	Baraga	1998	350	15
Saganing Eagles Landing	Standish	1993	800	6
Soaring Eagle	Mt. Pleasant	1993	4704	79
Turtle Creek Casino	Williamsburg	1993	100	0

Source: Michigan Gaming Control Board

TRAFFIC IMPACTS

A common concern of local governments is that the introduction of a major new facility like a casino will significantly increase traffic congestion. The larger the proposed facility is, the greater the concern is likely to be. This section considers the observed traffic impacts of the urban casinos and of some of the larger facilities that have been developed in rural areas.

Resort Casinos

A large resort casino[5] is often a significant activity center, offering entertainment and other amenities, potentially employing upward of 3,000 people and attracting twice that number of customers on a daily basis. Because a substantial number of these gamblers typically reside outside the immediate metropolitan area, an increase in auto and bus traffic can exacerbate existing traffic congestion problems. While perhaps more likely to be an issue in urban areas, rural casinos may also cause traffic problems. We first consider impacts of new casino developments on Detroit, as well as on Windsor and Niagara Falls, Ontario.

In all three cities, the resort casinos are located close to the city centers. Initially, temporary casino facilities were opened in all three cities. In Niagara Falls, the decision was made to retain the initial temporary casino and to build a second casino about 1.5 kilometers away. The two casinos are located in active tourist areas. The temporary Casino Windsor was located just west of the city center before the permanent facility was built at the eastern edge of the downtown, about 0.75 kilometers away from the original site. In both cities, the second locations are far enough away from the original sites to produce distinct traffic patterns.

The three temporary casinos in Detroit were located in existing buildings on the fringes of the central business district. After considerable debate and a failed attempt to create a casino district along the riverfront (directly opposite Casino Windsor), the sites selected for the permanent

---

5. The term "resort casino" is not used in Michigan; it is adopted here for convenience in referring to a large urban casino, regardless of which side of the border it is located.

Table 9.4 Change in Traffic Volumes near Caesars Windsor Casino

Windsor	1994	2001	2003	2004	2005	2006	2008
Riverside Dr. (north)	28,500	29,100		22,600			
Glengarry (east)	4,800	4,900				4,600	
McDougall (west)	——	7,000			7,100		
University (south)	3,900	8,500			6,700		
Ouellete			22,200				17,500
Wyandotte		20,700				23,200	

Source: City of Windsor Public Works, 2012

casinos were in close proximity (no more than two blocks away) to its temporary counterpart. All three permanent sites are adjacent to freeway interchanges.

In Windsor, data of traffic volumes indicate that there generally has been little change in traffic counts on the streets abutting the casino (Table 9.4). Data for 1994 precede the opening of the permanent casino, while the 2001 data reflect conditions after its opening. Riverside Drive and Glengarry Street experienced modest (about 2 percent) increases in traffic counts immediately after the casino opening, but volumes have subsequently declined. The widening and realignment of University Avenue initially brought a significant increase in traffic, although volume has declined over time here as well. There has certainly been no significant increase in traffic congestion or accidents in the vicinity. Table 9.4 also includes traffic counts for other streets in downtown Windsor (Ouellette and Wyandotte) that are not adjacent to the casino. These streets, as well as others in the city, have seen traffic volumes fluctuate with economic conditions. Most Windsor streets continue to provide acceptable levels of service.

Table 9.5 presents comparable data on traffic flows for Detroit streets close to the three permanent casino sites. Traffic counts are provided for the primary street on which each casino is located and for two locations

Table 9.5 Change in Traffic Volumes near the Detroit Casinos

	Street	Intersection	1998	1999	2005	2010	2011
Motor City Casino	Grand River	Lodge	11,200	10,000	14,800	8,700	11,600
	Lodge Fwy.	Grand River	112,000	106,000	106,000	58,600	86,100
		Michigan	96,000	98,900	83,500	81,200	66,400
		Grand Blvd.	*133,000*	*130,000*	*132,000*	*128,200*	*110,500*
MGM Grand	Michigan	Third	14,200	14,100	9,900	8,100	8,100
	Fisher Fwy.	Lodge	88,700	87,900	95,200	92,100	95,500
		Woodward	101,000	100,000	94,400	98,600	102,200
		Clark	*99,200*	*93,000*	*114,000*	*84,800*	*101,300*
Greektown	Chrysler Service Dr.	St. Antoine	10,100	10,000	na	12,900	10,100
	Chrysler Fwy.	Lafayette	45,800	45,500	48,900	36,300	36,300
		Mack	121,000	131,000	124,000	124,600	81,600
		Grand Blvd.	*192,000*	*170,000*	*176,000*	*169,200*	*150,500*

Source: Michigan Department of Transportation

on the major expressway providing access.[6] The third freeway traffic count (in italics) provides a point of reference at a location several miles from the casinos.

Over the past decade, traffic volumes in the vicinity of the three Detroit casinos have generally declined, typically by more than 15 percent. Grand River Avenue near the Motor City Casino and the Fisher Freeway close to the MGM Grand Casino are the only roads that experienced even modest increases. The freeway traffic counts further from the casinos show trends similar to those recorded close to the casinos—volumes on the Fisher are up (slightly) but down on the Lodge and the Chrysler freeways.

The Windsor and Detroit casinos have clearly not contributed to increased traffic congestion. Casino-bound traffic in these cities is

---

6. In most cases, the same traffic count locations could be used for the temporary casinos as well.

somewhat dispersed as a result of the twenty-four-hour operation of the casino, as well as the substantial number of tour buses that are used. The potential for adverse effects is mitigated by the significant unused road capacity in the CBDs of both cities.

Casino development in the city of Niagara Falls presents a different situation. Because the two casinos are located close to the Niagara Falls, one of the top tourist attractions in North America, traffic volumes and other activities around the casino sites were already high. Particularly during the summer months, there was little or no excess capacity available in the local street system prior to either casino opening. The opening of the first casino, on a site close to the international border crossing and the Clifton Hill tourist area, added more activity to a location already frequently congested by vehicle and pedestrian traffic.

The initial increases in average daily traffic counts attributable to the casinos in Niagara Falls have been marginal. The city of Niagara Falls has implemented a number of improvements (expanded capacity on several streets, new traffic controls, and shuttle buses from remote parking lots) to ease congestion. The 2011 Niagara Regional Transportation plan calls for about $32 million in road improvements, primarily in the vicinity of the second casino, to bring the quality of service to an acceptable level.[7]

Tribal Casinos

Figure 9.1 shows select traffic count data for some of the larger Michigan tribal casinos. Each of the casinos shown on the chart opened during the period presented on the chart (the opening year is represented by the large marker). It is thus possible to compare traffic volumes on the adjacent expressways, before and after the casino openings.

Two of the three large tribal casinos that opened during this period recorded substantial increases in expressway traffic immediately after they opened. Two years after their openings, traffic at the Gun Lake and Fire-Keepers casinos had increased by 19 percent and 12 percent, respectively.

---

7. The improvements in the area of the two casinos represent about 18 percent of $172 million in total planned road improvements.

Figure 9.1 Average traffic counts, select Michigan casinos

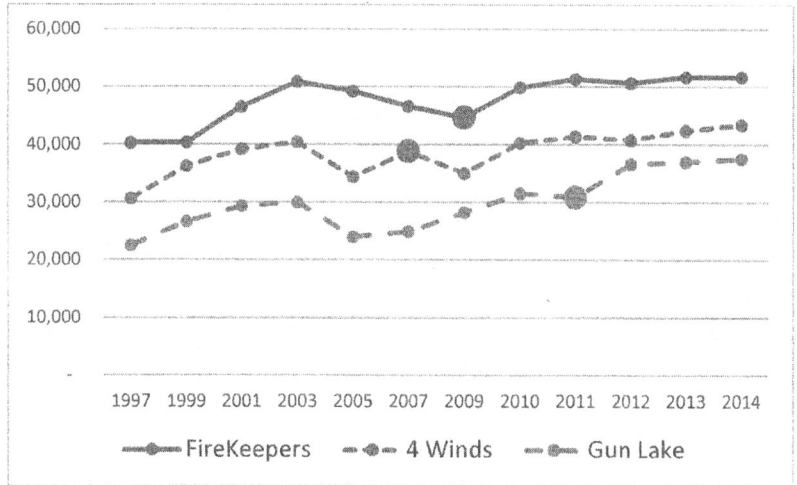

Source: Michigan Department of Transportation.

In subsequent years, both of these casino locations continued to experience small increases in traffic volumes. Despite a 10 percent drop following its 2007 opening, traffic at the Four Winds Casino location showed a 12 percent net increase by 2014.

While two of these three casinos recorded double-digit rates of increase in traffic volumes subsequent to their openings, there is little indication that the casinos have contributed significantly to higher levels of traffic congestion. Traffic volumes remain well below capacity and the levels of service are still good. Traffic volumes, moreover, have been highly variable throughout this period, generally following larger economic trends. Economic conditions in west Michigan, where the three tribal casinos are located, probably account for most of the increases in traffic volumes on the expressways.

ECONOMIC AND COMMUNITY DEVELOPMENT

Several metrics may be used to assess the economic and community development impacts of casinos: employment, retail and other commercial activity, and other subsequent development activity in the vicinity of the casinos. First we consider employment by the casinos themselves. Below, we look at changes in total employment in the casino communities.

Casino Employment

New casinos are obviously sources of additional employment when they first open. Casinos, especially those that include hotel and restaurant facilities, tend to have substantial numbers of employees. Positions include skilled and unskilled occupations. The nominal wage rates for many positions are often low. Employees who have direct contact with gamblers (dealers, hostesses, and the like) often receive substantial tip income. Indeed, some casinos withhold all of the floor personnel's wages to cover taxes on the tip income they receive.

The OLG resort and charity casinos and slot facilities provide a total of more than 17,000 jobs; this number has declined somewhat recently, as a result of the Great Recession. The three Detroit casinos employ a total of 12,000. The Michigan tribal casinos do not consistently report their employment totals; it is estimated that they employ an additional 8,000 persons, producing total direct casino employment in Michigan of just over 20,000, about 25 percent higher than in Ontario.

In licensing its three casinos, Detroit negotiated hiring quotas with the casino operators, who are obliged to hire Detroit residents to fill a minimum of half of their positions. This has worked well, with all three casinos regularly exceeding their quotas. These jobs not only are badly needed in economically distressed Detroit, but resident jobs also contribute more to municipal income tax collections. Such hiring requirements do not currently exist for any of the other categories of casinos. In several instances, the number of employees at the tribal casinos exceeds the total number of tribe members.

Land Use

Advocates of new casino development often argue that the casino will generate a variety of spinoff developments, particularly in areas adjacent to the casino facility. Typical examples of anticipated off-site benefits are businesses that cater to a tourist clientele that the casino will presumably

Figure 9.2 Motor City Casino adjacent land uses

attract: hotels, restaurants, and tourist-oriented retail. These new businesses would not only provide new employment opportunities for local residents but also contribute to the community's property tax base.

For the urban casinos, it would seem likely that adjacent developments might be more common. At least in theory, urban casinos provide an opportunity for gamblers to simply walk out the door and go to a different business. In Detroit and Windsor, there clearly has been little new development as a result of the permanent casinos. The MGM Grand and Motor City casinos in Detroit and Caesar's Windsor have spurred no new development, and there are still vacant lots and buildings adjacent to these facilities. The Fallsview Casino in Niagara Falls generally falls in the same category, although there are several other hotels adjacent, along with restaurants and commercial development.

The Greektown Casino in Detroit and Casino Niagara are each located in well-established restaurant and entertainment areas. Both of these commercial areas, which pre-date the casinos by decades, continue to serve their traditional clientele, with little indication that the casinos have directly contributed to increased business activity.

In most instances, anticipated benefits of casino development simply have not occurred. Even the most casual observation suggests that few, if any, spinoff developments are evident in the areas around the new

Figure 9.3 Caesars Windsor adjacent land uses

casinos. As seen in Figures 9.2 and 9.3, casinos in Detroit and Windsor have only managed to convert a few vacant lots into parking lots (for casino employees). Nearby commercial buildings generally remain vacant.

The Ontario charity casinos and the tribal casinos in Michigan have similarly produced few development spinoffs. Even casinos that have been open for more than a decade continue to be surrounded by farm fields. Casinos in rural areas are often on the outskirts of the town, where abundant land allows them to isolate themselves from other establishments that might distract gamblers before they lose all their money. As the aerial photographs in Figures 9.4 and 9.5 indicate, there are few places within comfortable walking distance of these casinos. Despite the large site sizes, several casinos have built parking decks; presumably so that gamblers will never be discouraged by the length of the walk into the casino.

There are occasional exceptions to the lack of development around rural casinos. For example, the Soaring Eagle Casino in Mt. Pleasant and the Odawa Casino Resort in Petoskey are located in areas where substantial new commercial development has occurred. It does not appear, however, that this new development has much connection to the casinos. Rather, it appears to be a situation where land uses with similar location requirements (including relatively large parcels of relatively

Figure 9.4 FireKeepers Casino, Battle Creek, MI

cheap land) have been developing independently of, but adjacent to, each other.

Data from the County Business Patterns reports provide a different perspective on the spinoff effects of the casinos. They provide data on employment, wages, and establishments at the two-digit North American Industrial Classification System level. This data series has a number of advantages, including providing consistent annual data for more than a decade. The data, however, are subject to the Census Bureau's disclosure rules, which are often a problem in geographic areas or NAICS categories with a limited number of firms. Another limitation is that comparable data are not available for the Canadian casino cities.

A benchmark for evaluating the changes occurring in the Michigan counties where casinos are located is provided by a separate group of counties similar in population size and in close proximity to the casino counties. The casino counties are home to the largest casinos in the state, based on the number of slot machines at each facility, including Allegan, Berrien, Calhoun in southwest Michigan; Manistee and Isabella in central Michigan; Emmett and Grand Traverse in the north; Menominee in the Upper Peninsula; and Wayne in southeast Michigan. These counties were aggregated for comparison to the following counties that do not have casinos: Van Buren, Jackson, and St. Joseph; Mason and Wexford; Charlevoix and Montcalm; Delta; and Oakland.

Figure 9.5 Change in county employment, 1998–2014

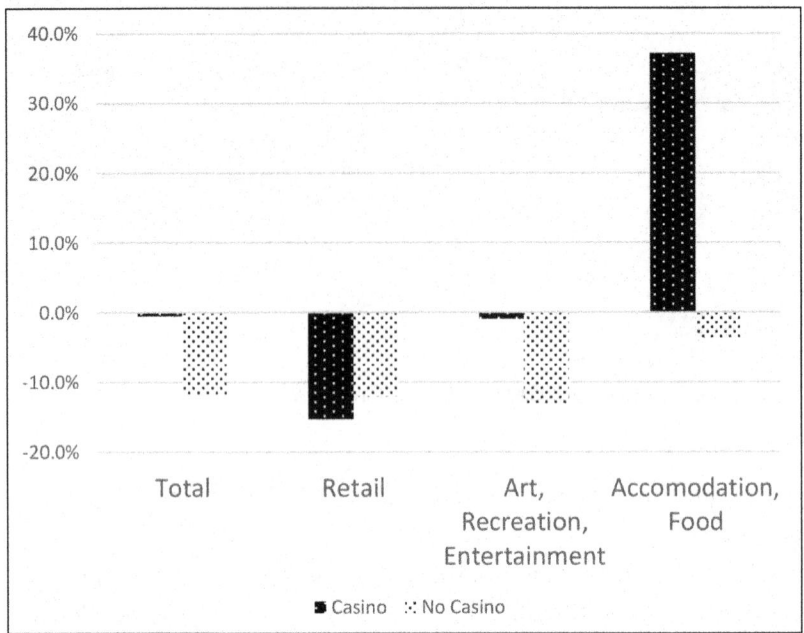

Source: County Business Patterns

The most populous counties, Wayne (which includes the Detroit casinos) and Oakland, reported declines in both the number of business establishments and employment, with the rate of decline in Wayne County double that of Oakland County. Although both of these counties had a net loss of retailing jobs, they experienced gains in arts, recreation, and entertainment as well as accommodations and food services employment. Wayne County had a larger increase in accommodation and food services job than did Oakland County.

In the lower population counties, the number of business establishments increased in three of the casino counties (Allegan, Emmet, and Isabella) but in only one of the comparison counties, Van Buren, between 1998 and 2014. All of the casino counties had a net gain in accommodations and food service employment, and four increased their employment in arts, recreation, and entertainment. Half of the non-casino counties recorded net losses of jobs in these two categories; however, when aggregated the non-casino counties lost jobs in both industries.

Figure 9.6 County unemployment before and after casino openings

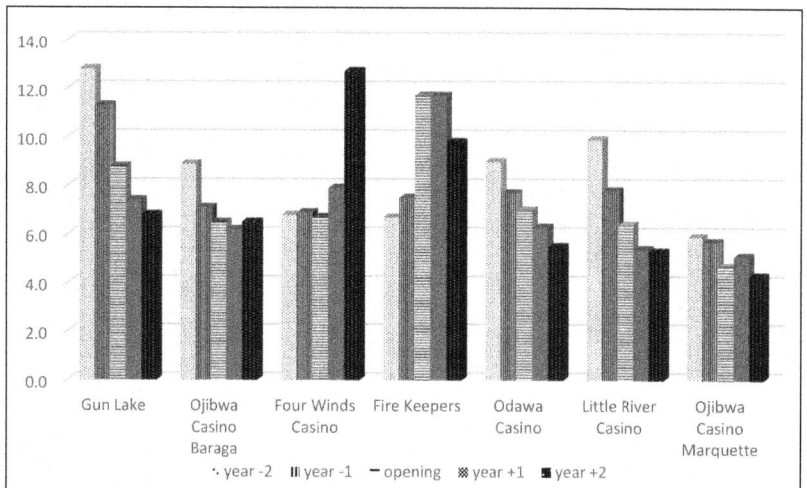

Source: Michigan labor market information system

These data suggest that, while the introduction of casino gambling had a positive effect on employment and business establishments, the effects were not sufficient to reverse the prevailing downward trends in both indicators. In most instances the casinos were only able to slow the rate of loss, especially in the smaller counties. In Wayne County, the casinos seem to have had a positive impact on employment in the accommodations and food services industry, but Oakland County continued to outperform Wayne on other measures.

Unemployment

Figure 9.6 shows the changes in the unemployment rate for the seven tribal casinos that opened between 1998 and 2011. Annual average county unemployment rates for the five-year period centered on the opening of the casino exhibit several consistent trends. In five instances, there was a net decline in unemployment over the five years, ranging from 6 percentage points in Allegan County (Gun Lake Casino) to 1.6 percentage points in Marquette County (Ojibwa Marquette Casino). Interestingly, the unemployment declines in these counties had actually started before the casino opened.

Table 9.6 Average Wage Rates, 1998 and 2014

		1998			2014		
		Casino	Non-Casino	Difference	Casino	Non-Casino	Difference
Wayne/Oakland	Mean Wage	$36,410	$39,462	-$3,052	$51,004	$56,878	-$5,875
Other	Mean Wage	$26,669	$26,251	$418	$40,977	$39,322	$1,655

Source: County Business Patterns

The unemployment rates in Berrien County (Four Winds Casino) and Calhoun County (FireKeepers Casino) increased subsequent to the casino openings, by 5.9 and 3.1 percentage points, respectively. The trend in the Berrien County unemployment rate was relatively flat prior to the casino opening, while Calhoun County's rate peaked in the year the casino opened. Although the casino openings apparently had little immediate effect, by 2015 the unemployment rates in these two counties had dropped to about 5 percent, almost half a percentage point below the Michigan average.

Wages

A common goal of local economic development programs is to raise income levels in the community. Increases in average wages may occur because jobs at a new development pay a higher-than-average wage or because the competition for labor pushes up wages generally. Table 9.6 presents summary data on average wage rates for the casino/non-casino counties. In 1998, the average wage in Oakland County was about $3,000 higher than in Wayne County. The 2014 data indicate that the difference in average wages almost doubled to $5,875.

The pattern is different for the smaller, counties outside of southeast Michigan that are included in Table 9.6. The casinos in these counties are likely to be among the largest local employers and thus have a greater impact on countywide wages. In 1998, the counties where casinos would be located had a mean wage rate slightly higher than the non-casino counties. In 2014, the difference had increased to $1,655, still favoring the casino counties.

CASINO REVENUES AND GOVERNMENT RECEIPTS

Perhaps the most important benefit of legalized casino gambling is the revenue generated on behalf of government entities at the state/provincial and municipal levels. With respect to casino gambling, the state may license private operators (as in Michigan) or it may undertake to operate the casinos directly (as in Ontario). In both countries, First Nations have a degree of sovereignty that allows them to operate casinos independently of the state. In Ontario and Michigan, however, the operators of tribal casinos have entered into formal agreements with the state. These agreements or compacts typically include a schedule of payments to the state or province, in exchange for the state's agreement not to authorize competitive developments. Privately owned casinos, including tribal casinos, generate public revenues through income taxes on winnings and on the gross profits of casino operators. The net receipts of Ontario's government-operated casinos are a source of additional revenue as well.

Ontario and Michigan have adopted quite different approaches to the government revenue arrangements. The province of Ontario, through the OLG, is the owner of both the resort and charity casinos, as well as the slot machines at the horse racing tracks around the province. The charity casinos and racetrack slot facilities are also operated by the OLG, but the operation and management of the resort casinos is contracted with private management companies. For example, the casino in Windsor is now Caesars Windsor and is operated by Caesars Entertainment.

The gross revenue (the difference between total amount wagered and the amount won by casino patrons) generated by the resort casinos is used to cover operating expenses of these facilities. In addition to costs such as wages and salaries, advertising (including comps) and operations, the host municipalities of Niagara Falls and Windsor each receive a fixed annual payment, currently $3 million, adjusted for inflation.

A different approach is used to allocate funds to municipal governments. By agreement, 2 percent of gross revenues are allocated to local

Figure 9.7 Gross revenues in millions, 2003–2012, by casino type

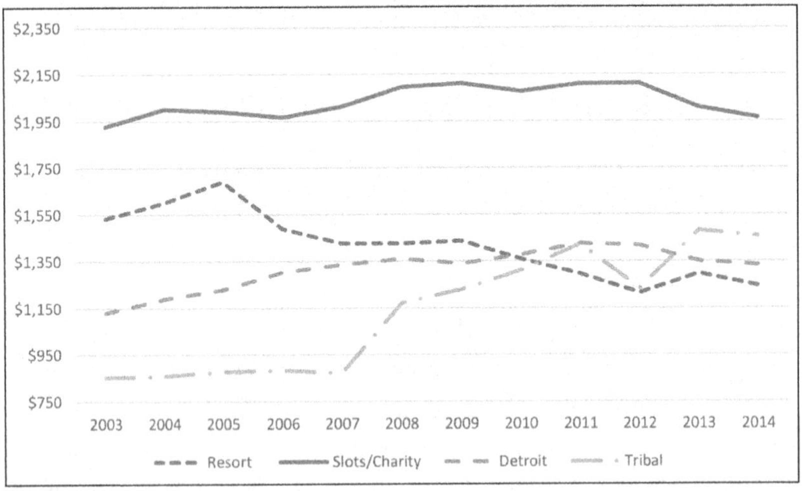

Sources: Ontario Lottery and Gaming Commission, Michigan Gambling Control Board

governments in the vicinity of the casinos. Funds are distributed in response to specific applications from local governments and public agencies. The allocation process is competitive and no agency is guaranteed an award.

The racetrack slot facilities divide their revenues among the tracks, the horse racing industry itself, and local and provincial government agencies. Although the arrangement may differ from racetrack to racetrack, typically the racing industry receives about four times as much as the track operators do.

Michigan casinos are authorized by the state government but owned and operated by either the Native American tribes or by private investors. As a result, the bulk of the casino profits do not accrue to the government (as in Ontario) but rather to these non-government entities. The State of Michigan as well as the local governments receive revenue based on predetermined taxes, resulting in a much smaller return than in Ontario.

The tribal casinos agreed in their 1994 compact with the State of Michigan to two separate taxes, both tied to gross revenues. Two percent of the gross revenue from the first 450 slot machines at each casino and 5 percent of revenue from any additional slot machines are placed in a fund for the benefit of local governments and public agencies. Revenue generated by table games, restaurants, and other ancillary facilities are not subject to this "tax." The tribal casinos also agreed to pay the State of Michigan 8 percent of gross gambling revenues in exchange for the state's promise to limit competitive facilities. When Michigan entered into a second compact in 1998, authorizing other tribes to establish more casinos, the tribes included in the first compact sued the state and stopped paying the 8 percent tax. The bands participating in the second compact are subject to the 2 percent tax and an addition levy of 4 percent to 12 percent of net winnings which the state uses for economic development programs.

Unlike the tribal casinos, the three investor-owned resort casinos authorized for the city of Detroit were required to obtain approval of both the city and the state. This allowed both levels of government to impose conditions including specific tax levies on these casinos. The city of Detroit, in addition to a license fee, also imposes fees to fund a special police unit to deal with gambling-related crimes and for assisting problem gamblers.[8] The city also required that at least half of the employees of each casino be Detroit residents and that, within a specified time frame, each casino would build a 400-room hotel as part of its facilities.

The largest tax, however, was based on a percentage of gross gambling revenues. Initially, while the casinos were in temporary facilities, the total tax rate was set at 18 percent, with 10.1 percent going to the city and the balance going to the state. When each casino operator opened its permanent facility, the total tax rate increased by 6 percentage points, with the state allocated a 4-percentage-point increase and the city 2 additional points.

The returns to the city of Detroit from this latter tax have been substantial. Over the past five years, the casino wagering tax has generated an average of about $200 million a year. The casinos are the second largest source of general fund revenue for the city, ahead of the property tax and the municipal income tax.

These various taxing schemes have produced a wide range of results. The province of Ontario has gained much more revenue from casino gambling

---

8. The casinos are also subject to property taxes.

than Michigan has. Detroit clearly has benefitted more from its three casinos than have Windsor and Niagara Falls. Detroit not only receives a much larger amount annually than the Ontario cities but the amount is tied in part to the amounts wagered, as opposed to a fixed amount adjusted for inflation. While the smaller municipalities in Michigan and Ontario have received benefits from the casinos, they are unable to rely on an annual payment but must compete for whatever funds are available.

CONCLUSIONS

While strong opposition to legalized gambling continues, it has become a fact of life throughout North America. For many communities, casino gambling is an important component of their economic development strategy. This study, while not conclusive, is indicative of the impacts that casino gaming may have on local communities. Below, we repeat the original research questions and summarize the most important findings.

Do new casino developments, particularly those located in urban areas, have significant adverse impacts on traffic congestion?

Despite the fact that a large casino may attract thousands of gamblers and employees each day, our analysis found that the answer is no. There is little indication that any of the casino developments examined have had substantial or long-lasting adverse traffic impacts on local streets. The primary reason for the limited impact is that most of the casinos have been located in economically depressed areas, where the existing street system has excess capacity. An exception to this would be casinos located in resort and tourist-oriented areas like Niagara Falls, Ontario, and Petoskey, Michigan. In both of these locations, traffic volumes have risen, resulting in increased levels of seasonal congestion. It should be noted, however, that peak season congestion would exist in these communities absent the casinos. Another factor mitigating the potential for traffic problems is the traffic management implicit in casino operations. These facilities often operate twenty-four hours a day and seldom generate peak hour traffic at times that coincide with other rush hour peaks.

Do new casino developments generate "spillovers," inducing additional investments and economic activity in the surrounding areas?

The answer here again is no. Whether in the city center or in a farm field along the interstate, none of the casinos examined appear to have attracted significant additional investment in surrounding areas. (The casinos in Niagara Falls and Mt. Pleasant may be exceptions.) For casino operators, this conclusion is an affirmation of their business model. The casino operators have little interest in seeing their customers spend money elsewhere. The high rate of taxation (see below) that is often imposed on the casinos seems to be an acceptable way to contribute to the community; encouraging potentially competitive developments does not.

Does casino development provide significant fiscal benefits to the host community?

The direct employment benefits of the casinos are substantial. OLG employs more than 18,000, with an average annual wage of $52,000. Specific data for Michigan casinos are not available, but total employment is estimated at about 20,000. Because casino development often occurs in depressed or declining areas, there are relatively few examples of net employment gains. The casinos do, however, appear to slow job losses. Moreover, there seems to be little evidence of a "Wal-Mart effect," where the casino has an adverse effect on existing local restaurants, bars, and other recreational opportunities, perhaps because the residents of the host community are not the primary market of the casinos.

The most important contribution that the casinos make to local and state/provincial governments is through the taxes they pay. Here the results vary widely, with the province of Ontario and the city of Detroit being the biggest beneficiaries.[9] These financial benefits are a function of the nature of the revenue agreement that is negotiated. Casinos do provide financial benefits to governments; how large the benefits are, and how they are apportioned among government entities, is far from a given.

---

9. The horse racing industry in Ontario also receives significant benefits from the slot machines at racetracks.

There are several additional considerations that emerged from this study that seem to merit closer examination. Casino gambling is not a limitless source of government revenue. The gambling market may in time become saturated; it is also subject to fluctuations in the overall economy. The Greektown Casino in Detroit was forced into bankruptcy by competition and the cost of building its permanent facility. The opening of new competitive facilities has consistently reduced the level of wagering at existing facilities: the Detroit and Windsor casinos are competitive with each other and with the new casino in Toledo, Ohio. A similar situation exists with the casinos in Niagara Falls, Ontario, and those in Buffalo and Niagara Falls, New York.

Looking at the revenues generated by the different type of facilities operated by OLG reveals that the more elaborate the development, the less revenue it produces for the province. Resort casinos have lost money in the last several years; charity casinos have, on occasion, also operated at a loss. The slot machines at racetracks (a single type of gaming in someone else's building) has consistently produced the highest return of the three. The provincial lottery has produced the best returns for the province, in part because of its low overhead.

In spite of clear empirical evidence, there continues to be heavy investment in flagship casinos, with hotels and multiple restaurants. With the potential for better returns from simply increasing the number of opportunities to play the slots, why is there repeated upgrading and expansion of existing commercial casinos? In part, the explanation relates to the differences in the types of facilities provided. The province of Ontario owns the resort casinos there, and the province receives most of its gaming revenue from this source. Similarly, the tribal casinos in Michigan contribute less to the state (or local governments) than do the resort casinos in Detroit. For most cities, particularly midsize communities and those that are non-rural, it does not appear that the *local* benefits are worth the cost, a finding supported by other work (Gross, 1998; Garrett, 2004; Florida, 2014).

10

Trends and Tendencies

[T]hese factors suggest that the Canadian experience is likely to be highly relevant to conditions in the United States.

Tomalty and Mallach, 2015, 2

In this concluding chapter we highlight the more important themes of the previous chapters and attempt to identify the public policies that might have an impact on the future prosperity of these urban areas. One thing that stands out is the rich variety that characterizes midsize Canadian cities. Our analysis suggests that there is not just a single road to prosperity. Clearly, one size does not fit all or, perhaps, even most.

The two decades covered in this research have seen significant changes among the midsize urban areas. At the beginning of the 1990s, Canada's midsize urban areas were home to more than one of every five Canadians. Through 2011, they experienced an average population increase of 24 percent, compared to the national population growth of just over 20 percent. Population increased in thirty-four of the forty-two midsize urban areas. There have been regional differences in the population growth rates. Half of the ten fastest growing urban areas, including Abbotsford and Kelowna in British Columbia and Lethbridge in Alberta, were in Western Canada. The strong economy of the Greater Toronto Area helped make Barrie the fastest growing midsize urban area, with population growth of 90 percent. Along with Oshawa and Guelph, Barrie benefitted from proximity to the strong economy (and high housing prices) of the Toronto Census Metropolitan Area. Sherbrooke and Drummondville in Quebec rounded out the top ten; their growth rates were more than three times larger than Montreal, and well above the other midsize urban areas in that province.

Of the eight urban areas that lost population between 1991 and 2011, five are in Ontario, but located far from Metropolitan Toronto. Shawinigan and Saguenay, both in Quebec, had declines in population of 12.7 percent and 4.2 percent, respectively. Saint John, NB, was the only other midsize community to lose population.

Not surprisingly, trends in employment over these two decades exhibit similar patterns. Between 1991 and 2011, the total number of jobs in Canada rose by almost 2.4 million (16.7 percent). While the three largest CMAs have about one-third of the Canadian population, they accounted for almost 64 percent of the job growth. Midsize urban areas accounted for about 22 percent of the employment growth. The average employment growth over the two decades was 27 percent. The communities with the highest and lowest rankings of employment change are the same as for population change. Sarnia and Greater Sudbury were the only urban areas that gained population (a modest 0.4 percent increase in both urban areas) but had a net loss of jobs (-10.6 percent and -1.7 percent, respectively). Moncton, NB, recorded stronger employment growth (38.9 percent) than the other midsize New Brunswick communities, Saint John (6.2 percent) and Fredericton (18.4 percent).

All of the midsize urban areas recorded increases in median household income between 1991 and 2011. On average, the median income rose by more than 54 percent; this is about the same as the national income growth. Median household income in 2011 was highest in Oshawa, Guelph, and Barrie. Of the seven urban areas with incomes below $50,000, six are in Quebec; Cornwall, ON, is the exception. The highest rate of income growth, 90 percent, was in Saskatoon; in Trois-Rivières, median household income increased by just 28 percent during the same period.

Trends in population, employment, and income during this period suggest that most midsize urban areas maintained an important role in the Canadian economy. Half of these urban areas experienced a decline in their Economic Prosperity Index (EPI).[1] The midsize communities

---

1. A negative change in EPI does not indicate an absolute decline; rather, it means that the change in the urban area falls short of the change in the national averages.

experiencing the largest relative increases in economic well-being were found across Canada, including Red Deer, AB, St. John's, NL, and Prince George, BC. The urban areas with the largest declines were all in Quebec. Next we will consider some of the factors that have contributed to these differences.

EMPLOYMENT RESTRUCTURING

How has deindustrialization affected Canada's midsize urban areas over the past twenty years?

Over these two decades, the Canadian economy experienced a substantial shift away from manufacturing. Since 1991, the number of manufacturing jobs in Canada has declined by 465,000. In 2011, manufacturing employment was just 9.2 percent of the total, compared to 14.7 percent in 1991. The aggregate manufacturing employment in Montreal, Toronto, and Vancouver metropolitan areas fell by 186,000 during the same period. Manufacturing employment in Montreal in 2011 was some 90,000 less than the 1991 total, a decline of almost 30 percent.

The aggregate change in manufacturing jobs between 1991 and 2011 for all midsize urban areas was a net decrease of about 79,000, or about 19 percent (Table 10.1). Two-thirds of the midsize metro areas experienced a decrease in manufacturing jobs between 1991 and 2011. Thunder Bay lost more than 61 percent of its manufacturing jobs during these two decades. Other remote urban areas with substantial declines in manufacturing employment include Greater Sudbury (48 percent), Saint John (45 percent), Sault Ste. Marie (45 percent), and North Bay (40 percent). Manufacturing declines were not confined to isolated communities, however. Despite their relative proximity to a large metropolitan area, Nanaimo and St. Catharines each lost half of their manufacturing job base; St. Catharines-Niagara had the largest absolute manufacturing job loss, more than 19,000.

Substantial increases in manufacturing employment occurred in several western Canadian communities, including Lethbridge, Red Deer, and Chilliwack with growth rates of 52 percent, 47 percent, and 43 percent, respectively. Each of these urban areas gained natural resources

Table 10.1 Trends in Manufacturing and Business Services Employment, 1991–2011

	Manufacturing			Business Services		
	1991	2011	Change	1991	2011	Change
Canada	2,084,115	1,619,295	-22.3%	802,405	1,240,850	54.6%
Three Largest CMA	775,520	589,100	-24.0%	394,005	607,215	54.1%
Midsize Urban Areas	452,025	367,400	-18.7%	136,350	208,225	52.7%

employment as well. Barrie (29 percent), Drummondville (25 percent), and Moncton (22 percent) also recorded increases in manufacturing employment.

What took the place of these lost manufacturing jobs?

Despite this evidence of widespread deindustrialization, only a handful of midsize urban areas actually experienced a net decline in total employment during this period, as job growth in other industries offset the loss of manufacturing jobs. As was the case across North America, deindustrialization has largely been offset by the rapid growth in services and the knowledge-based economy. Because the services sector is so broad, we focus on business services as a bellwether of employment restructuring. Canada's business services jobs tend to be concentrated in the largest metropolitan areas. Toronto accounted for over one-quarter of all Canadian business services in 1991; between them, Montreal and Vancouver contributed an additional 23 percent of the total. Over the next two decades, almost two-thirds of the growth in business services occurred in these three metropolitan areas. By 2011, Canada had 145 business service jobs for each 100 manufacturing jobs. Both Toronto and Vancouver had more than two such jobs for each manufacturing job; Montreal was slightly above the national average.

Midsize urban areas had a net gain of more than 72,000 business services jobs between 1991 and 2011. The growth in this industry tended to favor the larger of the midsize metro areas: almost half (49 percent) of the net gain in business services employment occurred in the nine urban areas with populations over 200,000. Kitchener had the largest absolute growth in business services employment, with a net gain of more than 14,000, followed by Oshawa (9,935), Victoria (9,070), and Halifax (8,265). Only two of the midsize urban areas, Belleville and Sault Ste. Marie, both in Ontario, had a net loss in the number of business service jobs.

Eleven of these urban areas had more business services jobs than manufacturing jobs in 1991; by 2011, there were twenty-four communities with more business service than manufacturing jobs, including seven of the ten largest. The eighteen urban areas with more manufacturing than business services jobs in 2011 are all located in Ontario or Quebec. In the aggregate, midsize urban areas had 113 business services jobs for every 100 manufacturing jobs in 2011. Of the fifteen urban areas with the highest ratio of business services jobs to manufacturing jobs (all of which are above the national average), thirteen are not close to a major urban area. Eight are in Western Canada, three in the Maritimes, and four in Ontario. Four are provincial capitals. The midsize urban areas with business service job growth are thus most likely to be found in remote areas, where they serve a more extensive hinterland, and in Western Canada, where manufacturing activities have traditionally been limited.

New business services jobs did not consistently replace lost manufacturing jobs. Six of the nine largest midsize urban areas recorded gains in both business services and manufacturing, led by Saskatoon, which had an increase of 7,500 manufacturing jobs and 6,100 business services jobs.

Did this employment restructuring bring about significant changes in the economic bases of these communities?

A community's economic base can be defined by the types of industries that exist there. This is not always the industrial sector with the most employees, but rather the one that makes the primary contribution to the overall community economy. Over the last two decades, the economic

Table 10.2 Economic Base Trends, 1991–2011

1991	2011					
	Natural Resources	Goods	Health/ Education	Other	Diverse	Total
Resources	5	0	0	0	3	8
Goods	0	7	1	0	4	12
Trade	1	0	1	1	3	6
Health/Education	1	0	0	0	5	6
Diverse	0	0	2	0	8	10
Total	7	7	4	1	23	42

Source: Statistics Canada

base of these communities was relatively stable. Twenty of the midsize urban areas had the same economic base in 2011 as they did in 1991 (Table 10.2). The majority of the natural resource, manufacturing, and diverse economies in 1991 remained in those categories. The energy boom in Western Canada helped to produce two new natural resource–based communities. No new manufacturing centers emerged during this period. Despite the substantial growth in business services noted above, this industry was not the economic base of any of the midsize urban areas in 1991 or 2011. None of the six urban areas that specialized in higher education and health care in 1991 retained this classification in 2011; however, four new communities moved into this category.

Of the twenty-two urban areas where the economic base changed, fifteen moved into the diversified category. Each of the categories (except business services) contributed to the increase in communities with a diversified economic base, including five health/education and four goods-producing economies. Faster growth in other industries (rather than declines in the once dominant industry) was generally responsible for the change. This trend toward less specialization in the economies of these communities is perhaps the most significant change during this period and potentially bodes well for their economic sustainability in the face of future global economic change.

What was the relationship between economic prosperity and economic base?

The relationship between a community's economic base and its prosperity can help in understanding the existing situation. It can also inform policy discussions by assisting in the identification of potentially effective economic development strategies. Here we consider both the Economic Prosperity Index and median household income data.

In 1991, the average EPI for urban areas with an economic base in higher education/health was 303, the highest among the five categories. Natural resource–based (294) and diverse (295) economies had the lowest average scores. Median household income was about $39,000 in all categories except natural resources ($37,000) and trade ($31,000).

Local economies with an economic base in natural resources in 2011 had the highest average EPI, regardless of their economic base in 1996. Median household income (one of the components of the EPI), at $64,600 on average, is highest for natural resource communities as well. Manufacturing centers had the lowest average EPI, 288, as well as the lowest median incomes, $55,000. These relatively low incomes in manufacturing communities reflect a bi-modal distribution in which Ontario urban areas have incomes considerably above those in Quebec. The other three economic base categories—diverse, health and higher education, and other—each had average EPI scores of about 294 and median household incomes ranging between $57,500 and $59,000.

The nature of a community's economic base provides only limited clues to understanding community prosperity. Both natural resource and manufacturing-based local economies tend to be cyclical, in terms of income and EPI. Moreover, as local economies lose their specializations and become more diverse, the differences between communities tend to narrow.

What community characteristics, other than economic base, are associated with higher levels of prosperity?

Population

Indicators of prosperity, such as incomes and job growth, often favor larger metropolitan areas. A similar pattern can be seen among the midsize urban areas. As a general rule, urban areas with populations above 200,000 were more likely to enjoy a greater relative prosperity than metro areas with populations below 100,000. The correlation between population and relative prosperity is not high, however. Smaller communities, such as St. John's, Medicine Hat, and Lethbridge, have high prosperity scores related to natural resources. Prosperity in slightly larger urban areas, such as Guelph and Barrie, seems to benefit from their proximity to Metropolitan Toronto.

It should also be noted that the relation between population and economic prosperity varied considerably between 1991 and 2011. St. John's prosperity has been cyclical; it surged between 1991 and 1996, then declined in 2001 before starting to rise once again. It is likely that the current weakness in the energy sector has had a negative effect on all of the energy-based economies. Other communities where the EPI exhibited a similar cyclical pattern were Brantford, Saint-Hyacinthe, and Thunder Bay.

Regional Location

For most measures of growth and prosperity, urban areas in Quebec lagged behind other parts of the country. The prosperity index for Montreal was the lowest of the three large metropolitan areas in each census year. The eight midsize Quebec urban areas have consistently had the lowest average Economic Prosperity Index scores of any region since 1996 (see Figure 10.1). In 2011, seven of the eight Quebec urban areas were in the bottom quartile when the midsize areas are ranked by their prosperity index scores; only Saint-Jean-sur-Richelieu escaped the bottom of the rankings. In the other three Canadian regions, relative prosperity of the midsize urban areas peaked in 1996. Despite declines in subsequent years, their average prosperity scores have generally remained well above those in Quebec. Western Canada and the Maritime provinces had the highest average EPI in 2011.

Proximity to a Large Metropolitan Area

Other things equal, a midsize urban area within commuting distance of a major metro was likely to fare better than more remote communities.

Figure 10.1 Regional trends in economic prosperity

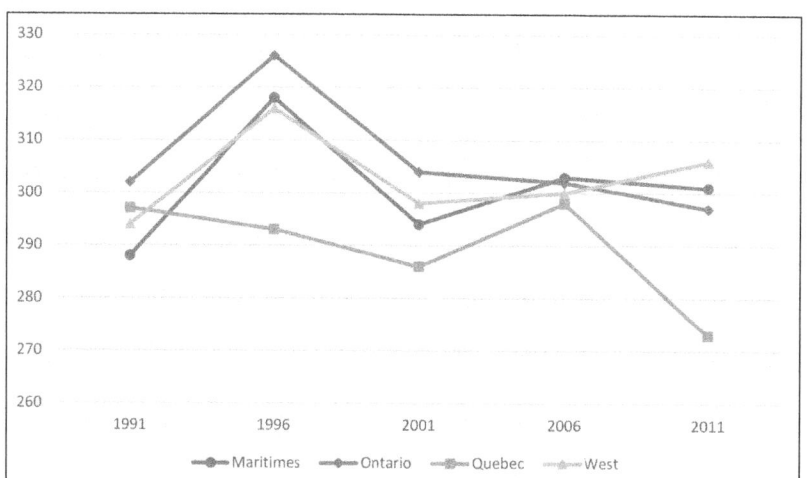

Urban areas such as Saint-Jean-sur-Richelieu, QC, and Abbotsford, BC, and even Barrie, ON, have benefitted from the spillover of economic activity and population from the nearby metropolis. Some of the new residents continue as commuters, trading off more time spent traveling to work for lower housing prices and a different lifestyle.

Higher Education

Post-secondary education is increasingly perceived as the minimum qualification for individual economic success. In Canada, four types of post-secondary educational institutions are commonly recognized. The different types of post-secondary educational institutions can reasonably be expected to have different effects on the economy of their host community. Universities with significant graduate enrollments are likely to be the most important.[2] Total employment at these institutions is typically high, both in total and per student. Many of these additional employees are skilled professionals who are supported by funded research.

---

2. *Maclean's* magazine in its annual ranking of Canadian universities employs three different categories: medical/doctoral, comprehensive, and primarily undergraduate. The first two of these correspond to research universities in the United States.

Universities with primarily undergraduate enrollment, with a focus on teaching rather than research, can be expected to have a lesser impact on the local economy. The economic spillovers from these undergraduate institutions may include spending by students at local business establishments. Canadian colleges (CEGEP in Quebec) primarily have responsibility for vocational and technical training, although most also offer some general education classes as well. A number of these colleges have, however, begun to offer four-year degrees, either independently or in conjunction with an established university in a different community.

Although their potential economic contributions are widely recognized, it is difficult to create a new research university for this purpose. Many of the leading universities in North America have been in existence for over a century. It is less difficult to expand these institutions incrementally than to build brand new facilities (and faculties), particularly in an era of limited public resources. There are some exceptions, however. The University of Waterloo is relatively young, established in 1957; nevertheless, it has become a world-class university, especially in engineering and computer science.

Establishing a new undergraduate institution can be less difficult. Several colleges in British Columbia have expanded their charters to offer four-year degrees. For example, Malispina College has become the University of Vancouver Island, and Fraser Valley College is now the University of the Fraser Valley. The University of Northern British Columbia was established in 1990 and was ranked first in 2016 among primarily undergraduate universities by *Maclean's* magazine. Another new university, Laurier Brantford, was established in 1999. While not one of the top-ranked universities, Laurier Brantford appears to have had a positive economic development impact on the Brantford city center by adding to its resident population.

Table 10.3 summarizes the relationship between post-secondary education and economic prosperity. Not only do urban areas with research universities have the highest average EPI, but they are also the only group that experienced an increase in the average score over the 1991 to 2011 period. Communities with four-year undergraduate institutions consistently outperform those with only a two-year college.

Table 10.3 Post-Secondary Education and Economic Prosperity

	Number of Metros	Avg. EPI 1991	Avg. EPI 2011	Change
Doctoral/Comprehensive	14	302	303	+1
Undergraduate	17	296	294	-2
College/CEGEP	11	293	287	-6

Municipal Amalgamation

David Rusk (1993) has argued that the consolidation of municipalities can make a substantial contribution to regional prosperity. The rationale for most governmental reorganizations is to promote economy and efficiencies in government operations. Amalgamations of suburban municipalities with the central city may eliminate unnecessary duplication of services, equalize public services, strengthen the central city tax base, and eliminate competition among municipalities for new development.

Between 1991 and 2011, almost half of the midsize urban areas were involved in amalgamations. While the anticipated benefits in terms of cost savings and increased efficiency may have been realized, amalgamations have made little contribution to community prosperity (Table 10.4). Indeed, the midsize urban areas that have been the location of recent amalgamation activities have experienced a substantial decline in their Economic Prosperity Index.

ECONOMIC DEVELOPMENT STRATEGIES

Next, we turn to an examination of the relationships between community economic well-being (as measured by EPI) in 1991–2011 and specific economic development strategies. While the characteristics outlined above are statistically related to economic prosperity, it may not be easy to turn them into effective economic development strategies. In some cases "place luck" may be more important than local economic development initiatives (Reese and Ye, 2011). The potential economic benefits of a milder climate, larger population, or proximity to a major urban area are not things that can be legislated by a local municipality. At best,

Table 10.4 Municipal Amalgamation and Economic Prosperity

	Number of Metros	Avg. EPI 1991	Avg. EPI 2011	Change
2000 or later	12	300	286	-14
1990–99	8	296	297	+1
Pre-1990 or none	22	296	299	+3

midsize urban areas can develop an economic strategy that focuses on their particular favorable attributes.

Nevertheless, there are a wide range of economic development strategies available to midsize urban areas. Not all of them, however, are appropriate in every instance. For example, although heritage buildings and tourism are common attributes of prosperous communities (Filion et al., 2004), urban areas such as Kamloops or Barrie lack a critical mass of heritage properties. Nanaimo's efforts to increase tourism by attracting cruise ships may have greater potential for success than efforts to make North Bay a tourist destination.

Equally important, however, is the fact that there is no guarantee that any particular strategy will be effective in all circumstances. Economic development initiatives are often successful only as long as they are innovative or unique. To cite an American example, Atlantic City's adoption of casino gambling was initially successful so long as there was little competition other than Las Vegas. As casinos proliferated in the Eastern United States, however, Atlantic City has lost its luster. With this in mind, the potential benefits of some of these strategies are summarized here.

Immigrants

This research found a significant and positive relationship between community economic health and its immigrant population. Immigration is the diversity variable that was most consistently related to economic health.[3]

---

3. Other research suggests that the direction of causality runs from immigrants to economic prosperity, rather than immigrants being attracted to prosperous locations.

Greater diversity among residents, particularly within the immigrant population, is significantly correlated with future economic health, even controlling for other demographic and employment factors. Other aspects of diversity—language, visible minority status, and religion—were also related to economic health; but only the correlation with the foreign born remained significant in multiple regression.

Population diversity appears to be more important than the presence of a particular immigrant group in its contribution to economic health. The presence of immigrants from different countries has only slightly different relationships to economic health. Immigration from Africa, the Middle East, East Asia, and Southeast Asia was most strongly related to health. However, any type of immigration was related to economic health, particularly when cities outside Quebec are considered.

Although there is a strong statistical correlation between the two measures, it is not possible to specify with certainty the causal elements in the relationship. It seems just as logical to argue that immigrants were drawn to prosperous communities as it is to argue that a large immigrant population is responsible for the prosperity. In the case of the Quebec urban areas, the limitations inherent in the provincial preference for francophone immigrants may be the most important factor.

These findings may be relevant to local public policy in two distinct ways. First, most of the Canadian efforts to utilize immigration as an economic development tool have primarily occurred at the national and, increasingly, provincial levels. Local government officials might do well to consider immigration and diversity as potentially important to economic development efforts. At present, few local governments have established immigrant attraction programs to augment federal and provincial efforts.

Programs to support immigrants once they have arrived are potentially another important aspect of local government economic development policies. Both the Waterloo region and Windsor have high proportions of foreign-born residents and well-developed public services to meet their needs. In Waterloo, the initiatives not only seek to attract immigrants but also to facilitate recognition of foreign professional certification. There is a conscious effort to allow immigrants to fully participate in and contribute to the local economy. In Windsor, on the other hand, most of the immigrant services seem to have been established to address the needs of foreign-born populations that have already located in the city.

Creative Class

Many cities across North America have turned to creative class strategies in their efforts to foster economic prosperity and growth. Unlike traditional economic incentive strategies, the creative class strategies focus on creating a milieu that is conducive to attracting talented people to the community. It is presumed that a tolerant, amenity-rich environment will attract talented, creative people. This pool of talent will attract New Economy employment, initiating a virtuous cycle of prosperity and growth.

Not surprisingly, individual communities have tended to focus on creativity and amenities, rather than attempting to make improvements in the more nebulous area of community tolerance. In particular, place making and third-place strategies (efforts to preserve and foster local identity [Mayer and Knox, 2006]) have become increasingly common. However, the definition of the key creative concepts is not always straightforward. The evaluation of these strategies requires the clear and consistent definition of the specific variables.

The data from the midsize urban areas fail to provide anything like a definitive basis for pursuing creative class economic development strategies, however. While racial and ethnic diversity and creative occupations were significantly correlated with concurrent Economic Prosperity Index scores, the relationships with technology employment were not. There were, moreover, no significant correlates with change in prosperity over time. This suggests that increases in the creative class population provide little assurance that increases in prosperity will follow.

These findings must be viewed cautiously, however. There is a possibility of misspecification of the key variables and a different time period might produce different results. Even if these results are robust to changes in variable specification and the time period examined, it is not easy to dismiss creative class strategies completely. Arguably, a community that is tolerant of different races, ethnicities, lifestyle choices, religions, and immigrants is a more attractive place in which to live. Investing in arts, culture, and special places will provide benefits for current community residents even if it does not contribute to population and economic growth. Creative class economic development strategies may not provide the ultimate answer to every community's economic development needs, but they seem unlikely to be harmful.

City Centers

Along with the widespread acceptance of creative class–based strategies, there is a growing interest in "place making." This includes not only ascribing greater importance to the public realm, but also to those locations providing opportunities for interactions with friends as well as strangers. Perhaps the most important of these special places is the city center, a community's downtown. For generations raised in bland suburban environments, the city center provides an important gathering place that offers not only a variety of entertainment and recreational activities but also a physical setting that is distinct from the suburban malls or entertainment centers surrounded by acres of parking. While heritage buildings can make a positive contribution to the city center environment, even an architecturally undistinguished physical setting can be sufficiently different from potential suburban competition.

The increasing importance of the city center as an entertainment and recreational hub coincides with the decline of the city center as a retail and sometimes employment center. The reimaging of downtowns as leisure activity centers takes advantage of the city centers' existing building stock (frequently vacant commercial space), its high degree of accessibility, and often a relatively substantial daytime population of office workers. For many local governments, making the city center a priority can take different forms, ranging from capital improvements such as parking facilities, sports facilities, and tourist attractions, to supportive development regulations and high quality public services.

A successful entertainment-oriented city center may rely on a private or quasi-governmental organization to guide the functioning of the opportunities and activities that will attract local visitors and tourists alike. Downtown Development Authorities (DDAs), Main Street initiatives, and Business Improvement Areas (BIAs) can play an important role in addressing city center needs. While the goals of these organizations may

be similar, the differences in their financing and governance can make a
significant difference in their success. A DDA that enjoys a substantial
and steady income from a tax increment financing district is better suited
for the development of substantial public infrastructure, such as parking facilities and street improvements. A BIA that relies on its members'
voluntary contributions is a more appropriate choice for supplementary
litter control and public safety initiatives. Perhaps most importantly, the
Ontario BIAs seem to be much more adaptable to changing circumstances and able to adopt new priorities when necessary.

It should also be noted that, while a great deal of attention has been
given to ensuring the quality of the city center environment, there is little
indication that a successful and well-regarded downtown provides any
guarantee of community-wide economic prosperity.

New Urbanism

There has also been increasing attention paid to the quality of the public realm in other parts of urban areas. The prescriptive physical design
standards proposed by the New Urbanism movement can be applied to
new peripheral neighborhoods and in-fill redevelopments, as well as to
city centers. While not explicitly an economic development strategy, the
emphasis on place making and linkages to walkable communities and
environmental quality all serve to link new urban developments to community quality.

Planned communities in Canada have a history dating back more
than a half-century. They have often provided prototypes for other developments. From Don Mills through the planned developments in Mississauga, suburban form (low density, single use, automobile oriented) has
dominated development in urban areas of all sizes.

Our examination of new urban developments in Ontario and Quebec suggests that, while New Urban developments have gained market
acceptance, the general public does not appear to value the pure forms
of New Urban development as much as the professional advocates do.
Local government officials may be reluctant to make a full commitment
to New Urban design principles, particularly rear lanes and public transit service. These features, however, were not always highly valued by

residents. Some of the most successful New Urban developments are priced somewhat below the prevailing market. Thus, it is not clear that the New Urban developments were able to command the price premium that is often required. While the mixing of residential and commercial services was generally accepted by residents, the economic viability of neighborhood commercial is by no means assured.

Casino Gambling

Regardless of any moral considerations, casino gambling can be a potentially lucrative source of revenue for governments. The traditionally high-profit margins of casinos allows governments to impose high tax rates on both their operations and the winnings of their customers. Taxes on wagering are not so much viewed as sin taxes (where punitive rates are used as a means of discouraging the activity) but rather as a voluntary form of taxation—people can easily avoid the taxes by refraining from gambling.

Because casino gambling falls within the purview of senior levels of government (state or provincial, in some cases national), the potential benefits to the local jurisdiction where the gambling facilities are located can vary considerably. In Ontario, a provincial agency collects the taxes and returns a portion of the revenue to local governments in the form of competitive grants or, in the case of the larger resort casinos, in fixed annual payments. The financial arrangements for sharing revenue from the tribal casinos between the state of Michigan and the local jurisdictions are similar. The three casinos in the city of Detroit, however, pay wagering taxes to both the state and to the city (roughly ten percent of gross operating income to each), in addition to employee income taxes, real property taxes, and licensing fees. This arrangement is highly beneficial to the city, with the casinos generating almost one-quarter of Detroit's general fund revenues. Before any midsize city should embrace gambling as an economic development tool, consideration must be given to the terms of the deal—the monetary/tax return for the city and hiring preferences for local residents, as well as the potential negative externalities in terms of burdens on local infrastructure and services in the forms of traffic and crime.

CONCLUSIONS

In our examination of the various public policies related to the economic prosperity of midsize Canadian urban areas, two important conclusions have emerged. First, there is little evidence that any of the strategies considered were actually very effective in maintaining or increasing prosperity. The most consistently reliable predictors of economic prosperity were the current and past prosperity levels in that community. Even in urban areas with a volatile economic base, such as those reliant on natural resources for their economic base, the correlations between past and current levels of prosperity were high.

Concluding that economic development strategies cannot be shown to have measurable impacts of future prosperity is not the same as concluding that such policies are completely without value, however. Indeed, the second important observation that can be drawn from these studies is that, while many public policies are not clearly effective in raising economic prosperity, they can nevertheless contribute to the quality of life of residents. For example, city center improvements, whether "clean and safe" initiatives, programmed activities such as concerts and fairs, or physical improvements from benches to banners, can make the city center more attractive for residents and visitors alike. Better urban design, heritage preservation, and improvements that encourage walkability are also beneficial.

As rates of natural population increase slow, immigrants are increasingly important sources of population growth. Programs to attract or support immigrants can also benefit the community as a whole. Ensuring that supportive services are available to the foreign born and that their occupational credentials are recognized, enabling them to contribute fully to community life, are strategies that are not only useful but may also be effective in attracting additional immigrants.

While the presence of a local university is not something midsize cities can easily control, the links between education levels and economic prosperity should not be ignored (Reese and Ye, 2011). Investment in local public schools is well within the control of city officials and will serve to improve the local employment base and make the city an attractive location for new residents, particularly families (Reese, 2012). Similarly, other research has shown that spending on local public services—police, fire, parks and recreation, public buildings—and public amenities—libraries and parks—is correlated with economic prosperity (Reese and Ye, 2011). Further, recent research has concluded that general quality of life indicators such as air quality, walkability, safety, and open spaces are significantly correlated with economic prosperity (Peach and Petach, 2016). Thus, investing in the basics of local government is something every city can and should do.

Among the economic development strategies for midsize urban areas that we have considered, the only one that does not appear to be worth exploring is casino gambling. While in some instances casinos may provide substantial community benefits, as noted previously, the gambling market appears to be reaching saturation and the proliferation of casinos significantly diminishes their potential value as tourist attractions. Certainly from a community perspective, the nature of the financial arrangements with the senior level of government is critical to determining if this strategy would be worthwhile.

As has been mentioned throughout, these midsize Canadian urban areas exhibit a number of common characteristics and similar trends. Generally, the two decades covered by this research have been a period of modest growth that has allowed them to enjoy average levels of economic prosperity. Most of these communities with manufacturing and natural resource based economies have maintained these specializations. The majority of these communities, however, were found to have a local economy with no dominant specialization in 2011. Nevertheless, important differences remain in characteristics such as proportion of foreign born, creative, and knowledge-based occupations. This diversity offers the potential for adaption of successful economic development strategies from other midsize communities.

Our primary conclusion is not, however, that economic development initiatives should be ignored. Rather, we would encourage communities to be realistic in their expectations of what can be achieved by their investments in economic development. There are no silver bullets that can offer a guarantee of economic prosperity. Nor are there economic development initiatives that would be equally effective in all circumstances. But if a community invests in those things that enhance the quality of life of its residents, the return on these investments may be justified, even if they do not lead directly to economic prosperity.

Appendix A. Metropolitan Area Data

Table A1 Demographics

1991				
Urban Area	Province	Population	Immigrants	University Degrees
Abbotsford	BC	59,578	15.3%	6.2%
Barrie	ON	92,165	12.5%	9.2%
Belleville	ON	95,000	8.6%	7.4%
Brantford	ON	97,106	13.8%	7.3%
Chilliwack	BC	60,251	15.6%	5.4%
Cornwall	ON	53,545	5.7%	6.0%
Drummondville	QC	60,092	1.3%	6.8%
Fredericton	NB	71,869	5.9%	18.7%
Granby	QC	56,835	2.2%	6.5%
Greater Sudbury	ON	157,613	8.1%	9.0%
Guelph	ON	97,213	19.2%	16.7%
Halifax	NS	320,501	6.5%	16.8%
Kamloops	BC	57,856	14.3%	7.6%
Kelowna	BC	111,846	14.9%	7.2%
Kingston	ON	136,401	13.1%	16.0%
Kitchener	ON	366,421	20.7%	11.9%
Lethbridge	AB	60,974	14.9%	11.6%
London	ON	381,522	18.5%	15.1%
Medicine Hat	AB	52,681	9.1%	6.2%
Moncton	NB	106,503	3.2%	10.3%
Nanaimo	BC	73,547	14.7%	7.4%
North Bay	ON	63,285	5.8%	8.9%
Oshawa	ON	240,104	17.0%	8.4%
Peterborough	ON	98,060	9.1%	9.6%

Table A1 1991 (*continued*)

Urban Area	Province	Population	Immigrants	University Degrees
Prince George	BC	69,653	11.6%	7.1%
Red Deer	AB	58,134	9.1%	8.1%
Regina	SK	191,692	8.3%	13.0%
Saguenay	QC	160,928	0.7%	8.3%
Saint-Hyacinthe	QC	49,333	1.8%	7.1%
Saint-Jean-sur-Richelieu	QC	68,378	3.2%	8.1%
Saint John	NB	124,981	4.2%	8.9%
Sarnia	ON	87,870	14.7%	9.5%
Saskatoon	SK	210,023	8.2%	14.2%
Sault Ste. Marie	ON	85,008	12.3%	8.4%
Shawinigan	QC	60,434	0.8%	5.2%
Sherbrooke	QC	139,194	3.7%	12.0%
St. Catharines-Niagara	ON	364,552	18.6%	9.2%
St. John's	NL	171,859	2.8%	13.2%
Thunder Bay	ON	124,427	13.0%	9.5%
Trois-Rivières	QC	136,303	1.3%	8.9%
Victoria	BC	287,897	19.2%	14.7%
Windsor	ON	262,075	20.5%	10.3%

1996						
Urban Area	Province	Population	Visible Minorities	Immigrants	University Degrees	Public Transit Commuters
Abbotsford	BC	136,480	12.7%	20.0%	13.5%	5.8%
Barrie	ON	118,695	2.6%	11.4%	13.8%	8.5%
Belleville	ON	87,871	2.7%	8.2%	11.9%	10.2%
Brantford	ON	84,754	5.0%	12.7%	10.9%	8.9%
Chilliwack	BC	66,254	0.0%	14.7%	4.1%	0.8%
Cornwall	ON	58,495	0.0%	5.8%	8.4%	4.2%
Drummondville	QC	65,119	0.7%	1.7%	11.9%	10.0%
Fredericton	NB	78,950	2.9%	6.0%	26.9%	13.2%
Granby	QC	58,872	0.9%	2.2%	12.9%	8.8%
Greater Sudbury	ON	165,648	5.2%	20.3%	23.3%	14.3%
Guelph	ON	105,420	21.2%	6.9%	25.9%	21.8%
Halifax	NS	332,518	1.4%	11.2%	15.4%	9.3%
Kamloops	BC	85,407	6.1%	16.7%	15.2%	8.4%
Kelowna	BC	136,541	4.6%	13.2%	21.4%	16.5%
Kingston	ON	144,528	23.6%	21.6%	17.5%	10.7%
Kitchener	ON	382,940	1.3%	13.8%	17.9%	9.2%
Lethbridge	AB	63,053	48.1%	19.0%	19.9%	14.2%
London	ON	398,616	0.4%	8.7%	10.9%	6.6%
Medicine Hat	AB	56,570	1.9%	3.2%	17.8%	10.8%
Moncton	NB	113,491	4.9%	15.5%	16.3%	11.3%
Nanaimo	BC	82,691	1.0%	5.7%	15.0%	16.8%
North Bay	ON	64,785	24.8%	16.4%	13.4%	10.1%
Oshawa	ON	268,773	0.8%	9.1%	14.9%	12.4%
Peterborough	ON	100,285	3.8%	13.4%	10.6%	8.3%
Prince George	BC	87,731	3.4%	9.5%	13.3%	10.2%
Red Deer	AB	60,080	17.2%	7.9%	21.5%	11.9%
Regina	SK	193,652	0.4%	0.7%	15.6%	9.3%
Saguenay	QC	160,454	0.2%	1.6%	13.3%	9.3%
Saint-Hyacinthe	QC	50,027	1.1%	2.6%	13.8%	11.9%

Table A1 1996 (*continued*)

Urban Area	Province	Population	Visible Minorities	Immigrants	University Degrees	Public Transit Commuters
Saint-Jean-sur-Richelieu	QC	75,451	3.3%	3.9%	15.9%	11.7%
Saint John	NB	125,705	2.1%	13.8%	14.1%	8.2%
Sarnia	ON	86,480	13.0%	7.5%	21.8%	13.6%
Saskatoon	SK	219,056	0.5%	11.8%	14.5%	10.6%
Sault Ste. Marie	ON	83,619	0.3%	0.6%	11.7%	11.3%
Shawinigan	QC	59,851	5.0%	4.3%	20.9%	13.5%
Sherbrooke	QC	147,384	9.1%	18.1%	13.4%	8.4%
St. Catharines-Niagara	ON	372,406	0.6%	7.4%	22.1%	9.4%
St. John's	NL	174,051	1.6%	2.9%	13.5%	11.9%
Thunder Bay	ON	125,562	2.1%	12.1%	16.2%	10.2%
Trois-Rivières	QC	139,956	0.9%	1.5%	18.0%	10.5%
Victoria	BC	304,287	7.5%	19.0%	24.4%	24.5%
Windsor	ON	278,685	9.9%	19.4%	16.8%	9.7%

2001						
Urban Area	Province	Population	Visible Minorities	Immigrants	University Degrees	Public Transit Commuters
Abbotsford	BC	147,370	17.5%	22.0%	9.7%	6.1%
Barrie	ON	148,480	4.0%	11.6%	10.2%	7.7%
Belleville	ON	87,395	2.8%	8.6%	8.8%	9.8%
Brantford	ON	86,417	5.2%	14.3%	8.2%	8.0%
Chilliwack	BC	69,776	3.8%	12.9%	7.7%	10.0%
Cornwall	ON	57,581	3.3%	6.4%	7.0%	10.1%
Drummondville	QC	68,451	0.7%	1.8%	8.8%	9.4%
Fredericton	NB	81,346	3.0%	5.5%	22.9%	11.0%
Granby	QC	60,264	1.0%	2.4%	9.4%	8.6%
Greater Sudbury	ON	155,601	2.0%	7.0%	10.9%	11.9%
Guelph	ON	117,344	10.6%	19.7%	21.9%	14.5%
Halifax	NS	359,183	7.0%	6.8%	21.1%	21.1%
Kamloops	BC	86,491	5.4%	10.2%	10.4%	9.8%
Kelowna	BC	147,739	3.9%	13.9%	10.6%	9.4%
Kingston	ON	146,838	4.6%	12.4%	18.7%	16.1%
Kitchener	ON	414,284	10.6%	22.1%	15.5%	9.9%
Lethbridge	AB	67,374	5.7%	11.9%	14.0%	8.4%
London	ON	432,451	8.9%	18.8%	16.1%	13.4%
Medicine Hat	AB	61,735	3.3%	7.5%	8.5%	6.9%
Moncton	NB	117,727	1.3%	2.9%	13.7%	10.5%
Nanaimo	BC	85,664	5.9%	15.5%	11.4%	10.7%
North Bay	ON	63,681	1.3%	5.1%	11.6%	14.7%
Oshawa	ON	296,298	7.0%	15.7%	11.0%	11.2%
Peterborough	ON	102,423	2.7%	8.9%	13.0%	12.2%
Prince George	BC	85,035	5.3%	9.8%	9.4%	7.6%
Red Deer	AB	67,707	5.2%	8.7%	10.6%	9.9%
Regina	SK	192,800	5.1%	7.4%	15.5%	11.0%
Saguenay	QC	154,938	0.6%	0.9%	10.8%	9.1%
Saint-Hyacinthe	QC	49,536	0.9%	1.9%	9.7%	13.5%

Table A1 2001 (*continued*)

Urban Area	Province	Population	Visible Minorities	Immigrants	University Degrees	Public Transit Commuters
Saint-Jean-sur-Richelieu	QC	79,600	1.1%	2.6%	9.4%	12.2%
Saint John	NB	122,678	2.6%	3.8%	12.8%	11.6%
Sarnia	ON	88,331	2.9%	12.7%	10.3%	6.8%
Saskatoon	SK	225,927	5.5%	7.6%	17.5%	12.3%
Sault Ste. Marie	ON	78,908	1.2%	11.4%	11.7%	10.7%
Shawinigan	QC	57,304	0.2%	0.9%	7.5%	11.6%
Sherbrooke	QC	153,811	2.5%	4.6%	15.3%	13.6%
St. Catharines-Niagara	ON	377,009	4.5%	17.8%	11.1%	7.9%
St. John's	NL	172,918	1.3%	2.9%	16.7%	8.8%
Thunder Bay	ON	121,986	2.2%	11.1%	12.7%	9.5%
Trois-Rivières	QC	137,507	0.9%	1.5%	12.3%	10.5%
Victoria	BC	311,902	8.7%	18.8%	19.8%	24.9%
Windsor	ON	307,877	12.8%	22.3%	16.0%	8.8%

2006						
Urban Area	Province	Population	Visible Minorities	Immigrants	University Degrees	Public Transit Commuters
Abbotsford	BC	159,020	22.5%	23.3%	11.6%	5.6%
Barrie	ON	177,061	5.7%	17.7%	12.6%	8.3%
Belleville	ON	91,518	3.8%	8.7%	10.3%	10.4%
Brantford	ON	124,607	5.4%	13.0%	11.1%	9.0%
Chilliwack	BC	82,465	4.2%	13.9%	8.8%	7.1%
Cornwall	ON	58,485	4.8%	8.0%	8.5%	8.7%
Drummondville	QC	78,108	2.1%	2.9%	10.3%	8.6%
Fredericton	NB	85,688	4.4%	6.9%	25.4%	12.4%
Granby	QC	68,352	1.9%	3.5%	10.8%	7.8%
Greater Sudbury	ON	158,258	2.1%	6.6%	13.2%	12.0%
Guelph	ON	136,698	12.6%	20.3%	23.9%	14.4%
Halifax	NS	372,858	7.4%	7.4%	24.0%	23.0%
Kamloops	BC	92,882	5.6%	10.4%	11.7%	10.6%
Kelowna	BC	162,276	5.1%	14.6%	12.6%	9.4%
Kingston	ON	152,358	5.6%	12.5%	21.7%	16.1%
Kitchener	ON	451,235	13.6%	22.8%	15.7%	11.5%
Lethbridge	AB	95,196	5.9%	12.1%	14.7%	9.2%
London	ON	457,720	11.0%	19.1%	18.3%	14.4%
Medicine Hat	AB	68,822	3.0%	7.6%	9.1%	6.7%
Moncton	NB	126,424	1.9%	3.4%	18.0%	11.4%
Nanaimo	BC	92,361	7.2%	15.5%	14.0%	11.3%
North Bay	ON	63,424	2.0%	5.7%	14.1%	15.5%
Oshawa	ON	330,594	10.2%	16.3%	13.1%	11.7%
Peterborough	ON	116,570	2.7%	9.4%	14.5%	12.6%
Prince George	BC	83,225	5.3%	9.3%	12.0%	8.5%
Red Deer	AB	82,772	7.0%	9.2%	11.4%	10.4%
Regina	SK	194,971	5.5%	7.6%	18.4%	11.4%
Saguenay	QC	156,305	0.9%	1.2%	12.5%	8.7%
Saint-Hyacinthe	QC	54,976	2.1%	4.1%	10.7%	12.9%

Table A1 2006 (*continued*)

Urban Area	Province	Population	Visible Minorities	Immigrants	University Degrees	Public Transit Commuters
Saint-Jean-sur-Richelieu	QC	87,492	1.5%	3.3%	11.4%	13.0%
Saint John	NB	122,389	3.1%	4.2%	14.1%	12.0%
Sarnia	ON	88,793	3.4%	12.6%	11.7%	9.0%
Saskatoon	SK	233,923	6.4%	7.7%	19.7%	12.3%
Sault Ste. Marie	ON	80,098	1.2%	10.3%	13.4%	12.1%
Shawinigan	QC	56,434	0.3%	0.7%	8.2%	10.4%
Sherbrooke	QC	186,952	3.7%	5.5%	17.6%	13.1%
St. Catharines-Niagara	ON	390,317	6.5%	18.0%	13.1%	8.0%
St. John's	NL	181,113	1.9%	2.9%	18.8%	9.7%
Thunder Bay	ON	122,907	2.7%	10.3%	14.8%	10.7%
Trois-Rivières	QC	141,529	1.6%	2.2%	13.6%	9.9%
Victoria	BC	330,088	10.3%	19.1%	23.6%	26.3%
Windsor	ON	323,342	15.8%	23.1%	17.8%	8.5%

	2011					
Urban Area	Province	Population	Visible Minorities	Immigrants	University Degrees	Public Transit Commuters
Abbotsford	BC	166,650	19.3%	23.4%	13.6%	2.3%
Barrie	ON	184,330	6.4%	12.1%	24.5%	4.3%
Belleville	ON	90,660	3.4%	7.0%	11.7%	2.2%
Brantford	ON	133,245	5.6%	11.3%	12.1%	2.6%
Chilliwack	BC	90,240	4.5%	12.7%	10.4%	1.2%
Cornwall	ON	57,420	5.4%	8.3%	9.3%	3.5%
Drummondville	QC	85,700	2.2%	2.7%	10.0%	0.8%
Fredericton	NB	93,085	4.8%	6.8%	28.4%	2.7%
Granby	QC	77,077	2.6%	4.1%	12.6%	1.0%
Greater Sudbury	ON	160,770	2.7%	6.2%	15.6%	4.4%
Guelph	OB	141,097	14.0%	19.7%	26.1%	5.4%
Halifax	NS	390,328	5.1%	4.6%	27.0%	11.7%
Kamloops	BC	96,610	6.3%	9.1%	15.3%	4.0%
Kelowna	BC	176,435	6.0%	13.9%	15.4%	3.1%
Kingston	ON	159,561	6.1%	11.8%	23.5%	4.8%
Kitchener	ON	469,935	16.2%	23.1%	21.6%	5.1%
Lethbridge	AB	102,785	7.3%	12.1%	17.9%	2.6%
London	ON	467,260	13.1%	18.8%	20.4%	6.4%
Medicine Hat	AB	71,070	4.3%	7.2%	11.2%	2.0%
Moncton	NB	138,644	3.4%	2.1%	19.2%	3.1%
Nanaimo	BC	98,021	7.0%	14.1%	16.5%	3.0%
North Bay	ON	62,705	2.6%	5.4%	16.6%	1.6%
Oshawa	ON	381,640	10.9%	14.7%	15.7%	8.0%
Peterborough	ON	116,175	3.4%	8.2%	17.8%	3.2%
Prince George	BC	84,232	6.6%	9.5%	13.2%	6.8%
Red Deer	AB	88,730	9.7%	10.6%	13.7%	4.2%
Regina	SK	207,215	10.6%	10.5%	21.2%	4.6%
Saguenay	QC	154,235	0.8%	1.1%	13.8%	2.2%
Saint-Hyacinthe	QC	54,570	3.3%	4.0%	11.8%	1.4%

Table A1 2011 (*continued*)

Urban Area	Province	Population	Visible Minorities	Immigrants	University Degrees	Public Transit Commuters
Saint-Jean-sur-Richelieu	QC	90,375	1.8%	2.9%	12.1%	5.4%
Saint John	NB	125,005	3.7%	4.3%	16.5%	4.5%
Sarnia	ON	88,180	4.1%	10.9%	12.7%	2.0%
Saskatoon	SK	256,435	11.2%	10.7%	16.9%	4.2%
Sault Ste. Marie	ON	78,480	1.6%	8.7%	15.3%	4.3%
Shawinigan	QC	56,009	0.4%	0.5%	8.6%	1.0%
Sherbrooke	QC	196,680	4.4%	6.2%	19.1%	4.0%
St. Catharines-Niagara	ON	383,970	7.0%	16.8%	14.6%	2.7%
St. John's	NL	193,830	2.5%	3.0%	22.0%	2.9%
Thunder Bay	ON	119,145	3.1%	9.1%	17.4%	3.4%
Trois-Rivières	QC	146,930	2.4%	2.8%	15.4%	2.2%
Victoria	BC	336,180	11.2%	17.9%	26.6%	10.2%
Windsor	ON	315,460	17.2%	22.3%	19.2%	2.8%

Table A2 Manufacturing and Business Services Employment, 1991–2011

Urban Area	Manufacturing			Business Services		
	1991	2011	Change	1991	2011	Change
Abbotsford	7,440	8,065	625	4,390	8,385	3,995
Barrie	8,485	10,925	2,440	5,310	10,465	5,155
Belleville	8,695	5,260	(3,435)	3,930	3,220	(710)
Brantford	12,440	11,545	(895)	3,860	5,910	2,050
Chilliwack	2,400	3,435	1,035	2,585	3,820	1,235
Cornwall	5,650	3,425	(2,225)	1,905	1,935	30
Drummondville	7,757	9,680	1,923	2,275	3,425	1,150
Fredericton	1,820	1,670	(150)	4,245	6,540	2,295
Granby	9,980	10,005	25	2,370	4,105	1,735
Greater Sudbury	6,345	3,295	(3,050)	6,195	7,790	1,595
Guelph	12,850	15,220	2,370	5,685	9,845	4,160
Halifax	12,015	10,285	(1,730)	21,875	30,140	8,265
Kamloops	2,895	2,605	(290)	2,830	5,305	2,475
Kelowna	4,265	5,460	1,195	5,520	12,350	6,830
Kingston	6,115	4,000	(2,115)	6,465	7,965	1,500
Kitchener	51,830	49,225	(2,605)	23,345	37,390	14,045
Lethbridge	3,080	4,670	1,590	2,580	5,740	3,160
London	33,425	28,670	(4,755)	25,750	32,490	6,740
Medicine Hat	1,830	1,545	(285)	1,600	4,085	2,485
Moncton	4,115	5,020	905	5,300	9,000	3,700
Nanaimo	3,635	1,670	(1,965)	3,375	5,445	2,070
North Bay	2,265	1,350	(915)	2,380	2,705	325
Oshawa	24,985	18,615	(6,370)	14,560	24,495	9,935
Peterborough	7,505	5,140	(2,365)	4,710	5,465	755
Prince George	5,465	3,765	(1,700)	2,820	4,110	1,290
Red Deer	2,735	4,010	1,275	2,695	5,535	2,840
Regina	8,205	6,060	(2,145)	13,195	16,640	3,445
Saguenay	11,205	9,035	(2,170)	5,995	7,375	1,380
Saint-Hyacinthe	5,505	4,850	(655)	2,415	3,085	670

Table A2 (*continued*)

Urban Area	Manufacturing			Business Services		
	1991	2011	Change	1991	2011	Change
Saint-Jean-sur-Richelieu	7,270	7,645	375	3,250	5,120	1,870
Saint John	9,655	5,300	(4,355)	5,670	6,945	1,275
Sarnia	9,340	5,190	(4,150)	3,590	3,925	335
Saskatoon	8,800	9,875	1,075	11,170	17,410	6,240
Sault Ste. Marie	8,275	4,560	(3,715)	3,040	2,850	(190)
Shawinigan	6,030	3,760	(2,270)	1,600	1,645	45
Sherbrooke	11,870	13,000	1,130	6,140	10,730	4,590
St. Catharines-Niagara	38,415	19,245	(19,170)	16,585	17,960	1,375
St. John's	4,730	4,375	(355)	8,180	11,540	3,360
Thunder Bay	7,745	2,975	(4,770)	5,235	5,940	705
Trois-Rivières	12,265	9,090	(3,175)	5,660	6,550	890
Victoria	7,255	6,065	(1,190)	16,765	25,835	9,070
Windsor	36,980	27,820	(9,160)	11,535	14,145	2,610
MID-SIZE	443,567	367,400	(76,167)	288,580	415,355	126,775
Canada	2,084,715	2,834,000	749,285	1,612,969	2,348,000	735,031

Source: Statistics Canada

Table A3 Economic Base

Urban Area	1991	1996	2001	2006	2011
Abbotsford	Natural Resources	Natural Resources	Natural Resources	Natural Resources	Natural Resources
Barrie	Trade	Trade	Diversified	Diversified	Diversified
Belleville	Trade	Trade	Diversified	Diversified	Diversified
Brantford	Manufac-turing	Manufac-turing	Manufac-turing	Manufac-turing	Manufac-turing
Chilliwack	Natural Resources	Natural Resources	Natural Resources	Natural Resources	Diversified
Cornwall	Diversified	Diversified	Manufac-turing	Diversified	Diversified
Drummondville	Manufac-turing	Manufac-turing	Manufac-turing	Manufac-turing	Manufac-turing
Fredericton	Higher Ed./Health	Health/ Education	Other Services	Other Services	Diversified
Granby	Manufac-turing	Manufac-turing	Manufac-turing	Manufac-turing	Manufac-turing
Greater Sudbury	Natural Resources	Natural Resources	Natural Resources	Natural Resources	Natural Resources
Guelph	Manufac-turing	Manufac-turing	Manufac-turing	Manufac-turing	Manufac-turing
Halifax	Higher Ed./Health	Health/ Education	Other Services	Diversified	Diversified
Kamloops	Trade	Trade	Diversified	Diversified	Natural Resources
Kelowna	Natural Resources	Natural Resources	Diversified	Diversified	Diversified
Kingston	Higher Ed./Health	Health/ Education	Higher Ed./Health	Higher Ed./Health	Diversified
Kitchener	Manufac-turing	Manufac-turing	Manufac-turing	Manufac-turing	Health/ Education
Lethbridge	Higher Ed./Health	Health/ Education	Higher Ed./Health	Natural Resources	Natural Resources
London	Diversified	Diversified	Higher Ed./Health	Diversified	Diversified

Table A3 (continued)

Urban Area	1991	1996	2001	2006	2011
Medicine Hat	Natural Resources	Natural Resources	Natural Resources	Natural Resources	Natural Resources
Moncton	Trade	Trade	Higher Ed./Health	Diversified	Other
Nanaimo	Trade	Trade	Diversified	Diversified	Diversified
North Bay	Trade	Trade	Higher Ed./Health	Higher Ed./Health	Health/Education
Oshawa	Manufacturing	Manufacturing	Diversified	Diversified	Diversified
Peterborough	Diversified	Services	Higher Ed./Health	Diversified	Diversified
Prince George	Natural Resources	Natural Resources	Natural Resources	Natural Resources	Natural Resources
Red Deer	Natural Resources	Natural Resources	Natural Resources	Natural Resources	Natural Resources
Regina	Higher Ed./Health	Health/Education	Higher Ed./Health	Diversified	Diversified
Saguenay	Diversified	Diversified	Higher Ed./Health	Diversified	Diversified
Saint-Hyacinthe	Manufacturing	Manufacturing	Manufacturing	Manufacturing	Manufacturing
Saint-Jean-sur-Richelieu	Manufacturing	Manufacturing	Manufacturing	Manufacturing	Manufacturing
Saint John	Diversified	Diversified	Diversified	Diversified	Diversified
Sarnia	Manufacturing	Manufacturing	Diversified	Diversified	Diversified
Saskatoon	Natural Resources	Natural Resources	Higher Ed./Health	Business Services	Diversified
Sault Ste. Marie	Diversified	Diversified	Higher Ed./Health	Diversified	Diversified
Shawinigan	Manufacturing	Manufacturing	Higher Ed./Health	Manufacturing	Diversified
Sherbrooke	Diversified	Diversified	Higher Ed./Health	Business Services	Health/Education

Table A3 (continued)

Urban Area	1991	1996	2001	2006	2011
St. Catharines-Niagara	Manufacturing	Manufacturing	Diversified	Diversified	Diversified
St. John's	Diversified	Diversified	Higher Ed./Health	Other Services	Diversified
Thunder Bay	Diversified	Diversified	Higher Ed./Health	Business Services	Health/Education
Trois-Rivières	Diversified	Diversified	Diversified	Diversified	Diversified
Victoria	Higher Ed./Health	Health/Education	Higher Ed./Health	Other Services	Diversified
Windsor	Manufacturing	Manufacturing	Manufacturing	Manufacturing	Manufacturing

Table A4 Creative Occupations

Urban Area	1991	2001	2011
Abbotsford	1.19%	1.13%	1.32%
Barrie	1.04%	1.26%	1.70%
Belleville	0.84%	0.95%	1.15%
Brantford	0.73%	1.02%	1.41%
Chilliwack	0.95%	1.16%	0.74%
Cornwall	0.72%	0.63%	0.24%
Drummondville	1.02%	0.93%	0.87%
Fredericton	1.00%	1.20%	1.53%
Granby	1.09%	1.26%	1.21%
Greater Sudbury	0.90%	0.80%	0.94%
Guelph	0.98%	1.45%	1.42%
Halifax	1.34%	1.71%	1.64%
Kamloops	1.10%	1.37%	1.12%
Kelowna	1.09%	1.60%	1.69%
Kingston	1.22%	1.36%	1.48%
Kitchener	1.19%	1.37%	1.11%
Lethbridge	1.03%	1.12%	1.09%
London	1.22%	1.27%	1.40%
Medicine Hat	0.90%	1.22%	1.22%
Moncton	0.87%	1.01%	1.20%
Nanaimo	1.14%	1.44%	1.84%
North Bay	1.15%	1.14%	0.94%
Oshawa	0.97%	1.14%	1.39%
Peterborough	1.13%	1.14%	1.32%
Prince George	0.84%	0.92%	0.93%
Red Deer	1.16%	1.12%	1.15%
Regina	1.45%	1.34%	1.34%
Saguenay	1.17%	0.79%	0.90%
Saint-Hyacinthe	1.14%	1.15%	0.50%
Saint-Jean-sur-Richelieu	0.87%	0.78%	0.99%

Table A4 (*continued*)

Urban Area	1991	2001	2011
Saint John	0.76%	1.10%	0.94%
Sarnia	0.87%	1.03%	0.76%
Saskatoon	1.27%	1.39%	0.99%
Sault Ste. Marie	0.72%	0.88%	1.06%
Shawinigan	0.73%	0.82%	0.52%
Sherbrooke	2.03%	1.16%	1.12%
St. Catharines-Niagara	1.18%	1.34%	1.52%
St. John's	2.00%	1.52%	1.52%
Thunder Bay	0.76%	0.94%	1.11%
Trois-Rivières	0.88%	1.16%	1.05%
Victoria	1.74%	2.43%	1.61%
Windsor	0.82%	0.82%	0.77%

APPENDIX A

Table A5 Components of the Economic Prosperity Index

| Urban Area | 1991 | | | |
	Median Household Income	Market Income	Employment Rate	Prosperity Index
Abbotsford	$35,991	87.6%	89.6%	291
Barrie	$39,198	90.3%	91.7%	305
Belleville	$39,710	87.3%	90.9%	302
Brantford	$35,819	86.4%	90.3%	290
Chilliwack	$36,230	84.9%	89.9%	289
Cornwall	$34,726	84.4%	89.9%	284
Drummondville	$38,104	84.5%	89.0%	292
Fredericton	$41,401	89.6%	89.9%	307
Granby	$34,560	86.8%	89.4%	286
Greater Sudbury	$36,580	88.5%	91.3%	295
Guelph	$44,967	90.6%	92.5%	321
Halifax	$38,023	90.4%	90.8%	301
Kamloops	$35,092	87.8%	87.3%	286
Kelowna	$40,269	84.6%	87.7%	296
Kingston	$43,858	89.4%	92.5%	316
Kitchener	$40,836	90.6%	91.0%	308
Lethbridge	$36,915	87.8%	90.7%	295
London	$38,491	89.5%	91.5%	302
Medicine Hat	$37,860	87.0%	91.8%	297
Moncton	$36,753	86.2%	88.6%	290
Nanaimo	$40,327	85.7%	86.9%	297
North Bay	$39,912	87.1%	91.4%	302
Oshawa	$47,044	91.7%	91.5%	326
Peterborough	$41,397	86.1%	91.5%	305
Prince George	$30,835	90.8%	87.2%	279
Red Deer	$36,189	89.9%	91.8%	296
Regina	$30,047	90.2%	92.8%	282
Saguenay	$51,731	87.0%	86.6%	327
Saint-Hyacinthe	$42,312	86.1%	90.7%	307

Table A5 1991 (*continued*)

Urban Area	Median Household Income	Market Income	Employment Rate	Prosperity Index
Saint-Jean-sur-Richelieu	$31,745	86.3%	88.8%	278
Saint John	$27,829	86.3%	88.6%	267
Sarnia	$33,557	89.8%	90.7%	288
Saskatoon	$40,362	89.2%	91.3%	306
Sault Ste. Marie	$39,656	85.1%	88.6%	296
Shawinigan	$40,481	79.6%	83.4%	286
Sherbrooke	$39,602	85.7%	89.1%	297
St. Catharines-Niagara	$45,904	86.7%	90.5%	316
St. John's	$33,385	86.9%	83.9%	277
Thunder Bay	$37,708	87.5%	90.5%	296
Trois-Rivières	$42,514	85.0%	86.7%	301
Victoria	$44,812	87.8%	92.3%	317
Windsor	$32,076	87.7%	88.2%	279

1996				
Urban Area	Median Household Income	Market Income	Employment Rate	Prosperity Index
Abbotsford	$43,232	85.1%	90.0%	329
Barrie	$46,358	87.3%	91.4%	343
Belleville	$40,259	83.0%	89.6%	300
Brantford	$40,092	83.8%	91.3%	328
Chilliwack	$37,351	82.8%	86.6%	275
Cornwall	$33,512	80.9%	87.6%	258
Drummondville	$31,380	82.4%	90.2%	282
Fredericton	$41,251	82.4%	90.2%	300
Granby	$33,003	87.5%	90.1%	289
Greater Sudbury	$42,142	85.0%	88.0%	336
Guelph	$47,651	88.8%	93.4%	351
Halifax	$49,619	87.6%	91.4%	337
Kamloops	$43,482	86.9%	88.7%	304
Kelowna	$38,222	83.0%	90.3%	324
Kingston	$42,459	86.0%	90.6%	339
Kitchener	$46,027	88.5%	91.9%	348
Lethbridge	$38,014	85.4%	93.2%	297
London	$42,287	86.6%	90.7%	343
Medicine Hat	$38,261	85.5%	92.7%	294
Moncton	$39,084	84.8%	90.3%	320
Nanaimo	$38,063	83.4%	87.9%	287
North Bay	$38,776	83.8%	89.0%	295
Oshawa	$53,331	89.2%	91.0%	360
Peterborough	$38,770	82.4%	89.3%	292
Prince George	$50,799	89.7%	88.3%	324
Red Deer	$40,118	88.0%	90.3%	304
Regina	$41,376	88.0%	92.7%	342
Saguenay	$36,444	82.1%	91.0%	313
Saint-Hyacinthe	$32,512	82.8%	89.3%	284
Saint-Jean-sur-Richelieu	$34,856	83.4%	86.9%	291

Table A5 1996 (*continued*)

Urban Area	Median Household Income	Market Income	Employment Rate	Prosperity Index
Saint John	$37,827	86.2%	89.3%	315
Sarnia	$44,767	87.0%	92.5%	347
Saskatoon	$37,825	83.5%	87.1%	332
Sault Ste. Marie	$39,737	76.8%	84.5%	291
Shawinigan	$27,042	83.4%	89.7%	258
Sherbrooke	$31,493	83.3%	90.1%	314
St. Catharines-Niagara	$40,191	84.0%	85.8%	327
St. John's	$46,872	84.1%	90.8%	316
Thunder Bay	$44,129	85.3%	89.3%	339
Trois-Rivières	$32,052	82.4%	88.0%	312
Victoria	$42,213	86.2%	92.3%	348
Windsor	$45,989	87.3%	91.9%	352

	2001			
Urban Area	Median Household Income	Market Income	Employment Rate	Prosperity Index
Abbotsford	$48,721	86.5%	91.8%	290
Barrie	$57,703	90.8%	94.7%	310
Belleville	$43,885	85.1%	92.5%	293
Brantford	$43,908	86.6%	93.2%	298
Chilliwack	$41,850	85.3%	87.6%	290
Cornwall	$37,758	83.2%	91.5%	275
Drummondville	$36,383	82.8%	92.7%	282
Fredericton	$47,049	84.1%	91.6%	301
Granby	$39,692	88.8%	91.8%	293
Greater Sudbury	$45,206	86.5%	90.8%	296
Guelph	$57,523	91.4%	94.9%	329
Halifax	$46,941	89.2%	92.8%	306
Kamloops	$46,337	86.8%	89.6%	292
Kelowna	$46,492	84.7%	91.2%	290
Kingston	$47,979	88.1%	93.1%	307
Kitchener	$55,528	91.2%	94.5%	322
Lethbridge	$44,105	86.9%	94.5%	293
London	$48,026	89.0%	93.3%	310
Medicine Hat	$44,399	87.1%	94.6%	292
Moncton	$43,766	86.7%	91.9%	291
Nanaimo	$40,858	84.1%	88.4%	283
North Bay	$43,568	85.8%	91.6%	291
Oshawa	$62,956	91.7%	94.0%	333
Peterborough	$43,469	85.6%	92.6%	293
Prince George	$52,826	89.8%	88.7%	309
Red Deer	$50,556	90.4%	94.8%	311
Regina	$47,757	89.2%	94.0%	311
Saguenay	$41,854	84.2%	93.3%	279
Saint-Hyacinthe	$37,103	85.9%	93.2%	289
Saint-Jean-sur-Richelieu	$40,284	85.6%	90.8%	294

Table A5 2001 (*continued*)

Urban Area	Median Household Income	Market Income	Employment Rate	Prosperity Index
Saint John	$41,596	87.6%	92.5%	287
Sarnia	$48,090	88.5%	93.3%	302
Saskatoon	$48,392	84.6%	90.5%	299
Sault Ste. Marie	$43,582	79.4%	88.2%	286
Shawinigan	$32,549	85.4%	93.1%	283
Sherbrooke	$36,744	86.3%	94.0%	289
St. Catharines-Niagara	$46,881	86.4%	88.7%	298
St. John's	$53,836	86.3%	92.9%	286
Thunder Bay	$42,849	86.4%	91.2%	303
Trois-Rivières	$38,969	83.8%	90.8%	277
Victoria	$46,381	87.5%	93.4%	312
Windsor	$54,442	90.4%	93.7%	318

2006					
Urban Area	Median Household Income	Market Income	Employment Rate	Prosperity Index	CBD Score
Abbotsford	$54,535	87.6%	94.5%	292	3.62
Barrie	$66,036	90.7%	94.1%	318	4.50
Belleville	$51,648	85.8%	94.0%	297	4.00
Brantford	$56,624	87.5%	94.0%	305	1.93
Chilliwack	$49,342	84.4%	91.3%	281	3.87
Cornwall	$42,782	82.1%	92.7%	269	3.00
Drummondville	$41,563	83.6%	92.8%	303	3.57
Fredericton	$52,864	83.6%	92.8%	296	5.50
Granby	$39,789	89.5%	93.3%	306	na
Greater Sudbury	$54,959	85.8%	95.0%	291	3.76
Guelph	$65,991	87.4%	92.2%	312	5.55
Halifax	$54,108	91.6%	94.9%	310	6.27
Kamloops	$53,669	90.2%	93.7%	301	4.50
Kelowna	$50,308	87.7%	93.8%	299	4.46
Kingston	$55,531	87.1%	94.9%	310	6.09
Kitchener	$63,984	88.8%	93.4%	320	3.95
Lethbridge	$52,931	91.4%	94.4%	300	4.25
London	$48,293	89.0%	95.9%	312	4.41
Medicine Hat	$57,426	89.3%	93.9%	320	4.50
Moncton	$50,405	90.3%	96.0%	299	4.50
Nanaimo	$47,242	87.8%	93.8%	283	3.08
North Bay	$48,969	85.3%	93.0%	292	4.12
Oshawa	$72,329	85.7%	92.7%	330	3.36
Peterborough	$59,785	86.8%	92.9%	297	5.27
Prince George	$60,576	86.8%	92.9%	312	3.25
Red Deer	$63,064	90.2%	92.4%	322	4.62
Regina	$55,629	92.8%	95.6%	320	4.12
Saguenay	$46,410	90.4%	95.2%	287	3.75
Saint-Hyacinthe	$43,290	86.9%	92.0%	292	2.75

Table A5 2006 (*continued*)

Urban Area	Median Household Income	Market Income	Employment Rate	Prosperity Index	CBD Score
Saint-Jean-sur-Richelieu	$48,609	84.1%	94.1%	291	5.09
Saint John	$49,091	86.1%	95.1%	301	2.50
Sarnia	$58,095	88.8%	93.0%	320	5.37
Saskatoon	$51,169	90.2%	94.8%	299	3.50
Sault Ste. Marie	$49,797	84.9%	91.9%	283	3.56
Shawinigan	$36,077	79.0%	91.4%	292	2.00
Sherbrooke	$42,262	85.2%	93.1%	330	4.25
St. Catharines-Niagara	$53,057	86.4%	93.8%	285	4.51
St. John's	$52,864	87.6%	90.0%	309	4.89
Thunder Bay	$54,893	86.4%	92.6%	307	2.20
Trois-Rivières	$40,617	83.4%	92.7%	286	5.00
Victoria	$53,310	89.7%	95.7%	266	6.30
Windsor	$59,974	89.1%	91.8%	291	4.43

2011				
Urban Area	Median Household Income	Market Income	Employment Rate	Prosperity Index
Abbotsford	$63,315	86.3%	91.8%	302
Barrie	$70,745	87.5%	91.6%	315
Belleville	$56,306	82.2%	92.3%	286
Brantford	$59,665	83.7%	92.4%	294
Chilliwack	$55,275	84.0%	93.3%	288
Cornwall	$46,833	78.4%	90.0%	264
Drummondville	$44,805	80.8%	92.4%	266
Fredericton	$60,627	88.8%	92.5%	301
Granby	$48,914	84.1%	93.9%	278
Greater Sudbury	$62,472	85.4%	92.2%	300
Guelph	$71,597	89.0%	93.4%	320
Halifax	$62,099	89.9%	92.8%	305
Kamloops	$61,639	87.1%	91.5%	300
Kelowna	$59,456	86.6%	91.9%	296
Kingston	$63,564	86.9%	91.9%	303
Kitchener	$68,906	88.5%	92.8%	314
Lethbridge	$63,345	89.0%	93.7%	307
London	$58,405	86.0%	91.4%	293
Medicine Hat	$63,757	89.0%	92.9%	307
Moncton	$57,458	87.4%	92.7%	294
Nanaimo	$54,071	84.3%	98.6%	292
North Bay	$60,089	84.4%	91.4%	294
Oshawa	$76,816	88.7%	91.1%	326
Peterborough	$58,314	83.8%	91.5%	290
Prince George	$65,265	88.4%	90.0%	305
Red Deer	$72,385	91.6%	93.7%	325
Regina	$71,213	91.2%	95.2%	324
Saguenay	$52,799	83.8%	93.0%	283
Saint-Hyacinthe	$46,629	82.7%	93.9%	273
Saint-Jean-sur-Richelieu	$55,412	85.3%	98.4%	295

Table A5 2011 (*continued*)

Urban Area	Median Household Income	Market Income	Employment Rate	Prosperity Index
Saint John	$58,377	87.2%	91.4%	294
Sarnia	$59,688	85.2%	89.8%	292
Saskatoon	$68,288	91.0%	94.5%	318
Sault Ste. Marie	$56,482	82.3%	89.5%	284
Shawinigan	$40,821	77.3%	91.8%	255
Sherbrooke	$46,195	83.6%	93.7%	273
St. Catharines-Niagara	$57,093	82.8%	91.2%	287
St. John's	$66,581	88.2%	92.4%	310
Thunder Bay	$59,469	84.0%	91.6%	293
Trois-Rivières	$41,025	82.3%	91.4%	260
Victoria	$61,553	89.1%	93.9%	304
Windsor	$57,942	84.1%	89.6%	288

Table A6 Employment by Industry

	1991						
Urban Area	TOTAL	Natural Resources	Goods Producing	Trade	Professional Services	Health Education	Other
Abbotsford	31,210	4.6%	22.4%	20.0%	9.7%	15.1%	28.1%
Barrie	50,425	2.1%	24.9%	20.8%	10.5%	14.4%	27.3%
Belleville	48,915	2.4%	23.9%	17.9%	8.0%	14.1%	33.5%
Brantford	48,925	2.4%	31.3%	20.4%	7.9%	15.9%	22.2%
Chilliwack	28,555	10.4%	17.3%	17.3%	6.0%	13.5%	35.4%
Cornwall	25,735	1.6%	29.1%	18.7%	7.4%	16.8%	26.4%
Drummondville	29,325	2.4%	33.1%	19.8%	7.8%	15.9%	21.1%
Fredericton	40,140	3.3%	10.7%	17.6%	10.6%	18.4%	39.5%
Granby	30,480	2.4%	38.6%	18.4%	7.8%	12.6%	20.3%
Greater Sudbury	80,025	10.9%	15.1%	18.1%	7.7%	18.6%	29.5%
Guelph	54,775	2.6%	29.6%	15.4%	10.4%	21.0%	21.0%
Halifax	177,895	1.3%	12.5%	17.6%	12.3%	18.2%	38.1%
Kamloops	35,685	6.2%	15.4%	20.6%	7.9%	15.5%	34.4%
Kelowna	54,330	6.6%	20.6%	19.5%	10.2%	14.4%	28.6%
Kingston	73,265	1.8%	15.1%	14.9%	8.8%	25.5%	33.9%
Kitchener	198,065	1.7%	32.8%	18.0%	11.6%	15.0%	20.9%
Lethbridge	31,545	3.1%	16.2%	19.9%	8.2%	20.7%	31.9%
London	208,915	2.6%	22.3%	18.2%	12.3%	20.3%	24.3%
Medicine Hat	26,905	13.9%	13.9%	17.0%	5.9%	17.0%	32.2%
Moncton	54,735	1.6%	13.1%	22.5%	9.7%	17.4%	35.7%
Nanaimo	36,000	5.5%	19.3%	20.4%	9.4%	14.7%	30.7%
North Bay	31,350	1.5%	15.0%	17.7%	7.6%	19.3%	38.9%
Oshawa	130,225	1.6%	30.0%	16.4%	11.2%	14.3%	26.6%
Peterborough	48,655	3.1%	23.3%	19.0%	9.7%	19.3%	25.7%
Prince George	38,245	7.3%	20.6%	18.5%	7.4%	14.5%	31.8%
Red Deer	31,940	8.4%	15.4%	19.6%	8.4%	18.7%	29.4%
Regina	103,690	3.6%	12.2%	18.0%	12.7%	17.5%	36.1%

Table A6 1991 (*continued*)

Urban Area	TOTAL	Natural Resources	Goods Producing	Trade	Professional Services	Health Education	Other
Saguenay	72,375	2.6%	25.0%	17.8%	8.3%	18.9%	27.4%
Saint-Hyacinthe	25,070	3.5%	27.3%	18.6%	9.6%	18.3%	22.7%
Saint-Jean-sur-Richelieu	35,445	1.7%	26.9%	17.1%	9.2%	15.6%	29.6%
Saint John	60,565	1.8%	22.4%	18.5%	9.4%	17.7%	30.2%
Sarnia	44,790	2.9%	29.7%	17.4%	8.0%	15.3%	26.6%
Saskatoon	110,850	6.2%	13.7%	18.7%	10.2%	21.4%	29.8%
Sault Ste. Marie	40,940	1.9%	25.6%	16.7%	7.4%	18.7%	29.7%
Shawinigan	25,255	2.3%	38.4%	23.0%	9.0%	18.5%	8.8%
Sherbrooke	69,525	1.8%	22.7%	17.3%	8.8%	24.4%	25.0%
St. Catharines	183,875	3.8%	28.0%	17.3%	9.0%	14.8%	27.2%
St. John's	87,415	2.0%	12.2%	18.6%	9.4%	22.0%	35.9%
Thunder Bay	65,155	3.5%	18.7%	16.8%	8.0%	19.4%	33.6%
Trois-Rivières	64,800	1.9%	25.6%	17.0%	8.7%	18.7%	28.1%
Victoria	149,105	2.8%	11.9%	16.2%	11.2%	19.5%	38.3%
Windsor	130,740	1.5%	33.0%	16.7%	8.8%	16.7%	23.3%

1996						
Urban Area	TOTAL	Natural Resources	Goods Producing	Trade	Professional Services	Health Education	Other
Abbotsford	65,515	9.3%	22.7%	17.2%	9.0%	16.2%	25.6%
Barrie	60,470	2.0%	22.3%	20.6%	11.0%	15.7%	28.4%
Belleville	44,140	2.9%	21.9%	19.9%	7.1%	16.2%	31.9%
Brantford	48,240	2.1%	30.2%	19.4%	7.8%	17.4%	23.1%
Chilliwack	30,605	8.4%	16.7%	18.4%	7.7%	16.4%	32.4%
Cornwall	27,895	2.2%	26.1%	17.9%	7.5%	19.3%	26.9%
Drummondville	31,280	2.2%	32.9%	18.8%	8.6%	15.1%	22.4%
Fredericton	43,095	3.8%	11.2%	16.5%	11.0%	19.0%	38.4%
Granby	29,200	1.8%	35.5%	19.4%	7.9%	13.3%	22.0%
Greater Sudbury	76,230	10.2%	12.7%	19.5%	8.3%	19.7%	29.6%
Guelph	57,190	2.1%	29.8%	15.8%	10.2%	20.0%	22.0%
Halifax	173,735	1.2%	11.3%	17.7%	13.4%	19.5%	37.1%
Kamloops	43,855	6.8%	15.9%	19.1%	8.3%	17.8%	32.2%
Kelowna	67,280	5.2%	21.0%	19.5%	10.8%	15.7%	27.8%
Kingston	71,415	1.8%	13.7%	16.1%	9.5%	26.8%	32.1%
Kitchener	202,925	1.5%	32.0%	17.1%	12.8%	15.7%	21.0%
Lethbridge	32,740	3.2%	15.4%	21.1%	8.2%	21.9%	30.2%
London	203,295	2.5%	21.2%	17.8%	12.7%	21.6%	24.2%
Medicine Hat	29,260	12.6%	16.3%	18.5%	6.5%	16.6%	29.5%
Moncton	58,445	1.5%	14.5%	20.6%	10.4%	18.6%	34.3%
Nanaimo	41,580	5.2%	17.9%	19.6%	10.4%	17.3%	29.6%
North Bay	31,705	1.3%	15.6%	19.4%	8.9%	20.2%	34.6%
Oshawa	184,395	1.1%	19.9%	12.1%	9.1%	11.6%	46.3%
Peterborough	46,290	2.5%	20.7%	19.6%	8.4%	22.5%	26.3%
Prince George	41,300	6.7%	20.0%	18.6%	9.5%	15.5%	29.7%
Red Deer	29,260	12.6%	16.3%	18.5%	6.5%	16.6%	29.5%
Regina	101,595	3.1%	11.7%	17.9%	13.7%	18.5%	35.2%
Saguenay	69,805	2.9%	20.7%	18.2%	8.8%	19.8%	29.6%

Table A6 1996 (*continued*)

Urban Area	TOTAL	Natural Resources	Goods Producing	Trade	Professional Services	Health Education	Other
Saint-Hyacinthe	23,270	1.4%	26.0%	19.7%	9.6%	19.3%	24.1%
Saint-Jean-sur-Richelieu	36,850	1.8%	24.6%	20.4%	10.0%	15.9%	27.5%
Saint John	58,815	2.4%	19.2%	17.9%	10.0%	18.6%	32.0%
Sarnia	41,225	2.1%	25.1%	17.3%	8.7%	17.7%	29.1%
Saskatoon	113,275	5.9%	14.9%	17.9%	9.9%	21.2%	30.1%
Sault Ste. Marie	38,270	2.2%	21.8%	17.8%	7.5%	20.6%	30.1%
Shawinigan	23,850	2.9%	25.5%	17.2%	7.8%	18.7%	27.9%
Sherbrooke	71,400	1.9%	23.0%	16.4%	9.6%	25.9%	23.1%
St. Catharines-Niagara	177,395	3.6%	25.2%	17.6%	9.0%	16.9%	27.7%
St. John's	83,145	2.2%	10.9%	18.4%	10.2%	24.3%	33.9%
Thunder Bay	62,810	3.5%	17.8%	17.6%	7.7%	21.6%	31.7%
Trois-Rivières	63,385	1.9%	24.0%	17.6%	8.5%	21.0%	27.0%
Victoria	157,710	2.4%	11.3%	15.3%	11.9%	20.7%	38.3%
Windsor	138,545	1.5%	33.8%	15.0%	8.9%	16.4%	24.4%

	2001					
Urban Area	**TOTAL**	**Natural Resources**	**Goods Producing**	**Trade**	**Professional Services**	**Health Education**	**Other**
Abbotsford	73,595	9.4%	20.3%	15.6%	8.8%	16.1%	29.9%
Barrie	79,310	1.2%	24.4%	19.1%	9.8%	14.0%	31.5%
Belleville	43,050	1.5%	21.3%	19.6%	7.6%	15.3%	34.7%
Brantford	45,890	0.9%	31.2%	14.4%	7.2%	14.1%	32.2%
Chilliwack	32,645	7.6%	16.8%	17.1%	8.2%	17.0%	33.3%
Cornwall	21,370	1.6%	12.8%	17.0%	7.5%	22.9%	38.3%
Drummondville	34,610	2.2%	34.6%	17.1%	7.7%	14.5%	23.9%
Fredericton	45,635	2.6%	9.9%	13.8%	11.2%	19.4%	43.1%
Granby	33,170	1.5%	37.1%	19.9%	6.4%	12.7%	22.4%
Greater Sudbury	75,900	7.1%	12.2%	16.6%	7.9%	19.3%	36.9%
Guelph	66,410	1.2%	29.6%	14.0%	11.1%	19.9%	24.3%
Halifax	194,715	1.2%	10.4%	16.0%	13.1%	19.0%	40.3%
Kamloops	45,275	5.6%	13.7%	18.3%	8.7%	17.3%	36.4%
Kelowna	72,865	4.2%	17.8%	17.1%	12.2%	17.2%	31.6%
Kingston	74,940	1.6%	13.5%	14.6%	9.1%	25.0%	36.1%
Kitchener	230,895	1.0%	31.5%	16.0%	12.6%	14.4%	24.4%
Lethbridge	36,695	2.6%	16.8%	17.2%	9.4%	21.9%	32.1%
London	227,010	2.0%	21.4%	16.0%	12.2%	19.9%	28.5%
Medicine Hat	33,240	13.4%	17.4%	15.6%	7.1%	16.3%	30.2%
Moncton	64,495	1.1%	14.0%	18.4%	11.0%	17.0%	38.6%
Nanaimo	41,230	3.3%	13.5%	19.1%	10.9%	18.0%	35.0%
North Bay	31,120	2.0%	12.9%	17.7%	9.2%	21.2%	37.0%
Oshawa	158,250	1.1%	24.7%	16.7%	11.7%	15.4%	30.4%
Peterborough	49,820	2.1%	19.6%	15.8%	9.5%	20.8%	32.2%
Prince George	46,805	6.7%	18.1%	15.9%	9.2%	16.8%	33.3%
Red Deer	39,570	9.2%	16.6%	17.7%	9.6%	17.6%	29.4%
Regina	105,105	2.3%	10.3%	16.0%	13.6%	18.2%	39.6%
Saguenay	71,490	2.5%	22.5%	16.4%	8.3%	19.6%	30.7%

Table A6 2001 (*continued*)

Urban Area	TOTAL	Natural Resources	Goods Producing	Trade	Professional Services	Health Education	Other
Saint-Hyacinthe	25,465	2.5%	27.4%	16.9%	9.3%	18.7%	25.2%
Saint-Jean-sur-Richelieu	41,370	1.6%	26.1%	15.9%	8.9%	16.7%	30.8%
Saint John	60,290	2.0%	15.7%	16.3%	9.4%	18.9%	37.7%
Sarnia	44,030	2.6%	23.0%	14.1%	7.9%	15.9%	36.4%
Saskatoon	120,900	5.1%	14.3%	16.2%	10.3%	21.4%	32.8%
Sault Ste. Marie	36,990	1.8%	20.1%	15.4%	7.8%	19.9%	34.9%
Shawinigan	24,535	2.9%	27.7%	14.4%	6.8%	18.0%	30.2%
Sherbrooke	78,630	2.0%	25.1%	14.9%	9.1%	22.9%	26.0%
St. Catharines-Niagara	189,290	3.1%	22.9%	16.1%	8.3%	15.1%	34.5%
St. John's	87,670	3.7%	9.8%	16.5%	22.4%	22.0%	25.6%
Thunder Bay	67,380	3.1%	24.1%	13.5%	7.5%	19.3%	32.5%
Trois-Rivières	64,842	1.7%	22.9%	16.2%	8.2%	20.5%	30.3%
Victoria	163,865	1.8%	9.6%	14.3%	23.7%	20.6%	30.0%
Windsor	157,060	1.1%	33.6%	13.4%	8.0%	15.1%	28.9%

2006						
Urban Area	TOTAL	Natural Resources	Goods Producing	Trade	Professional Services	Health Education	Other
Abbotsford	83,220	8.8%	21.1%	14.5%	24.5%	14.7%	16.5%
Barrie	98,070	2.0%	22.6%	18.6%	21.8%	15.4%	19.6%
Belleville	46,705	2.2%	20.2%	18.4%	21.6%	15.5%	22.1%
Brantford	66.660	3.5%	27.4%	15.8%	20.1%	16.2%	17.0%
Chilliwack	40,020	7.2%	19.7%	15.4%	19.2%	16.3%	22.1%
Cornwall	26,900	1.7%	22.3%	16.1%	23.3%	18.2%	18.4%
Drummondville	40,060	3.1%	32.8%	16.5%	15.5%	16.1%	16.0%
Fredericton	48,360	4.2%	9.8%	13.9%	25.6%	18.7%	27.9%
Granby	36,850	2.4%	34.6%	18.0%	14.8%	14.6%	15.6%
Greater Sudbury	79,960	8.4%	12.7%	17.1%	25.1%	14.1%	22.6%
Guelph	72,830	2.5%	28.1%	14.0%	20.1%	19.4%	15.9%
Halifax	210,135	1.7%	10.8%	16.0%	27.1%	19.4%	25.0%
Kamloops	50,540	5.9%	15.0%	16.7%	22.7%	17.3%	22.4%
Kelowna	85,630	4.5%	17.8%	17.3%	24.4%	16.6%	19.4%
Kingston	79,035	1.7%	11.5%	14.6%	19.1%	26.7%	26.4%
Kitchener	254,545	1.5%	28.8%	16.1%	23.7%	15.8%	14.1%
Lethbridge	52,220	7.1%	23.4%	14.6%	17.9%	18.7%	18.3%
London	246,385	2.8%	20.5%	15.4%	24.0%	20.5%	16.8%
Medicine Hat	39,290	15.9%	15.8%	15.6%	16.4%	15.7%	20.5%
Moncton	70,135	2.3%	12.4%	17.9%	29.1%	17.9%	20.5%
Nanaimo	46,620	3.8%	14.8%	17.9%	23.7%	18.8%	20.9%
North Bay	31,595	2.7%	11.9%	17.3%	24.0%	21.7%	22.5%
Oshawa	178,890	3.7%	21.3%	16.4%	24.6%	16.4%	17.5%
Peterborough	59,910	3.6%	17.7%	16.0%	20.6%	21.4%	20.7%
Prince George	47,515	7.0%	17.5%	15.9%	21.7%	17.9%	20.1%
Red Deer	50,770	12.8%	17.2%	16.7%	18.9%	16.4%	18.0%
Regina	110,620	3.7%	10.7%	16.3%	25.7%	18.4%	25.2%
Saguenay	73,655	4.2%	19.5%	17.1%	16.5%	21.4%	21.3%

Table A6 2006 (*continued*)

Urban Area	TOTAL	Natural Resources	Goods Producing	Trade	Professional Services	Health Education	Other
Saint-Hyacinthe	29,785	4.5%	25.6%	18.2%	17.2%	17.5%	16.9%
Saint-Jean-sur-Richelieu	46,875	1.8%	24.4%	16.5%	20.9%	17.6%	18.8%
Saint John	63,075	3.6%	15.5%	17.7%	26.6%	18.6%	18.0%
Sarnia	45,445	4.0%	22.5%	14.6%	21.7%	16.1%	21.0%
Saskatoon	130,985	5.8%	14.6%	15.6%	21.6%	22.1%	20.3%
Sault Ste. Marie	39,185	1.8%	17.5%	14.5%	21.0%	20.3%	24.9%
Shawinigan	24,380	3.1%	28.0%	15.0%	12.2%	19.2%	22.5%
Sherbrooke	96,555	2.2%	22.2%	15.0%	17.6%	24.3%	18.7%
St. Catharines-Niagara	202,140	3.5%	19.5%	15.2%	20.5%	15.9%	25.4%
St. John's	95,735	4.4%	10.0%	16.2%	23.8%	21.6%	23.9%
Thunder Bay	62,975	4.5%	13.5%	15.4%	20.9%	23.4%	22.3%
Trois-Rivières	69,130	3.7%	19.9%	15.4%	16.0%	20.2%	24.9%
Victoria	181,140	1.7%	10.9%	14.0%	24.7%	19.4%	29.2%
Windsor	162,590	1.6%	29.3%	14.3%	17.9%	17.2%	19.6%

Urban Area	TOTAL	Natural Resources	Goods Producing	Trade	Professional Services	Health Education	Other
						2011	
Abbotsford	87,275	7.0%	19.7%	15.2%	9.6%	16.6%	16.6%
Barrie	100,835	1.1%	18.8%	18.0%	10.4%	17.9%	17.9%
Belleville	45,425	1.1%	16.9%	17.7%	7.1%	18.2%	18.2%
Brantford	69,300	2.4%	23.2%	16.6%	8.5%	18.0%	18.0%
Chilliwack	43,855	5.7%	17.3%	16.0%	8.7%	18.4%	18.4%
Cornwall	26,790	0.9%	18.9%	16.0%	7.2%	19.6%	19.6%
Drummondville	44,525	4.3%	28.2%	17.8%	7.7%	16.5%	16.5%
Fredericton	52,785	1.4%	9.5%	13.9%	12.4%	20.3%	20.3%
Granby	40,760	2.9%	30.7%	17.3%	10.1%	16.3%	16.3%
Greater Sudbury	82,095	8.9%	10.9%	16.3%	9.5%	23.0%	23.0%
Guelph	78,630	1.4%	24.4%	14.3%	12.5%	20.8%	20.8%
Halifax	221,260	1.0%	10.6%	15.5%	13.6%	20.2%	20.2%
Kamloops	51,985	6.0%	12.9%	17.0%	10.2%	20.3%	20.3%
Kelowna	94,575	2.8%	16.3%	17.4%	13.1%	18.9%	18.9%
Kingston	83,545	0.9%	10.7%	13.9%	9.5%	28.1%	28.1%
Kitchener	261,585	1.1%	24.9%	16.4%	14.3%	17.3%	17.3%
Lethbridge	58,500	5.8%	17.1%	16.0%	9.8%	21.9%	21.9%
London	246,170	1.6%	17.4%	14.9%	13.2%	22.9%	22.9%
Medicine Hat	39,190	11.6%	13.4%	15.0%	10.4%	18.9%	18.9%
Moncton	78,050	1.4%	12.2%	18.1%	11.5%	19.1%	19.1%
Nanaimo	49,155	3.2%	12.4%	18.3%	11.1%	20.8%	20.8%
North Bay	32,625	2.6%	10.2%	19.2%	8.3%	25.3%	25.3%
Oshawa	188,310	0.8%	16.6%	16.8%	13.0%	18.7%	18.7%
Peterborough	56,360	2.1%	16.2%	13.9%	9.7%	24.0%	24.0%
Prince George	46,045	5.9%	16.2%	15.9%	8.9%	19.7%	19.7%
Red Deer	52,445	9.6%	16.4%	18.0%	10.6%	18.2%	18.2%
Regina	122,150	2.3%	12.9%	15.8%	13.6%	18.7%	18.7%
Saguenay	78,920	2.4%	18.5%	17.1%	9.3%	21.4%	21.4%

Table A6 2011 (*continued*)

Urban Area	TOTAL	Natural Resources	Goods Producing	Trade	Professional Services	Health Education	Other
Saint-Hyacinthe	29,185	3.3%	22.5%	17.7%	10.6%	19.5%	19.5%
Saint-Jean-sur-Richelieu	49,840	1.1%	21.7%	16.9%	10.3%	18.5%	18.5%
Saint John	66,205	1.9%	16.0%	16.7%	10.5%	19.9%	19.9%
Sarnia	42,715	3.0%	20.4%	15.5%	9.2%	18.7%	18.7%
Saskatoon	150,085	5.2%	15.1%	15.7%	11.6%	22.1%	22.1%
Sault Ste. Marie	39,045	1.1%	18.7%	15.1%	7.3%	22.2%	22.2%
Shawinigan	23,495	2.0%	22.9%	16.2%	7.0%	22.3%	22.3%
Sherbrooke	101,395	1.5%	18.8%	15.4%	10.6%	26.6%	26.6%
St. Catharines-Niagara	194,375	2.5%	16.6%	16.5%	9.2%	17.6%	17.6%
St. John's	107,515	3.4%	10.7%	16.2%	10.7%	22.6%	22.6%
Thunder Bay	61,270	3.0%	11.6%	15.1%	9.7%	24.8%	24.8%
Trois-Rivières	73,535	1.4%	18.2%	15.6%	8.9%	23.6%	23.6%
Victoria	186,430	1.1%	10.0%	14.2%	13.9%	21.7%	21.7%
Windsor	147,760	1.5%	24.1%	14.0%	9.6%	21.0%	21.0%

Table A7 Employment Share Information Technology and Creative Occupations

Urban Area	Computer Science	Information	Design	Arts	Total
		1991			
Abbotsford	0.51%	0.64%	0.13%	1.11%	2.38%
Barrie	1.15%	1.42%	0.30%	0.84%	3.71%
Belleville	1.07%	1.16%	0.22%	0.70%	3.16%
Brantford	0.77%	0.87%	0.13%	0.63%	2.39%
Chilliwack	0.24%	0.43%	0.26%	0.76%	1.70%
Cornwall	0.70%	0.91%	0.11%	0.65%	2.36%
Drummondville	0.21%	0.38%	0.08%	0.99%	1.66%
Fredericton	2.16%	4.07%	0.20%	0.83%	7.26%
Granby	1.19%	1.33%	0.27%	0.87%	3.67%
Greater Sudbury	0.56%	1.22%	0.27%	0.71%	2.76%
Guelph	1.80%	3.37%	0.32%	0.81%	6.30%
Halifax	1.66%	2.79%	0.37%	1.15%	5.97%
Kamloops	0.75%	1.01%	0.41%	0.79%	2.97%
Kelowna	0.46%	0.75%	0.34%	0.90%	2.46%
Kingston	1.24%	3.12%	0.25%	1.04%	5.66%
Kitchener	1.89%	2.67%	0.28%	1.01%	5.84%
Lethbridge	0.64%	1.69%	0.42%	0.80%	3.54%
London	1.36%	2.27%	0.24%	1.09%	4.96%
Medicine Hat	0.50%	0.31%	0.18%	0.81%	1.80%
Moncton	1.15%	0.82%	0.24%	0.73%	2.94%
Nanaimo	0.78%	0.14%	0.31%	0.90%	2.13%
North Bay	0.69%	0.34%	0.32%	0.90%	2.25%
Oshawa	2.07%	0.20%	0.23%	0.82%	3.33%
Peterborough	0.67%	0.64%	0.20%	0.99%	2.51%
Prince George	0.40%	0.20%	0.19%	0.69%	1.49%
Red Deer	0.48%	0.26%	0.23%	1.01%	1.99%
Regina	2.16%	0.81%	0.27%	1.33%	4.56%
Saguenay	0.88%	0.56%	0.37%	0.83%	2.64%
Saint-Hyacinthe	0.80%	0.30%	0.26%	0.94%	2.30%

Table A7 1991 (*continued*)

Urban Area	Computer Science	Information	Design	Arts	Total
Saint-Jean-sur-Richelieu	1.11%	0.32%	0.13%	0.77%	2.33%
Saint John	1.19%	0.40%	0.14%	0.66%	2.39%
Sarnia	1.11%	0.21%	0.13%	0.74%	2.19%
Saskatoon	1.06%	1.33%	0.18%	1.15%	3.71%
Sault Ste. Marie	1.02%	0.18%	0.14%	0.61%	1.95%
Shawinigan	0.62%	0.14%	0.19%	0.54%	1.49%
Sherbrooke	0.27%	0.25%	1.08%	1.01%	2.61%
St. Catharines-Niagara	0.99%	0.22%	0.22%	1.00%	2.44%
St. John's	1.59%	1.24%	1.08%	1.03%	4.94%
Thunder Bay	0.91%	0.65%	0.22%	0.59%	2.38%
Trois-Rivières	3.69%	0.72%	0.17%	0.73%	5.31%
Victoria	0.90%	0.86%	0.30%	1.50%	3.56%
Windsor	0.41%	0.53%	0.13%	0.73%	1.80%

1996					
Urban Area	**Computer Science**	**Information**	**Design**	**Arts**	**Total**
Abbotsford	0.60%	0.30%	0.50%	0.63%	2.03%
Barrie	1.22%	0.26%	0.71%	0.64%	2.83%
Belleville	1.08%	0.12%	0.30%	0.50%	2.01%
Brantford	0.70%	0.37%	0.37%	0.51%	1.95%
Chilliwack	0.31%	0.22%	0.50%	0.64%	1.66%
Cornwall	0.76%	0.13%	0.36%	0.69%	1.94%
Drummondville	0.66%	0.27%	0.58%	0.76%	2.28%
Fredericton	2.87%	2.16%	0.82%	0.93%	6.78%
Granby	1.42%	0.21%	0.72%	0.45%	2.79%
Greater Sudbury	0.84%	0.64%	0.31%	0.51%	2.31%
Guelph	1.81%	1.39%	0.62%	0.74%	4.55%
Halifax	1.71%	1.25%	0.70%	0.90%	4.56%
Kamloops	0.84%	0.39%	0.39%	0.62%	2.24%
Kelowna	0.72%	0.37%	0.69%	0.75%	2.53%
Kingston	1.29%	1.99%	0.60%	0.76%	4.64%
Kitchener	2.22%	0.95%	0.58%	0.70%	4.45%
Lethbridge	0.52%	0.74%	0.46%	0.75%	2.46%
London	1.53%	1.09%	0.55%	0.75%	3.92%
Medicine Hat	0.60%	0.29%	0.39%	0.60%	1.88%
Moncton	2.78%	0.98%	0.43%	0.80%	5.00%
Nanaimo	0.60%	0.37%	0.81%	0.58%	2.36%
North Bay	1.34%	0.53%	0.56%	0.56%	2.99%
Oshawa	2.20%	0.37%	0.38%	0.62%	3.57%
Peterborough	0.86%	0.70%	0.47%	0.91%	2.94%
Prince George	0.62%	0.49%	0.40%	0.63%	2.14%
Red Deer	0.63%	0.12%	0.73%	0.89%	2.37%
Regina	2.45%	0.97%	0.64%	0.94%	5.01%
Saguenay	0.72%	0.69%	0.20%	0.59%	2.19%
Saint-Hyacinthe	2.46%	0.34%	0.55%	0.40%	3.75%
Saint-Jean-sur-Richelieu	1.26%	0.26%	0.49%	0.71%	2.71%

Table A7 1996 (*continued*)

Urban Area	Computer Science	Information	Design	Arts	Total
Saint John	1.34%	0.46%	0.35%	0.58%	2.73%
Sarnia	1.13%	0.17%	0.43%	0.69%	2.41%
Saskatoon	1.03%	1.31%	0.57%	0.87%	3.77%
Sault Ste. Marie	1.15%	0.50%	0.47%	0.81%	2.92%
Shawinigan	0.37%	0.27%	0.33%	0.29%	1.28%
Sherbrooke	0.41%	0.59%	0.53%	0.71%	2.25%
St. Catharines-Niagara	0.83%	0.51%	0.52%	0.79%	2.64%
St. John's	1.83%	1.53%	0.52%	0.93%	4.80%
Thunder Bay	0.88%	0.78%	0.47%	0.57%	2.71%
Trois-Rivières	0.78%	1.03%	0.49%	0.43%	2.72%
Victoria	1.72%	1.03%	0.75%	0.97%	4.48%
Windsor	1.10%	0.62%	0.42%	0.56%	2.70%

2001					
Urban Area	Computer Science	Information	Design	Arts	Total
Abbotsford	1.12%	0.49%	0.56%	0.59%	2.76%
Barrie	1.89%	0.37%	0.65%	0.71%	3.62%
Belleville	2.70%	0.52%	0.42%	0.55%	4.19%
Brantford	1.49%	0.38%	0.55%	0.49%	2.92%
Chilliwack	0.75%	0.37%	0.66%	0.51%	2.28%
Cornwall	1.28%	0.19%	0.30%	0.33%	2.10%
Drummondville	0.79%	0.21%	0.61%	0.39%	2.00%
Fredericton	3.98%	1.70%	0.79%	0.46%	6.93%
Granby	2.35%	0.34%	0.69%	0.57%	3.94%
Greater Sudbury	1.18%	0.70%	0.37%	0.51%	2.76%
Guelph	2.90%	1.59%	0.74%	0.75%	5.98%
Halifax	2.97%	1.19%	0.75%	1.04%	5.95%
Kamloops	0.87%	0.24%	0.71%	0.74%	2.56%
Kelowna	1.65%	0.32%	0.83%	0.83%	3.63%
Kingston	2.25%	1.82%	0.53%	0.87%	5.48%
Kitchener	3.41%	1.07%	0.65%	0.76%	5.89%
Lethbridge	0.78%	0.99%	0.49%	0.77%	3.03%
London	2.64%	1.02%	0.59%	0.73%	4.97%
Medicine Hat	0.97%	0.13%	0.54%	0.75%	2.39%
Moncton	3.09%	1.87%	0.33%	0.77%	6.06%
Nanaimo	0.89%	0.29%	0.69%	0.78%	2.66%
North Bay	2.03%	0.76%	0.43%	0.74%	3.96%
Oshawa	3.25%	0.31%	0.60%	0.60%	4.77%
Peterborough	1.55%	0.67%	0.42%	0.80%	3.44%
Prince George	0.97%	0.46%	0.32%	0.65%	2.39%
Red Deer	1.01%	0.30%	0.58%	0.56%	2.46%
Regina	3.46%	0.99%	0.43%	0.98%	5.86%
Saguenay	1.13%	0.67%	0.37%	0.46%	2.63%
Saint-Hyacinthe	1.42%	0.29%	0.56%	0.63%	2.90%
Saint-Jean-sur-Richelieu	2.01%	0.31%	0.41%	0.39%	3.12%

Table A7 2001 (*continued*)

Urban Area	Computer Science	Information	Design	Arts	Total
Saint John	3.02%	1.43%	0.45%	0.69%	5.60%
Sarnia	1.61%	0.21%	0.40%	0.68%	2.90%
Saskatoon	1.79%	1.20%	0.53%	0.91%	4.43%
Sault Ste. Marie	1.91%	0.29%	0.37%	0.54%	3.10%
Shawinigan	0.66%	0.22%	0.59%	0.23%	1.70%
Sherbrooke	1.80%	1.12%	0.56%	0.61%	4.09%
St. Catharines-Niagara	1.44%	0.55%	0.65%	0.73%	3.38%
St. John's	2.63%	1.47%	0.60%	1.01%	5.72%
Thunder Bay	0.99%	0.68%	0.43%	0.59%	2.70%
Trois-Rivières	1.09%	0.72%	0.67%	0.49%	2.97%
Victoria	3.58%	1.20%	1.07%	1.42%	7.27%
Windsor	1.79%	0.54%	0.39%	0.47%	3.19%

2006				
Urban Area	Computer Science	Information	Design	Arts	Total
Abbotsford	0.79%	0.34%	0.44%	0.48%	2.05%
Barrie	1.34%	0.43%	0.66%	0.63%	3.06%
Belleville	1.12%	0.28%	0.45%	0.70%	2.55%
Brantford	0.95%	0.41%	0.50%	0.62%	2.48%
Chilliwack	0.50%	0.34%	0.55%	0.65%	2.04%
Cornwall	0.65%	0.20%	0.89%	0.41%	2.16%
Drummondville	0.77%	0.17%	0.56%	0.42%	1.93%
Fredericton	2.93%	2.04%	0.74%	0.86%	6.57%
Granby	1.38%	0.34%	0.62%	0.41%	2.75%
Greater Sudbury	0.92%	0.85%	0.46%	0.56%	2.79%
Guelph	2.29%	1.57%	0.81%	0.91%	5.57%
Halifax	2.24%	1.49%	0.75%	1.13%	5.61%
Kamloops	0.79%	1.19%	0.68%	0.68%	3.34%
Kelowna	0.98%	0.58%	0.50%	0.86%	2.92%
Kingston	1.77%	1.94%	0.58%	0.87%	5.16%
Kitchener	2.86%	1.13%	0.64%	0.75%	5.39%
Lethbridge	0.65%	0.86%	0.64%	0.67%	2.82%
London	1.79%	1.06%	0.61%	0.72%	4.17%
Medicine Hat	0.33%	0.18%	0.57%	0.36%	1.44%
Moncton	2.08%	0.91%	0.60%	0.64%	4.23%
Nanaimo	0.87%	0.48%	0.82%	1.04%	3.21%
North Bay	0.98%	0.60%	0.40%	0.38%	2.36%
Oshawa	2.44%	0.51%	0.63%	0.70%	4.28%
Peterborough	0.99%	0.93%	0.62%	1.08%	3.63%
Prince George	0.56%	0.64%	0.42%	0.38%	2.00%
Red Deer	0.58%	0.28%	0.53%	0.60%	1.99%
Regina	2.82%	1.19%	0.65%	1.00%	5.66%
Saguenay	1.20%	0.63%	0.50%	0.35%	2.68%
Saint-Hyacinthe	0.94%	0.25%	0.39%	0.34%	1.91%
Saint-Jean-sur-Richelieu	1.66%	0.42%	0.43%	0.36%	2.87%

Table A7 2006 (*continued*)

Urban Area	Computer Science	Information	Design	Arts	Total
Saint John	2.01%	0.75%	0.59%	0.72%	4.07%
Sarnia	1.07%	0.36%	0.50%	0.61%	2.53%
Saskatoon	1.22%	1.26%	0.52%	0.85%	3.85%
Sault Ste. Marie	1.15%	0.38%	0.41%	0.59%	2.53%
Shawinigan	0.57%	0.37%	0.37%	0.21%	1.52%
Sherbrooke	1.31%	1.23%	0.54%	0.65%	3.73%
St. Catharines-Niagara	0.95%	0.54%	0.65%	0.80%	2.93%
St. John's	2.12%	1.38%	0.62%	0.91%	5.02%
Thunder Bay	0.77%	0.89%	0.45%	0.69%	2.80%
Trois-Rivières	0.95%	0.85%	0.43%	0.46%	2.69%
Victoria	3.07%	1.39%	1.01%	1.43%	6.90%
Windsor	1.56%	0.68%	0.53%	0.57%	3.34%

2011					
Urban Area	Computer Science	Information	Design	Arts	Total
Abbotsford	0.52%	0.47%	0.64%	0.68%	2.31%
Barrie	0.69%	0.27%	0.87%	0.93%	2.77%
Belleville	0.63%	0.35%	0.40%	0.76%	2.13%
Brantford	0.42%	0.50%	0.85%	0.61%	2.38%
Chilliwack	0.22%	0.61%	0.42%	0.35%	1.59%
Cornwall	0.22%	0.28%	0.16%	0.08%	0.74%
Drummondville	0.29%	0.45%	0.52%	0.34%	1.60%
Fredericton	1.09%	1.82%	0.59%	1.03%	4.53%
Granby	0.40%	0.41%	0.90%	0.31%	2.02%
Greater Sudbury	1.07%	0.88%	0.44%	0.53%	2.92%
Guelph	1.04%	1.85%	0.81%	0.64%	4.34%
Halifax	0.93%	1.36%	0.70%	1.00%	3.99%
Kamloops	0.39%	1.14%	0.56%	0.57%	2.66%
Kelowna	0.65%	0.72%	0.91%	0.85%	3.14%
Kingston	0.67%	3.30%	0.63%	0.89%	5.50%
Kitchener	1.75%	1.17%	0.73%	0.45%	4.10%
Lethbridge	0.32%	1.11%	0.69%	0.45%	2.57%
London	0.78%	1.20%	0.66%	0.79%	3.42%
Medicine Hat	0.11%	0.28%	0.80%	0.42%	1.61%
Moncton	0.61%	1.12%	0.68%	0.57%	2.99%
Nanaimo	0.66%	1.25%	0.90%	1.00%	3.82%
North Bay	0.30%	0.88%	0.44%	0.53%	2.15%
Oshawa	1.06%	0.57%	0.78%	0.66%	3.07%
Peterborough	0.59%	0.89%	0.63%	0.70%	2.80%
Prince George	0.37%	0.71%	0.47%	0.53%	2.08%
Red Deer	0.40%	0.28%	0.65%	0.55%	1.89%
Regina	0.87%	1.18%	0.58%	0.85%	3.47%
Saguenay	0.41%	0.70%	0.45%	0.47%	2.04%
Saint-Hyacinthe	0.34%	0.38%	0.36%	0.14%	1.21%
Saint-Jean-sur-Richelieu	0.56%	0.34%	0.66%	0.33%	1.90%

Table A7 2011 (*continued*)

Urban Area	Computer Science	Information	Design	Arts	Total
Saint John	0.70%	0.65%	0.47%	0.47%	2.29%
Sarnia	0.46%	0.11%	0.37%	0.39%	1.33%
Saskatoon	0.65%	1.30%	0.61%	0.44%	3.00%
Sault Ste. Marie	0.79%	0.66%	0.75%	0.31%	2.51%
Shawinigan	0.16%	0.32%	0.27%	0.25%	0.99%
Sherbrooke	0.42%	1.21%	0.60%	0.56%	2.79%
St. Catharines-Niagara	0.59%	0.67%	0.87%	0.72%	2.86%
St. John's	0.70%	1.66%	0.63%	0.99%	3.98%
Thunder Bay	2.11%	1.01%	0.46%	0.67%	4.25%
Trois-Rivières	0.32%	0.90%	0.60%	0.50%	2.32%
Victoria	1.17%	1.52%	0.99%	0.70%	4.39%
Windsor	0.59%	0.76%	0.13%	0.69%	2.17%

Appendix B. Factor Loadings

Factor analysis is a statistical technique that is often used to reduce the number of variables in instances where the individual variables are highly correlated. In essence, factor analysis creates a new index variable (factor) by the linear addition of two or more measures. When two or more factors are extracted, they are constructed so that the correlation between factors is minimized. As a result, the variables included in each factor can be interpreted as representing a different concept. Both exploratory and confirmatory factor analyses were performed using creative class indicator measures derived from previous creative class research.

The results of these analyses are provided below, indicating the individual variables in each factor, along with the associated factor loading.

CREATIVE CLASS

Creative Factor Loadings

Gay/Creative		Diversity		Engineering	
Same sex households	.68	Black	.82	Engineering	.78
Design	.70	Hispanic	.92	R &D	.78
Computer services	.64	Arabic	.87	*Computer/Aerospace*	
Scientific services	.60	Asian	.86	Computer mfg.	.94
Arts Company	.62	Foreign born	.96	Aerospace	.94
Arts Independent	.84			*Medical*	
				Pharmaceuticals	.80
				Medical equipment	.80

Amenities Factor Loadings

Unique Amenities		Generic Amenities	
Local bookstores	.86	chain bookstores	.85
Local coffeehouses	.91	chain coffeehouses	.93
Local restaurants	.90	chain restaurants	.94
Major movies/cinemas[1]	.67	fairs/festivals	.62
Museums/zoos/aquariums	.85		
Art galleries/studios	.91		
Theaters/concert halls	.72		
Art supply stores	.50		

IMMIGRANT

Immigrant Origin Factor Loadings

1996	Factor Loading	2001	Factor Loading	2006	Factor Loading
Less Industrial		*Less Industrial*		*Pacific*	
Central America	.77	Central America	.73	Central America	.89
Eastern Europe	.78	Eastern Europe	.80	US	.70
Africa	.85	Africa	.83	East Asia	.65
Middle East	.84	Middle East	.88	Oceania	.93
Southeast Asia	.75	Southeast Asia	.68	*Europe*	
More Industrial		*More Industrial*		Western Europe	.93
Western Europe	.73	Western Europe	.84	Eastern Europe	.93
US	.72	US	.71	Middle East	.73

---

1. While both major and independent movie houses were initially coded, there were few independents and their presenece was highly correlated with major/chain movie theaters. Thus, they were combined for subsequent analysis.

Table (*continued*)

1996	Factor Loading	2001	Factor Loading	2006	Factor Loading
East Asia	.63	East Asia	.67	*Asia/Africa*	
South Asia	.69	South Asia	.51	Africa	.78
Oceania	.92	Oceania	.93	Southeast Asia	.63
				South Asia	.63

Minority Population Factor Loadings

	VM Hispanic/ Asian	VM Black/Arab
Chinese	**.83**	.08
Korean	**.65**	.20
Filipino	**.80**	.17
Hispanic	**.68**	.32
Southeast Asian	**.80**	.26
Arab	.34	**.85**
Black	.13	**.92**

NEW URBAN

Preference Factor Loadings

Factor	Variable	Loading	% variance
Diversity	Housing Variety	.671	16.409
	Price Variety	.697	
	Diversity	.920	
	Live in Neighborhood	.697	
	Neighbors	.659	
Public Realm	Style	.784	13.681
	Neighborhood Appearance	.822	
	Landscaping	.723	

Table (*continued*)

Factor	Variable	Loading	% variance
	Traffic	.506	
Child Friendly	Recreation	.756	12.009
	Playground	.779	
	Sidewalks	.499	
	Schools	.658	
Accessibility	Shopping	.807	10.488
	Cafe	.524	
	Public Transportation	.762	
House	Size of Home	.693	8.057
	Cost of Home	.800	
Yard	Front Yard	.626	7.700
	Back Yard	.803	
TOTAL			68.442

Satisfaction Factor Loadings

Factor	Variable	Loading	% of variance
Urban Design	Neighborhood Appearance	.780	18.166
	Parks	.737	
	Privacy	.569	
	Open Space	.691	
	Trails	.509	15.757
Own House	House Size	.855	
	Yard Size	.876	
Traffic	Parking	.800	15.545
	Congestion	.742	
	Vehicle Traffic	.770	
Access	Shopping	.783	11.905
	Schools	.732	
Walkability	Walkability	.899	9.026
TOTAL			70.399

References

Abbott, C. 1993. Five downtown strategies: Policy discourse and downtown planning since 1945. *Journal of Policy History* 5, 5–27.

Abu-Laban, Y., and Garber, J. A. 2005. The construction of the geography of immigration as a policy problem: The United States and Canada compared. *Urban Affairs Review* 40 (4): 520–61.

Alesina, A., Devleschauwer, A., and Easterly, W. 2002. Fractionalization. Working Paper no. 9411, NBER.

Alesina, A., and La Ferrera, D. 2005. Ethnic diversity and economic performance. *Journal of Economic Literature* 43, 762–800.

Alexander, L., ed. 1986. *Downtown Improvement Districts*. New York, NY: Downtown Research & Development Center.

American Gaming Association. 2012. *State of the States*. www.american gaming.org/ sites/default/files/uploads/docs/sos/aga_sos_2012_web.pdf. Accessed March 25, 2013.

Anderson, M. 1964. *The Federal Bulldozer*. Cambridge, MA: MIT Press.

Anderson, P. L., Cotton, C. S., and Watkins, S. O. 2003. *Market and Economic Impacts of a Tribal Casino in Wayland Township, Michigan*. Lansing, MI: Anderson Economic Group.

Andrews, R. R. 1963. Mechanics of the urban economic base: Historical development of the base concept. *Land Economics* 29 (2): 161–67.

Association of Atlantic Universities. 2010. *Universities May Hold the Key to Successful Immigration*. Public Policy Paper Series. public.atlanticuniversities.ca/ PublicPolicyPaperSeries/AAUSPublicPolicyPaperSeriesIssue/tabid/62/ ArticleID/2/Default.aspx.

Baird, J., Adelman, R. M., Reid, L. W., and Jaret, C. 2008. Immigrant settlement patterns: The role of metropolitan characteristics. *Sociological Inquiry* 78 (3): 310–34.

Bates, T. 2006. The urban development potential of black-owned businesses. *Journal of the American Planning Association* 72 (2): 227–37.

Baycan-Levent, T., and Nijkamp, P. 2009. Characteristics of migrant entrepreneurship in Europe. *Entrepreneurship & Regional Development* 21 (4): 375–97.

Bell, D., and J. Binnie. 2004. Authenticating queer space: Citizenship, urbanism and governance. *Urban Studies* 41 (9): 1807–20.

Berridge Lewinberg Greenberg Ltd. 1991. *Guidelines for the Reurbanization of Metropolitan Toronto.* Toronto, ON: Municipality of Metropolitan Toronto.

Beyard, M. D. 2001. *Developing Retail Entertainment Destinations.* Washington, DC: Urban Land Institute.

Billings, S. B., and Leland, S. 2009. Examining the logic behind the self-help, self-taxing movement: Business improvement district formation. *Public Budgeting and Finance* (Winter): 108–24.

Binkley, C. 2008. *Winner Takes All.* New York: Hyperion.

Birch, E. L. 2002. Having a longer view on downtown living. *Journal of the American Planning Association* 68 (1): 5–21.

Black, J. T., Howland, L., and Rogel, S. L. 1983. *Downtown retail development: Conditions for success and project profiles.* Washington, DC: Urban Land Institute.

Blakeley, E. J. 1994. *Planning local economic development theory and practice.* 2nd ed. Thousand Oaks, CA: Sage Publications.

Blakely, E., and Snyder, M. 1997. *Fortress America: Gated Communities in the United States.* Washington, DC: Brookings Institution Press.

Blumenfeld, H. 1955. The Economic Base of the Metropolis: Critical remarks on the "basic"–"non-basic concept. *Journal of the American Institute of Planners* 21 (4): 112–32.

Bois-Franc a Saint-Laurent. 2006. A new city style. www.boisfranc.com Accessed November 25, 2006.

Bookout, L. 1992. New Urbanist Town Planning: A New Vision for the Suburbs. *Urban Land* 51, 1:20–26.

Borg, M. O., Mason, P. M., and Shapiro, S. I. 1991. The incidence of taxes on casino gambling: Exploiting the tired and poor. *American Journal of Economics and Sociology* 50: 323–33. doi: 10.1111/j.1536–7150.1991.tb02299.x.

Borjas, G. J. 1995. The economic benefits from immigration. *Journal of Economic Perspectives* 9: 3–22.

Bourdieu, P. 1984. *Distinction.* Cambridge, MA: Harvard University Press.

Bourne, L. 2007. *New Urban Divides: How Economic, Social, and Demographic Trends Are Creating New Sources of Urban Difference in Canada.* University of Toronto: Centre for Urban and Communities Studies, Research Bulletin 33. www.urbancentre.utoronto.ca

Bousefield, J. R. 1992. New avenues to draft approvals. *Plan Canada* (May): 17–20.

Brandford, S. 1993. TNDs selling? *Builder* 16 (10): 76–79.

Briffault, R. 1999. A government for our time? Business improvement districts and urban governance. *Columbia Law Review* 99 (2): 365–477.

Brindley, T. 2003. The social dimension of the urban village. *Urban Design International* 8, 53–65.

Brown, B., and Cropper, V. 2001. New urban and standard suburban subdivisions. *Journal of the American Planning Association* 76 (4): 402–19.

Bunting, T., and Filion, P. 1999. Dispersed city form in Canada: A Kitchener CMA case study. *Canadian Geographer* 43, 268–87.

Bunting, T. and Filion, P. eds. 2006. *Canadian Cities in Transition.* 3rd edition. Toronto: Oxford University Press.

Bunting, T. E. and Millward, H. 1999. A tale of two CBDs II: The internal retail dynamics of downtown Halifax and downtown Kitchener. *Canadian Journal of Urban Research*, 8(1): 1–27.

Burayidi, M. A., ed. 2001. *Downtowns: Revitalizing the centers of small communities.* New York: Routledge.

Burayidi, M. A. 2001. Keeping faith: What we know about downtown revitalization in small urban centers. In M. Burayidi, ed., *Downtowns: Revitalizing the centers of small communities* (pp. 291–96). New York: Routledge.

Burchell, R., Listokin, D. and C. Calley. 2000. Smart growth: more than a ghost of urban policy past, less than a bold new horizon. *Housing Policy Debate* 11 (4): S21–79.

Bureau of Municipal Research. 1973. *The Toronto Region's Privately Developed New Communities.* Toronto: Bureau of Municipal Research.

Business Builds a City. 1954. *Architectural Forum* 100(6): 147–51

Calthorpe, P. 1993. *The Next American Metropolis.* Princeton, NJ: Princeton Architectural Press.

Camarota, S. A., and Keeley, J. 2001. The new Ellis Islands: Examining non-traditional areas of immigrant settlement in the 1990s. *Backgrounder.* Washington, DC: Center for Immigration Studies. www.cis.org

Cameron, S., and Field, A. 2000. Community, ethnicity and neighbourhood. *Housing Studies* 15: 827–43.

Campbell, C. C. 1976. *New Towns: Another Way to Live.* Reston, VA: Reston Publishing Company.

Canadian Broadcasting Corporation. 2004. Cinder blocks enforce Quebec subdivision parking rule. CBC.CA News. www.cbc.ca/stories/print/2004/07/03noparking040703.

Canadian Broadcasting Corporation. 2010. Immigrant settlement funds cut for Ontario. December 23.

Canadian Broadcasting Corporation. 2011. Immigrant centre cuts spark city hall protest. January 28.

Carey, E. 2003. Toronto is leading the way: 905 regions increasingly home to immigrants, Toronto still has world's highest rate of newcomers. *Toronto Star*, January 22.

Carlson, K. 2006. Back to the future urbanism. *Canadian Geographic*. www. canadiangeographic.ca/Magazine/mj06/indepth/communities.asp.

Carmon, N. 1999. Three generations of urban renewal policies: Analysis and policy implications. *Geoforum* 30: 145–58.

Caruso, D., and Sands, G. 2003. Problems in implementing New Urbanism. Landscape Architectural Boards Foundation. *Strategies for Safe and Sustainable Communities* (pp. 111–28). Vienna, VA: The Architectural Boards Foundation.

Carver, H. 1962. *Cities in the Suburbs*. Toronto: University of Toronto Press.

Casino City. 2014. *Casino and Gaming Directory*. www.casinocity.com. Accessed November 18, 2014.

Cervero, R. 1986. *Suburban Gridlock*. New Brunswick, NJ: Rutgers University Center of Urban Policy Research.

Chapin, F. S., and Kaiser, H. J. 1979. *Urban Land Use Planning*. 2nd ed. Urbana: University of Illinois Press.

Chappele, K., Markusen, A. Schrock, G., Yamamoto, D., and Yu, P. 2004. Gauging metropolitan "high tech" and "i-tech" activity. *Economic Development Quarterly* 18 (February): 10–29.

Christensen, C. 1986. *The American Garden City and the New Towns Movement*. Ann Arbor, MI: UMI Research Press.

Church, G., Greenberg, K., and McPhedran, M. 1997. Toronto: An Urban Alternative. In R. Geddes, *Cities in Our Future: Growth and Form, Environmental Health and Social Equity*. Washington, DC: Island Press. 93–109.

City of Toronto Archives. 1998. *After the Sprawl? Suburban Pasts and Futures in the Greater Toronto Area*. Toronto: City of Toronto Archives.

Clark, T. N. 2011. *The city as an entertainment machine*. Oxford: Elsevier.

Clark, T. N., Lloyd, R., Wong, K. K., and Jain, P. 2002. Amenities drive urban growth. *Journal of Urban Affairs* 24: 493–515.

Clarke, S. E., and Gaile, G. L. 1992. The next wave: Postfederal local economic development strategies. *Economic Development Quarterly* 6: 187–98.

Coffey, W. J. 2000. Canadian cities and shifting fortunes of economic development. In T. Bunting and P. Filion, eds., *Canadian cities in transition*, 2nd ed. (pp. 121–50). New York: Oxford University Press.

Coffey, W. J., and Shearmur, R. 1996. *Employment Growth and Change in the Canadian Urban System*. Ottawa: Canadian Policy Research Network.

Coffey, W. J., and Shearmur, R. 2006. Employment in Canadian Cities. 249-271. In *Canadian Cities in Transition*, 2nd Edition, T. Bunting and P. Filion, eds. Toronto: Oxford University Press.

Congress for the New Urbanism. 2004. *Charter of the new urbanism*. www.cnu. org/aboutcnu/.

Cullen, J. B., and Levitt, S. D. 1999. Crime, urban flight, and the consequences for cities. *Review of Economic and Statistics* 81: 159–69.

Cuomo, A. 1997. Interview. *Architecture* 86 (August): 44–49.

Dane, S. G. 1997. *Main Street success stories*. Washington, DC: National Main Street Center.

Department of Housing and Urban Development. 2000. *Principles for Inner City Neighborhood Design: HOPE VI and the New Urbanism*. Washington, DC: HUD User.

Don Mills, the Planned Industrial Community near Toronto. 1961. *Architectural Forum* 107(1): 63-66.

Don Mills: Nearly a "New Town." 1961. *Town and Country Planning*. 29 (2): 66–71.

Donegan, M., Drucker, J. Goldstein, H., Lowe, N., and Malizia, E. 2008. Which indicators explain metropolitan economic performance best? *Journal of the American Planning Association* 74: 180–95.

Downs, A. 1994. *New Visions for Metropolitan America*. Washington, DC: Brookings Institution.

Dreher, C. 2002. Be creative—or die. *Salon* (June 6). www.salon.com. Accessed September 11, 2006.

Duany, A. 2000. A New Theory of Urbanism. *Scientific American* 283 (December): 6.

Duany, A., Plater-Zyberk, E., et al. n.d. Cornell Ontario. (Project tear sheet) www.dpz.com/projects.aspx. Accessed December 9, 2006.

Duany, A., Plater-Zyberk, E., and Speck, J. 2000. *Suburban Nation: The Rise of Sprawl and the Decline of the American Dream*. New York: North Point Press.

Duderstadt, J. J. 2005. *A Roadmap to Michigan's Future*. Ann Arbor: University of Michigan Press.

Duderstadt, J.J. 2015. *Tilting at Windmills: Policy Battles Won, Lost and Long Forgotten*. Ann Arbor: The University of Michigan Millenium Project.

Eakin, E. 2002. The cities and their new elite. *New York Times* 1 (June): B7–B9.

Eisinger, P. K. 1988. *The Rise of the Entrepreneurial State*. Madison: University of Wisconsin Press.

Elfring, T., and Hulsink, W. 2003. Networks in entrepreneurship: The case of high technology firms. *Small Business Economics* 21: 409–22.

Erichek, G. A., and McKinney, H. 2004. "Small city blues": Looking for growth factors in small and medium-sized cities. Working Paper 04-100. Kalamazoo, MI: Upjohn Institute for Employment Research.

Fainstein, S. S. 2005. Cities and diversity: Should we want it? Can we plan for it? *Urban Affairs Review* 41 (3): 3–19.

Faludi, E. G. 1950a. Designing New Canadian Communities Theory and Practice. *Journal of the American Institute of Planners* 16 (2): 71–79.

Faludi, E. G. 1950b. Designing New Canadian Communities Theory and Practice. *Journal of the American Institute of Planners* 16 (3): 140–47.

Feehan, D. 2006. The Vision-Driven Downtown Organization. In D. Feehan and M. D. Feit (eds.), *Making Business Districts Work*. New York: Hayworth Press.

Feser, E. J. 2003. What regions do rather than make: A proposed set of knowledge based occupation clusters. *Urban Studies* 40 (10): 1937–1358.

Filion, P. 1993. Factors of evolution in the content of planning documents: Downtown planning in a Canadian city, 1962–1992. *Environment and Planning B* 20: 459–78.

Filion, P. 2010. Growth and decline in the Canadian urban system. *GeoJournal* 75 (6): 517–35.

Filion, P., Bunting, T., and Warriner, K. 1999. The entrenchment of urban dispersion: Residential preferences and location patterns in the dispersed city. *Urban Studies* 36, 1317–1347.

Filion, P. and Hoernig, H. 2003. Downtown past, downtown present, downtown yet to come: decline and revival in middle-size urban areas. *Plan Canada*, 43(1), 31–34.

Filion, P., Hoernig, H., Bunting, T., and Sands, G. 2004. The successful few: Healthy core areas of small metropolitan regions. *Journal of the American Planning Association* 70: 328–43.

Fleischmann, A., Green, G. P., and Kwong, T. M. 1992. What's a city to do? Explaining the differences in local economic development policies. *Western Political Quarterly* 27: 677–99.

Florida, R. 2002a. Bohemia and economic geography. *Journal of Economic Geography* 2: 55–71.

Florida, R. 2002b. *The rise of the creative class*. New York: Basic Books.

Florida, R. 2005a. *The flight of the creative class*. New York: Harper Business.

Florida, R. 2005b. *Cities and the creative class*. New York: Routledge.

Florida, R. 2014. The creative class and economic development. *Economic Development Quarterly* 28 (3): 196–205.

Florida, R., and Gates, G. 2001. *Technology and Tolerance: The Importance of Diversity to High-tech Growth*. Washington, DC: Brookings Institution Press.

Fogelson, R. M. 2001. *Downtown: Its Rise and Fall, 1880–1950*. New Haven, CT: Yale University Press.

Ford, L. 2003. *American's New Downtowns: Revitalization or Reinvention.* Baltimore: Johns Hopkins University Press.

Forgey, F. 1993. Tax increment financing: Equity, effectiveness, and efficiency. *Municipal Yearbook.* Washington, DC: International City/County Management Association.

Frieden, B., and Sagalyn, L. 1989. *Downtown Inc.: How America Rebuilds Its Cities.* Cambridge, MA: MIT Press.

Friedman, J., Hakim, S., and Weinblatt, J. 1989. Casino gambling as a "growth pole strategy and its effect on crime. *Journal of Regional Science,* 29: 615–23. doi: 10.1111/j.1467–989.tb01247.x

Friedman, T. 2005. *The World Is Flat.* New York: Farrar, Straus and Giroux.

Frumkin, H., Frank, L., and Jackson, R. 2004. *Urban Sprawl and Public Health.* Washington, DC: Island Press.

Fulton, W. 1996. *The New Urbanism: Hope or Hype for American Communities?* Cambridge, MA: Lincoln Instate of Land Policy.

Gamble, S. 2014. Laurier buys Market Square Mall. Brantford Expositor. September 11. http://www.brantfordexpositor.ca/2014/09/11/city-hall-laurier-buys-market-square-mall

Ganning, J. P. 2016. Arts stability and growth amid redevelopment in U.S. shrinking cities' downtowns: A case study. Economic Development Quarterly: DOI 10.1177/0891242415626277.

Garrett, T. A. 2004. Casino gaming and local employment trends. *Review-Federal Reserve Bank of St. Louis* 86 (1): 9–22.

Gertler, M. S., Florida, R., Gates, G., Vinodrai, T. 2002. *Competing on creativity: Placing Ontario's cities in North American context.* Ontario Ministry of Enterprise, Opportunity, and Innovation and the Institute for Competitiveness and Prosperity.

Gillette, H. 1985. The evolution of the planned shopping center in suburb and city. *Journal of the American Planning Association* 51, 449–60.

Glaeser, E. L., Kallal, H., Scheinkman, J., Schlief, A. 1992. Growth in cities. *Journal of Political Economy* 100: 1126–52.

Glaeser, E. L., Kolko, J., and Saiz, A. 2001. Consumer city. *Journal of Economic Geography* 1: 27–50.

Glaeser, E. L., and Mare, D. C. 2001. Cities and skills. *Journal of Labor Economics* 19 (2): 316–42.

Glazer, L., and Grimes, D. R. 2005. *A new path to prosperity? Manufacturing and knowledge-based industries as drivers of economic growth.* Ann Arbor, MI: Michigan Future, Inc.

Goldberg, M. A., and Mercer, J. 1986. *The Myth of the North American City.* Vancouver, BC: University of British Columbia Press.

Gomez-Insausti, R. 2006. Canada's leading retailers: Latest trends and strategies for their major chains. *Canadian Journal of Regional Science* 29 (3): 359–74.

Goodman, R. 1979. *The last entrepreneurs: America's regional wars for jobs and dollars.* New York: Simon & Schuster.

Gordon, D., and Vipond, S. 2005. Gross Density and New Urbanism. *Journal of the American Planning Association* 74 (1): 41–54.

Gordon, P., and Richardson, H. W. 1997. Are compact cities a desirable planning goal? *Journal of the American Planning Association* 63 (1): 95–106.

Goshorn, J. 1999. In a TIF: Why Missouri needs tax increment financing reform. *Washington University Law Quarterly* 77: 919–46.

Gotham, K. F. 2002. Marketing Mardi Gras: Commodification, spectacle and the political economy of tourism in New Orleans. *Urban Studies* 39 (10): 1735–56.

Gottdiener, M., and Klephart, G. 1991. The multinucleated metropolitan region: A comparative analysis. In R. Kling, S. Olin and M. Poster (eds.), *Postmodern California: The Transformation of Orange County since World War II* (pp. 31–54). Berkeley: University of California Press.

Gottlieb, P. 1995. Residential Amenities, Firm Location and Economic Development. *Urban Studies* 32 (9): 1413-36.

Greater Toronto Area Task Force. 1996. *Report.* Toronto: Queen's Printer for Ontario.

Gross, J. S. 2005. Business improvement districts in New York City's low-income and high-income neighborhoods. *Economic Development Quarterly* 19: 174–89.

Gross, J. S. 2010. The 'localization' of migrant's inclusion in multi-ethnic cities: The London case paper prepared for presentation at the annual meeting of the American Political Science Association, Washington, DC. Available from Jill Gross, Hunter College.

Gross, M. 1998. Legal gambling as a strategy for economic development. *Economic Development Quarterly* 12 (3): 203–13.

Gruen, V. 1964. *The Heart of Our Cities: The Urban Crisis, Diagnosis and Cure.* New York: Reinhold.

Gyourko, J., and Rybczynski, W. 2000. Financing New Urbanism projects: Obstacles and solutions. *Housing Policy Debate* 11 (3).

Hackler, D., and Mayer, H. 2008. Diversity, entrepreneurship, and the urban environment. *Journal of Urban Affairs* 30 (3): 273–307.

Halseth, G. 2003. Attracting growth 'back' to an amenity rich fringe: Rural-urban fringe dynamics around metropolitan Vancouver, Canada. *Canadian Journal of Regional Science* 26: 297–318.

Hancock, M. 1965. New towns: Are they the answer to current urban sprawl? *Journal of Housing* 22: 469–72.

Hannigan, J. 1998. *Fantasy City: Pleasure and Profit in the Postmodern Metropolis.* New York: Routledge.

Haque, A. 2001. Does size matter? Successful economic development strategies of small cities. In *Downtowns: Revitalizing the centers of small urban communities,* Michael Burayidi, ed. 275–95. New York, NY: Routledge.

Harris, R. 1996. *Unplanned Suburbs: Toronto's American Tragedy.* Baltimore: Johns Hopkins University Press.

Hartley, D. A., Kaza, N., and Lester, T. W. 2016. Are America's inner cities competitive? Evidence from the 2000s. *Economic Development Quarterly* 30 (2): 137–58.

Hempstead, K. 2005. *Mobility of the Foreign-born Population in the United States, 1995–2000: The Role of Gateway States.* Center for State Health Policy, Rutgers University, New Brunswick, NJ. Unpublished manuscript. www.cshp. rutgers.edu

Henriksson, L. E. 1996. Hardly a quick fix: Casino gambling in Canada. *Canadian Public Policy / Analyse de Politiques* 22 (2): 116–28.

Henry, F. 1994. *The Caribbean Diaspora in Toronto: Learning to Live with Racism.* Toronto: University of Toronto Press.

Heritage Canada the National Trust. 2014. *Main Street Canada.* www.heritage canada.org /en/resources/regeneration/main-street.

Hertel, S. 1999. Cornell: Looking forward or backward? *Ontario Planning Journal* 14 (4): 5–7.

Hiebert, D. 2000. Immigration and the changing Canadian city. *Canadian Geographer* 44: 25–43.

Hiebert, D. 2006. Winning, losing and still playing the game: The political economy of immigration in Canada. *Tijdschrift voor Economische en Sociale Grogragie* 97: 38–48.

Hiebert, D., Schuurman, N., and Smith, H. 2007. *The Social Geography of Immigrant and Visible Minority Populations in Montreal, Toronto, and Vancouver, Projected to 2017.* Centre of Excellence for Research on Immigration and Diversity Work Paper 07–12. riim.metropolis.net.

Hill, E. W., and Brennan, J. F. 2000. A methodology for identifying the drivers of industrial clusters. *Economic Development Quarterly* 14: 65–96.

Hobson, G. 2002. Immigrant population soars 121% in 90s decade. *Kansas City Star,* May 22.

Hodge, G. 1998. *Planning Canadian Communities: An Introduction to the Principles, Practice, and Participants.* Toronto: ITP Nelson.

Horváth, C., and Paap, R. 2012. The effect of recessions on gambling expenditures. *Journal of Gambling Studies* 28 (4): 703–17.

Hou, F., and Bourne, L. S. 2006. The migration-immigration link in Canada's gateway cities: A comparative study of Toronto, Montreal, and Vancouver. *Environment and Planning A* 38: 1505–25.

Houston, L. 1998. Urban awakening. *Urban Land* 57 (10), pp. 34–41.

Howard, E. 1965 [1902]. *Garden Cities of Tomorrow.* Cambridge, MA: MIT Press.

Hoyman, M., and Faricy, C. 2010. It takes a village. *Urban Affairs Review* 44 (3): 311–33.

Hoyt, L. 2003. The business improvement district: An internationally diffused approach to revitalization. Mimeograph, department of Urban Studies, Massachusetts Institute of Technology.

Hoyt, L. 2006. Importing ideas: The transnational transfer of urban revitalization policy. *International Journal of Public Administration* 29: 221–43.

Huey, L., Ericson, R., and Haggerty, K. 2005. Policing fantasy city. In D. Cooley, ed., *Re-imagining Policing in Canada* (pp. 140–208). Toronto: University of Toronto Press.

Immigration in Canada: A smaller welcome mat. 2010. *Economist* (December 18): 55.

Institute for Competitiveness and Prosperity. 2002. *Measuring Ontario's prosperity: Developing an economic indicator system.* Working Paper no. 2. Toronto: University of Toronto Rothman School of Business.

Jackson, K. 1985. *Crabgrass Frontier.* New York: Oxford University Press.

Jacobs, J. 1961. *The Death and Life of Great American Cities.* New York: Random House.

Janke, J., and Gerlach, J. 2010. Native American casino gambling in Wisconsin and Minnesota. *Focus on Geography* 47 (2): 14–20.

Joh, K., Nguyen, M. T., and Boarnet, M. G. 2011. Can built and social environmental factors encourage walking among individuals with negative walking attitudes? *Journal of Planning Education and Research* 32 (2): 219–36.

Johnson, C., and Mann, J. 2001. *Tax increment financing and economic development: Uses, structures, and impact.* Albany: State University of New York Press.

Jones, T., Barrett, G., and McEvoy, D. 2000. Market potential as a decisive influence on the performance of ethnic minority business. In J. Rath, ed., *Immigrant Businesses: The Economic, Political and Social Environment* (pp. 37–53). Houndmills: Macmillan.

Kantor, P., and Savitch, H. 1998. Can politicians bargain with business? A theoretical and comparative perspective on urban development. In D. Judd and P. Kantor, eds., *The Politics of Urban America* (pp. 288–96). Needham Heights, MA: Allyn & Bacon.

Katz, P. 1994. *The New Urbanism: Toward Architecture of Community*. New York: McGraw-Hill.

Kearney, M. S. 2005. *The Economic Winners and Losers of Legalized Gambling*. Washington, DC: Brookings Institution.

Keating, W. D., and Krumholz, N. 1991. Downtown plans of the 1980s: The case for more equity in the 1990s. *Journal of the American Planning Association* 57: 136–52.

Kelbaugh, D. 1999. *Common Place: Toward Neighborhood and Regional Design*. Seattle: University of Washington Press.

Kelly, P., and Lusis, T. 2006. Migration and the transnational habitus: Evidence from Canada and the Philippines. *Environment and Planning A* 38: 831–47.

Kent, T., and Brown, R. 2009. *Flagship Marketing*. New York: Routledge.

Knack, R. E. 1989. Repent, Ye Sinners, Repent. *Planning* 55 (8): 4–13.

Knack, R. E. 1998. Downtown is where the living is easy: From New York to Aiken, South Carolina, downtown housing is hot. But will it do all it's supposed to? *Planning* 64: 4–9.

Knack, S. 2002. Social capital and the quality of government: Evidence from the states. *American Journal of Political Science* 46 (4): 772–85.

Kobayashi, A. 1993. Multiculturalism: Representing a Canadian institution. In J. Duncan and D. Ley, eds., *Place/Culture/Representation* (pp. 205–31). London: Routledge.

Kresl, P. K., and Singh, B. 1999. Competitiveness and the urban economy: Twenty-four large US metropolitan areas. *Urban Studies* 36: 1017–28.

Kunstler, J. H. 1993. *The Geography of Nowhere*. New York: Simon and Schuster.

Lang, R. 2003. Edgeless Cities: Exploring the Elusive Metropolis. Washington: Brookings

Langdon, P. 1994. *A Better Place to Live*. Amherst: University of Massachusetts Press.

Lautier, V., and Varin, F. 2007. *Commercial Urbanism in the Context of Sustainable Development*. Montreal: La Fondation Rues Principales.

Law Development Ltd. 1998. *Cornell Markham*. Thornhill, ON: Law Development Ltd.

Lee, C. K., Kang, S. K., Long, P., and Reisinger, Y. 2010. Residents' perceptions of casino impacts: A comparative study. *Tourism Management* 31 (2): 189–201.

Lee, N. 2011. Ethnic diversity and employment growth in English cities. *Urban Studies* 48 (2): 407–25.

Lee, T. 2000. Place Making in Suburbia. *Urban Land* 59 (10): 72–79.

Lehnen, R., and Johnson, C. 2001. The impact of tax increment financing on school districts: An Indiana case study. In C. Johnson and J. Mann (eds.), *Tax*

Increment Financing and Economic Development: Users, Structures, and Impact (pp. 137–54). Albany: State University of New York Press.

Leigh, R. 1963. The use of location quotients in urban economic base studies. *Land Economics* 46 (2): 202–5.

Leinberger, C. 2001. *Financing New Urbanism*. Cambridge, MA: Harvard University Joint Center for Housing Studies.

Lerner, M. 2007. Survey: Buyers driven to buy in the suburbs. *Washington Times*. March 23, p. F1.

Lever, W. F. 2002. Correlating the knowledge-base of cities with economic growth. *Urban Studies* 39: 859–70.

Levine, J. C. 1998. Rethinking accessibility and jobs housing balance. *Journal of the American Planning Association* 64 (2): 133–49.

Levine, R., and Serbeh-Dunn, G. 1999. Mosaic vs. melting pot. *Voices: Publication of the Victoria Immigrant and Refugee Centre Society* 1 (4). www.darren duncan.net/ archived_ web_work/voices/voices_v1_n4/mosaic.html. Accessed May 20, 2015.

Lewis, N. M. 2010. Grappling with governance: The emergence of business improvement districts in a national capital. *Urban Affairs Review* 27 (August): 180–217.

Ley, D. 2003. Artists, aestheticisation and the field of gentrification. *Urban Studies* 40 (12): 426–41.

Ley, D. 2007. *Multiculturalism: A Canadian defense. Research on Immigration and Integration in the Metropolis*. Working Paper 07–04. Vancouver Centre of Excellence. www.prostate.centre.com.

Ley, D. 2008. Post-multiculturalism? In L. M. Henley, B. A. Ruble, and A. M. Garland, eds., *Renegotiating the City: Concepts of Immigration and Integration in Urban Communities* (pp. 177–96). Washington, DC: Woodrow Wilson International Center Press.

Li, P. 1996. *The Making of Postwar Canada*. Toronto: Oxford University Press.

Lichter, D.T., 2012. Immigration and the new racial diversity in rural America. Rural Sociology, 77 (1), pp. 3–35.

Lin, J. 1998. Globalization and the revalorizing of ethnic places in immigration gateway cities *Urban Affairs Review* 34 (2): 313–39.

Lippert, R. 2007. Urban revitalization, security, and knowledge transfer: The case of broken windows and kiddie bars. *Canadian Journal of Law and Society* 22: 29–54.

Lippert, R. 2010. Mundane and mutant devices of power: Sanctuaries and business improvement districts. *European Journal of Cultural Studies* 13 (4): 477–94.

Lippert, R., and Sleiman, M. 2012. Ambassadors, business improvement district governance and knowledge of the urban. *Urban Studies* 49 (1): 61–76.

Lipset, S. M. 1990. *Continental Divide: The Values and Institutions of the United States and Canada*. New York: Routledge.

Lloyd, W. J. 1991. Changing suburban retail patterns in metropolitan Los Angeles. *Professional Geographer* 43, 335–44.

Lofland, L. H. 1998. *The Public Realm*. New York: Aldine de Gruyter.

Longhi, S., Nijkamp, P., and Poot, J. 2010. Meta-analyses of labour-market impacts of immigration: Key conclusions and policy implications. *Environment and Planning C: Government and Policy* 28 (5): 819–33.

Lorch, B. J., and Smith, M. J. 1993. Pedestrian movement and the downtown enclosed shopping center. *Journal of the American Planning Association* 59: 75–86.

Lorimer, J. 1978. *The Developers*. Toronto: Lorimer.

Loukaitou-Sideris, A., Blumenberg, E., and Ehrenfeucht, R. 2004. Sidewalk democracy: Municipalities and the regulation of public space. In E. Ben-Joseph and T. Szolc, eds., *Regulating place*. New York: Routledge.

Loukaitou-Sideris, A., and Soureli, K. 2012. Cultural tourism as an economic development strategy for ethnic neighborhoods. *Economic Development Quarterly* 26 (1): 50–72.

Luce, T. 2003. Reclaiming the intent: Tax increment finance in Kansas City and St. Louis metropolitan areas. Washington, DC: Brookings Institution.

Luciani, P. 2006. Creative cities . . . the latest urban economic fad. *AIMS Commentary*. September.

MacDonald, H. 1999. BIDs really work. *City Journal* 6: 29–42.

Madden, J. F. 2001. Do racial composition and segregation affect economic outcomes in metropolitan areas? In E. Anderson and D. S. Massey, eds., *Problem of the century: Racial stratification in the United States* (pp. 290–316). New York: Russell Sage Foundation.

Malecki, E. 1997. *Technology and Economic Development: The Dynamics of Local, Regional and National Competitiveness*. Harlow: Addison, Wesley, Longman.

Mallach, A. 2010. Economic and social impact of introducing casino gambling: A review and assessment of the literature. Philadelphia: Federal Reserve Bank. www.philadelphiafed.org/ community-development/publications/discussion -papers/discussion-paper_casino-gambling.pdf.

Markusen, A., Wassall, G. H., DeNatale, D., and Cohen, R. 2008. Defining the creative economy: Industry and occupational approaches. *Economic Development Quarterly* 22 (1): 24–45.

Martin, D. G., and Holloway, S. R. 2005. Organizing diversity: Scales of demographic change and neighborhood organizing in St. Paul, MN. *Environment and Planning A* 17: 1091–1112.

Mattila, J. M., and Thompson, W. R. 1955. The Measurement of the Economic Base of the Metropolitan Area. *Land Economics* 31 (3): 215–28.

Mayer, H., and Knox, P. L. 2006. Slow cities: Sustainable places in a fast world. *Journal of Urban Affairs* 28 (4): 321–34.

Mayer, M. 1978. *The Builders: houses, people, neighborhoods, government, money.* New York: Norton.

McDougall, D. 2000. The New Urban Legend. *National Post.* September 30. N1.

McIssac, E. 2003. Immigrants in Canadian cities: Census 2001: What do the data tell us? *Policy Options* 24 (May): 58–63.

McNally, M. G., and Ryan, S. 1992. Accessibility of neotraditional neighborhoods: A review of design concepts, policies and recent literature. UCTU Working paper no. 141. Berkeley: University of California Transportation Center.

Means, A. C. 1997. Downtown revitalization in small cities. *Urban Land* 55 (1): 27–31, 56.

Meltzer, R. 2011. Understanding business improvement district formation: An analysis of neighborhoods and boundaries. *Journal of Urban Economics* 71: 66–78.

Michigan Gambling Control Board. Various Years. Annual Reports. www.michigan.gov/ mgcb/0,4620,7–120–57063_57067—,00.html. Accessed February 1, 2013.

Milder, D. 1997. *Niche Strategies for Downtown Revitalization: A Hands-on Guide to Developing, Strengthening and Marketing Niches.* New York: Downtown Research and Development Center.

Miller, G. 1997. Promises, Promises . . . Are municipalities in the GTA delivering the goods for a livable region? Canadian Urban Institute Roundtable Breakfast Series, December 11, no. 4.

Ministry of Housing. 1974. *The North Pickering Project: A New Community.* Toronto: Queen's Printer for Ontario.

Ministry of Municipal Affairs. 1993. Guideline directory: A listing of provincial policies and guidelines related to land development. Toronto: Queen's Printer for Ontario.

Ministry of Municipal Affairs and Housing. 1995. Making Choices: Alternative Development Standards Guideline. Toronto: Queen's Printer for Ontario.

Ministry of Municipal Affairs and Housing. 1997. *Breaking Ground: An Illustration of Alternative Development Standards in Ontario's New Communities.* Toronto: Queen's Printer for Ontario.

Mitchell, J. 2001. Business improvement districts and the management of innovation. *American Review of Public Administration* 31: 201–17.

Mitchell, J. 2008. *Business Improvement Districts and the Shape of American Cities.* Albany: State University of New York Press.

Moon, Z. K., Farmer, F. L., Miller, W. P., and Abreo, C. 2014. Identification and attenuation of barriers to entrepreneurship: Targeting new destination Latino migrants. *Economic Development Quarterly* 28 (1): 61–72.

Moore, C. G., and Siskin, C. 1985. *PUDS in Practice.* Washington, DC: ULI–The Urban Land Institute.

Moos, M., and Skaburskis, A. 2010. Workplace restructuring and urban form: The changing national settlement patterns of the Canadian workforce. *Journal of Urban Affairs* 32 (1): 25–53.

Morazain, J. 2002. New Life for Town Centres. Forces. 135: 66-69.

Morcol, G., and Wolf, J. F. 2010. Understanding business improvement districts: A new governance framework. *Public Administration Review* (November/December): 906-13.

Morgan, G., and Ren, X. 2012. The creative underclass: Culture, subculture, and urban renewal. *Journal of Urban Affairs* 34 (2): 127–30.

Morrow-Jones, H., Irwin, E., and Roe, B. 2005. Consumer preferences of neotraditional neighborhood characteristics. *Housing Policy Debate* 5 (11): 171–202.

Morse, E. A., and Goss, E. P. 2009. *Governing Fortune: Casino Gambling in America.* Ann Arbor: University of Michigan Press.

Moss, M. L. 1997. Reinventing the central city as a place to live and work. *Housing Policy Debate* 8 (2): 471–90.

Moufakkir, O. 2002. Changes in selected economic and social indicators associated with the establishment of casinos in the city of Detroit. PhD diss., Michigan State University.

Murdie, R. A. 1997. The welfare state, economic restructuring and immigrant flows: Impacts on sociospatial segregation in Greater Toronto. In S. Musterd and W. Ostendorf (eds.), *Urban Segregation and Social Exclusion in Western Welfare States.* London: Routledge.

Musterd, S., Andersson, R., Galster, G., and Kauppinen, T. M. 2008. Are immigrants' earnings influenced by the characteristics of their neighbours? *Environment and Planning A* 40: 785–805.

Musterd, S., and Salet, E. 2003. *Amsterdam Human Capital.* Amsterdam: Amsterdam University Press.

Myers, D., and Gearin, E. 2001. Current Preferences and Future Demand for Denser Residential Environments. *Housing Policy Debate* 12 (4): 633–74.

Myers, M. B., and Rosenbloom, R. S. 1996. Rethinking the role of industrial research. In R. S. Rosenbloom and W. J. Spencer, eds., *Engines in Innovation: US Industrial Research at the End of an Era* (pp. 209–28). Boston: Harvard Business School Press.

NAHB Research Center. 1993. *Proposed Model Land Development Standards and Accompanying Model State Enabling Legislation.* Washington, DC: U.S. Department of Housing and Urban Development Office of Policy Development and Research.

National Main Street Center. 1988. *Revitalizing downtown, 1976–1986.* Washington, DC: NMSC.

Nationwide overhaul of land use laws needed. 2001. *New Urban News* 6 (1): 2.

Navin, J. C., and Sullivan, T. S. 2007. Do riverboat casinos act as competitors? A look at the St. Louis market. *Economic Development Quarterly* 21 (1): 49–59.

Nelson, A. C., Dawkins, C. J., Ganning, J. P., Kittrell, K. G., and Ewing, R. 2016. The association between professional performing arts and knowledge class growth: Implications for metropolitan economic development. *Economic Development Quarterly* 30 (1): 88–98.

New urban projects on a neighborhood scale in the United States. 2002. *New Urban News* 7 (6): 1–6.

Ninette, K., and Trebilcock, M. 1998. *The Making of the Mosaic.* Toronto: University of Toronto Press.

Oakville, Town of Planning Services Department. 1998. Uptown core community profile. Oakville, ON: Oakville Planning Services Department.

Oldemberg, R. 1991. *The Great Good Place.* New York: Marlowe & Company.

Oldham, J. 1960. Don Mills: Today's New Town. *Urban Land* 19 (1): 3–9.

Ontario Lottery and Gaming Corporation. Various Years. Annual Performance Reports. www.olg.ca/about/public_disclosure/performance_highlights.jsp?con tentID=about_performance_highlights Accessed February 1, 2013.

Ontario Ministry of Urban Affairs and Housing. 2006. *Places to Grow.* Toronto: Municipal Affairs and Housing.

Orfield, M. 1998. *Metropolitics.* Washington, DC: Brookings Institution.

Osgood, J. L., Opp, S. M., and Bernotsky, R. L. 2012. Yesterday's gains versus today's realities: Lessons from 10 years of economic development practice. *Economic Development Quarterly* 26 (4): 334–50.

Ottaviano, G. I. P., and Peri, G. 2005. Cities and cultures. *Journal of Urban Economics* 58: 304–37.

Palma, D. 2000a. Downtown revitalization. In R. L. Kemp, ed., *Main Street Renewal: A Handbook for Citizens and Public Officials* (pp. 158–63). Jefferson, NC: McFarland.

Palma, D. 2000b. Ten myths about downtown revitalization. In R. Kemp, ed., *Main Street Renewal.* Jefferson, NC: McFarland.

Palma, D., and Hyett, D. 1997. Born again: Downtown revivals offer salvation for cities. *American City and Country* (July): 26–29.

Paradis, T. W. 2000a. Conceptualizing small towns as urban places: The process of downtown redevelopment in Galena, Illinois. *Urban Geography* 21: 61–82.

Paradis, T. W. 2000b. Main street transformed: Community sense of place for non-metropolitan tourism business districts. *Urban Geography,* 21: 609–39.

Patriquin, M. 2016. New Brunswick: A Drive-Through Province. *Maclean's Magazine.* March 21, 14-17.

Paumier, C. B. 2004. Creating a vibrant city center: urban design and regeneration principles. Washington: Urban Land Institute.

Peach, N. D., and Petach, L. A. 2016. Development and quality of life in cities. *Economic Development Quarterly* 30 (1): 32–45.

Peck, J. 2005. Struggling with the creative class. *International Journal of Urban and Regional Research* 29 (4): 740–70.

Peters, A., and Fisher, P. 2005. The failure of economic development incentives. *Journal of the American Planning Association* 70: 27–37.

Philips, R. 2002. *Concept Marketing for Communities.* Westport, CT: Praeger.

Picot, G. 2004. The deteriorating economic welfare of Canadian immigrants *Canadian Journal of Urban Research* 13: 25–45.

Pink-Harper, S. A. 2015. Educational attainment: An examination of its impact on regional economic growth. *Economic Development Quarterly* 29 (2): 167–79.

Plaine, M. 2007. Big Plans for small places: Downtown revitalization on Main Street. *Heritage Magazine* (Summer). www.heritagecanada.org/sites/heritagecanada.org/files/magazines/2007/summer/Summer2007_MainStreet.pdf.

Polese, M., and Shearmur, R. 2002. The Periphery in the Knowledge Economy. Moncton and Montreal: INRS Urbanisation, Culture et Societe and Canadian Institute for Research on Regional Development.

Pressman, N. 1976. *Planning New Communities in Canada.* Ottawa: Ministry of State for Urban Affairs.

Putnam, R. D. 2000. *Bowling Alone.* New York: Simon and Schuster

Qadeer, M. 2005. Ethnic segregation in a multicultural city. In D. P. Varady, ed., *Desegregating the City: Ghettos, Enclaves and Inequality* (pp. 45–61). Albany: State University of New York Press.

Randolph Group Management Consultants. 1997. *Town of Oakville Economic Development Strategy Final Report.* Oakville ON: Town of Oakville.

Rath, J. 2005. *Tourism, Ethnic Diversity and the City.* London: Routledge.

Rausch, S., and Negrey, C. 2006. Does the creative engine run? A consideration of the effect of creative class on economic strength and growth. *Journal of Urban Affairs* 28 (5): 473–89.

Reese, L. A. 2004. Same governance, different day: Does metropolitan reorganization make a difference? *Review of Policy Research* 21: 595–611.

Reese, L. A. 2006. Do we really need another typology? Clusters of local economic development Strategies. *Economic Development Quarterly* 20 (4): 368–76.

Reese, L.A. 2012. Creative Class or Procreative Class: Implications for Local Economic Development, *Theoretical and Empirical Research in Urban Management* (February): 5-26.

Reese, L. A., Faist, L., and Sands, G. 2010. Measuring the creative class: Do we know it when we see it? *Journal of Urban Affairs* 32: 345–66.

Reese, L. A., and Rosenfeld, R. A. 2002. *The Civic Culture of Local Economic Development.* Thousand Oaks, CA: Sage Publications.

Reese, L. A., and Rosenfeld, R. A. 2004. Local economic development in the U.S. and Canada: Institutionalizing policy approaches. *American Review of Public Administration* 34: 277–92.

Reese, L. A., and Sands, G. 2007a. Making the least of our differences? Trends in Canadian and US local economic development, 1990–2005. *Canadian Public Administration.* 50: 79–99.

Reese, L. A., and Sands, G. 2007b. *Public Act 198 Industrial Facilities Tax Abatements: Current Practices and Policy Recommendations.* Report 2007–09. East Lansing: Michigan State University Land Policy Institute.

Reese, L. A., and Ye, M. 2011. Policy versus Placeluck: Achieving Local Economic Prosperity. *Economic Development Quarterly* 25 (3): 221–36.

Reese, L.A. and Zalewski, M. 2015. Substantive and procedural tolerance: Are diverse communities really more tolerant? *Urban Affairs Review* 51: 781-818.

Rich, M. A. 2013. From coal to cool: The creative class, social capital, and the revitalization of Scranton. *Journal of Urban Affairs* 35 (3): 365–84.

Robertson, K. A. 1993. Pedestrianization strategies for downtown planners: Skywalks versus pedestrian malls. *Journal of the American Planning Association* 59: 361–70.

Robertson, K. A. 1995. Downtown redevelopment strategies in the United States: An end-of-the-century assessment. *Journal of the American Planning Association* 61: 429–37.

Robertson, K. A. 1999. Can small-city downtowns remain viable? A national study of development issues and strategies. *Journal of the American Planning Association* 65: 270–83.

Robertson, K. A. 2001. Downtown development principles for small cities. In M. Burayidi, ed., *Downtowns: Revitalizing the Centers of Small Communities* (pp. 9–22). New York: Routledge.

Robinson, D. 2010. The neighbourhood effects of new immigration. *Environment and Planning A* 42: 2451–66.

Ross, B. H., and Levine, M. A. 2001. *Urban Politics: Power in Metropolitan America*. 6th ed. Itasca, IL: F. E. Peacock.

Rossback, A., Fessenden, F., and Ashkenas, J. 2014. The Crowded Market for Casino Gambling. *New York Times*, August 10. A14.

Rougier, H. 2003. *The Canadian Mosaic*. Ottawa: Statistics Canada.

Rubin, H. J., and Rubin, I. 1987. Economic development incentives: The poor (cities) pay more. *Urban Affairs Quarterly* 23: 37–62.

Ruffin, F. A. 2010. Collaborative network management for urban revitalization. The business improvement district model. *Public Performance and Management Review* 33 (3): 459–87.

Rupasingha, A., Goetz, S. J., and Freshwater, D. 2002. Social and institutional factors as determinants of economic growth: Evidence from United States counties. *Papers in Regional Science* 81: 139–55.

Rushbrook, D. 2002. Cities, queer space, and the cosmopolitan tourist. *GLQ: A journal of lesbian and gay studies*, 8(1), 183–206.

Rusk, D. 1993. *Cities without Suburbs*. Washington, DC: Woodrow Wilson Center Press.

Sands, G. 1982. *Land-Office Business*. Lexington, MA: Lexington Books.

Sands, G. 2005. Assessing the health of core areas of mid-sized cities in Ontario and Michigan. *International Journal of Canadian Research* 35: 69–89.

Sands, G. 2007a. Economic health and new economy jobs. Paper presented at the ACSUS Biennial Meeting, Toronto. November.

Sands, G. 2007b. No Finer Place. *Journal of Sustainable Planning and Development* 2 (2): 1–11.

Sands, G. 2010. Prosperity and the new economy in Canada's major city regions. *GeoJournal* 75 (6): 539–51.

Sands, G., and Caruso, D. 2002. Land use and traffic impacts of urban casinos. Chicago: Association of Collegiate Schools of Planning Annual Conference. November.

Sands, G., and Reese, L. A. 2008. Cultivating the creative class: And what about Nanaimo? *Economic Development Quarterly* 22: 8–23.

Sands, G. and Reese, L.A. 2012. *Money for Nothing: Industrial Tax Abatements and Economic Development*. Lanham MD: Lexington Books.

Sands, G., Reese, L.A. and Filion, P. 2014. Keeping the Doors Open *International Business Research*. 7(6): 18-29.

Sands, G., Reese, L. A., and Trudeau, K. 2007. Tips for TIFs: Policies for Neighborhood Tax Increment Financing Districts. *Journal of the Community Development Association* 38 (Summer): 68–86.

Sanez, R., Donato, K., Gouveia, L., and Torres, C. 2003. Latinos in the South: A glimpse of ongoing trends and research. *Southern Rural Sociology* 19: 1–19.

Schubert, S. F., Matias, Á., and Costa, C. M. G. 2011. Optimality of Casino Taxation—The Case of Portugal. *Tourism Economics* : 231–43.

Schwartz, Z. 2015. Best of the best: Introducing the 2016 Maclean's university rankings. October 29. www.macleans.ca/education/best-of-the-best-intro ducing-the-2016-macleans-university-rankings. Accessed January 13, 2016.

Scott, A. J. 2006. Creative cities: Conceptual issues and policy questions. *Journal of Urban Affairs* 28: 1–17.

Scott, D. M., Coomes, P. A., and Izyumov, A. I. 2005. The location choice of employment-based immigrants among U.S. metro areas. *Journal of Regional Science* 45: 113–45.

Sewell, J. 1993. *The Shape of the City.* Toronto: University of Toronto Press.

Sharp, E. B. 1991. Institutional manifestations of accessibility and urban economic development policy. *Western Political Quarterly* 44: 129–47.

Sharp, E. B. 2007 Culture, segregation, and tolerance in urban America. Paper presented at the annual meeting, American Political Science Association, Chicago.

Sharp, E. B., and Joslyn, M. R. 2008. Culture, segregation, and tolerance in urban America. *Social Science Quarterly* 89: 573–91.

Shaw, G. A. and Williams, M. 1994. *Critical issues in tourism: a geographical perspective.* London: Blackwell Publishers.

Shearmur, R., and Polese, M. 2005. Diversity and employment growth in Canada, 1971–2001: Can diversification policies succeed? *Canadian Geographer* 49 (3): 272–90.

Sheridan, M. B., and Cohn, D. 2001. Immigrating in, settling out. *Washington Post*, April 25.

Simmons, J., and McCann, L. 2000. Growth and transition in the Canadian urban system. In T. Bunting and P. Filion, eds., *Canadian Cities in Transition: The Twenty-first Century* (pp. 97–120). Toronto: Oxford University Press.

Singer, A. 2004. The rise of new immigrant gateways. Brookings Institution Center on Urban and Metropolitan Policy. The Living Cities Census Series (February). www.brookings.edu.

Skaburskis, A. 2006. New Urbanism and Sprawl. *Journal of Planning Education and Research* 25 (3): 233–48.

Skelcher, B. 1992. What are the lessons learned from the Main Street pilot project, 1977–1980? *Small Town* 22 (4): 15–19.

Smerk, G. M. 1965. *Urban transportation: The federal role.* Bloomington: Indiana University Press.

Smith, H. 2004. The evolving relationship between immigrant settlement and neighborhood disadvantage in Canadian cities, 1991–2001. Vancouver:

Research on Immigration and Integration in the Metropolis Working Paper 04–18. mbc.metropolis.net.

Smith, R. C. 2006. *Mexican New York: Transitional Lives of New Immigrants.* Berkeley: University of California Press.

Sohmer, R. 1999. Downtown housing as an urban redevelopment tool: Hype or hope? *Housing Policy Debate* 10: 477–505.

Sohmer, R., and Lang, R. E. 2001. *Downtown rebound.* Washington, DC: Fannie Mae and Brookings Institution Center on Urban and Metropolitan Policy.

Soja, E. 1996. *Thirdspace.* London: Basil Blackwell.

Southworth, M., and Ben-Joseph, E. 1995. Street standards and the shaping of suburbia. *Journal of the American Planning Association* 61: 65–81.

Sparber, C. 2006. Racial diversity and aggregate productivity in US industries: 1980–2000. *Southern Economic Journal* 75 (3): 829–57.

Spurr, P. 1976. *Land and Urban Development.* Toronto: Lorimer.

Statistics Canada. 1991, 1996, 2001, 2006, 2011. Census of Population.

Statistics Canada. 2002. Community profile: Ville St-Laurent. www.statisticscanada.ca.

Statistics Canada. 2003. Immigrants choice of destination. www.statcan.gc.ca/pub/89–611-x/4152881-eng.htm.

Statistics Canada 2011. National Household Survey.

Stern, M.J. and Seifert, S. 2007. From creative economy to creative society. *Progressive Planning,* Winter.

Steuteville, R. 1996. New urbanism catches on in Canada. *New Urban News* 2 (2): 1, 4–7.

Steuteville, R., and Langdon, P. 2003. *New Urbanism.* Ithaca, NY: New Urban News.

Stokes, R. J. 2007. Business improvement districts and small business advocacy: The case of San Diego's citywide BID program. *Economic Development Quarterly* 21: 278–91.

Suchman, D. 2002. *Successful Infill Housing,* Washington: ULI—The Urban Land Institute:

Sutro, S. 1990. *Reinventing the Village: Planning, Zoning and Design Strategies.* Planning Advisory Services Report 430. Washington, DC: American Planning Association.

Symes, M., and Steel, M. 2003. Lessons from America: The role of business improvement districts as an agent of urban regeneration. *Town Planning Review* 74 (3): 301–13.

Talen, E. 2000. Measuring the public realm. *Journal of Architectural and Planning Research* 36 (8): 344–60.

Talen, E. 2001. Traditional urbanism meets residential affluence. *APA Journal* 67 (2): 199–216.

Talen, E. 2002. The social goals of new urbanism. *Housing Policy Debate* 13 (1): 165–88.

Talen, E. 2005. *New urbanism and American planning: The conflict of cultures.* London: Routledge.

Taylor, Z. 2014. If different, then why? Explaining the divergent political development of Canadian and American local governments. *International Journal of Canadian Studies* 40: 53–79.

Teaford, J. C. 1990. *The Rough Road to Renaissance: Urban revitalization in America, 1940–1985.* Baltimore: Johns Hopkins University Press.

Teaford, J. C. 1993. *The Twentieth-century American City.* 2nd ed. Baltimore: Johns Hopkins University Press.

Teixeria, C. 2001. Community resources and opportunities in ethnic economies: A case study of Portuguese and Black entrepreneurs in Toronto. *Urban Studies* 38: 2055–78.

Teixeria, C., Lo, L., and Truelove, M. 2005. Immigrant entrepreneurship, institutional discrimination, and implications for public policy: A case study of Toronto. *Environment and Planning C: Government and Policy* 25 (2): 176–93.

Theodore, N., and Martin, N. 2007. Migrant civil society: New voices in the struggle over community development. *Journal of Urban Affairs* 29 (3): 269–87.

Thin, T., and Hsu, C. H. 2012. Opinions on Riverboat Casinos and the Perceived Impacts on Community Quality by Quad Cities' Residents. *UNLV Gaming Research & Review Journal* 1 (2). Retrieved from digitalscholarship. unlv.edu/grrj/vol1/iss2/1.

Thomas, E., Lambert, T. E., Srinivasan, A. K., Dufrene, U., and Min, H. 2010. Urban location and the success of casinos in five states. *International Journal of Management and Marketing Research* 3 (3): 1–16.

Thomas, J. M., and Darnton, J. 2006. Social diversity and economic development in the metropolis. *Journal of Planning Literature* 21: 153–68.

Thompson, W. 1967. *A Preface to Urban Economics.* Baltimore: Johns Hopkins University Press.

Thompson, W. N. 2011. Why they say no (casi-no): Countries that reject legalized casino gambling. *UNLV Gaming Law Journal* 2: 195.

Tobocman, S. 2010. An immigration strategy to transform local economies. *Michigan Planner* 14 (November/December): 1–7.

Tomalty, R. 1997. *The Compact Metropolis: Growth Management and Intensification in Vancouver, Toronto, and Montreal.* Toronto: ICURR Publications.

Tomanty, R., and Mallach, A. 2015. *America's Urban Future: Lessons from North of the Border.* Washington: Island Press.

Toronto Real Estate Board. 2015. Community Housing Market Report York Region: Markham. http://www.trebhome.com/market_news/market_watch/2015/Q1/York/MarkhamQ12015.pdf#search="markham"

Town of Markham. 1995. Official Plan for the Town of Markham Planning Area Amendment no. 5 Municipal Housing Statement Study/Urban Area Expansion Study.

Town of Markham Development Services. n,d, *New Urbanism: Myth and Reality.*

Traub, J. 1996. Can associations of businesses be true community builders? *Responsive Community* 29: 28–32.

Turner, R. S. 2002. The politics of design and development in the postmodern downtown. *Journal of Urban Affairs* 24: 533–48.

Turner, R. S., and Rosentraub, M. 2002. Tourism, Sports and the Centrality of Cities. *Journal of Urban Affairs,* 24 (5), 487–92, 2002.

UN Habitat. 2012. *State of the World Cities Report 2012/2013: Prosperity of Cities.* Nairobi: UN Human Settlements Program.

Upall, S., and LaRochelle-Cote, S. 2013. Employment changes across industries during the downturn and recovery. Catalogue no. 75–008-X. Ottawa: Statistics Canada.

Urban Land Institute. 2000-2008. *Development Handbook Series: Multifamily Development* (2000), *Business Parks and Industrial Development (2001), Mixed Use Development* (2003), *Residential Development* (2004), and *Retail Development* (2008). Washington DC: Urban Land Institute.

Valpy, M. 2007. Cracks begin to show in Canada's suburban dream. *Toronto Globe and Mail.* March 18.

Van Delft, H., Gorter, C., and Nijkamp, P. 2000. In search of ethnic entrepreneurship opportunities in the city: A comparative policy study. *Environment and Planning C: Government and Policy* 18 (4): 429–51.

Vertovec, S. 2007. Super-diversity and its implications. *Ethnic and Racial Studies* 30 (6): 1025.

Volk, L., and Zimmerman, T. 2001. Comment on Myers and Gearin. *Housing Policy Debate* 12 (4): 675–709.

Voytek, K., and Ledebur, L. 1991. Is industry targeting a viable economic development strategy? In R. D. Bingham and R. Mier, eds., *Dilemmas of urban economic development* (pp. 171–94). Thousand Oaks, CA: Sage.

Walker, D. 1999. Legalized casino gambling and the export base theory of economic growth. *Gaming Law Review* 3 (2–3): 157–63.

Walker, D. 2007. *The Economics of Casino Gambling.* New York: Springer.

Walker, D. 2011. Casino revenues and retail property values: The Detroit case. *Journal of Real Estate Finance and Economics* 42 (1): 99–14.

Walker, D., and Jackson, J. 1998. New goods and economic growth: Evidence from legalized gambling. *Review of Regional Studies* 28: 47–69.

Wang, Q. 2015. Foreign-born status, gender, and Hispanic business ownership across U.S. metropolitan labor markets: A multilevel approach. *Economic Development Quarterly* 29 (4): 328–40.

Ward, K. 2006. Policies in motion, urban management and state restructuring: The trans-local expansion of business improvement districts. *International Journal of Urban and Regional Research* 30 (1): 54–75.

Weber, R. 2003. Equity and entrepreneurialism the impact of tax increment financing on school finance. *Urban Affairs Review* 38: 619–44.

Weissman, S. 2000. Lawyering the New Urbanism. *Urban Land* (October).

Wells, B. 2000. *Downtown Revitalization in Urban Neighborhoods and Small Cities.* Washington: Northeast- Midwest Institute.

West, D. M., and Orr, M. 2003. Downtown malls as engines of economic development, community spirit, and political capital. *Economic Development Quarterly* 17 (2): 193–204.

White, R. 2016. *Planning Toronto.* Vancouver: University of British Columbia Press.

Whyte, W. H. 1988. *City: Rediscovering the Center.* New York: Doubleday.

Wial, H., and Friehoff, A. 2006. *Bearing the Brunt: Manufacturing Job Loss in the Great Lakes Region, 1995–2005.* Washington, DC: Brookings Institution Metro Economy Series.

Wilson, J. Q., ed. 1966. *Urban Renewal: The Record and the Controversy.* Cambridge, MA: MIT Press.

Wojan, R. R., Lambert, D. M., and McGranahan, D. A. 2007. The emergence of rural artistic havens: A first look. *Agricultural and Resource Economics Review* 36 (1): 53–70.

Wolman, H. 1996. The politics of local economic development. *Economic Development Quarterly* 10: 115–50.

Yeates, M. 1988. *The North American City.* 5th ed. New York: Longman.

Index

Lightning Source UK Ltd.
Milton Keynes UK
UKOW01f2137241017
311561UK00008B/734/P